Washington County Maryland Church Records of the 18th Century 1768–1800

Hagerstown, Clearspring, Williamsport, Leitersburg, Funkstown, Cearfoss

F. Edward Wright

WILLOW BEND BOOKS
2007

WILLOW BEND BOOKS
AN IMPRINT OF HERITAGE BOOKS, INC.

Books, CDs, and more—Worldwide

For our listing of thousands of titles see our website
at
www.HeritageBooks.com

Published 2007 by
HERITAGE BOOKS, INC.
Publishing Division
65 East Main Street
Westminster, Maryland 21157-5026

Copyright © 1988 F. Edward Wright

All rights reserved. No part of this book may be reproduced or transmitted in any form or by any means, electronic or mechanical, including photocopying, recording or by any information storage and retrieval system without written permission from the author, except for the inclusion of brief quotations in a review.

International Standard Book Number: 978-1-58549-115-2

INTRODUCTION

This is a collection of vital records taken from German churches at Hagerstown (Lutheran and Reformed); Salem (Reformed), Cearfoss Pike; Funkstown (Lutheran and Reformed); St. Paul's near Clearspring (Lutheran and Reformed); Jacob's near Leitersburg (Lutheran) and Williamsport (Lutheran); and excerpts from the Vestry minutes of the Episcopal Church of St. John's at Hagerstown. In most cases, copies or transcripts are held by the Maryland Historical Society; Washington County Free Library, Hagerstown; D.A.R. Library, Washington, D.C., and the Maryland State Archives.

In using German church records of Maryland one must realize that the Lutheran and the Reformed congregations frequently shared the same church building at some time in their histories. These were called union churches. Although each denomination was distinct and independent of the other, members frequently used the minister of the other denomination; sometimes records of the two congregations were combined.

St. John's Lutheran Church at Elizabethtown (later Hagerstown), was organized in 1770. The first pastor was Rev. Wildban. In 1795, when a new building was erected, the congregation numbered 108. The first records begin with baptisms in 1768. The Maryland State Archives holds the originals and a copy of the earliest records on microfilm, microcopy M1182. A portion of the record, 1793-1818, is translated by two different translators. Transcripts are also held by the Western Maryland Room of the Washington County Free Library and the D.A.R. Library, Washington, D.C.

Zion Reformed Church of Elizabeth-town (later Hagerstown) was founded around 1771. Originals of the baptisms, beginning in 1771, are held by the church itself. Transcripts are held by the Western Maryland Room, Washington County; the D.A.R. Library, Washington, D.C.; and the Maryland Historical Society, Baltimore, Md.

Records of the Salem Reformed Church begin with baptisms performed in 1771. Two transcripts are held by the Maryland Historical Society: one covering the period 1771-1783; and a second portion of the records, beginning with 1787, which was copied by Miss Electa Ziegler. The Pennsyvlania German Society Quarterly indicates that the originals are held by the church. In addition copies are held by the Western Maryland Room, Washington County and the D.A.R. Library, Washington, D.C.

St. Paul's Reformed Church, near Clearspring, was founded around 1747; the Lutheran Congregation, using the same church building, was founded around 1760. The baptism records for the Reformed congregation and the Lutheran congregation are combined and begin in 1788. There are two sets of translations for St. Paul's Lutheran and Reformed Church held by the Maryland Historical Society. One set was copied by "Mrs. Warren D. Miller, Historian." The second set was translated by Bertha B. Heinemann and identified as "Church Register for both the Evangelical Lutheran and The Reformed Church Congregations in Washington County, Provinz, Maryland." Transcripts are also held by the Western Maryland Room, Washington County Free Library, Hagerstown; and the D.A.R. Library, 1776 D. Street, Washington, D.C.

The records for Jacobs Lutheran Church, several miles north of Leitersburg, near the Pennsylvania border, south of Waynesboro, Pennsylvania begin in 1791. The records recorded in this book were taken from the translation by Matilda Ripple Detrich, made in 1929.

The records for the Old Reformed Church, Funkstown (formerly Jerusalem) were translated by Mrs. Louise L. Miller and Mrs. Kurt Lande. The Penn. German Society Quarterly refers to a union church here from 1771.

Zion Luthern Church, Williamsport, began around 1791. For fifteen years pastors of St. John's Lutheran Church of Hagerstown served the Williamsport Church. Around 1798 the Williamsport congregation built a small log church. In 1806 they adopted the name, "Zion German Evangelic Lutheran Congregation, in and about William's Port, Washington, County, Maryland." Copies of the early records are held by the Maryland Historical Society and the Washington County Free Library.

Of the German churches existing in Washington County in the 18th century there are no known records or copies for Trinity Reformed, at Boonsboro, founded around 1775; and Trinity Lutheran founded around 1774 as Ringer's Church, west of Boonsboro.

The Episcopal records for the period are limited to the Vestry Proceedings of St. John's Parish. This parish encompassed all of the newly established Washington County.

Presbyterians - There are no known records of the Presbyterian Church in Hagerstown until 1817 although Rev. Thomas McPherrin was called to the pastorate of the Presbyterian Congregation west of South Mountain in 1774. As early as 1768 people of this vicinity were requesting preaching supplies from the Donegal Presbytery.

Methodists - There was a congregation of Methodists in Hagerstown as early as 1793; however there are no known records extant for the 18th century.

Catholics - Catholics built their first church in Hagerstown in 1794. No records are known to exist for the 18th century.

Information is given on sources of Maryland German Church records in the following.
1. Quarterly of the Pennsylvania German Society, vol. 14, # 2, April 1980. (From which much of the founding dates were taken for this introduction. This excellent article titled, "Eighteenth Century German Church Records From Maryland: A Checklist," provides information on the location of the originals, copies, and dates of the churches were founded and other background.
2. Directory of Maryland Church Records, 1988 (Family Line Publications) provides information on the location of records of all known church records up and into the 20th century.

Abbreviations used:

b = born
bapt = baptized
d = died

spon = sponsor
wit = witness

Suggestions and comments are welcomed.

F. Edward Wright
Silver Spring, Maryland

Evangelical Lutheran Church at Elizabethtown (Hagerstown)

From the microfilm copy held by the Maryland State Archives (M1182)
Baptisms of infants
Frederic of Jacob Schuvv (Schupp) and Christina Margar. b Dec 30 1767; bapt Feb 1768
John Jacob of Jacob Schuvv (Schupp) and Christina Margar. b Jul 8 1770; bapt Aug 5 1770
Elisabeth of Christian Leiter and Elisabeth b Apr 13 1758; bapt Apr 13 1770
Katharine of Lewis Russel and Mary b Jun 5 1768; bapt Jun 4 1770
John George of Kaspar Hofmann and Margareth b Nov 6 1769; bapt Jun 4 1770
George Adam of Adam Huber and Katharina b Jun 25 1769; bapt Apr 13 1770
Jacob of William Weil and Ann Sophia b Oct 10 1769; bapt Apr 13 1770
Sarah of Martin Reitenauer & wife b Feb 3 1772; bapt Mar 27 1772
Eva of Lewis Reitenauer and Rosina b Apr 3 1773; bapt Apr 5 1773
John George of Matias Ellinger and Katharina b Jan 19; bapt Apr 30
John Henry of Frederic Sallate and Regina b Jan 15 1774; bapt Apr 3 1774
John Jacob of Jacob Berlin and Magdalene b Mar 8; bapt Apr 4
John Niclas of Matth. Reitenauer and wife b Aug 15 1755
Henry of Matth. Reitenauer and wife b Oct 17 1757
Jacob of Matth. Reitenauer and wife b Jan 11 1759
John of Matth. Reitenauer and wife b May 5 1762
Eva of Matth. Reitenauer and wife b Dec 24 1764
Rosina of Matth. Reitenauer and wife b Mar 30 1766
Mathis of Matth. Reitenauer and wife b Mar 11 1770
Daniel of Matth. Reitenauer and wife b Oct 5 1773
--- of Matth. Reitenauer and wife b Nov 20 1775
Michael of John Stadler and Eva b Sep 23 1774; bapt Apr 10 1774
Juliana of Henry Storzmann and Eva b Mar 21; bapt Apr 10
Elisabeth of Frederic Alter and Margareth b Jan 29 bapt Apr 10
Katharina of Kaspar Stehr and Mary b (?) bapt Apr 12
John Jacob of Matias Nied and Katharina b Nov 18 1773 bapt Apr 12 1774
George Peter of Nicolas Enderns and Barbara b Mar 20 bapt Apr 16 1774
Frederic of Jacob Deible and Ann Mary b Mar 18 bapt Apr 24
Jacob of John Mueller and Fronica b Apr 9 bapt Apr 4
Michael of Christopher Ehret and Katharina b Dec 24 1773 bapt Apr 24 1774
John Henry and Margareth of George Maurer and Magdalene b Apr 3 and bapt Apr 24 1774
Nicolas of Martin Zeitner and Margarethe b Sep 1 1773 bapt Apr 24 1774
Mary Margaratha of Peter Bell and Elisabeth b Jun 28 1773; bapt May 8 1774
Jacob of Jacob Leitert and Juliana b Jul 6 1773; bapt May 8 1774
Ann Elisabeth of John Adam Weiss and Margaretha b Apr 26 1774; bapt May 1 1774
Era Christina of Gottlieb Glassbrenner and Margaretha b May 8; bapt May 11
Henry of John Sattles and Mary Barbara b May 19; bapt May 22
Mary Elisabeth of Josseph Faerer and Ann Mary b Oct 7 1773; bapt May 24 1774
Jacob of Antony Bell and Mary b Mar 24 1774; bapt May 29 1774
Elisabeth of Nicolas Russ and Ann Katharina b Jan 11, bapt Jun 12
Peter of Peter Ried and Ann Katharina b Jun 3; bapt Jun 19
Jacob of Jacob Damm and Barbara b Apr 13; bapt Jun 3
George of George Zinn and Ann Mary b Jan 14; bapt Jul 3
John of Peter Foesslich and Ann Mary b Jun 17; bapt Jul 3
John George of Andrew Mueller and Ann Mary b Jun 28; bapt Jul 10
Peter of Jacob Hoss and Magdalene bapt Jul 31
Elisabeth of Peter Wirth and Elisabeth b May 23; bapt Aug 24
William of Abraham Ritter and Margaretha b Jul 27 1774; bapt Aug 24 1774
John of Mathes Rapp and Mary Margareth bapt Sep 4

Evangelical Lutheran Church at Elizabethtown (Hagerstown)

John of Peter Flieger and Elisabeth b Aug 26; bapt Sep 18
Nicholas of Philip Krieg and Katharina b Jun 5 bapt Aug 24
Michael of Michel Ott and Margaretha b Sep 22 bapt Oct 23
John Adam of Adam Wohlfahrt and Elisabeth b Sep 11 bapt Oct 23
Salome of George Schmidt and Magdalena b Aug 23 bapt Oct 23
Martin of George Feigeli and Sophronia b Sep 26 bapt Nov 6
Ann Mary b Gustav Alter and Johanna b Oct 28; bapt Nov 20
Frederic of Andrew Nemminger and Ann Mary b Oct 9; bapt Nov 2
Ann Mary of John Reinhard and Eva Elisabeth b Nov 10; bapt Nov 20
Philippina of Jacob Valentine and Margaretha b Aug 28 1770; bapt Nov 20 1774
John of Jacob Valentine and Margarathe b Apr 28 1773; bapt Nov 20 1774
Frederic of Jacob Valentine and Margarethe b Jun 26 1774; bapt Nov 20 1774
George of Peter Volz and Mary b Oct 26 1774; bapt Jan 1 1775
Jacob of Abraham Leiter and Katharina b Dec 18 1774; bapt Feb 12 1775
Margaretha of Berhard Fad and Zanna b Jan 20 1775; bapt Jun 4 1775
John of George Jung and Margaretha b Dec 25 1774; bapt Jan 8 1775
Elisabeth of Martin Reitenauer and Katharina b Mar 15 1775; bapt Apr 9 1775
John George of John Braun and Katharina b Feb 19; bapt Apr 17
Peter of Peter Hoss and Salome b Apr 26; bapt Apr 30
Elisabeth of Georg Zinn and Anna Maria b Apr 6; bapt May 28
Katharina of John Wetzstein and Eve b Apr 20; bapt Jun 4
Michel of Michel Foss and Christina b May 12; bapt Jun 18
John of Frederic Heistkell and Katharina b Jun 19; bapt Jun 25
Christian of George Weiss and Anna Eve b Jun 23; bapt Jun 25
Mary Elisabeth of Baltasar Goll and Mary Elisabeth b Jun 10; bapt Jul 16
Margareth Barbara of Martin Seidner and Margaretha b Jun 5; bapt Jul 16
Elisabeth of George Jung and Elisabeth b Jun 17; bapt Jul 30
Elisabeth of Christoph Zueroher and Margareth b Jul 16; bapt Aug 13
Anna Margaretha of Jacob Berlin and Magdalene b Aug 27; bapt Sep 24
Magdalaene of George Schmidt and Magdalene b Nov 9; bapt Dec 17
Mary Magdalene of Adam Schmidt and ---; bapt Dec 12
Margareth of Frederic Tuerder and Margareth b Nov 22 1775; bapt Jan 14 1776
Henry of Melchior Beltzhuber and Elisabeth b Jan 10 1776; bapt Jan 14 1776
Ann Mary of Philipp Dussing and Ann Mary b Dec 31 1775; bapt Jan 27 1776
Jacob of George Theil and Fronica b Dec 12 1775; bapt Jan 28 1776
Katharina of Philipp Rippel and Angelica b Nov 13 1775; bapt Feb 1 1776
Mary Helen of John Fadler and Mary Eva b Jan 27 1776; bapt Feb 11 1776
Rosina of Frederic Reitenauer and Rosina b Jan 4; bapt Mar 24
Katharina of George Dingler and Ann Mary b Feb 7; bapt Mar 14
Jacob of Andrew Freyberger and Ann Katharine b Aug 3 1775; bapt Mar 26 1776
Ann Katharina of Michael Devilbiess and Margaretha b Apr 26 1776; bapt May 5 1776
Michael of Nicholas Rus and Katharina b Nov 16 1775; bapt May 19 1776
Christoph of Michael Fadele and Katharine b Dec 10 1775; bapt May 26 1776
John Frederic of Michael Dohmer and Ann Mary b Apr 20 1776; bapt May 26 1776
Ann Mary of George Freund and Mary b Apr 6 1775; bapt Jun 2 1776
George Henry of Henry Rauk and Mary b Mar 5 1776; bapt Jun 16 1776
--- of Michael Walter and Katharina b Jun 25 1776; bapt Jul 14 1776
John George of Jacob Kuebler and Ann Margaretha b Jul 11 1776; bapt Jul 28 1776
Elisabeth of Jacob Belzhuber and Magdalena b ---; bapt Sep 20 1776
Margarethe of Christoph Alter and Susanna b Sep 16; bapt Sep 22
Elizabeth of Wendel Wolf and Dorothea b Sep 13; bapt Oct 27
Jacob of Balthasar Mandi and Ann Mary b Sep 8; bapt Oct 27
Christine of Jacob Deibele and Ann b Sep 26; bapt Nov 10

Evangelical Lutheran Church at Elizabethtown (Hagerstown)

John Jacob of John Uensell and Ann Mary; b -; bapt Dec 4 1777
Ann Margarethe of Henry Mahninger and Elisabeth b Oct 29 1776; bapt Nov 24 1776
Elisabeth of John Wetzstein and Eva b Oct 5; bapt Nov 24
John of George Rauch and Elisabeth b Oct 18; bapt Dec 8
Katharina of Peter Flieger and Elisabeth b Sep 16 1776; bapt 8 (?) 1777
John of Henry Weidel and Susanna b Dec 7 1776; bapt Jan 5 1777
John of Gottfred Stempel and Mary Margareth b Nov 7 1776; bapt Feb 2 1777
Christine Margareth of Frederic Alter and Margarethe b Jan 15 1777; bapt Mar 16 1777
Mary of William Boxe (Bope?) and Katharine b Dec 9 1776; bapt Mar 16 1777
Daniel of Henry Stortzmann and Eve b Jan 1 1777; bapt Mar 30 1777
John of Jacob Reitenauer and Rebecca b Jan 15 1777; bapt Mar 30 1777
Katharina of Andrew Vogler and Ester b Nov 15 1776; bapt Mar 30 1777
Jacob of Peter Leiter and Eve b Aug 14 1776; bapt Mar 30 1777
Rosina of Adam Wohlfahrt and Elisabeth b Feb 2 1777; bapt Apr 12 1777
Adam of Henry Reitenauer and Margarethe b Feb 14; bapt Apr 27
Ann of Anton Bell and Mary b Feb 5; bapt Jul 20
Mary Elisabeth of Christian Schad and Magdalene b Mar 27 1777; bapt Mar 8 1778
Elisabeth of Valentine Ebert and Elisabeth b Apr 14 1775; bapt Aug 31 1777
Katharine of Valentine Ebert and Elisabeth b Sep 18 1776; bapt Aug 31 1777
Daniel of Peter Bell and Mary Elisbeth b Jul 12 1777; bapt Sep 14 1777
Mary Ann of Abraham Leiter and Johanna Kathar. b Jul 9 1777; bapt Sep 14 1777
Johanna of John Reb and Elisabeth b Aug 24; bapt Sep 21
Jacob of Philip Werner and Magdalene b Sep 5; bapt Oct 4
Johanna of Georg Kiessman and Elisabeth b Nov 13; bapt Dec 7
John of Jonas Pennerich and Margaretha b Jan 6 1778; bapt Feb 1 1778
John of Adam Schmidt and Mary b Feb 27 1778; bapt Mar 16 1778
Simon of Georg Schmidt and Magdalana b Nov 14 1777; bapt Mar 15 1778
Magdalene of Nicholas Fach and Elisabeth b Feb 9 1778; bapt Apr 5 1778
Mary of Peter Foss and Salome b Feb 22; bapt Apr 19
Elisabeth of Philipp Kring and Mary b Jul 12 1777; bapt sometime in Sep 78
Ann Katharina of Andrew Freyberger and Ann Katharina b Nov 16 1777; bapt May 10 1778
George of Jacob Foss and Magdalene b Apr 26 1778; bapt May 10 1778
Michel of Michel Walter and Katharina b Mar 30; bapt May 24
Magdalene of Mickel Fadel and Katharina b May 31; bapt Jun 21
Elisabeth of Theobold Kehlhofer and Ann Mary b May 5; bapt Jun 21
Susanna of Philipp Dussing and Ann Mary bapt Oct 20 1778; bapt soon after
Mary Katharina of Adam Weiss and Margaretha b Jun 28; bapt Jul 5
Elisabeth of Frederic Tuerdes and Margarethe b May 27; bapt Jul 5
Magdalene of Adam Hoblitzel and Christine b Jun 20; bapt Jul 5 1778
John of Georg Zinn and Ann Mary b Jul 24; bapt Oct 4
George(?) of Georg New and Magdalene b Sep 12; bapt Oct 25
Elisabeth of Philipp Oisseder and Dorothea b Sep 25; bapt Oct 25
Katharina of Lewis Reitenauer and Rosina b Apr 3 1778; bapt Apr 25 1778
Magdalene of Christoph Alter and Susanna b Oct 17; bapt Nov 26
Juliana of Christian Schad and Margarethe bapt Dec 25 1778
Elisabeth of John Reb and Elisbeth b Jan 2 1779; bapt Jan 10 1779
Elisabeth of Henry Weidel and Susanna b Nov 28 1778; bapt Jan 10 1779
Susanna of Thomas Reinhard and Eve Elisabeth b Dec 1 1778; bapt Jan 17 1779
John of Jonathan Haeger(?) and Ann Sophie b Feb 6 1779; bapt Feb 14 1779
John of Paul Christman and Magdalena b - 1779; bapt Feb 14 1779

Evangelical Lutheran Church at Elizabethtown (Hagerstown)

Martin of Leonhard Pseiser (Pheifer?) and Mariana b Dec 7 1778; bapt Feb 28 1779
Elisabeth of Jacob Reitenauer and Rebeca b Oct 1778; bapt Feb 28 1779
Katharina of Theobold Rau and Elisabeth b Mar 7 1779; bapt Mar 28 1779
John of John Fadler and Eva b Dec 10 1778; bapt Mar 14 1779
Abraham of Jakob Leiter and Juliana b Feb 9 1779; bapt Mar 28 1779
Jacob of Michael Deibelbiss and Margaretha b Apr 5; bapt May 2
Margaretha of Andreas Kleinsmidt b Nov 15 1778; bapt Dec 1778
George Michael of George Adam Haushalter and Margaretha b May 8; bapt May 23
George Frederick of Frederick Feisskel and Katharina b May 5; bapt May 28
John Phillip of Jacob Zieger and Judith b May 29; bapt Jun 21
Maria Rebeca of George Schoengel and Katharina b May 26; bapt Jun 20
Anna Maria of John Foss and Katharina b May 6; bapt Jul 3
Anna Katharina of George Shoengel and Christina b Jan 7; bapt Jan 21
Gerhard of Gerhard Steinback and Anna Maria b May 25; bapt Jan 21
Simon of Michael Kademann and Elisabeth b Jan 9; bapt Jul 4
Maria of Valentin Ebert and Elisabeth b Mar 22; bapt Jul 18
Anna Katharina of Jonas Ennereis and Anna Marga. b Aug 15; bapt Sep 26
Magdalena of Nicolaus Reitenauer and Katharina b Sep 2; bapt Oct 10
Jacob of Jacob Fentz and Christina b Aug 28; bapt Sep 10
Anna Maria of Jacob Nef and Rebeca b Aug 18
Jacob of Jacob Weyrick and Christina bapt Jan 1 1780
Jacob of Adam Schmidt and Maria Anna b Oct 28 1779; bapt Jun 9 1780
Jacob of Henry Reitenauer and Eva b Dec 20 1779; bapt Feb 13
Elisabeth of Jacob Edenberger and Eva b Mar 4; bapt Mar 7
John of Jacob Deible and Anna b Feb 8; bapt Mar 12
Anna Maria of Jacob Ott and Katharina b Oct 22 1779; bapt Mar 12 1780
Eva of Henry Rotzman and Eva b Nov 21 1779; bapt Mar 26 1780
Sara of Ludwig Reitenauer and Rosina b Sep 22 1779; bapt Mar 26 1780
Juliana of Nicolaus Fachi and Elisabeth b Mar 28; bapt Apr 23
Jacob of Jonathan Fager and Mary b Mar 23 ; bapt Apr 23
-- of Adam Theil and Maria Dorothea b Apr 20; bapt May 14
Anna Maria of Benjamin Feiskel and Anna Margaretha b Mar 4; bapt May 14
Anna Maria of Philip Werner and Magdalena b Mar 13; bapt May 14
Margaretha of Nathanael Morgan and Magdalena bapt May 4
John of Nicolaus Entzminger and Katharina b Jun 3; bapt Jul 2
Jacob of George Dengler and Anna Maria b Apr 22; bapt Jul 2
Anna Maria of Leonhard Pseister (Pfeister?) and Katharina b May 1; bapt Jul 2
John of Abraham Leiter and Katharina b Jun 12; bapt Jul 9
Katharina of Georg Shafal and Rebeca b Jul 17; bapt Jul 30
Elisabeth of Tobias Freund and Margareth b Jun 3; bapt Jul 30
Maria Elisabeth of Thomas Reinhard and Elisabeth b Jul 7; bapt Jul 30
Samuel of George Jung and Margareth b Jul 15; bapt Jul 30
Anna Maria of Michael Banart and Margaretha b Jul 20; bapt Aug 6
Anna Dorothea of Wendel Wolf and Anna Dorothea b Jul 20; bapt Aug 13
Jacob of Martin Ferrjanior and Susana b Jul 15; bapt Aug 13
Friedrick of Adam Ott and Juliana b Jul 11; bapt Aug 13
Susanna of John Fadler and Maria Eva b Sep 22; bapt Oct 8
John of Andreas Klenshmidt and Rebeca b Sep 5; bapt Oct 8
Katharina of John Sted and Katharina b Aug 28; bapt Oct 8
Fenrick of Fenrick Mahninger and Elisabeth b Sep 4; bapt Oct 8
Jacob of Philip Miller and Christina b May 7; bapt May 10
Elisabeth of Adam Edanberger and Dorothea b Jun 1; bapt Jun 21
Rosina of John Kaussler and Christina b Sep 1; bapt Oct 22

Evangelical Lutheran Church at Elizabethtown (Hagerstown)

Rosina of John Kaussler and Christina b Sep 1; bapt Oct 22
Anna Maria of Peter Zinn and Jane b Oct 8; bapt Nov 19
Eva Katharina of Jonas Emmerich and Margareth b Nov 23 bapt Dec 17
- Michael Jadel and Magd. b Sep 26; bapt Dec 25
Eva Katharina of Nicolaus Reitenauer and Katharina b Nov 7; bapt Dec 25
Susanna of Theobold Kau and Elisabeth b Oct 12; bapt Dec 25
Anna Katharina of David Koch and Katharina b Dec 24 1780; bapt Jan 14 1781
Margaretha of John Roe bapt Jan 14 1781
William of George Esher and Elisabeth b Nov 23 1780; bapt Jan 17 1781
Maria of Simon Bauman and Magdalena b Oct 26 1780
Jacob of Peter Flieger and Elisabeth; bapt Aug 6 1780; bapt Jan 26 1781
Katharina of John Reb and Elisabeth b Nov 14; bapt Feb 25 1781
David of John Wetzstein and Eva b Dec 16; bapt Feb 25
Christina Elisabeth of Friedrich Bauer and Katharina b Feb 17; bapt Mar 25
John George of Christian Fachy and Juliana b Feb 19; bapt Mar 25
John of Jacob Reitenauer and Rebeca b Nov 6 1780; bapt Mar 25 1781
Katharina of Fenrick Weidel and Susana b Jan 14; bapt Mar 25
Elisabeth of George Neu(?) and Magdalena b Feb 25; bapt Apr 15
John of Fenrick Reitenauer and Eva b Apr 5; bapt May 3
Elisabeth of Dietrich Ebert and Elisabeth b Mar 6; bapt May 6
Anna Margaretha of Simon Kisseder and Maria Elisabeth b Apr 21; bapt May 20
Johanna of John Hermann and Anna Maria b Nov 3 1780; bapt May 7 1781
Eva Elisabeth of Michael Stein and Eva Katharina b Jul 11; bapt Aug 26
Maria Sara of Friedrich Alter and Margaretha b Jul 20; bapt Aug 26
Philip of George M. Hausshalter and Susana b Jun 30 bapt Aug 26
John Jacob of David Feun (Ferin?) and Anna Marga. b Sep 26; bapt Oct 7
John of Christoph Shrob and Dorothea b Jul 31 1780; bapt Oct 7 1781
Eva of Christoph Alter and Johanna b Oct 26; bapt Dec 25
Liberty of Henry Shryotz (Shryok?) and Katharina b Jan 14 1782; bapt Jan 18 1782
Martha of Maria Barbara Mantelin b Dec 10 1781; bapt Jan 20
John of Martin Fern and Susana b Jan 17; bapt Feb 17
Elisabeth of Andreas Langberger and Anna Katharina b Jul 31 1781; bapt Feb 23 1782
Margaretha of Jacob Nepf and Barbara b Feb 18; bapt Mar 17
John Fenrick of John Reb and Elisabeth b Dec 4 1781; bapt Mar 31 1782
Margaretha of John Geiger and Fronia b Mar 10; bapt Apr 14
Jacob of Ludwig Kernkaum and Regina b Oct 12; bapt Apr 14
Maria of John Feucht and Anna Maria b Feb 21; bapt Apr 25
Dorothea of Georg Shmidt and Magdalena b Mar 19; bapt Apr 28
Anna Rebeca of Jacob Fentz and Christina b Feb 21; bapt Apr 28
David of Ludwig Reitenauer and Rosina b Jan 3; bapt Apr 28
John George of John George Neu and Magdalena b Mar 16; bapt May 19
Magdalena of David Koch and Chatarina b Apr 5; bapt May 19
John Michael of Adam Walfahrt and Elisabeth b Feb 11; bapt May 19
Susana of Fenrick Stortzman and Eva b Apr 5; bapt Jun 9
Anna of Herrman Hellman and Magdalen b Apr 17; bapt Jun 22
Friedrick of John Hofmann and Maria Rebeca b Jun 16; bapt Jun 23
John of Conrad Ester and Eva b Apr 20; bapt May 19
Michael of Nicolaus Shnengel and Elisabeth b May 24; bapt Jun 23
Maria of George Kirshmann and Elisabeth b Mar 13; bapt Jul 7
John of Matheiss Reitenauer and Katharina b Jun 25; bapt Jul 21
John of Peter Weberle and Maria b Apr 10; bapt Jul 21
Susana of Paul Christmann and Magdalena b Apr 24; bapt Aug 4
Friedrick of Friedrick Bauer b Jun 6; bapt Aug 4

Evangelical Lutheran Church at Elizabethtown (Hagerstown)

Friedrick of Nicolaus Reitenauer and Katharina b Apr 30; bapt Aug 4
Martin of Jacob Reitenauer and Susana b Jul 5; bapt Aug 4
Christina of Jacob Weyrich and Christina b Jun 13; bapt Aug 18
William of George Zinn and Ann Maria b Jul 18; bapt Sep 1
John of Philip Dussing and Anna Maria b Apr 27; bapt not long after
Katharina of Philip Bethele and Magdalena b Jul 23; bapt Sep 1
George of Nicolaus Fachy and Elisabeth b Jul 16; bapt Sep 15
George of Michael Bauart and Margaretha b Sep 16; bapt Sep 21
John David of Christian Fetzminger and Margaretha b Aug 12; bapt Sep 26
Jacob of Leonhard Pseister (Pfeister?) and Elisabeth b Mar 31; bapt Sep 29
Jacob of Jacob Bauer and Katharina b Sep 24; bapt Oct 13
Katharina of Adam Bauer and Rosina b Sep 6; bapt Oct 13
Anna Margaret of Adam Stortzman and Elisabeth b Sep 2; bapt Oct 13
Jacob of Balthasar Maudi and Anna Maria b Jul 29; bapt Oct 16
Jacob of John Kaussler and Christina b Oct 11; bapt Nov 24
Rosina of Fenrick Reitenauer and Eva b Oct 8 1782; bapt Nov 10
Katharina of Martin Krebs and Magdalena b Nov 18 1782; bapt Jan 5 1783
Jacob of Jacob Ferre and Maria Elisabeth b Jan 7; bapt Feb 2
Margaretha of John George Young and Margaretha b Feb 5; bapt Feb 27
John Peter of Peter Fluger and Elisabeth b Feb 19; bapt Apr 5
George of Jacob Greber and Anna Maria b Jan 28; bapt Mar 2
Conrad of David Reitenauer and Sarah b Feb 21; bapt May 11
John George of George Reitenauer and Katharina bapt May 25
Simon of George Michael and Susana b May 14; bapt Jun 22
-- of Ludwig Reitenauer b May 18; bapt Jul 6
Anna Maria of John Reb and Elisbeth b Mar 5; bapt Jul 6
John of John Klein and Katharina b Jun 5; bapt Aug 3
Elisabeth of John Geiger and Franida b Jul 31; bapt Sep 7
John of George Nef and Elisabeth b Aug 14; bapt Sep 7
Anna Maria of Fenrich Geiger and Kathrina b Sep 4; bapt Sep 14
Margaretha of Georg Shal b Aug 30 1783; bapt Sep 28 1783
Sally of Friedrick Keisskell and Katharina b Aug 23; bapt Nov 9
Anna Maria of John Brotzmann and Anna Maria b Nov 14; bapt Nov 30
Maria Margaretha of David Koch and Katharina b Nov 14; bapt Dec 15
George of Christoph Alter and Susana b Dec 18; bapt Dec 25
Magdalena of John Frucht and Maria b Sep 24 1783; bapt Jan 4 1784
John George of Peter Zinn b Nov 12 1783; bapt Jan 11 1784
Rosina of Jonas Emmerich and Margaretha b Dec 5 1783; bapt Feb 15 1784
Elisabetha of Martin Ferre and Susana b Jan 19; bapt Mar 7
Susana of George Neu and Magdalena b Oct 26 1783; bapt Mar 7
David of Peter Stortzmann and Margaretha b Jan 12; bapt Mar 22
Fenrich of Peter Feigele and Katharina b Dec 5; bapt Apr 4
John Christoph of Jo. Christoph Jopsele and Elisabeth b Jan 29; bapt Mar 21
John of David Ferre and Anna Margaretha b Mar 7; bapt Apr 4
John Jacob of Charls Fassele and Katharina b Feb 1; bapt Apr 11
Elisabeth of Nicolaus Reitenauer and Katharina b Nov 19 1783; bapt Apr 11 1784
-- of Jacob Pitry bapt Apr 11
John of Fenrich Shnell and Margaretha b Jan 7; bapt Apr 15
John of Christian Fichy and Juliana b Mar 19; bapt May 9
Philippina of Fenrich Reitenauer and Eva b Apr 11; bapt May 16
Andreas of John Neid and Katharina b Jan 18; bapt May 16
Samuel of John Ferre and Elisabeth b Jul 22; bapt Aug 22
Magdalena of Jacob Bauer and Katharina b Jul 23; bapt Aug 29
John of John Fentz b Jun 22; bapt Aug 29

Evangelical Lutheran Church at Elizabethtown (Hagerstown)

George of George Shal and Margaretha b Sep 16; bapt Oct 3
Felix of Jacob Shapp and Maria b Feb 1784; bapt Nov 2
George of Jacob Ferre and Maria Elisabeth b Sep 30; bapt Nov 21
Susana of Daniel Vold and Susana b Aug 5; bapt Dec 12
-- of William Lania(?) b Aug 5
Rosina of Jacob Reitenauer and Susana b Sep 14 1784; bapt Jan 9 1785
Michael of George Neu and Magdalena b Dec 2 1784; bapt Feb 13 1785
David of Fenrich Gramlich b Dec 11 1784
Anna Margaretha of Michael Bauart and Margaretha b Feb 4; bapt Feb 27
Katharina of John Reb and Elisabeth b Dec 29 1784; bapt Apr 17 1785
George of Fenrich Weidel b Mar 16; bapt May 15
Anna Maria of David Koch and Katharina b May 13 bapt Jun 12
Maria of Fenrich Kau and Maria b Oct 18 1784; bapt Jun 25 1785
Christina of Andreas Fryberger and Anna Katharina b May 13 1784; bapt Jun 26 1785
John of Thomas Shuman and Susana b May 28; bapt Jul 21
Elisabeth of Adam Muller and Katharina b Apr 28; bapt Jul 24
George of Fenrich Geiger and Katharina b Jun 30; bapt Jul 24
John Fenrich of William Fess and Magdalena b Jul 22; bapt Aug 14
Katharina of David Reitenauer and Sarah b Jul 23; bapt Aug 21
Anna Maria of Carl Fassele and Katharina b Aug 28; bapt Oct 9
Samuel Stedinger of Friedrich Heiskkell and Katharina b Sep 25; bapt Oct 18
Peter of Peter Feigele and Katharina b Sep 6; bapt Nov 6
Elisabeth of John Ferre and Elisabeth b Nov 6; bapt Dec 4
Eva Katharina of Peter Stortzmann and Margaretha b Oct 18; bapt Dec 25
George of Michael Deibelbiess and Margaretha b Jan 15 1786; bapt Feb 12
Anna Margaretha of David Ferre and Anna Marg. b Feb 14; b apt Feb 26
Maria Magdalena of George Neu and Magdalen b Dec 26 1785; bapt Feb 26
Rebeca of Valentin Haslich and Anna Maria b Jan 14; bapt Feb 12
Elisabeth of John Reisser and Magdalena b Feb 27; bapt Mar 12
Philip of Philip Frand b Mar 9; bapt Apr 14
Samuel of Christoph Alter and Susana b Apr 5; bapt Apr 16
Michael of Nicolaus Reitenauer and Katharina b Nov 26 1785; bapt Apr 16
Mary of Huen (Kuen?) Montgomery and Eva b Jun 14 1785; bapt Apr 16
John of Fenrich Muller and Ester b Feb 10; bapt Apr 16
Katharina of Christian Stempfle and Magdalena b Mar 14; bapt Apr 23
George of Martin Ferre and Susana b Apr 3; bapt Apr 23
Elisabeth of Philip Dussing and Anna Maria b Apr 7; bapt May 28
John of Carl Gelloids(?)/Gebl.ids?) and Maria Barbara b May 6; bapt Jun 5
John Adam of Paul Christmann b Apr 28; bapt Jun 18
Jacob of Fenrick Leissinger and Margaretha b Sep 9 1780; bapt Jun 21 1786
Fenrich of Konrad Brendlinger and Dorothea b Jun 9; bapt Jun 19
Elisabeth of Fenrich Zeister and Katharina b Jun 1; bapt Jul 3
-- of Fenrich Geed and Katharina b May 5; bapt Jul 9
Katharina of Philip Munch and Elisabeth b Aug 15; bapt Aug 27
Elisabeth of George Netz and Elisabeth b Sep 29; bapt Oct 22
Katharina of Jacob Bauer b Sep 15; bapt Oct 22
Katharina of Simon Baumann and Magdalena b Dec 28 1786
Sarah of Fenrich Werle b Sep 3; bapt Oct 22
Jacob of John Theil and Sarah b Aug 3; bapt Nov 12
Fenrich of Fenrich Alter and Margaretha b Oct 29; bapt Nov 12
Samuel of Zacharias Mohls and Susana b Nov 3; bapt Dec 3
Jacob of Fenrich Geiger and Katharina b Jan 10 1787; bapt Feb 11
Elisabeth of Theobold Teissinger and Katharina b Jan 13; bapt Feb 11
Sarah of John Kaussler and Christina b Feb 2; bapt Mar 25

Evangelical Lutheran Church at Elizabethtown (Hagerstown)

Christian of Peter Flidinger and Taborah b Mar 27; bapt May 19
Elisabeth of Fenrich Reitemann and Margaretha b Mar 16; bapt May 20
David of George W. Hausshalter and Susana b May 13; bapt Jul 29
Katharina of George Shend and Katharina b Aug 19; bapt Sep 2
Daniel of Peter Zinn b Aug 2; bapt Sep 2
Anna Maria of Peter Hoslich and Margaretha b Jul 29; bapt Sep 2
Elizabeth of Jacob Young and Odelia b Aug 26; bapt Oct 5
Fenrich of Peter Feigele b Sep 30; bapt Nov 11
Morgan of Nathan Morgan b Oct 10; bapt Nov 25
Elisabeth of Jacob Geyer and Dorothea b Oct 30; bapt Dec 2
Anna Maria of Friedrich Seidner and Maria b Sep 10; bapt Dec 5
Samuel of Fenrich Weidel b Oct 20; bapt Dec 26
Anna Maria of Martin Ferre and Susana b May 8; bapt Jun 22
Maria Magdalena of Peter Jenanein (Jenawein?) and Christiana b Sep 8 1787; bapt Jun 22 1788
Katharina of John Reusser and Magdalena b May 20; bapt Jun 22
Peter of John Ferre and Elisabeth b Apr 7; bapt Jul 20
Katharina of Peter Kraft and Katharina b Jan 7; bapt Jul 20
Susanah of Carl Gelluds and Barbara b Jun 24 ; bapt Aug 17
Katharina of Jacob Weil and Susanah b Jun 15; bapt Aug 17
Maria Magdalena of Christian Stempfle and Magdalena b Jul 30; bapt Sep 14
Anna Maria of George Shend b Sep 27; bapt Oct 12
Maria Elisabeth of Thomas Reinhardt b Aug 29; bapt Oct 12
Sarah of Thomas Shumann and Susanah b Jul 10; bapt Sep 10
Peter of John Geiger and Fronida b Sep 27; bapt Nov 9
Salome of Peter Fassel and Salome b Sep 23; bapt Nov 16
Michael of Melchior Bonder and Anna Maria b Dec 12 1788; bapt Jan 20 1789
Rebeca of Christian Langenader and Anna Margaretha b Feb 14; bapt Mar 8
Katharina of George Neu and Magdalena b Dec 27 1788; bapt Mar 8 1789
Margareth of Christian Fachy and Juliana b Feb 2; bapt Mar 29
Anna Maria of Jacob Ferre and Maria Elisab. b Feb 15; bapt May 3
David of Mathes Reitenauer b Apr 14; bapt May 31
Daniel of Fenrich Alter b May 1; bapt May 31
James of Frantz Eltzrinth b Apr 24; bapt May 31
Jacob of Peter Hoflich and Margaretha b Jun 28; bapt Aug 23
Sarah of Fenrich Weh and Maria b Dec 1; bapt Feb 8 1790
Samuel of David Theil and Margaretha b Dec 11 1788; bapt Feb 1
Hanna of John Reb and Elisabeth b Nov 4 1788; bapt Feb 8 1789
George Michael of George M. Hausshalter and Susanah b Jun 26; bapt Sep 13
Katharina of John Reitenauer and Elisabeth b Jul 27; bapt Sep 26 1790
Elizabeth of David Stempel and Eva Katharina b Feb 10 1790; bapt Sep 23 1790
Katharina of Leonhard Nest and Elisabath b Sep 19; bapt Oct 23
George of George Shmid and Katharina b Dec 17 1790; bapt Jan 1 1791
Eleonorah of George Young and Susanah b May 22; bapt Jul 1
Samuel of George Shmid and Katharina b Mar 5 1793; bapt Mar 23

"These children, who Pastor Young had neglected entering for some years.
Maria of John Regen and Lilia b Sep 9 1777; bapt Dec 24 1777
Lilia of John Regen and Lilia b Sep 3 1779; bapt Sep 24 1779
John of John Regen and Lilia b Feb 17 1781; bapt Mar 10 1781
Elisabeth of John Regen and Lilia b Oct 1 1783; bapt Nov 11 1783
George of John Regen and Lilia b Jul 4 1789; bapt Aug 20 1789
William of John Regen and Lilia b May 4 1791; bapt Jul 20 1791
Jacob of Peter Vrolss, and Maria b Oct 29 1772; bapt Apr 20 1773
George of Peter Vrolss, and Maria b Oct 26 1774; bapt Jan 1 1775

Evangelical Lutheran Church at Elizabethtown (Hagerstown)

John of Peter Vrolss and Maria b Nov 28 1776; bapt Dec 22 1776
Michael of Peter Vrolss and Maria b Jul 13 1779; bapt Jul 18 1779
Margaretha of Peter Vrolss and Maria b Apr 25 1782; bapt Jun 24 1782
Otto of Peter Vrolss and Maria b Sep 28 1784; bapt Dec 18 1784
Hishia of Peter Vrolss and Maria b Jul 8 1788; bapt Nov 16 1788
Melito of Peter Vrolss and Maria b Sep 8 1790; bapt Dec 10 1790
Jesse of Peter Vrolss and Maria b Dec 18(?) 1792; bapt Mar 2 1793
Henry of Konrad Lilendlinger and Dorodea b Jun 9 1780; bapt Jun 24 1780
Konrad of Konrad Lilendlinger and Dorodea b Nov 12 1788; bapt Nov 26
Jacob of Konrad Lilendlinger and Dorodea b Sep 11 1790; bapt Sep 24 1790
John George of Konrad Lilendlinger and Dorodea b Feb 1792; bapt Mar 1 1792
Jacob of Jacob Graber and Magdalena b Dec 26 1778; bapt Feb 18 1779
John of Jacob Graber and Magdalena b Jan 1 1781; bapt Feb 23
George of Jacob Graber and Magdalena b Jan 28 1783; bapt Feb 18 1783
Katharina of Jacob Graber and Magdalena b Dec 21 1788; bapt Jan 11 1789
Samuel of Jacob Graber and Magdalena b Apr 27 1791; bapt May 1
Elisabeth of Andreas Lind and Magdalena b Mar 27 1775; bapt Apr 11 1775
Peter of Andreas Lind and Magdalena b Jan 23 1777; bapt Feb 11 1777
Anna Maria of Henry Grieger and Anna Maria b Jul 8 1781; bapt Jul 9 1781
John of Henry Grieger and Anna Maria b Jul 26 1783; bapt AJun 20 1785
Henry of Henry Grieger and Anna Maria b Mar 20 1786; bapt Apr 20 1786
George of Henry Grieger and Anna Maria b May 21 1788; bapt Jun 20 1788
Daniel of Henry Grieger and Anna Maria b Oct 9 1790; bapt Nov 10 1790
William of Henry Grieger and Anna Maria b Jun 17 1793; bapt Jul 20 1793
John of John Gader and Anna Maria b Jan 20 1788; bapt Feb 14 1788
Anna Maria of John Gader and Anna Maria b Jan 15 1789; bapt Jul 10 1789
Georg of James Shumann and Susana b Jul 9 1790; bapt Jul 15 1790
Henry of Henry Shryock and Katharina b Oct 13 1768; bapt Dec 13 1768
Samuel of Henry Shryock and Katharina b Jan 26 1780; bapt Feb 6 1780
Amilia of Henry Shryock and Katharina b Jan 2 1783; bapt Jan 10 1783
July of Henry Shryock and Katharina b Sep 30 b 1785; bapt Oct 10 1785
Anna Barbara of Henry Shryock and Katharina b Jun 10 1788; bapt Jul 4 1788
Elisabeth of George Nef and Elisabeth b Dec 2 1789; bapt Feb 28 1790
George and Jacob of George Nef and Elisabeth b Oct 16 1792; bapt Dec 11 1792
Jacob of John Rochel and Susana b Jul 10 1793; bapt Jul 21 1793
Elisabeth of Christian Langrender and Margaretha b Dec 14 1784; bapt May 10 1785
David of Christian Langrender and Margaretha b Dec 8 1786; bapt Jan 6 1787
John of Jacob Ott and Katharina b Oct 29 1793; bapt Feb 12 1794
Juliana of Jacob Ott and Katharina b Jan 9 1790; bapt Apr 11 1790
Jacob of Jacob Ott and Katharina b May 24 1795; bapt Aug 12 1795
George of Jacob Ott and Katharina b May 10 1777; bapt Jun 5 1777
Margaretha of Jacob Ott and Katharina b Oct 17 1779; bapt Nov 16 1779
Katharina of Jacob Ott and Katharina b Feb 15 1782; bapt Mar 5 1782
Elizabeth of Jacob Ott and Katharina b Jun 23 1785; bapt Jul 15 1785
Elisabeth of Christian Sachy and Juliana b Oct 13 1793; bapt Oct 17 1793
John Jacob of Christian Sachy and Juliana b Aug 11 1786; bapt Aug 20 1786
Barbara of Leonhard Streit and Barbara b Sep 9 1787; bapt Oct 12 1787
Anna Maria of Leonhard Streit and Barbara b Aug 26 1780; bapt Sep 5 1780
Christina of John Reydenauer and Eva b Aug 9 1791; bapt Sep 11 1791
Mathias of John Reydenauer and Eva b Mar 7 1793; bapt May 7 1793
Nicholaus of Simon Kiesieder and Elisabetha b May 18 1789; bapt Jul 1 1791
Philip of Simon Kiesieder and Elisabetha b Dec 20 1792; bapt Jan 6 1793
Henry of Henry Weidel and Susana b Feb 14 1783; bapt Apr 13 1783
Jacob of --- Feurer b Mar 6 1790; bapt Jun 4 1790

Evangelical Lutheran Church at Elizabethtown (Hagerstown)

-- of Melder Bender and Anna Maria b Feb 3 1795; bapt Aug 10 1795
Johanes of Simon Kiesieder(?) and Elisabeth b May 18 1790; bapt Jul 2 1790
John Jacob of Simon Kiesieder(?) and Elisbeth b Dec 20 1792; bapt Feb 13 1793
John of Jacob Shupp and Chris. Marg b Feb 12 1773(?); bapt Mar 6 1773(?)
Katharina of Jacob Shupp and Chris. Marg b May 3 1776; bapt May 6 1776
Emmerich of Jacob Shupp and Chris. Marg b Jan 31 1779; bapt Feb 12 1779
Elisabeth of Jacob Shupp and Chris. Marg b Jun 10 1784; bapt Aug 11 1784
David of Jacob Shupp and Chris. Marg b Sep 22 1787; bapt Oct 8 1787
Daniel of Jacob Shupp and Chris. Marg b Sep 1 1789; bapt Oct 22 1789
John Jonathan of Jacob Shupp and Chris. Marg b Mar 9 1791; bapt Apr 10 1791
George of Friedrich Shupp and Eva b Jun 16 1791; bapt Jun 19 1791
Anna Maria of Joh. Gasser and wife Anna Maria/dau b 22 Dec 1792 bapt 30 Jul 1793; spon: John Biel, wife
Bezie of Tomas Schuman and wife Sus. dau b 26 May 1793, bapt 10 Jul 1793;spon: Bezi Wolz(?)
Susanna of Joh. Weil and wife Cath. dau b 19 Apr 1793; bapt 3 Aug 1793; spon: Jacob Weil and wife Sus.
Joh. Jacob of Simon Kiesecker and wife Elis. b 20 Dec 1794; bapt 13 Feb 1793; spon: Philip Kiesecker and wife Dorrothea
Wilhelm of Jacob Trislet and wife Magd. b 9 Jun 1793; bapt 10 Aug 1793; spon: parents
Eva of David Volck and wife, Anna Maria b 2 Jul 1793; bapt 4 Aug 1793; spon: parents
Anna Maria of Peter Feigele and wife Anna Maria Cath. b 20 Jul 1793; bapt 1 Sep 1793 spon: Anna Maria Barbara Hessin
dau of Peter Zimmerman and wife Barbara b 11 Aug 1792; bapt 11 Sep 1793; spon: Daniel Volck and wife Maria
Samuel of Jacob Schupp and wife Christ. Marg. b 15 Feb 1793; bapt 15 Mar; spon: David Herre and wife Marg.
Jacob of Friderich Schupp and wife Eva b 9 May 1793; bapt 21 Jul 1793; spon: Jacob Schupp and wife Anna
dau of Samuel Rigerain and wife Magd. b 10 Oct 1791; bapt 14 Aug 1793; spon: parents
Rebeca of Christoph Dorfin and wife Barbara b 12 Nov 1793; bapt 11 Sep 1793 spon: parents
Elis Susanna of Joh. Gander wife Anna Maria b 29 Mar 1793; bapt 11 Aug 1793; spon: Georg Beigler and wife Elis.
Abraham of Samuel Fried and wife Maria b 26 Aug 1793; bapt 22 Sep; spon: parents
Samuel of Jacob Leh and wife Anna b 11 Feb 1793; bapt 22 Sep; spon: parents
Sibile of Hennerich Warly and wife Sabina Maria b 18 Sep 1793; bapt 23 Sep; spon: parents
son of Joh. Miller and wife Anna Maria b 19 Sep 1793; bapt 22 Sep; spon: parents
"In all this year there were only 15 children recorded by the old guest preacher for me."
dau of Peter Schleiss (Schlius ?)and wife, Anna Maria b 21 Sep 1793; bapt 5 Jan; spon: Sus. Miller
Samuel of Joh. Schruyack and wife Anna Maria b 23 Sep 1793; bapt 2 Feb; spon: parents
Johannes of Joh. Biel and wife Eva b 12 Oct 1793; bapt 5 Feb; spon: Joh. Gasser and wife Anna Maria
dau of Jacob Goyer and wife Dorrothea b 8 Jan 1794; bapt 8 Feb 1794; spon: parents

Evangelical Lutheran Church at Elizabethtown (Hagerstown)

dau of Conrad Blendlinger and wife Dorrothea b 8 Jan 1794; bapt 8 Feb; spon: parents
Wilhelm of Friderick Beck and wife Juliana b 20 Dec 1793; bapt 2 Feb 1794; spon: Conrad Kaffroth and wife Magd.
Marg. of Hennerich Heffele and wife Sus. b 30 Dec 1793; bapt 10 Jan; spon: Friderich Alter and wife Marg.
Cath. of Christoph Schwab and wife Cath. b 22 Dec 1793; bapt 10 Jan; spon: Adam Arnold and wife Anna
Samuel of Tobias Ritter and wife Eva b 11 Jan 1794; bapt 12 Mar; spon: Jacob Jackel
Anna Maria of Ludwig Jung and wife Cath. b 20 Nov 1793; bapt 16 Mar; spon: parents
Cath. of William Starr and wife Elis. b 4 Mar 1794; bapt 16 Mar; spon Susanna Miller
Elis. of Georg Reiss and wife Barbara b 8 Dec 1793; bapt 2 Feb 1794; spon: parents
Margaretha of Christian Fechtig and wife Susanna b 23 Oct 1792; bapt 12 Mar; spon: parents
Michael of Hennerich Miller and wife Rosina b 4 Jan 1794; bapt 16 Mar; spon: Michael Bauart and wife Marg.
Lana of Peter Miller and wife Christ. b 27 Nov 1793; bapt 19 Aug 1794; spon: Johannes Hoffman and wife Barbara
Anna Maria Cath. of Balzer Goll and wife Cath. b 27 Nov 1793; bapt 6 Dec 1793; spon: Anna Maria Salome Weimarn
Joh. Christian of Joh. Georg Griessman and wife Cath. b 28 Jan 1794; bapt 9 Mar; spon: Johannes Kiesecker
Samuel of Christian Hacken and wife Juliana b 26 Oct 1793; bapt 26 Dec 1793; spon: Johannes Schaffer
David of Leonard Streit and wife Barbara b 5 Feb 1794; bapt 9 Feb 1794; spon: Johannes Kaussler and wife
dau of Casper Mundus and wife Elis. b 16 Jul 1793; bapt 8 Jun; spon: parents
dau of William McKormick and wife Marg. b 5 May 1794; bapt 8 Jun(?); spon: Georg Grisinger and wife Cath.
Cath of Mathews Reydenauer and wife Cath. b 19 Jun 1794; bapt 20 Jul 1794; spon: Barbara Feque
Elis. of Christoph Weimar and wife Ester b 2 Mar 1794; bapt 2 Aug; spon: parents
Christian of Christian Fechtig and wife Sus. b 6 Feb 1794; bapt 20 Mar; spon: parents
son of Jonadan Hager and wife Anna b 28 Apr 1794 bapt 8 Jun; spon: Adam Off and wife Juliana
Margaretha of Jacob Kraft and wife Eva b 1 Jul 1794; bapt 12 Aug; spon: Martin Volck and wife Cath.
Eva Elis. of Martin Volck and wife Cath. b 26 Dec 1794(?); bapt 12 Aug; spon: Jacob Kraft and wife Eva
Johannes of Martin Schutz and wife Maria b 31 Mar 1794; bapt 13 Aug; spon: Joh. Hardman
Johannes of Peter Storzman and wife Marg. b 5 Dec 1794; bapt 13 Jan 1796; spon: Melchar Wickert and wife Barbara
Maria Magdalena of Ludwig Stolz and wife Margaretha b 12 May 1794; bapt 24 Sep; spon: Hennerich Huber and wife Anna Maria
Sovia of Jacob Weil and wife Susanna b 21 Mar 1794; bapt 24 Sep; spon: Eitel Gerhard and wife Sovia
Hennerich of Jacob Trapp and wife Cath. b 1 Aug 1794; bapt 21 Sep; spon: Stophel Trapp and wife Barbara

Evangelical Lutheran Church at Elizabethtown (Hagerstown)

David of Peter Arz and wife Anna Maria b 26 Oct 1793; bapt 7 Nov 1794; spon: parents
Friderich of Hennerich Geyer and wife Cath. b 26 Jul 1794; bapt 5 Oct; spon: Peter Feygele and wife Cath.
Johannes of Georg Bidinger and wife Mag. b 16 Feb 1794; bapt 24 Oct; spon: Johannes Weil
William of Rabert Hukens and wife Cath. b 11 Jul 1794; bapt 8 Nov; spon: parents
Johannes of Georg Bügler and wife Elis. b 27 Oct 1794; bapt 23 Nov; spon: Johannes Gander and wife Magd.
Magd. of Jacob Jung and wife Atthilia b 6 Jul 1794; bapt 26 Nov 1794; spon: parents
son of Michael Basel and wife Dorrothea b 30 Sep 1794; bapt 6 Dec; spon: parents
dau of Joh. Reydenauer and wife Eva b 10 Oct 1794; bapt 30 Nov; spon: Mathias Reydenauer and wife Anna Maria
Cath. of Andreas Luz and wife Julianna b 31 Mar 1794; bapt 7 Dec; spon: Jacob Bunckele and wife Cath.
Tomas of Tomas Reed and wife Vronica b 22 Jan 1794; bapt 23 Dec; spon: Jacob Arban
Hennerich of Herman Lorshbach and wife b 13 Nov 1794; bapt 7 Mar; spon: parents
Anna Maria of David Herre and wife Margaretha b 6 Sep 1794; bapt 20 Sep 1794; spon: Anna Maria Bishoff
Christian of Peter Becher and wife Anna Maria b 22 Jan 1794; bapt 23 Dec; spon: Christian Langenecker and wife Anna Marg.
Elis. of Georg Beck and wife Barbara; b 9 Dec 1794; bapt 10 Jan; spon: Peter Arz and wife Maria
Elis. of Benjamin Marsteller and wife Maria b 10 Jan 1795; bapt 10 Feb; spon: Elis. Kramer
Anna Maria of Benjamin Reydenauer and wife Maria b 4 Jan 1795; bapt 12 Apr; spon: parents
Anna Maria of Jacob Bauman and wife Sus. b 21 Nov 1794; bapt 12 Apr; spon: parents
Susanna of Jacob Schonefelt and wife Elis. b 17 Feb 1795; bapt 12 Apr; spon: Christian Becker
Samuel of Jacob Herre and wife Elis. Maria b 25 Feb 1795; bapt 29 Mar; spon: Johannes Geiger and wife Susanna
Jacob Salede of Casper Scheffner and wife Cath. b 26 Jan 1795; bapt 23 Mar; spon: Jacob Wreyack and wife Amilia
Jonadan of Antonie Hauret and wife Maria b 18 Nov 1794; bapt 25 Mar; spon: parents
Magdalena of Duvalt Kennel and wife Elis. b 9 Nov 1794; bapt 25 Mar; spon: parents
Cath. of Leonhart Streitt and wife Barbara b 19 Mar 1795; bapt 15 Apr; spon: Hennerich Fuhrohr and wife Anna Maria
Sara of Andreas Refschneider and wife Elis. b 12 Dec 1794; bapt 19 Apr; spon: Matheus Kessler and wife Eva
Hennerich of Jacob Mayer and wife Elis. b 4 Dec 1794; bapt 13 Jan; spon: Hennerich Schapp and wife
Samuel of Matheus Kesler and wife Eva b 4 Dec 1794; bapt 21 Apr; spon: Samuel Hackmeyer and his sister Maria
Agatha Reydenauer brought an illegally born child and gave Conrad Hackmeyer, Jun. for the father. Born 10 Apr 1794, bapt 21 Apr Conrad Genant. Spon: Conrad Hackmeyer Sen. wife, Mary Magd.

Evangelical Lutheran Church at Elizabethtown (Hagerstown)

Elis. of Elias Rotter and wife Marg. b 1 Feb 1795; bapt May 25; spon: Jacob Jung and wife Otilia
Rosina of Valentin Eckeberger and wife Rosina b 30 Oct 1794; bapt 25 May; spon: Eva Reidenauer
Sly(?) son of Hennerich Weickel and wife Susana b 28 Oct 1792; bapt 25 May; spon: parents
Daniel of Hennerich Weickel and wife Sus. b 24 Apr 1795; bapt 25 May; spon: Jacob Gayer and wife Dorroth.
Susana of Jacob Schupp and wife Anna b 31 Jan 1795; bapt 8 Jun; spon: Tomas Schuman and wife Susana
Cath. of Joh. Annewald and wife Susana b 13 Oct 1794; bapt 14(?) Jun; spon: Jacob Binckle and wife Cath.
Scharlotta of Philip Empig and wife Juliana b 19 Dec 1794; bapt 15 Jul; spon: Daniel Nied and wife Anna Maria
Jacob Goring of Balzer Goll and wife Cath. b 17 Mary 1795; bapt 15 Jun; spon: Jacob Goering and wife Bezi
John Hennerich of Jonas Emerich and wife Anna Margaretha b 6 Apr 1795; bapt 14 Jun; spon: Johannes Kiesecker
Joh. Georg of Hennerich Straus and wife Christ. b 11 Jun 1795; bapt 28 Jun; spon: Georg Glassbrenner
Anna of Abraham Peter and wife Cath. b 8 Apr 1793; bapt 18 Jul; spon: parents
Cath. of Joh. Russel and wife Susana b 26 Apr 1795; bapt 11 Aug; spon: Balzer Goll and wife Cath.
Jonathan of Joh. Knodel and wife Elis. b 6 Mar 1795; bapt 24 Aug; spon: parents
Anna Maria of Peter Wolz and wife Anna Maria b 3 Jul 1795; bapt 30 Aug; spon: parents
Cath. of Peter Schleiss and wife Elis. b 22 Apr 1795; bapt 3 Oct; spon: Michale Ox and wife Elis.
Beky of Joh. Schaw and wife Eva b 16 Oct 1794; bapt 24 Sep; spon: parents
Joh. Hennerich of Joh. Hennerich Krieger and wife Anna Maria b 12 Aug 1795; bapt 3 Oct; spon: parents
Daniel of Jacob Loch and wife Nenzi b 26 Mar 1795; bapt 7 Nov; spon: Daniel Klein
Johannes of Joh. Teiss and wife Elis. b 3 Oct 1795; bapt 15 Oct; spon: Philip Kiesecker and wife Dorrothea
Adam of Georg Neu and wife Magd. b 25 Jul 1795; bapt 6 Aug; spon: Jacob Herre and wife Maria Elis.
Ferdinand of Georg Schmucker and wife Cath. b 12 Jul 1795; bapt 12 Jul; spon: parents
Elis. of Jonadan Tutweiler and wife Barbara b 30 Nov 1795; bapt 10 Dec; spon: Dewald Eichelberger and wife Barbara
Cath. of Joh. Miller and wife Anna Maria b 19 Nov 1795; bapt 19 Dec; spon: Hennerich Warly and his sister Cath.
Maria of Adam Boraf and wife Elis. b 24 Aug 1795; bapt 19 Dec; spon: Hennerich Strauss and wife Christina
Sara of Peter Arz and wife Maria b 2 Nov 1795; bapt 19 Dec; spon: Philip Krieger and wife Barbara
Georg Peter and Joh. Gander and wife Maria b 8 Oct 1795; bapt 26 Dec; spon: Peter Miller and wife Anna Maria
(The following entry written in pencil) Elis. of Georg Schenck and wife Cath b 5 Jan 1795; bapt 14 Feb; spon: Peter Miller and wife A. Maria
Twin daughters of Jonas Hackmeyer and wife Susana b 2 May 1798; bapt the older Susana, the youger Cath. 20 Jun; spon: parents

Evangelical Lutheran Church at Elizabethtown (Hagerstown)

Simon Kiesecker and wife Elis. b 1 Feb 1796; bapt 11 Feb; spon: George Schmucker and wife Catharina
Susanna of Adam Bauer and wife Rosina b 1 Aug 1795; bapt 12 Feb 1796 ; spon: parents
Wilhelm of Willhelm Storr and wife Elis. b 19 Dec 1795; bapt 12 Feb 1796; spon: Jacob Kraft and wife Eva
Johann Peter of Daniel Nied and wife Anna Maria b 7 Jan 1796; bapt 12 Feb; spon: Joh. Peter Hefflich and wife Barbara
Anna Maria of Michael Haun and wife Anna Maria b 13 Jan 1796; bapt 12 Feb; spon: parents
Elis. of Georg Schenck and wife Cath. b 5 Jan 1796; bapt 12 Jan; spon: Peter Miller and wife Anna Maria
Johannes of Georg Stamm and wife Glora b 8 Jan 1796; bapt 12 Feb; spon: Wilhelm Hess and wife Magdalena
Anna Maria of Peter Miller and wife Christina b 1 Feb 1796; bapt 28 Feb; spon: Susana Brendner
Joh. Georg of Georg Klein and wife Elis. b 21 Dec 1796 (1795?); bapt 16 Mar 1796; spon: Mathais Wolfort
Anna Maria of Simon Wart and wife Sibile b 15 Dec 1796 (1795?); bapt 16 Mar 1796; spon: Anna Maria Schweyere
Loisa Fredericka of Georg Keck and wife Anna Cath. b 1 Jan 1796; bapt 2 Mar; spon: parents
Catharina of Friderich Hoss and wife Marg. b 1 Dec 1795; bapt 2 Mar 1796;
Wilhelm of Willhelm Bender and wife Marg. b 2 Mar 1796; bapt 14 Mar; spon: Christoph Alter and wife Susana
Jacob of David Weil and wife Philipina (committed suicide), born illigitimatly 5 Dec 1795; bapt 14 Mar 1796; spon: Jacob Weil and wife Susana
Samuel of Peter Feigele and wife Cath. b 25 Jan 1796; bapt 20 Mar; spon: parents
Sara of Peter Starzman and wife Marg. b 11 Sep 1795; bapt 10 Apr 1796; spon: Juliana Starzman
Eva of Jacob Irig and wife Cath. b 2 Oct 1795; bapt 16 Apr 1796; spon: Matheus Kessler and wife Eva
Cath. of George Biegler and wife Elis. b 17 Apr 1769; bapt 10 May; spon: Georg Schenck and wife Cath.
Joh. Hennerich of Martin Starzman and wife Sus. b 12 Jul 1795; bapt 14 Feb 1796(?); spon: Hennerich Starzman and wife Eva
Jacob of Jacob Geyer and wife Dorrothea b 4 Jan 1796; bapt 21 Feb; spon: Dewalt Schefer and wife Rosina
Andreas of Michael Bauart and wife Marg. b 24 Mar 1796; bapt 22 Apr; spon: Andreas Miller and wife Anna Maria
George of Georg Schon and wife Cath. b 2 Dec 1795; bapt 8 May 1796; spon: parents
Anna Maria of Dewald Leisinger and wife Cath. b 10 Mar 1796; bapt 16 Apr; spon: parents
Joseph of Joseph Klark and wife b 9 Jun 1792; bapt 22 Mar 1796; spon: parents
Margaretha of Joseph Klark and wife b 19 May 1794; bapt 22 Mar 1796; spon: parents
William of Joseph Klark and wife b 22 May 1794(?); bapt 22 Mar 1796; spon: parents
Maria of Andreas Kleinschmidt and wife Barbara b 12 Feb 1796; bapt 28 May; spon: parents

Evangelical Lutheran Church at Elizabethtown (Hagerstown)

Hennerich of Hennerich Miller and wife Rosina b 18 Jan 1796; bapt 19 May; spon: Andreas Miller
Wilhelm of Wilhelm Hess and wife Magd. b 20 Apr 1796; bapt 12 Jun; spon: parents
Samuel of Tomas Schuman and wife Sus. b 11 Apr 1796; bapt 17 May; spon: Simon Bauman and wife Mag.
Litia of Jacob Jung and wife Othilia b 10 Feb 1796; bapt 28 Jun; spon: parents
Littia of Leonhard Kuhn and wife Elis. b 1 Jun 1796; bapt 3 Jul; spon: Friderich Alter and wife Marg.
George of Herman Lorshbach and wife Elis. b 30 Apr 1796; bapt 9 Jul; spon: parents
Elis. of Christoph Hess and wife Marg. b 17 Jan 1796; bapt 17 Jul; spon: Elis. Belshuber
Elis of Joh. Paulus Wagele and wife Elis. b 2 Jul 1795; bapt 2 Jun 1796 spon: parents
Catharina of Hennerich Heffele and wife Susann b 29 Jun 1796; bapt 24 Jul; spon: Friderich Alter and wife Marg.
Sovia of George Nef and wife Elis. b 6 Jun 1796; bapt 9 Jul; spon: Dewald Eichelberger and wife Barbara
Adam of Jacob Stam and wife Magd. b 29 Jul 1796; bapt 3 Aug; spon: parents
Amilia of Georg Schaal and wife Marg. b 17 Jul 1796; bapt 26 Jul; spon: William Krebs and wife Anna
Johannes of Friderich Storr and wife Maria Marg. b 14 Mar 1792; bapt 10 Aug 1796; spon: Adam Off and wife Juliana
Samuel of Frederick Spiegler and wife Maria b 20 Sep 1792; bapt 10 Aug; spon: parents
Salome of Frederick Spiegler and wife Maria b 20 Nov 1793; bapt 10 Aug; spon: parents
Friederich of Frederick Spiegler and wife Maria b 20 Nov 1795; bapt 10 Aug; spon: Friderick Schwengel and wife Eva
Philip of Philip Sprecher and wife Mag. b 26 May 1796; bapt 10 Aug; spon: Philip Schwengel
Cath. of Johannes Frey and wife Elis. b 13 Apr 1796; bapt 12 Aug; spon: Marg. Voltz
Hennerich of Ludwig Franckeberger and wife Marg. b 4 Aug 1796; bapt 17 Sep; spon: Hennerich Sackman and wife A. Maria
Elis. of Hennerich Gross and wife Marg. b 29 Apr 1796; bapt 31 Aug; spon: Christ. Schreyack in
Wilhelm of Wilhelm Bauer and wife Sovia b 10 Sep 1796; bapt 18 Sep; spon: parents
Joh. Georg of William McOrmick and wife Cath. b 2 Nov 1796; bapt 16 Nov; Spon: Gottlieb Glassbrenner and wife Margaretha
Daniel of Zacharias Molls and wife Sus. b 26 Oct 1796; bapt 20 Nov; spon: Georg Schenck and wife Cath.
Michael of Georg Knod and wife Cath. b 31 Jan 1796; bapt 14 Oct; spon parents
Cath. of Jacob Mayer and wife Elis. b 16 Sep 1796; bapt 16 Oct; spon: Cath. Urban
William of Martin Schauncker and wife Cath b 7 Oct 1796; bapt 31 Oct; spon: parents
Jonas of Joh. Reidenauer and wife Eva b 15 Oct 1796; bapt 20 Dec; spon: Hennerich Reidenauer and wife Eva
Cath. of Daniel Reidenauer and wife Elis b 17 Nov 1796; bapt 20 Dec; spon: Catha. Pfeiffer

Evangelical Lutheran Church at Elizabethtown (Hagerstown)

Susana of Michael Lauri and wife Barbara b 27 Sep 1796; bapt 21 Dec; spon: Cath. Urban
Johannes of Peter Klein and wife Magd. b 28 Nov 1796; bapt 24 Dec 1796; spon: Peter Klein, Sen.
Elis., an illigitimatley born child of Samuel Filson and Magd. Braun b 7 Nov 1794; bapt 8 Dec 1796; spon: Cath. Leicht
Salome of Philip Hornish and wife Cath. b 26 Nov 1796; bapt 7 Jan 1797; spon: Dewald Scheffer and wife Rosina
Johannes of Abraham Ritter and wife Cath. b 25 Oct 1796; bapt 27 Nov 1796; spon: Nicholaus Reidenauer and wife A. Cath.
son of Georg Martini and wife b 19 Oct 1796; bapt 19 Nov 1796; spon: father Georg Martini and A. Maria Matini
Cath. of Georg Reiss and wife Barbara b 28 Nov 1796; bapt 20 Mar; spon: parents
Georg of Georg Schauncker and wife Cath. b 29 Jan 1797; bapt 1 Mar; spon: parents
Lidia of Peter Miller and wife An. Maria b 29 Dec 1796; bapt 12 Mar; spon: Georg Miller and wife Christina
A. Marg. of Hennerich Strauss and wife Christina b 8 Jan 1797; bapt 29 Jan; spon: Gottlieb Glassbrenner and wife A. Marg.
Georg of Jacob Mong and wife Barbara b Jan 2 1797; bapt 19 Feb; spon: parents
Martini of Andoni Hauret(?) and wife Maria b 21 Dec 1796; bapt 20 Feb 1797; spon: Martin Kershner
Sally of Joh. Hedinger and wife Bethina b 3 Feb 1797; bapt 10 Feb; spon: parents
Magdalena of Joh. Bayer and wife Elis. b 17 Dec 1796; bapt 1 Apr 1797; spon: parents
Johannes of Nicolaus Gauer(Garier?) and wife Cath b 13 Oct 1796; bapt 8 Mar 1797; spon: parents
Martin of Hennerich Bar and wife Marg. b 29 Dec 1796; bapt 8 Apr 1797; spon: Jacob Brietinstein and wife Dorrothea
Salome of Jacob Bauer and wife Cath. b 27 Dec 1796; bapt 16 Apr 1797; spon: parents
son of Nicolaus Schmidt and wife Cath. b 3 Mar 1796; bapt 1 Apr 1797; spon: Nicholaus Schmidt Sen. and wife Barbara
Jacob of Philip Keickerle and wife Elis. b 18 Mar 1797; bapt 2 Apr; spon: Jacob Binckele and wife Eva
Jacob of Benjamin Schwengel and wife Eva b 2 Apr 1797; bapt 17 Apr; spon: Nicolaus Schmidt and wife Barbara
M. Magd. of Georg Neu and wife M. Magd. b 5 Apr 1797; bapt 25 Apr; spon: Conrad Hackmeyer and wife Maria Magd.
Hanna of Jacob Herre and wife Maria Elis. b 24 Jan 1797; bapt 28 Mar; spon: David Reidenauer and wife Sara
Georg of Georg Hamer and wife Cath. b 22 Feb 1797; bapt 24 Apr; spon: parents
Johannes of Georg Roth and wife Cath. b 19 Oct 1796; bapt 3 May 1797; spon: Jacob Bauer and with Cath.
Adam of Adam Fassnacht and wife Barbara b 18 Jan 1797; bapt 18 Apr; spon: parents
Susana of Peter Startzman and wife Marg. b 5 Jan 1797; bapt 18 May; spon: Heffele (Hennerich) and wife Susana
David of Hennerich Startzman and wife Elis. b 11 Mar 1797; bapt 21 May; spon: Peter Startzman and wife Marg

Evangelical Lutheran Church at Elizabethtown (Hagerstown)

Johannes of Zacharias Bard and wife A. Maria b 28 Jan 1779; no bapt date given; spon: parents
Elisabeth of Zacharias Bard and wife A. Maria b 1 Apr 1781; no bapt date given; spon: parents
Georg of Zacharias Bard and wife A. Maria b 3 Mar 1783; no bapt date given; spon: parents
Cath. of Zacharias Bard and wife A. Maria b 21 Dec 1786; no bapt date given; spon: parents
Sus. of Zacharias Bard and wife A. Maria b 6 Apr 1788; no bapt date given; spon: parents
Maria of Zacharias Bard and wife A. Maria b 24 Apr 1791; no bapt date given; spon: parents
Sally of Zacharias Bard and wife A. Maria b 13 Nov 1793; no bapt date given; spon: parents
Zacharias of Zacharias Bard and wife A. Maria b 9 Mar 1795; no bapt date given; spon: parents
Elis of Georg Michael Haushalter and wife Cath. b 20 Jul 1796; bapt 5 Jun 1797; spon: Joh. Teise and wife Elis.
Bally of Georg Grissman and wife Cath. b 15 Apr 1797; bapt 28 May; spon: Bally Off in
Rebeca of Balzer Goll and wife Cath. b 10 Apr 1797; bapt 29 May; spon: Georg Beigler and wife Elis.
A. Cath. of Hennerich Sumer and wife A. Barbara b 10 Nov 1796; bapt 19 Jun 1797; spon: parents
Feronica of Joh. Geiger and wife Susana b 21 Apr 1797; bapt 24 Jun; spon: Georg Neu and wife Magd.
Georg of Joh. Schmidt and wife Maria b 14 May 1797; bapt 3 Jul; spon: parents
Amalia of Georg Binckly and wife Eva b 3 May 1797; bapt 18 Jun; spon: Jacob Pitri and wife Barbara
Elis. of Arthur Withny and wife A. Maria b 14 Mar 1797; bapt 29 July; spon: Georg Weiss and wife Eva
Jacob of Georg Stam and wife Clara b 11 Jun 1797; bapt 6 Aug; spon: Jacob Stam and wife M. Magd.
Michael of Zacharias Bard and wife Maria b 7 May 1797; bapt 20 Aug; spon: Michael Bard and wife Cath.
Elis. of Philip Agustin and wife Cath. b 21 Jun 1797; bapt 12 Sep; spon: parents
Johannes of Hennerich Schrader and wife Cath b 7 Dec 1796; bapt 2 Aug; spon: Christian Borstler and wife Dorrothea
Susana of Ludwig Wiessman and wife Elis. b 3 Feb 1797; bapt 25 Sep; spon: Joh. Miller and wife A. Maria
Georg of Joh. Klekam and wife Drusilla b 15 Jun 1797; bapt 6 Sep; spon: parents
David of Joh. Bayer and wife Elis. b 26 Jul 1797; bapt 22 Sep; spon: parents
Samuel of Isaac Miller and wife Eva b 7 May 1797; bapt 22 Sep; spon: parents
Magd. of Friderich Hoss and wife Marg. b 25 Apr 1797; bapt 12 Jul; spon: Jacob Hoss and wife Magd.
Johannes of Jonas Zeller and wife Elis. b 25 Jan 1797; bapt 12 Jul; spon: Joh. Wachtel and wife Elis.
Johannes of Melcher Bauder and wife A. Maria b 7 Sep 1797; bapt 16 Oct; spon: parents
Sara of Abraham Peter and wife Cath. b 10 Dec 1796; bapt 3 Nov 1797; spon: parents

Evangelical Lutheran Church at Elizabethtown (Hagerstown)

Georg of Cooper Schneider and wife Elis. b 24 Feb 1797; bapt 3 Nov; spon: Michael Wolf and wife Philippina
Susana of Tomas Cowin and wife Elis b 15 Jun 1797; bapt 3 Nov; spon: parents
M. Eva of Adam Osswald and wife Maria b 14 Sep 1797; bapt 14 Nov; spon: Eva Osswald
Johannes of Georg Walch and wife A. Maria b 4 Sep 1797; bapt 14 Nov; spon: Joh. Bauer and wife Hanna
Joh. Georg of Christ Fischer and wife Cath. b 6 Feb 1797; bapt 14 Nov; spon: William Storr and wife Elis.
Barbra of William Storr and wife Elis. b 26 Sep 1797; bapt 14 Nov; spon: Barbara Schmidt
A. Maria of Joh. Kausler and wife Christina b 18 Oct 1797; bapt 2 Nov; spon: Johannes Schleich and wife A. Maria
Magd. of Georg Merckel and wife Cath. b 24 Oct 1797; bapt 12 Dec; spon: Abraham Konig and wife Magd.
Maria of John. Ronnels and wife Maria b 29 Apr 1797; bapt 18 Dec; spon: parents
Anmaria of Hennerich Schon and wife Cath. b 2 Sep 1797; bapt 24 Dec; spon: parents
Marg. of John Schmals and wife Sara b 21 Mar 1795; bapt 4 Jan 1798; spon: parents
Rubin of John Schmals and wife Sara b 18 Jan 1797; bapt 4 Jan 1798; spon: parents
Friderick of Conrad Blendlinger and wife Dorrothea b 23 Jun 1797; bapt 24 Dec 1797; spon: parents
Hennerich of Georg Drill and wife Elis b 29 Nov 1797; bapt 24 Dec 1797; spon: Dewalt Kelhofer and wife A. Maria
Elisabeth of Joseph Leinbach and wife Bally b 19 Sep 1796; bapt 5 Jan 1798; spon: Joh. Brotzman and wife A. Maria
Hanna of Joseph Leinbach and wife Bally b 19 Dec 1797; bapt 5 Jan 1798; spon: Maria Berry
Cath. Clem. of Jacob Kurtz and wife Sus. b 19 Jan 1798; bapt 3 Mar; spon: parents
Juliana of Jacob Off and wife Cath. b 20 Mar 1796; bapt 12 Dec 1798; spon: Bally Fischer
Tomas of Tomas Herris and wife Dina b 5 Oct 1797; bapt 19 Jan 1798 spon: parents
Jonathan of Peter Feigele and wife Cath. b 24 Sep 1797; bapt 8 Jan 1798; spon: parents
Georg of Hennerich Gnadig and wife Elis. b 23 Jul 1797; bapt 8 Jan 1798; spon: Peter Hoss and wife Sus.
Mary of Tomas Parekee and wife Elis b 13 Jun 1795; bapt 22 Feb 1798; spon: parents
Samuel of Tomas Parekee and wife Elis. b 17 Mar 1797; spon: Jacob Graber and wife A. Maria
Sofia of Peter Artz and wife Maria b 22 Oct 1797; bapt 25 Jan 1798; spon: Matheus Kessler and wife Eva
Elis. of Peter Lantz and wife Elis. b 23 Sep 1797; bapt 4 Mar 1798; spon: parents
Cath. of Mathias Kessler and wife Eva b 7 Sep 1797; bapt 16 Jan 1798; spon: Joh. Nicolaus Spickler (?) and wife Elis.
Salome of Peter Hoss and Sus. b 3 Jan 1798; bapt 26 Mar 1798; spon: parents
Sara of Adam Borahf and wife Elis. b 3 Aug 1797; bapt 4 Feb 1798; spon: Maria Zeller

Evangelical Lutheran Church at Elizabethtown (Hagerstown)

Eva Marg of Hennerich Strauss and wife Christ. b 4 Mar 1798; bapt 25 Mar; spon: Gottlieb Glassbrenner and wife Marg.
Today, date 16th March Cath. Urban and her mother brought an illegitimate child to me for baptism, who gave one Joh. Miller as the father. b 8 Jan 1798; bapt 16 Mar; spon: Maria Urban
Daniel of Dewald Leysinger and wife Cath. b 27 Feb 1798; bapt 19 Mar; spon: parents
Marg. of Georg Schenck and wife Cath. b 25 Feb 1798; bapt 29 Mar; spon: Georg Biegler and wife Elis.
Georg of Georg Bender and wife Marg. b 7 Apr 1798; bapt 15 Apr; spon: Christoph Alter and wife Susana
Regina of Georg Roth and wife Cath. b 1 Apr 1798; bapt 26 Apr; spon: Ludwick Kernetam and wife Regina
Cath., an illegitimate child of Jacob Danner and Eva Mayer b 31 Jan 1798; bapt 26 Apr; spon: Margaretha Mayer
Elis. of Hennerich Lillich(?) and wife Christ. b 21 Apr 1798; bapt 27 Apr; spon: parents
Maria Dorrothea of Leonhart Kuhn and wife Elis. b 26 Mar 1798; bapt 27 Apr; spon: Friederich Alter and wife Maria Marg.
Susana of Jacob Geyer and wife Dorrothea b 12 Feb 1798; bapt 7 Apr; spon: Tomas Schuman and wife Susana
Samuel of Joh. Winders and wife Elis. b 11 Nov 1797; bapt 6 May 1798; spon: parents
Elis. of Joh. Mandi and wife Rosina b 30 Sep 1797; bapt 6 May 1798; spon: Cath. Trapp in
Sara of Christian Fogler and wife Sus. b 8 Oct 1797; bapt 12 May 1798; spon: parents
Cath. of Jacob Flager and wife Marg. b 25 Aug 1797; bapt 25 May 1798; spon: parents
Mary of William Ferin & wife Marg. b 24 May 1797; bapt 27 May 1798; spon: parents
Nancy of Simon Tyle and wife Elis b 3 Dec 1797; bapt 27 May 1798; spon: Reger Ryle and wife, Nanzi
Elis. of Jacob Weil and wife Sus. b 30 dec 1797; bapt 27 May 1798; spon: Mathias Kessler and wife Eva
Samuel of Hennerich Wolfahrt and wife Cath. b 17 Mar 1797; bapt 17 Jun 1798; spon: Joh. Geiger and wife Sus.
Bally of Adam Alt and wife Magd. b 1 May 1797;bapt 10 Jun 1798; spon: parents
Lidia of Benjamin Kugel and wife Dorrathea b 13 May 1798; bapt 20 Jun; spon: parents
Samuel of Hennerich Krieger and wife A. Maria b 14 Mar 1798; bapt 20 May 1798; spon: parents
Bally of George Nic. Abold and wife Maria b 9 Apr 1798; bapt 20 May; spon: parents
Samuel of Jacob Ehrhart and wife Maria b 12 Apr 1798; bapt 1 Jul; spon: Michael Kapp and wife Cath.
Christina of Philip Springer and wife Magd. b 25 Jan 1798; bapt 25 Jul 1798; spon: Georg Walch and A. Maria
Jacob of Hennerich Heffele and wife Sus. b 29 May 1798; bapt 27 Jul; spon: Jacob Tutweiler
Elis. of Georg Bishof and wife Elis. b 27 Jun 1798; bapt 6 Jul; spon: parents
Daniel of And. Schefer and wife A. Maria b 10 Apr 1798; bapt 10 Aug; spon: parents

Evangelical Lutheran Church at Elizabethtown (Hagerstown)

William of Herman Lorshbach and wife Elis. b 26 Jul 1798; bapt 26 Aug; spon: parents
dau of Joh. Hettinger and wife Betyna b 4 Apr 1798; bapt 13 Aug; spon: parents
Elis. of Joh. Miller and wife Bolly b 15 Mar 1798; bapt 19 Aug; spon: Barbara Krieger
Maria Louisa of Carl Fried. Gelwicks and wife Maria b 18 Aug 1798; bapt 3 Sep; spon: Carl Gelwicks and wife M. Barbara
Sovia of Gottlieb Zimerman and wife Eva b 15 Jul 1798; bapt 18 Aug; spon: Sovia Zimmerman
Theodor of Theodor Tyle and wife Marg. b Jan 9 1798; bapt Sep 3; spon: parents
Johannes of Philip Studer and wife Elis b 17 Oct 1797; bapt 2 Sep 1798; spon: Balzer Bauman and wife Sabina
Samuel of Nicholas Spickler and wife Elis. b 22 Jul 1798; bapt 12 Sep; spon: Samuel Spickler
Cath. of David Weil and wife Philippina b 29 Aug 1797; bapt 3 Sep 1798; spon: Matheus Kessler and wife Eva
Joh. Georg of Joh. Georg Knode and wife Cath. b 31 Jul 1798; bapt 18 Sep; spon: parents
Rebecca of Jonas Hackmeyer and wife Sus. b 6 Mar 1798; bapt 17 Sep; spon: parents
Barbara of Nicolaus Schmidt and wife Cath. b 31 Aug 1798; bapt 22 Sep; spon: Nicolaus Schmidt sen. and wife Barbara
Hesekiel of Joh. Miller and wife A. Maria b 10 Aug 1798; bapt 22 Sep; spon: parents
Eva Anna of Tobias Ritter aand wife Eva Cath. b 16 Jul 1798; bapt 20 Oct; spon: parents
Mihle of Willhelm Rotter and wife Sara b 7 Oct 1798; bapt 2 Nov; spon: parents
Samuel of Jacob Mayer and wife Elis. b 17 Aug 1798; bapt 13 Dec; spon: Jacob Schupp and wife Anna
Susana Lidia of Joh. Ganter and wife Maria b 27 Aug 1798; bapt 12 Dec; spon: Joh. Geiger and wife Susana
David of Joh. Reiser and wife Maria Magd. b 4 Nov 1797; bapt 1 Dec 1798; spon: parents
Mickella, dau of Walter Boyd and wife Anna b 21 oct 1798; bapt 25 Nov; spon: Elena Krokerly; Georg Price
Matilda of Joh. Ronnold and wife Magd. b 17 May 1798; bapt 4 Dec; spon: parents
Sarah of Michael Bauart and wife A. Marg. b 22 Nov 1798; bapt 22 Dec.; bapt Jacob Gerhart and wife Christina
Cath (twin) of Jacob Jung and wife Otilia b 28 Sep 1798; bapt 5 Dec; spon: parents
Otilia (twin) of Jacob Jung and wife Otilia b 28 Sep 1798; bapt 5 Dec; spon: parents
Jacob of Daniel Nied and wife A. Maria b 9 Oct 1798; bapt 16 Nov; spon: parents
Imanuel of Hennerich Brua and wife Cath. b 29 Oct 1798; bapt 7 Jan 1799; spon: parents
Rebecca of Peter Miller and wife Christina b 8 Dec 1798; bapt 7 Jan 1799; spon: parents
Cath. of Michael Laury and wife Barbara b 4 Nov 1798; bapt 19 Feb 1799; spon: Cath. Laury

Evangelical Lutheran Church at Elizabethtown (Hagerstown)

Sus. of Joh. Rossel and wife Sus b 16 Dec 1798; bapt 2 Feb 1799; spon: parents
Magraretha of Georg Martini and wife Sus. b 28 Nov 1798; bapt 16 Feb 1799; spon: Samuel Buler and wife Magd.
Joh. Jacob of Peter Wolf and wife Magd. b 5 Oct 1798; bapt 13 Mar 1799; spon: Christoph Hanly
Sara of Jacob Fischer and wife Cath. b 1 Sep 1798; bapt 17 Mar 1799; spon: parents
Maria Dorrothea of Joh. Tyre and wife Bezi b 4 Mar 1799; bapt 23 Mar; spon: parents
Georg Matheus of Peter Miller and wife A. Maria b 13 Feb 1799; bapt 31 Mar; spon: Georg Schenck and wife Cath.
Johannes of Friederich Klepper and wife Sarah b 4 Mar 1799; bapt 12 Apr; spon: parents
Rosina of Anthony Hauret and wife Maria b 16 Mar 1799; bapt 6 Apr; spon: Maria Kershner and Georg Kershner
Susana of Martin Startzman and wife Magd b 11 Feb 1799; bapt 20 Apr; spon: Christina Keller
Anna of Conrad Blendlinger and wife Dorrothea b 23 Apr 1799; bapt 5 May; spon: parents
Jacob of Peter Startzman and wife Marg. b 2 Jan 1799; bapt 12 May; spon: parents
Cath. of Joh. Bauser and wife Magd. b 11 Nov 1798; bapt 28 May; spon: parents
Cath. of Isaac Miller and wife Eva b 29 Jan 1799; bapt 28 May; spon: parents
Elis. of Jacob Trap and wife Cath. b 14 Jan 1799; bapt 29 May; spon: Michael Strahn and wife Elis.
Joh. Jacob of Jacob Flager and wife Marg. b 2 Mar 1799; bapt 2 Jun; spon: Martin Kufer
Magd., illegitimate child of Jacob Hoss and Cath. Jegly b 17 May 1799; bapt 4 Jun; spon: Cath. Jegly, mother
Elis. of Benjamin Reitenauer and wife A. Maria b 10 Jun 1798; bapt 14 Jun 1799; spon: Juliana Trisher
Johannes of Jacob Bauer and wife Cath. b 8 Feb 1799; bapt 28 May; spon: parents
Barb. of Peter Hisson and wife Barb. b 11 Mar 1799; bapt 19 May; spon: Adam Fassnacht and wife Barbara
Nathanael of Nathaneal Morgan and wife Judith b 28 Jan 1799; bapt 26 May; spon: Georg Schaal and wife Marg.
Anna of Wilhelm Haus and wife Bezi b 8 May 1799; bapt 1 Jun; spon: Fried. Alter and wife Maria Marg.
Cath. of Jacob Jegly and wife Elis. b 17 Feb 1799; bapt 22 Jun; spon: Cath. Fogelgesang
Johannes of Joh. Beyerly and wife Barb. b 4 Jun 1799; bapt 22 Jun; spon: parents
Samuel Simon of Georg Schmucker and wife Cath. b 28 Jan 1799; bapt 16 Mar; spon: Simon Kiesecker and wife and Samuel Gross and wife Elisabeth
Samuel of Ludwich Yung and wife Cath. b 17 May 1799; bapt 5 Aug; spon: parents
Elis. of Hennerich Zimmerman and wife Marg. b 31 Oct 98; bapt 21 Jul 1799; spon: parents
Samuel of Georg Bauder and wife Marg. b 10 Jul 1799; bapt 20 Jul; spon: Stophel Alter and wife Sus.
Magd. of Isaac Gulsen and wife Marg. b 20 Apr 1799; bapt 23 Aug; spon: Margaretha Grosskopf

Evangelical Lutheran Church at Elizabethtown (Hagerstown)

Bally of Joseph Hamilton and wife Barbara b 5 May 1799; bapt 23 Aug; spon: Maria Kernekam
Cath. of Jacob Miller and wife Elis. b 1 Sep 1799; bapt 6 Oct; spon: Cath Hauslerin
Cath. of Franz Streithof and wife Cath. b 15 Dec 1798; bapt 13 Nov 1799; spon: Joh. Reiser and wife Magd.
Cath. of Fried. Hoss and wife Marg. b 5 Aug 1799; bapt 20 Oct; spon: parents
Ellenora of Joh. Geiger and wife Sus. b 2 Jul 1799; bapt 24 Sep; spon: parents
Johannes of Willhelm Storr and wife Elis. b 28 Jul 1799; bapt 10 Sep; spon: Jacob Bienkle and wife Cath.
Maria of Georg Hamer and wife Cath. b 24 Jul 1799; bapt 26 Sep; spon: parents
Elis. of Hennerich Arnold and wife Bally b 4 Aug 1799; bapt 1 Dec; spon: Simon Bauman and wife Magd.
Sus. of Abraham Peter and wife Cath. b 4 Jan 1799; bapt 4 Dec; spon: parents
Polly of Reinherd M'Donnol and wife Polly b 9 Sep 1799; bapt 2 Dec; spon: parents
Cath. of Christ. Vogelgesang and wife Barb b 13 Oct 1799; bapt 26 Dec; spon: Georg Vogelgesang and wife Cath.
Philipp of Adam Schneider and wife Cath. b 13 Aug 1799; bapt 29 Oct; spon: parents
William of Arder. Withny and wife A. Maria b 31 Jul 1799; bapt 3 Nov; spon: George Weiss and wife Eva
Johannes of Joh. Anderson and wife Elis b 23 Oct 1799; bapt 4 Jan 1800; spon: Samuel Hackmeyer
Elis. of Peter Hooss and wife Sus. b 1 Dec 1799; bapt 17 Jan 1800; spon: Elis. Gnadig
Elis. of Nicolaus Schmidt and wife Cath. b 13 Jan 1800; bapt 27 Jan; spon: Elis. Schmidt
Samuel of Hennerich Lillig and wife Christ. b 11 Jan 1800; bapt 28 Jan; spon: Cath. Stattler and the father of the child
Johannes of Joh. Roynolds and wife Charlotta b 12 Dec 1799; bapt 30 Jan; spon: Georg Woltz and wife
Rebecca of Georg Deil and wife Elis. b 19 Jan 1800; bapt 18 Feb; spon: Dewald Kelhofer and wife A.Maria
Maria of Hennerich Kelhofer and wife Elis. b 13 Jan 1800; bapt 13 Feb; spon: Dewald Kelhofer and wife A. Maria
Prudens of Zacharias Molls and wife Sus. b 17 Nov 1799; bapt 16 Feb; spon: Judit Brendlinger
Susana of Jacob Herre and wife M. Elis. b 3 Dec 1799; bapt 6 Mar 1800; spon: Joh. Geiger and wife Susana
Joh. Jacob of Peter Suder and wife Cath. b 13 Feb 1800; bapt 1 Apr; spon: Joh. Jacob Urban
Andres of Joh. Jegly and wife Sus. b 26 Dec 1799; bapt 17 Mar 1800; spon: Cath. Jegly
Juliana of Georg Roth and wife Cath. b 9 Jan 1800; bapt 27 Mar; spon: parents
Susana of Joh. Bayer and wife Elis. b 12 Nov 1799; bapt 5 May 1800; spon: parents
Cath. of Georg Reider and wife Cath. b 20 Dec 1799; bapt 14 May; spon: George Faber and wife Cath
son of Hennerich Purman and wife Cath. b 8 Nov 1797; bapt 14 May 1800; spon: parents

Evangelical Lutheran Church at Elizabethtown (Hagerstown)

dau of Hennerich Purman and wife Cath. b 5 May 1800; bapt 14 May; spon: parents
Sovia of George Biegler and wife Elis. b 8 Mar 1800; bapt 19 May; spon: parents
Cath. of Matheus Strein and wife Fronika b 6 Jul 1799; bapt 3 May 1800; spon: Cath. Wachtel
Magd. of Ludwick Kernetam and wife Cath. b 23 Jan 1800; bapt 25 May; spon: parents
Bernd of Adam Fasenacht and wife, Barb. b 2 Jan 1800; bapt 2 Jun; spon: parents
Elis. of Isaac Jones and wife Marg. b 3 Jun 1800; bapt 9 Jul; spon: parents
Polly of Bernhart Fastenacht and wife Elis. b 11 Feb 1800; bapt 18 Jul; spon: Adam Fastenacht and wife Barbara
Elis. of Joh. Koch and wife Cath. b 16 Apr 1800; bapt 19 Jun; spon: parents
Levi of Samuel Trabinger and wife Polly b 10 Mar 1800; bapt 16 Jun; spon: Philip Moyer and wife Cath.
Daniel of Hennerich Schon and wife Cath. b 6 Jun 1799; bapt 5 Jul; spon: parents
Marg. Ludwick Kernetam and wife Cath. b 23 Jan 1800; bapt 25 May; spon: parents
Daniel of Martin Starzman and wife Magd. b 6 Jun 1800; bapt 16 Jun; spon: Hennerich Startzman and wife Eva
Johannes of Georg Schenck and wife Cath. b 12 Apr 1800; bapt 22 May; spon: Abrah. Leiter and wife Elis.
Jacob of Dewald Leysinger and wife Cath. b 19 Jun 1800; bapt 23 Jun; spon: parents
Johannes of Martin Schourcker and wife Cath. b 8 Jun 1800; bapt 1 Aug; spon: parents
Jonathan of Benjamin Kugel and wife Dorrothea b 24 Apr 1800; bapt 24 Jul; spon: parents
Johannes of Peter Krout and wife Elis. b 20 Jan 1800; bapt 26 Jul; spon: parents
son of Conrad Hackmeyer and wife Cath. b 24(?) Jul 1800; bapt 3 Aug; Samuel Hackmeyer
Daniel of Joh. Weiss and wife Christ. b 5 Aug 1800; bapt 17 Aug; spon: parents
Willhelm of Philip Hornish and wife Cath. b 5 Sep 1800; bapt 15 Sep; spon: Adam Fockler
Johannes, an illigitimate child brought by widow Reidenauer and (who) gave Joh. Oss for the father; b 9 Nov 1798; bapt 24 Sep 1800; spon: mother
Jacob of Jacob Carl and wife Christ. b 14 Mar 1800; bapt 26 Jul; spon: parents
Georg of Jacob Geyer and wife Dorrothea b 9 Jul 1800; bapt 6 Sep; spon: Peter Feygele and wife Cath.
Elis. of David Lefever and wife Sus. b 8 Dec 1799; bapt 8 Sep 1800; spon: Jacob Zouck and wife Elis.
A. Maria of Peter Artz and wife A. Maria b 30 Jun 1800; bapt 6 Oct; spon: parents
Maria of Gottlieb Zimerman and wife Eva b 21 Aug 1800; b 21 Aug 1800; bapt 15 Nov; spon: Dewald Eichelberger and wife Lora
Susana of Hennerich Krieger and wife A. Maria b 10 Sep 1800; bapt 15 Nov; spon: Georg Matiny and wife
Sara of Henrich Arnold and wife Polly b 2 Oct 1800; bapt 2 Dec; spon: Tomas Schuman and wife Sus.

Evangelical Lutheran Church at Elizabethtown (Hagerstown)

George of Christ Schmidt and wife Cath. b 15 Oct 1800; bapt 26 Dec; spon: Georg Binckle and wife Eva
Henrich of Henrich Heffele and wife Sus. b 3 Nov 1800; bapt 17 Dec; spon: Georg Neff and wife Elis.
of Joh. Hamel and wife Maria b 28 Aug 1800; bapt 30 Nov; spon: parents
Henrich of Jacob Schupp and wife Sus. b 14 Feb 1800; bapt 30 Nov; spon: parents
Hanna of Peter Schupp and wife Elis. b 19 Mar 1800; bapt 30 Dec; spon: Jacob Schupp and wife Anna
Joh. Georg of Henrich Strauss and wife Christ. b 12 Oct 1800; bapt 15 Dec; spon: parents
Susana of Hennerich Schon and wife Cath. b 14 Jun; bapt 1 Mar; spon: Betty Gross
Sus. of Willh. Rotter and wife Sara b 29 Nov 1800; bapt 14 Jan 1801; spon: parents
Elias of Joh. Miller and wife Maria b 19 Dec 1800; bapt 1 Mar 1801; spon: parents
Johannes of Georg Hemel and wife Cath. b 16 Mar 1800; bapt 4 Apr; spon: Christ. Schwab & wife Cath.
Andreas of Mathias Kessler & wife Eva b 15 Oct 1800; bapt 3 Jan 1801; spon: Georg Neu and wife Magd.
Samuel of Andreas Carl and wife Nanzi b 26 Dec 1800; bapt 8 Mar 1801; spon: parents
Samuel of Joh. Paul Wagele and wife Marg. b 5 Oct 1800; bapt 12 Mar 1801; spon: parents
Maria Magd. of Jacob Burckhardt and wife Cath. b 30 Juan 1796; bapt 3 May 1801; spon: parents
Joh. Georg of Jacob Burckhardt and wife Cath. b 23 Apr 1798; bapt 3 May 1801; spon: George Reinhard and wife
Cath. of Jacob Fischer and wife Cath. b 25 Oct 1800; bapt 28 Jul 1801; spon: parents
Sally of Joh. Ehrhart and wife Cath. b 27 Jun 1799; bapt 27 May 1801; spon: Cath Brendel
Johannes of Joh. Mecklu and wife Hanna b 21 Aug 1799; bapt 13 Mar 1801; spon: Joh. Rossel and wife Sus.
Hanna of Joh. Mecklu and wife Hanna b 20 Oct 1797; bapt 13 Mar 1801; spon: Joh. Rossel and wife Sus.
Anna of Jacob Bauer and wife Cath. b 2 Apr 1800; bapt 12 Mar 1801; spon: parents
Jacob of Henrich Sumers & wife Barb. b 20 Oct 1800; bapt 12 May 1801; spon: parents
Polly of Philip Weitturst and wife Cath. b 5 Jul 1798; bapt 3 Dec 1801; spon: Math. Heckman and wife Maria
Lidia of Georg Geck and wife Cath. b 20 Jan 1799; bapt 2 Jan 1802; spon: parents
Johannes of Joseph Reitenauer and wife Anna b 14 Mar 1800; bapt 13 Jan 1802; spon: parents
Nanzi of David Huber and wife Elis. b 25 Sep 1793; bapt 6 Jun 1803; spon: Jacob Weil and wife Sus.
Samuel of David Huber and wife Elis. b 22 May 1796; bapt 6 Jun 1803; spon: Georg Neu and Magd.
Cath. of David Huber and wife Elis. b 19 Jun 1798; bapt 6 Jun 1803; spon: parents
David of David Huber and wife Elis. b 20 Dec 1802; bapt 6 Jun 1803; spon: David Kessler and wife Susanna

Evangelical Lutheran Church at Elizabethtown (Hagerstown)

Jacob of Michael Heffele and wife Elis. b 22 Jun 1796; bapt 13 Nov 1803; spon: Henrich Heffele and Susana
A. Maria of Michael Heffele and wife Elis. b 2 Sep 1798; bapt 13 Nov 1803; spon: Henrich Heffele and Susana
Elias of Michael Heffele and wife Elis. b 1 Sep 1800; bapt 13 Nov 1803; spon: mother
dau of Michael Heffele and wife Elis. b 13 Sep 1802; bapt 13 Nov 1803; spon: mother
Peter of Peter Wagner and wife A. Maria b 26 Dec 1796; bapt 23 Nov 1803; spon: Lorentz Schich
Cath. of Jacob Fischer and wife Cath. b 25 Oct 1800; bapt 28 Jul 1801; spon: parents
Joh. Jacob of Jacob Schupp and wife Anna b 28 Jul 1770
Johannes of Jacob Schupp and wife Anna b 12 Feb 1773
Henrich of Jacob Schupp and wife Anna b 31 Jan 1779
Elisabeth of Jacob Schupp and wife Anna b 10 Jun 178-
David of Jacob Schupp and wife Anna b 22 Sep 1787
Daniel of Jacob Schupp and wife Anna b 1 Sep 1789
Jonathan of Jacob Schupp and wife Anna b 9 Mar 1791
Samuel of Jacob Schupp and wife Anna b 15 Feb 1793
Susana of Jacob Schupp and wife Anna b 31 Jan 1795
Simon Peter of Jacob Schupp and wife Anna b 24 Jan 1801
Christian of Christ. Fechtig and wife Sus. b 6 Feb 1794; bapt 24 Aug 1804; spon: parents
Georg of Christ. Fechtig and wife Sus. b 28 Aug 1797; bapt 24 Aug 1804; spon: parents
Johannes of Christ. Fechtig and wife Sus. b 24 Mar 1799; bapt 24 Aug 1804; spon: parents
Jacob of Christ. Fechtig and wife Sus. b 3 May 1802; bapt 24 Aug 1804; spon: parents
Samuel of Peter Schleiss & wife A. Maria b 3 Mar 1799; bapt 14 Mar 1805; spon: parents
Elizabeth of Maxwell Welsh and wife Marg. b 4 Jul 1794; bapt 17 Aug 1807; spon: parents
James Maxwell of Maxwell Welsh and wife Marg. b 27 Aug 1801; bapt 17 Aug 1807
Susanna of Jacob Mayer and wife Susana b 29 Nov 1799; bapt 29 Nov 1808(?); spon: parents
Ra(c)hel illegitimate child of John Scot & Eliz. Wilson b 4 Oct 1799; bapt 26 Jul 1809; spon: Juliana Hackin

"Register of the Marriages by me J. Georg Schmucker for the year of Christ, 1794." [The abbreviations, W.L., L., L.W., etc. probably refer to those marriages with and without licenses.]
1794
Aug 3 Philip Ringer and Eliz Bayer
3 Walter Eikeberger and Susana Schneider
5 Samuel Reed & Bezy Forter
10 Joh. McCormick & Elis. McCormick W.L.
10 Lauman & Marg. Bellin
Sep 28 Abraham Frey & Marg. Schmeissern(?)
Oct 6 Benjamin Schwengel and Eva Schmidt in . W.L.
6 Hennerick Strauss and Christina Glasbrenner n W.L.
10 James Reed and Cath. Ringer W.L.
Nov 16 Joh. Tyse and Elis. Kiesecker W.L.

Evangelical Lutheran Church at Elizabethtown (Hagerstown)

Dec. 2 Nedren Schmalzer and Cath Cau (Kau). W.L.
1795
Jan 4 Benjamin Heffner and Barbara Menzer
5 Johannes Haushulter and Hanna McHarry
Feb 15 Geo. Gabriel Escher and Jacobina Hauck in.
Mar 12 Joh. Ronals and Mary Welz. W.L.
17 Michael Baker and Mollena Hose W.L.
20 Leonhard Kuhn and Eliz. Alter W.L.
20 Jacob Schock and Eliz. Deal W.L.
23 Tomas Cresap and Mary Briscoe W.L.
29 John Earhart and Cath. Brindel W.L.
" Abraham Langenecker and Nenzi Kneberger
" James Slater and Mary Formar
" Georg Stumpf and Elis Walter
Apr 3 Elias Murry and Ellender Freeborn
4 Joh. Georg Pflatzgraf and Elis. Miller n
24 Adam Kizmiller and Elis. Ax.
Jacob Weil and Elis. Tomas
Franz Scheffer and Elis. Schuin
Samuel Neith and Elis. Benns
30 David Little and Elis. Wolz W.L.
May 2 Joh. Boerson and Mary Miller W.L.
2 Joseph Scherah(?) and Elis BezMar(?) W.L.
11 Andru Sillinger and Amotia Robars W.L.
13 Jonathan Jabson & Charity Walter W.L.
23 Georg Pender & Rebecca Alter W.L.
26 Peter Lanz & Elis. Schlimmer
27 David Weil & Philipina Weber n
27 Daniel Conrad & Easter Ruth
28 Hennerich Jegly & Marg. Lesig
29 John Ferrall & Mary Coroy W.L.
Jun 4 Robert Purdgard(?) and Peggy Dowlar W.L.
6 George Mangard & Haty Hawz W.L.
6 Georg Schnel & Rebecca Molloth W.L.
23 Joh. Peck & Cath. Biard W.L.
25 Conrad Heyberger & Cath. Wolf W.L.
28 Joh. Skils and Christ. Bez
Jul 28 George Confair and Eva Nouse W.L.
Aug 25 Joh. Frey and Elis. Schley W.L.
27 Benjamin Tyson and Marg Morgon W.L.
16 Jams Wood and Cath Flinger
8 Michael Beard and Hanna Hose W.L.
20 Jacob Funck and Sus. Ronk W.L.
Dec 18 Jacob Hanker and Cath. Butterbach W.L.
13 Jospeh Linebach and Maria Schaw L.W.
14 Wil. Kreps and Fanny Adams W.L.
18 George Farmar and Christ. Yunker W.L.
1796 Jan and Feb
4 Nathan Jackson and Mary Hemton W.L.
6 William Kennedy and Cath. Daily W.L.
8 Joh. Bayer and Elis. Kensinger
26 Adam Deyle and Cath. Updegraff W.L.
12 John Oharrough and Elis. Huiez W.L.
Mar
14 Manrall(?) Baker and Elis. McEvon W.L.

Evangelical Lutheran Church at Elizabethtown (Hagerstown)

9 Joh. Houk and Elis. Fiere W.L.
12 William Reynolds and Sus. Brendlinger W.L.
20 Harvy Schauer and Martha Lowman W.L.
Apr 2 James Burke and Elis. Ferrel W.L.
5 Peter Stihelader and Eva Leighter W.L.
Samuel Little and Lyday Roberts W.L.
12 Joh. Bouyrer and Magd. Bayer W.L.
15 Joh. Whittle and Charity Forrest W.L.
" Georg Mann and Maria Gebhart
" Michael Miller and Mag. Zimer
9 Joh. Kiesecker and Cath. Wolf W.L.
May 7 Joseph Pursel and Jane Jans W.L.
4 Jacob Boyer and Elis. Sigmond W.L.
Joh Graffort and Agatha Reydenauer
addenda: 18 Apr - Benjamin Moser and Mary Lethurman W.L.
Jun 4 Jacob Bergman and Cath. Miller W.L.
13 Richan Allender and Sarah McCanedy W.L.
2 George Roads and Cath. Fasnacht W.L.
4 George Bonebrake and Cath. Barkdull W.L.
5 Joh. Carter and Rebecca Feabran W.L.
25 Abraham Winter and Cath. Langenecker W.L.
20 David Reydenauer and Cath. Fiscus W.L.
Jul 2 Jacob Bayer and Barb. Anderson W.L.
Aug 6 Christian Whooer and Susy Antbebbrozgez W.L.
Oct 4 Jacob Feight and Cath. Henavel W.L.
9 Joh. Bayer and Elis. Bauser
15 Salomon Tile and Christina Farmer
1 Jacob Hurshman and Easter Gaver W.L.
Nov 22 Jacob Kitsmiller and Rosina Wolfort W.L.
Dec 12 William Smith and Eliz. Smith W.L.
30 Jacob Haynes and Mary Pisbet W.L.
6 David Flenner and Susana Bruva L.W.
16 Jacob Bruva and Mary Angle L.W.
1797
Jan 10 Jacob Flager and Marg. Foltz
7 Christian Backer and Nancy Stout L.W.
28 George Doyl and Eliz. Kelhoover L.W.
Martin Motz and Cath. Tard W.L.d. 28 March
March 28 George Bowsler and Motlaka Metty W.L.
Apr
19 Martin Meyer and Cath. Angle W.L.
May 19 Benjamin Koogle and Dorly Rudenauer W.L.
9 Daniel Mirker and Becke Vach W.L.
Mar
5 John Kitchen and Mary McCulloch W.L.
22 John Muntsh(?) and Margaret Reed W.L.
Jun 5 Christ Metz and Elis. Bergdoll W.L.
24 Andrew Boughman and Elis. Erich W.L.
26 Joseph Fiery and Magdalen Ridenauer W.L.
Jul 24 John Benter and Mary Willhelm L. (Wash)
29 Jacob Piper and Polly Amen L. (Wash)
Aug
3 William Hanes and Eliz. Brunner W.L.
Oct
26 Wendel Oyer and Cath. Cook W.L.

Evangelical Lutheran Church at Elizabethtown (Hagerstown)

28 Henry Syster and Barbara Waitman W.L.
27 Henry Cow and Mary Zimerman L.Wash
Michael Schwab and Polly Braun
Joh. Georg Hatfiel and Cath. Hausshalter
Nov
6 Nicolas Haysoni and Eliz. Flenner W.L.
10 John Shupp and Eliz. Conrad W.L.
9 Francis Cunningham and Margaret Hughes W.L.
Dec
2 Frederick Waver and Elis. Maggin W.L.
30 Thomas Caywood and Sarah Mastallen W.L.
3 Christian Fogelgesang & Susana Arnold W.L.
3 Friederich Leschurr and Maria Yunker
Michael Schmidt and Cath. Tim (Dim?)
Joh. Brunner and Marg. Schmidt in
1798
Jan 20 Francis Oyer and Peggy Coock L. Wash
11 Seth Lane and Cath Woltz L.
4 Andrew Hocker and Sus. Cow L.
Feb
13 Hennry Coock and Mary Schutz L.
13 Joh. Sherrick and Ann Weyant L.
6 Robert Davison and Sus. Burkart(?) L.
17 Gottlieb Zimerman and Eva Hann L.
Mar
Christ Schmidt and Eva Flori
Daniel Reidenauer and Barbara Kershner L.W.
Adam Housholder and Cath Davis L.W.
Adam Reidenaur and Cath. Tudweiler
Henry Mu..ar & Marg.Coon L.W.
Georg Flori and Eva Enderson
Isaac Tyler and Sus. Dengler
Apr
Jacob Fiery and Sus Startzman W.L.
Johann Hefflich and Magd. Alter W.L.
Friederich Clopper and Sarah Becker W.L.
Abrah. Ritter and Cath. Bayer
Jacob Jegly and Sus. Vogelgesang
May
Martin Startzman and Molly Keller L.
James Cunningham and Fanny Startzman L.
Andrew Charles and Margaret Vogelgesang W.L.
Jun
David Spesserd and Eva Hoise L.
Richard Hadley and Sarah Jobson
Jul
Abraham Leighter and Elis. Dusinger W.L.
Samuel Slohn and Elis. Hason
Alex. Clarch and Sus. Swailes L.W.
Aug
Joh. Byerly and Barbara Brendle W.L.
Adam Dusing and Cath. Buzzard W.L.
Sep
Henry Arnold and Mary Bowman W.L.
Joh. Obermeyer and Feni Carter

Evangelical Lutheran Church at Elizabethtown (Hagerstown)

Joh. Grau and Sus. Juques
Oct
Christ. Deal and Mary Werner L.
Nov
Peter Cookerly and Elina Boyd Price L.
Samuel Moon and Christ. Humbet L.
Dec
John Brandstater and Marg. Kifer
Joh. Wentling and Christ. Koler L.
1799
Jan
Joh. Schmidt and Cath Bar L.W.
Jacob Borckel and Juliana Fasnacht L.
David Lefebre and Sus. Crisinger
Col. (?) --- Moorehead and Esther Toneray L.
Feb
Christ. Palmer and Mary Kelly L.
Henry Ensminger and Rachel McIntire L.
William Draber and Mary Tise
Francis Kaar and Sally Klarck
Joh. Koch and Cath. Lora
Jacob Fisler and Cath. Griffer
Mar
Jacob Stack and Baggy Davis W.L.
Joh. Schumfeld and Barbara Schneider L.
Gottfried Mattick and Sus. Miller L.
Leonhard Knebel and Elis. Cow L.
Michael Schauma(?) and Polly Kepling L.
James Russel and Sarah Lepten L.
Jacob Fessler and Cath. Geisser L.
Jacob Knodel and Barb. Dusaler
Joh. Miller and Beggy Schreiber
Apr
Hennerich Kelhofer and Elis. Kuker
Jacob Cruist (?) and Cath.Diel L.
Levi Housley and Cath. Welty L.
Peter Sutter and Cath. Urban
Bernard Fasnacht and Elis. Wolf L.
May
Hennerich Sydel and Mary Weaddle L.
Michael Christman and Cath. Heik L.
Jacob Snavely and Elis. Stoner L.
Jun
Joh. Brown and Nanzi Dorman
Aug
Jacob Gantz and Sus. Langenecker L.
Peter Barckdall and Mary Musselman L.
Sep
James Wallace and Sus. Stack L.
Abraham Schmetz and Cath Fye L.
Joh. Logne and Ana Martin L.
Willhelm Stack and Esther Zerckman L.
Oct
Fried. Hausholter and Cath. Lefner L.
Joh. Hamel and Maria Curnicam L.

Evangelical Lutheran Church at Elizabethtown (Hagerstown)

Herman Wort and Sus. Miller L.
Albin Fenick and Elis. Pryer L.
Joh. Jegly and Sus. Miller L.
Nov
Georg Hatte(Halle?) and Cath Oxx L.
Dec
Georg Brendel and Elis. Grove L.
Peter Bayer and Maria Bowser L.
1800
Jan
Jams Blackiton and Christina Deyl L.
Martin Kefer and Mary Varner L.
Casper Kinckel and Sus. Grove
Joh. Lifler & Christ. Hausholter
Feb
Jacob Waltz and Sus. Fessler L.
Andreas Carl and Nancy Brunner L.
Mar
Joh. Meyers (Meyus?) and Cath. Albreith L.
Christoph Reidenauer and Elis. Bauers L.
Jacob Myers and Mary Schonefeld L.
Apr
Jacob Berckdoll and Sus. Muselman
Joh. Miller and Mary Robey L.
David Wusteberger and Sus. Ox L.
Joh. Schrader and Rebecca Lane L.
May
Joh. Beckey and Nancy Morris L.
Jun
Tom Forbes and Cath. Selser L.
Price Fisher and Mary Youngers L.
Jul
Lorenz Schick and Elis. Ebbert L.
Georg Schram and Sarah Alter L.
Conrad Franckeberger and Nelly Boyd L.
Aug
Jacob Keplinger and Elis. Highsho L.
William Green and Elis. Henry L.
Peter Shull and Elis Shacks(?) L.
Andreas Ocks and Maria Fiscbach L.
Joh. Schmidt and Sovia Vogelgesang L.
Tom Hudson and Sarah Walter L.
Joh. McKinly and Nancy Bell L.
Sep
Nathan Coldman and Elis. Dempster L.
Joh. Schlegel and Rebarbara Yelivichs(?) L.
Joh. Kitsmuller and Elis. Wolford L.
Joh. Yunter and Cath. Leise (obl.)
Nov
Phil Colp and Elis Cramer L.
George Spa---ys and Sarah Eakle L.
Joh. Hoffman and Cath. Eakle L.
Peter Bernhard and Barb. Metz L.
Michael Yerzer and Marg. Scholl L.
Robert Tembers and Cath. Heiss
Ludwig Ersminger and Polly Wyand L.

Salem Reformed Church

Baptismal Register (1771-1783)

1770, the 8th of April, was born into the world to Henrich Schnebeli a little young son: He received thereafter the sacrament of Holy Baptism, from N. Henop, Pastor, at present, in Fredericktown, but who has preached here. The little son received the name David.
1769. the 10th. February, was born to Hann Nicolaus Schaefer a daughter, and was on the 4th of July 1770, publicly baptised by the Pastor Henop. The godmother was Georg Shaefer's first daughter Elisabetha. The child received the name Sussanna.
1770, the 14th of January, was born to Jacob Mueller a son, and he was publicly baptised, July 13th, by Pastor Nicodemus. The godfather was Conrad Mueller, and he received the name Conrad.
Henrich of Johannes Anselt and mother Anna Maria b 10 Dec 1770, bapt 20 Jan 1771; wit: Henrich Schreyack and his housewife Catharina.
Maria Sara of Niclos Reis, and the mother Maria b 21 Sep 1770; bapt 20 Jan 1771; wit: Johan Niclos Werner and his housewife Maria.
Anna Susanna of Christian Mantel and mother Barbara b 27 Jan 1771, bapt 8 Feb 1771; wit: Fridrich Stats, and housewife Sibila
Johan Wilhelm of Georg Paulus Christman (Christ?) and mother Magdalena b 12 Jan 1771; bapt 3 Feb; wit: Wilhelm Heyser and housewife Anna
Jacob of Baltzer Gol and mother Maria Elisabetha, married, b 1771 and bapt
---
Maria Eva of Christian Fogelgesang and Maria Barbara, married, b 18 Jan 1771; bapt 16 Feb; wit: Frances Michael Fey and his housewife Maria Eva
Maria Catharina of Conrath Ham and Maria Gertrauta, married, b 26 Jan 1771; bapt 16 Feb; wit: Gabriel Baecker and his housewife Maria Cathrina
Johan Henrich, of Henrich Startzman and Eva, married, b 2 Jan 1771 and bapt 17 Feb; wit: Henrich Mueller and housewife Catharina
Johan Georg of Georg Jacob Oster and Juliana, married, born 9 Jan 1771, bapt 28 Mar; wit: Johann Georg Wird, godfather. Mar: Elib: Jungin
Anna Elisabetha of Niclos Bender and Susanna, married, b 8 Feb 1771; bapt 28(29?) Mar; wit: Baltzer Mauti and his housewife Elisabeth
Johannes of Georg Schaefer and Christina, married, b 8 Feb 1771; bapt 28 Mar; wit: Georg Schaefer and his housewife Maria
Eva Elisabetha of George Kirschner and mother Anna Maria, married, b 15 Feb; bapt 27 Mar 1771; wit: Eva Hipschin
Elisabetha of Johannes Kirschner and Elisabetha, married, b 24 Feb 1771; bapt 29 Mar; wit: Georg Kirschner and housewife Anna Maria and Anna Maria Hixin
David of Rutholf Flenner and Magdalena, married, b 10 Dec 1770; bapt 29 Mar 1771; wit: held by same in Holy Baptism
Maria of Jacob Schuander and Catharina, married, b 3 Mar 1771; bapt 1 Apr 1771; wit: Maria Schaeferin
Martin of Rutholf Hofman and Doratea, married, b 12 Oct 1769; bapt 1 Apr 1771; wit: Vellendin Lidman and his housewife Catharina
Jonathan of Rutholf Hofman and Doratea, married, b 9 Jun 1770; bapt 1 Apr 1771; wit: Henrich Esch, and his housewife Catharina
Catharina of Jacob Bautz and Anna Elisabeth, married, b 10 Apr 1771; bapt 5 May; wit: Christian Vogelgesang and his housewife Maria Barbara
Catharina of Detrich Dieter and Margretha, married; b 4 Apr 1771; bapt 5 May; wit: Ana Elisabetha
Henrich of Jacob Krup b 27 Apr 1771; bapt 5 May; wit: Henrich Reidenauer and his housewife

Salem Reformed Church

Jacob of Canrath Bueckle and Margretha, married; b 10 Aug 1770; bapt 19 May 1771; wit: Jacob Zoeller

Martin of Henrich Canterman and Barbara, married; b 4 Apr 1771; bapt 19 May; held by same

Nansi of Wilhelm Sitzler and Elisabetha, married; b 27 Jan 1771; bapt 2 Jun; wit: Johannes Schwepser and Nansi Warein

Georg of Michael Quickel and Fronica, married; b 2 Nov 1770; bapt 2 Jun 1771; held by same

Michael of Peter Schwieder and Elisabeth, married, b 15 Apr 1771; bapt 2 Jun; wit: Michael Quickel and his housewife Fronica

Maria Susana of Henrich Heinisch and Maria Elisabeth, married; b 27 Jan 1771; bapt 2 Jun; wit: Georg Schaefer and his housewife Anna Maria

Wilhelm of Adam Jung and Maria Elisabeth, married; b 12 Dec 1770; bapt 2 Jun 1771; wit: Wilhelm Reber

David of David Kirschner and Elisabetha Ollinger, unmarried, b 30 Jan 1771; bapt 9 Jul, illegitimate; wit: David Ollinger

Cathrina of Joseph Wohlgenerich(?) and Juliana Ollinger, unmarried; b 2 Jan 1771; bapt 9 Jul, illegitimate; wit: Elisabetha Ollingerin

Maria Elisabetha of Michael Russ and Elisabetha, married, b 7 May 1771; bapt 20 Jul; wit: Andoni Russ; housewife Anna Maria

Abraham of Johannes Wilige (Wibge?) and Elisabeth, married; b 2 Feb 1771; bapt 20 Jul; wit: Abraham Troxel

Abraham of Peter Richter and Maria Catharina, married; b 2 Jun 1771, bapt 28 Jul; held by same

Johann Georg of Gotfrid Bender and Margretha, married; b 31 Aug 1771; bapt 13 Sep; wit: Johan Georg Rauch and Juliana Osterin

Georg of Wilhelm Clety and Magdalena, married, b 3 May 1771; bapt 13 Sep; held by parents

Joh. Adam, of Adam Etelman and Eva; married; b 29 Jul 1771; bapt 15 Sep; wit: Adam Kaufman

Jacob of Reinharth Reblogel and Barbara, married; b 29 Aug 1771; bapt 13 Sep; wit: held by same

Johann Jacob of Samuel Moser and Elisabetha, married; b 29 Aug 1771; bapt 27 Oct; wit: Jacob Grub and his housewife Elisabetha

Maria Elisabetha of Georg Bernhart and Frantzcisca Appolonia; b 22 Jul 1771, bapt 17 Nov; wit: Baltzer Mauti   and his housewife Elisabetha

Peter of David D. Schons and Susana; b 1 Sep 1771; bapt 17 Nov; wit: held by same

Johannes of Henrich Teis and mother, married; b 27 Sep 1771; bapt 5 Jan 1772; wit: Johannes Flenner and his house wife

Jacob of Mattheis Wilberger and Margretha, married, b 19 Nov 1771; bapt 19 Jan 1772; wit: Jacob Zoelter and his housewife Magdalena

Vallentein of Peter Wirt and Elisabetha, married; b 4 Dec 1771; bapt 19 Jan 1772; wit: Vallentein Oster, and his housewife, Maria

Catharina, of Jacob Claesner and Catharina Elisabetha, married; b 25 Mar 1771; bapt 19 Jan 1772; wit: Jacob Schneider and his housewife Catharina

Rosina of Conrath Kirschner and Hanna, married, b 23 Sep 1771; bapt 12 Apr 1772; wit: Elisabeth Kirschner

Martin of Gotfried Stempfel and Margretha, married; b 3 Feb 1772; bapt 19 Apr; wit: Adam Hauer, and his housewife Anna Maria

Johan Georg of Georg Canderman and Rahel, married; b 11 Mar 1770; bapt 20 Apr; held by same

Joh: Adam of Baltzer Mauti and Elisabeth, married; b 1 Mar 1772; bapt 19 Apr; wit: Henrich Gerlach, and his housewife Magthalena

Salem Reformed Church

David of Henrich Readenauer and Margretha, married; b 31 Mar 1772; bapt 10 May; wit: Martin Raudenauer, and his housewife Catharina

Joh: Jacob of Johannes Schneider and Anna Maria, married; b 30 Mar 1772; bapt 10 May; wit: Niclos Baron and his housewife Catharina

Catharina of Wilhelm Schons(?) and Anna Maria, married; b 19 Jan 1772; bapt 12 May; wit: Daniel Schneid and his housewife Catharina

Johannes of Jacob Hoster and Ablonia, married; b 23 Jun 1770; bapt 8 Jun 1772; held by same

Joh: Adam of Johannes Gelbert and Catharina, married; b 23 Dec 1771; bapt 8 Jun 1772; wit: Georg Schultz

Abraham of Johannes Riter and Sara, married; b 23 Feb 1772; bapt 8 Jun; wit: Abraham Riter and Magthalena Magfetschrin

Sofia of Abraham Brauer and Maria, married; b 15 Apr 1765; bapt 4 Apr 1772; wit: Elisabeth Hauserin

Rahel of Abraham Brauer and Maria, married; b 6 Apr 1769; bapt 4 Apr 1772; wit: Elisabeth Hauserin

Sara of Abraham Brauer and Maria, married; b 13 Oct 1771; bapt 4 Apr 1772; wit: Barbara Hauserin

Georg of Johannes Hutfelt and Catharina, married; b 22 Jun 1772; bapt 5 Jul 1772

Margretha of Andreas Rensch and Elisabetha, married; b 20 Sep 1771; bapt 5 Jun 1772; wit: Elisabeth Renschin

Margretha of Frantz Philipi and Margretha, married; b 25 Apr 1772; bapt 5 Jul; held by same

Susana of Eutel Gerhart and Sofia, married; b 21 Apr 1772; bapt 5 Jul; wit: Henrich Stoll, and his housewife Anna

Jacob of Mathaeus Rap and Christina, married; b 23 Jun; bapt 10 Jul; wit: Jacob Hans, and his housewife Margretha

Margretha of Adam Leydi and Rosina, married; b 19 Jun 1772; bapt 2 Aug; wit: David Tschons (Johns), and his housewife Margretha

Magthalena of Georg Rincke and Magtalena, married; b 16 Jun 1772; bapt 2 Aug; wit: Barbara Tirrin

Margretha of Martin Suder and Margretha, married; b 11 May 1771; bapt 2 Aug 1772; held by same

Johan Peter of Peter Moser and Margretha, married; b 6 Jul 1772; bapt 16 Aug; wit: Martin Lang and his housewife Angnes

Johannes of Johannes Kirschner and Anna Maria; b 18 Apr 1772; bapt 16 Aug; wit: Georg Krischner and his housewife Anna Maria

Elisabeth of Conrath Buechli and Margretha, married; b 28 Mar 1772; bapt 30 Aug; wit: Catharina Eschi

Adam of Johannes Kamrer and Margretha, married; b 18 Mar 1771; bapt 12 Sep 1772; wit: held by same

Johan Georg of Lucas Schalle and Margretha, married; b 15 Sep 1772; bapt 27 Sep; held by same

Johannes of Georg Werner and Margretha, married; b 14th; bapt 4 Oct 1772; wit: Johannes Schweitzer and his housewife Anna

Rahel of Henrich Erlenbach and Anna Maria, married; b 7 Feb 1771; bapt 12 Nov 1772; held by same

Joh: Peter of Henrich Erlenbach and Anna Maria, married; b 1 May 1771(?); bapt 12 Nov 1772; held by same

Georg of Christian Angena and Elisabetha, married; b 16 Oct 1772; bapt 12 Nov; wit: Georg Schaefer

Anna of Jacob Fischer and Anna Maria, married; b 27 Sep 1772; bapt 20 Dec; wit: Henrich Stal and his housewife Anna

Salem Reformed Church

Daniel of M. Henrich Schnebly, Doc: and Elisabeth born Schaeferin, married; b 3 Oct 1772; bapt 20 Dec; wit: Daniel Hister and his housewife Rosina who, however, could not be present. M. Schnebly's wife instead.
Rahel of Georg Conterman and Rahel, married; b 18 May 1772; bapt 25 Dec; wit: Georg Schaefer and his housewife Margretha
Cath. Elisabetha of Georg Schaefer and Christina, married; b 9 Jun 1772; bapt 25 Dec; wit: Georg Call and his housewife Elisabetha
Joh: Peter of Vallentin Oster and Elisabeth, married; b 18 Nov 1772; bapt 25 Dec; wit: Peter Wagner, and his housewife Margretha
Anna Margretha of Andreas Wolf and Magtalena, married; b 24 Dec 1772; bapt 22 Jan 1773; wit: Elisabeth Schultze
Elisabetha of Theobald Angenor and mother; b 4 Dec 1772; bapt 28 Feb 1773; wit: Elisabeth Rufin
Anna Maria of Fridrich Altvater and Magthalena, married; b 13 Jan 1773; bapt 28 Feb 1773; held by same
Caspar of Caspar Cofman and Margretha, married; b 26 Dec 1772; bapt 28 Feb 1773; wit: Baltzer Mauti, and his housewife Elisabeth
Rosina of David Kirschner and Elisabeth, married; b 28 Oct 1772; bapt 28 Feb 1773; wit: Henrich Zoeller and his housewife Margretha
Margretha of Johannes Rolli and Maria; b 10 Jan 1773; bapt 28 Feb; wit: Henrich Stoll and his housewife Anna
Anna Magthlena of Jost Zimmerman and Margretha, married, b 15 Sep 1772; bapt 14 Mar 1773; wit: Catharina Traxel
Catharina of Johannes Roth and Juliana, married; b --- 1772; bapt 28 Mar 1773; wit: Catharina Traxel
Anna Maria of Conrath Sam and Gertraut, married; b 25 Dec 1772; bapt 8 Apr; wit: Wilhelm Tschons (Johns) and his housewife Anna Maria
Johannes of Henrich Seitz and Anna, married; b 25 Dec 1772; bapt 11 Apr 1773; wit: Dr. Schnebly and his housewife
Georg Michael of Fridrich Schoenenfelt and Magdalena; b 6 Jan 1773; bapt 11 Apr; wit: Michel Tirr and his housewife
David of Johanes Schaf and Fronica, married; b 13 Jan 1773; bapt 11 Apr; wit: Theobalt Angena and his housewife
Catharina of Nicolaus Ruf and Catharina, married; b 4 Feb 1773; bapt 24 Apr; wit: Christophel Esron and his housewife Catharina
Daniel of Rutholf Flenner and Magtalena, married; b 24 Dec 1773; bapt 23 May; held by same
Henrich of Henrich Braun and Maria Salome, married; b 8 Jan 1773; bapt 23 May; wit: Fridrich Defern(?) and his housewife Maria Barbara
Anna Maria of Wendel Heims and Philipine, married; b 24 Dec 1772; bapt 23 May 1773; wit: Johannes Schneid and his housewife Anna Maria
Anna Christina of Georg Dany and Elisabeth, married; b 14 Apr 1773; bapt 19 Jun; held by same
Joh: Henrich of Daniel Schneid and Anna, married; b 29 Apr 1773; bapt 19 Jun; held by same
Magtalena of Niclos Schefer and Magtalena, married; b 10 Nov 1772; bapt 1 Aug 1773; held by same
Elisabeth of Michael Tirr and Catharina, married; b 14 Jun 1773; bapt 1 Aug 1773; held by same
Johannes of Jacob Ganner and Susanna, married; b 26 Jul 1772; bapt 1 Sep 1773; wit: Josua Schwoegter and his housewife Christina
Elias of Georg Kirschner and Eva, married; b 30 Jun; bapt 10 Oct; wit: Johannes Flenner and his housewife
Anna Maria of Johannes Schweitzer and Anna Maria, married; b 1 Sep 1773; bapt 15 Oct; wit: Anna Maria, the mother in law of Johannes Schweitzer

Salem Reformed Church

Johannes of Matheis Wilberger and Margretha, married; b 13 Dec 1773; bapt 31 Dec; wit: Johannes Kirschner and his wife Maria
Henrich of Eutel Gerhart and Sovia, married; b 16 Oct 1773; bapt 1 Jan 1774; wit: Henrich Stall, and his housewife
Henrich of Nicolaus Rau and Elisabeth, married; b 10 Oct 1773; bapt 1 Jan 1774; wit: Johannes Mueller and his housewife Magtalena
Joh: Jacob of Joh: Jacob Seibert and Elisabetha, married; b 6 Feb 1774; bapt 13 Mar; wit: Henrich Batarf(?)
Johannes of Johannes Flenner and Cathrina, married; b 21 Nov 1773; bapt 13 Mar 1774; held by same
Magtalena of Henrich Eoller and Margretha, married; b 6 Dec 1773; bapt 27 Mar 1774; wit: Jacob Zoller and his housewife Magtalena
Susana of Wilhelm Tschons (Johns) and Anna Maria, married; b 2 Feb 1774; bapt 27 Mar; wit: Georg Mueller and his housewife
Henrich of Adam Esch and Catharina, married; b 22 Jan 1774; bapt 3 Apr; wit: Henrich Esch, and his housewife Catharina
Elisabetha of Andreas Rensch and Elisabetha, married; b 14 Dec 1773; bapt 10 Apr 1774; held in baptism by same
Johan Philip of Joh: Philip Ripel and Engel, married; b 6 Mar 1774; bapt 10 May 1774; wit: Daniel Schneid and his wife Anna
Catharina of David Kirschner and Elisabetha, married; b 8 Feb 1774; bapt 8 May 1774; wit: Adam Kaufman and his housewife Catharina
Susana of Henrich Deiss and Elisabeth, married; b 26 Mar 1774; bapt 22 May; held by same
Johannes of Michael Hauck and Elisabetha, married; b 13 Mar 1774; bapt 5 Jun 1774; wit: Jacob Hauck, and his housewife
Daniel of Reinhart Reblogel and Barbara; b 24 Sep 1773; bapt 19 Jun 1774
Jacob of Jacob Fischer and Anna Maria, married; b 18 May 1774; bapt 19 Jun; wit: Henrich Stal and his housewife Anna
Abraham of Mathaus Schwertzol and Catharina Barbara, married; b 9 Mar 1774; bapt 19 Jun; wit: Abraham Traxel and his housewife Catharina
Henrich of Tam Feth(?) and mother, married; bapt 10 Jul 1774; wit: Henrich Stal and his housewife Anna
Maria of Jacob Laut and Eva, married; b 3 Mar 1774; bapt 10 Jul; wit: Georg Schoefer and his wife Elisabeth
Ana Catharina of Christian Cohr and Barbara, married; b 11 Apr 1773; bapt 28 Aug 1774; wit: Jonathan Heger, Cathrina Shunkin
David of Jacob Oster and Juliana, married; b 21 Jun 1774; bapt 11 Sep; wit: Fridrich Hirsch and his wife Christina
Maria Margretha of Johannes Gilbert and Catharina, married; b 22 Aug; bapt 11 Sep; wit: Friderich Remer(?) and his wife Maria Margretha
Catharina Elisabetha of Johannes Schneider and Anna Maria, married; b 31 Aug bapt 11 Sep; wit: Catharina Elisabetha Sichwaltin
John Georg of Johannes Schneider and Anna Maria; b 1 Sep; bapt 11 Sep; wit: Georg Schefer and his housewife
Johannes of Caspar Schneid and Anna Maria, married; b 13 Sep 1774; bapt 19 Oct; wit: Johannes Fritz and his housewife Elisabeth
Anna Maria Margretha of Philip Reblogel and Anna Maria, married; b 5 Aug 1774; bapt 19 Oct; wit: Margretha Stolzin
Barbara of Adam Leidy and Rosina, married; b 7 Sep 1774; bapt 6 Nov; wit: Fridrich Leidy and his housewife Barbara
Anna Maria of Gottfried Stempfel and Margretha, married; b 10 Sep 1774; bapt 2 Nov); Wit: Andani (i.e. Anthony); Hauer and his housewife Anna Maria
Anna Maria of Niclos Bender and Susana, married; b 10 Oct 1779; bapt 12 Nov; wit: Fridrich Huersch, and his housewife

Salem Reformed Church

Susana of Vallentin Oster and Maria Elisabeth, married; b 7 Aug 1774; bapt 12 Nov; wit: Peter Wird and Susana Tschonsin (i.e. Johns)
Joh: Jacob of Conrath Ham and Maria Gertraud, married; b 17 Sep 1774; bapt 4 Dec; wit: Joh: Jacob Esbischi:
Jacob of Henrich Seytz and Anna, married; b 5 Dec 1774; bapt 20 1774; wit: Lorentz Dirr (or Tirr, or Duer) and his wife
Jacob of Peter Moser and Margreth, married; b 27 Nov 1774; bapt 20 Dec; wit: Jacob Stadler and his wife Anna
Anna Maria of Jacob Tider and Eva, married; b 27 Nov 1774; bapt 20 Dec; wit: Jacob Schenck and his wife Catharina
Joh: Adam of Niclos Baron and Catharina, married; b 18 Aug 1774; bapt 26 Dec; wit: Georg Jung and his housewife Elisabetha
Anna Maria of Henrich and Cathrina, married; b 5 Oct 1774; bapt 26 Dec 1774; wit: Adam Leidy and his housewife Rosina
Anna Magthalena of Rutholph Flenner and Magthalena, married; b 14 Oct 1774; bapt 15 Jan 1775; held by same
Barbara of Marthin Kirschner and Elisabeta, married; b 23 Jul 1774; bapt 5 Feb 1775; wit: Johannes Kirsch, and his housewife Maria
Hanna of Georg Hertzog and Juthit., married; b 15 Dec 1774; bapt 5 Feb 1775; wit: Georg Denler and his housewife Anna Maria
--- of --- Schmeiser and mother, married; b 1775; bapt 23 Apr; wit: ---- Barrit[?] and his house wife
Michael of Simon Hoech and Maria, married; b 21 Feb 1775; bapt 22 Apr; wit: Georg Schaefer and his housewife Margretha
Jacob of Henrich Zeller and Margretha, married; b 7 Mar 1775; bapt 22 Apr; wit: Jacob Zeller and his housewife
Barbara of Jacob Pfad and Barbara, married; b 13 Apr 1774; bapt 22 Apr 1775; held by same
Lenhart of Stefan Manen and Anna Maria, married; b 24 May 1775; bapt 28 Jun 1775; wit: Lenhart Stal
Johannes of Henrich Esch and mother; b 8 Feb 1775; bapt 13 Aug; held by same
Johannes of Jacob Seibert and Anna Maria, married; b 1 Jun 1775; bapt 13 Aug; held by same
Johannes of Jacob Seibert and Elisabeth, married; b 20 Mar 1775; bapt 13 Aug; held by same
Jacob of Jacob Hens and Elisabeta, married; b 12 Mar 1775; bapt 13 Aug; wit: Johannes Rau and his housewife Catharina
Caspar of Daniel Schneid and Anna, married; b 3 Apr 1775; bapt 13 Aug; wit: Caspar Lederman
Johan Peter of Baltzer Manti and N--, married; b 4 Aug 1775; bapt 15 Oct 1775; wit: Johannes Mueller and his housewife Eva
Susana of Johannes Hoeger and Catharina, married; b 9 Sep 1775; bapt 22 Oct; wit: Jacob Has and his housewife Christina
Peterus of Nicolaus Kau and Elisabeth, married; b 22 Sep 1775; bapt 22 Oct; wit: Peter Has and his housewife Agnes
Johannes of Fridrich Roemer and Margretha, married; b 26 Feb 1775; bapt 5 Nov; wit: Johannes Roemer
Johan Henrich of Caspar Pol(?) and Catharina, married; b 17 Aug 1775; bapt 6 Nov; wit: Michael Walter and housewife Catharina
Johan Georg of Caspar Schneider and Anna Maria, married; b 14 Oct 1775; bapt 5 Nov; wit: Georg Mueller and his houswife Catharina
Anna Maria of Johannes Kirschner and Anna Maria, married; b 9 Jul 1775; bapt 5 Nov; wit: Jacob Hix and his housweife Barbara
Henrich of Johannes Wicke and Elisabeth, married; b 29 Apr 1775; bapt 5 Nov; wit: Henrich Schreyack and his housewife Catharina

Salem Reformed Church

Susana of Adam Gerlach and Christiana, married; b 16 Nov 1775; bapt 3 Dec; wit: Maria Angena-in
Magthalena of Henrich Conterman and Barbara, married; b 10 Nov 1775; bapt 3 Dec; wit: Magtalena Flenner-in
Rosina of Christian Cor and Barbara, married; b 31 Oct ; bapt 10 Dec 1775; wit: Daniel Hister, his wife Rosina, and Jonathan Hoeger
Elisabetha of Jonathan Tschons (Johns) and Elisabeth, married; b 24 Oct 1775; bapt 31 Dec; wit: Henrich Deiss and his housewife
Jonathan of Johannes Flenner and Catharina, married; b 14 Nov 1775; bapt 28 Jan 1776; wit: Jonathan Tschons (i.e. Johns) and his housewife Elisabetha
Peter of Henrich Stoltz and Anna Barbara, married; b 22 Feb 1776; bapt 18 1776; held by same
--- of Gall and mother; b ---; bapt 28 Feb 1776; wit: Henrich Esch and his wife
Martin of Georg Kirschner and Anna Maria, married; b 12 Dec 1775; bapt 10 Mar 1776; wit: Martin Krischner and his housewife
Christiana of David Kirschner and Elisabeth, married; b 8 Jan 1776; bapt 10 Mar; held by same
David of Jost Prua and Magtalena, married; b 13 Jan 1776; bapt 24 Mar 1776; wit: Theobald Angena and Margretha
Elisabeth of Martin Kirschner and Elisabeth, married; b 26 Jan 1776; bapt 20 May; held by same
Elisabeth of Henrich Deiss and Elisabeth, married; b 8 Mar 1776; bapt 20 May; held by same
Margareth(?) of Abraham Gebel and Rebecca; b 2 Sep 1774; bapt 20 May 1776; held by same
Alexander of John Mars and Elisabetha; b 1 Nov 1775; bapt 20 May 1776; held by same
Mary of Ewin (?) Daubein and Margretha b 6 Apr 1775; bapt 20 May 1776; held by same
Georg Lenhart of Georg Kurbel and Catharina, married; b 6 Oct 1775; bapt 20 May; held by same
Joh: Georg of Adam Leid (Leydi) and Rosina, married; b 6 May 1776; bapt 16 Jun; held by same
Michael of Georg Gall and Elisabeth, married; b 2 Dec 1775; bapt 28 Jul 1776; wit: Henrich Esch and his housewife Catharina
Elisabeth of Johannes Golbert and Catharina, married; b 14 May 1776; bapt 28 Jul; wit: Georg Goll and his housewife
Jacob Lams and Regina, married; b 11 May 1776; bapt 28 Jul; wit: Anna Maria Schultzin
Johannes of Johannes Mueller and Anna Maria, married; b 8 Mar 1776; bapt 31 Oct; wit: Johanes Schweitzer and his housewife Anna
Johannes of Johannes Schweitzer and Anna, married; b 13 Jul 1776; bapt 31 Oct; wit: Johannes Mueller and his housewife Anna Maria
Susana of Jacob Hix and Anna Maria, married; b 5 May 1776; bapt 31 Oct; wit: John Kirschner and his housewife Anna Maria
Elisabetha of Conrath Kirschner and Hanna, married; b 16 Mar 1776; bapt 26 Nov; wit: Johannes Kirschner and his housewife Anna Maria
Henrich of Johannes Hager and Barbara, married; b 18 Feb 1777; bapt 16 Mar; wit: Henrich Stal and his housewife
Abraham of Peter Has and Anna, married; b 21 Jan 1777; bapt 16 Mar; wit: Abraham Mueller
Eva of Peter Wirt and Elisabetha, married; b 12 Oct 1776; bapt 30 Mar 1777; wit: Georg Ruch and his housewife

Salem Reformed Church

Anna Maria of Jacob Hems and Elisabetha, married; b 24 Jun 1776; bapt 30 Mar 1777; wit: Margretha Roemerin

Joh: Georg, of Vallentein Sichrist and Susana, married; b 10 May 1776; bapt 30 Mar 1777; wit: Georg Schaefer and his housewife

Jacob of Wilhelm Tschons (Johns) and Anna Maria, married; b 23 Dec 1776; bapt 30 Mar 1777; wit: Joseph Prua and his housewife Margretha

Georg of Lutwig Stoltz and Margretha F., married; b 3 Jan 1777; bapt 30 Mar; wit: Philip Krim

Jacob of Peter Kraut and Magtalena, married; b 13 Nov 1776; bapt 25 Apr 1777; held by same

Margreth of Rutholf Flenner and Magthalena, married; b 26 Feb 1777; bapt 27 Apr; wit: Margretha Zoeller

Margretha of Abraham Riter and Margretha, married; b 15 Nov 1776; bapt 27 Apr 1777; wit: Johannes Wetzstein and his Eva

Jacob of Jacob Schneid and Hanna, married; b 25 Nov 1776; bapt 27 Apr 1777; wit: Philip Ripel and his Catharina

Daniel of Daniel Schnied and Anna, married; b 15 Apr 1777; bapt 1 May; wit: Caspar Lederman

Johannes of Jacob Seiler and Christina, married; b 27 Feb 1777; bapt 1 May; held by same

Johannes of Jonathan Tschons(Johns) and Elisabeth, married; b 13 May 1777; bapt 3 Aug; wit: Johannes Flenner and his wife

Eva Barbara of Peter Moser and Margretha, married; b 14 Aug 1777; bapt 12 Sep; wit: Christian Kor and his wife Barbara

Christian of Johannes Heger and Elisabetha, married; b 4 aug 1777; bapt 12 Sep; wit: Christian Cor and his housewife Barbara

Anna Maria of Joh: Georg Jung; and Elisabeth, married; b 25 Jul 1777; bapt 28 Sep; wit: Anna Catharina Jungin

Fridrich, of Joh: Sallomon Mueller and Eva, married; b 2 May 1777; bapt 28 Sep; wit: Fridirch Remer and his wife Margreth

Joh: Jacob of Jacob Seibert and Anna Maria, married; b 15 Feb 1777; bapt 28 Sep; held by same

William of Bab English and Catharina, married; b 2 Feb 1777; bapt 28 Sep; wit: Johannes Wetzstein

Jacob of Jeams Strang and Magthalena, married; b 18 Feb 1777; bapt 9 Nov; wit: Georg Schaefer and his housewife

Christina of Christian Pfeifer and Doretea, married; b 6 Mar 1777; bapt 9 Nov; wit: Engelhart and Christina Neuin

Johannes of Lucas Schalli and Margretha, married; b 20 Oct 1777; bapt 9 Nov; held by same

Johannes of Gottfrit Bender and Margretha, married; b 14 Jun 1777; bapt 22 Nov; wit: Jacob Weimar and his housewife Sallome

Margretha of Joh: Deiszschnug(?) and N.--, married; b 2 Apr 1777; bapt 15 Feb 1778; held by same

Salomon of Johannes Kirschner and Maria, married; b 1 Oct 1777; bapt 15 Feb 1778; held by same

Anna of mother Catharina b 6 Jul 1777; bapt 22 Feb 1778; held by same

Susana of Rutholph Hofer and Catharina, married; b 13 Jan 1778; bapt 7 Mar; wit: Peter Hergert and his housewife Susana

Daniel of Johannes Flenner and Elisabeth, married; b 10 Sep 1777; bapt 7 Mar 1778; wit: Rutholph Flenner and his wife Magtalena

Magthelena of Thomas Tschons (Johns) and Magtalena, married; b 2 Oct 1777; bapt 10 Mar 1778; held by same

Joh: Georg of Georg Kirschner and Maria, married; b 28 Feb 1778; bapt 15 Apr; held by same

Salem Reformed Church

Elisabeth of Jacob Hentz and Elisabetha, married; b 14 Feb 1778; bapt 26 Apr; wit: Georg Kems(?) and his wife Elisabetha
Susana of Georg Oster and Anna, married; b 6 Dec 1777; bapt 26 Apr; wit: Magtalena Wirtin
Peter of Daniel Mueller and Juliana, married; b 15 Feb 1778; bapt 26 Apr; held by same
Susana of Jost Prua and Magthalena, married; b 12 May 1778; bapt 12 Jun; wit: Matheis Ott and his housewife Elisabetha
Elisabetha of Johannes Mueller and Anna Maria, married; w 31 Jan 1778; bapt 3 Jul; held by same
Johannes of Caspar Schneid and N., married; b 3 Jun 1778; bapt 5 Jul; wit: Joh: Sallomon Miller and his wife Eva
Catharina of Georg Kurbel and Catharina, married; b 21 Aug 1777; bapt 5 Jul 1778; wit: Martin Batorff and his wife Maria Barbara
Catharina of Georg Wolg and Catharina, married; b 24 Jun 1778; bapt 5 Jul; wit: Caspar Schneid and his housewife
Georg of Martin Batorff and Maria Barbara, married; b 14 Apr 1778; bapt 5 Jul; wit: Georg Kurbel and his housewife Catharina
Johannes of Matheis Schmeiser and Anna Engel, married; b 18 Mar 1778; bapt 26 Jul; wit: Joh: Salmon Mueller and his housewife Eva
Eva of Joseph Feuer and Anna Maria, married; b 2 Mar 1778; bapt 26 Jul; wit: Catharina Rauin
Anna Catharina of Henrich Hoenisch and Maria Elisabetha, married; b 19 Oct 1777; bapt 26 Jul 1778; wit: Catharina Schaefer
Susana of Georg Schuck and Catharina, married; b 30 Mar 1778; bapt 26 Jul; wit: Michael Wetzstein and his housewife Susana
Samuel of Jacob Wolf and Christina, married; b 21 May 1778; bapt 11 Feb 1779; held by same
Elisabetha of Ludwig Heriot(?) and M. Marg: B:, married; b 10 Dec 1778; bapt 11 Feb 1779; wit: Eva Hafner-in
Margretha of Vallentin Citman and Margretha, married; b 10 Nov 1778; bapt 14 1779; held by same
Maria of Henrich Mueller and Philibina, married; b 1 Sep 1778; bapt 14 Feb 1779; wit: Michael Schaefer and his housewife Eva
Elisabeth of Hn. Lehnart Bruner and Charlota, married; b 16 Oct 1778 ; bapt 17 Mar 1779; wit: Elisabet Klecan(?)
Maria Eva of Joh: Salmon Mueller and Eva, married; b 8 Jan 1779; bapt 17 Mar; wit: Caspar Schneid and his housewife Anna Maria
Jacob of Christophel Tomas and Susana; b 11 Apr 1777; bapt 17 Mar 1779; held by same
Johannes of Johannes Stadler and Catharina Barbara, married; b 2 Mar 1779; bapt 21 Mar; wit: Johannes Michel
Elisabeth of Johannes Schweitzer and Anna, married; b 20 Sep 1778; bapt 16 May 1779; held by same
Rahel of Emis\and Sabina b 3 Mar 1778; bapt -- 10 1779; held by same
Anna Margretha of Adam Fischer and Susana, married; b 9 Apr 1778; bapt 10 May 1779; wit: Wilhelm Tschons (Johns) and his housewife
Johannes of Martin Straner(?) and Elisabeth, married; b 6 May 1779; bapt 10 Jun; wit: Georg Schaefer, and his housewife
Joh: Fridrich of Andreas Volck and Christina, married; b 13 Apr 1779; bapt 6 Jun 1779; wit: Lucas Schally and his housewife
Johannes of Joseph Tschorsch (ie. George) and mother; b 1 Aug 1779; bapt 27 Nov
Maria Sabina of Johannes Schnebly and Barbara, married; b 17 Oct 1779; bapt 21 Nov; wit: Christian Cau and his housewife Barbara

Salem Reformed Church

Johannes of Thomas Tschons (ie. Johns) and Magthalena, married; b 28 Jul 1779; 5 Dec; held by same
Elisabeth of Stephan Manan and Anna Maria, married; b 3 Oct 1779; bapt 9 Dec; wit: Eutol Gerharth and his housewife Sophia
David of Jeams Strang and Magtalena, married; b 27 Sep; bapt 26 Mar 1780; wit: Theobalt Gegner and his housewife Margretha
Jacob of Jonathan Tschons (i.e. Johns) and Elisabeth B:, married; b 23 Jul 1779; bapt 15 Apr 1780; wit: Wilhelm Tschons (ie. Johns) and his housewife Magtalena
Michael of Herrich Tauss and Elisabetha, married; b 29 Mar 1780; bapt 17 May; held by same
Anna of Adam Leidi (Leydi or Leidy) and Rosina, married; b 25 Mar 1780; bapt 17 May; held by same
Elisabeth of Jacob Weider and Maria, married; b 24 Apr 1780; bapt 26 May; wit: Christofel Weider and his housewife Maria
Peter of Georg Lang and Catharina, married; b 7 Oct 1779; bapt 26 May 1780; wit: Canrath Lang and his housewife Maria
Anna Maria of Ludwig Barner and Gertraut, married; b 31 Aug 1779; bapt 4 Jun 1780; held by same
Johannes of William McFerin and Anna Leidi, married; b 7 Mar 1780; bapt 4 Jun; wit: Johannes Schneider and his housewife Anna Margretha
Emanuel of Jonathan Meier and Elisabetha, married; b 27 Oct 1779; bapt 4 Jun 1780; wit: Balthasar Mauti and his housewife Anna Maria
Jacob of Johannes Kirschner and Anna Maria, married; b 12 Dec 1779; bapt 13 Aug 1780; held by same
David of Georg Kirschner and Anna Maria, married; b 10 Jun 1780; bapt 13 Aug; wit: David Kirsch and his housewife
Sarah of Jacob Hix and Barbara, married; b 29 Jan 1780; bapt 13 Aug; wit: Henrich Stal(?) and his housewife Rosina
Johannes of Peter Oster and Anna Eisabetha, married; b 28 May 1780; bapt 16 Sep 1780; wit: Gottfried Band, and his housewife Margretha
Margretha of Martin Kirschner and Elisabeth, married; b 2 Dec 1779; bapt 24 Sep 1780; held by same
--- of Johannes Flenner and Catharina, married; b --; bapt 24 Sep 1780; wit: Georg Kirschner and his wife N. (M?)
David of Johannes Heger and Elisabeth, married; b 24 Sep 1780; bapt 17 Dec; wit: Georg Michel Haushalter and his housewife Susana
Elisabet and Catharina of Rutholf Hofer and Maria Catharina, married; b 21 Nov 1780; bapt 17 Dec; wit: David Schneid and Elisabeth Rau/Daniel Schneid and his wife Catharina
David of Daniel Mueller and Juliana, married; b 15 Dec 1780; bapt 25 Feb 1781; wit: David Traxel
Joh: Jacob of Johannes Schweitzer and Anna, married; b 29 Jan 1780; bapt 7 Sep 1781; held by same
Jacob of Jacob Kirschner and Margretha Angener, unmarried; b 3 Nov 1781; bapt 3 Jan 1782; wit: Adam Gerlach and his housewife Christina
Elisabeth of Johannes Oster and Magthalena Schmit-in, unmarried; b 14 Aug 1781; bapt 3 Jan 1782; wit: Fridrich Hirsch and his wife Christina
Christina Magthelena of Johannes Schnebly and mother N., married; b 10 Dec 1781; bapt 17 Feb 1782; wit: Adam Gerlach and his housewife Christian
Henrich of Adam Leidy and Rosina, married; b 6 Mar 1782; bapt 25 Mar; held by same
Henrich of Jacob Weiter and Maria, married; b 4 Nov 1781; bapt 26 Mar 1782; wit: Christofel Weiter and his housewife Maria

Salem Reformed Church

Jacob of Martin Kirschner and Elisabeth, married; b 18 Oct 1781; bapt 16 Aug 1782; held by same
Joh: Jacob of Georg Schwert(?) and Anna Elisabeth, married; b 16 Oct 1781; bapt 19 Aug 1782; held by same
Doretea of Michael Beickman and Eva, married; b 20 Aug 1782; bapt 19 Aug; wit: Doretea Brackgumier (ie. Bracumier)
Josoha (i.e. Josua) of Johannes Statler and Maria Barbara, married; b 31 Jan 1782; bapt 10 Nov; wit: Joh: Eberhart Michel and his housewife Anna Maria
Elisabetha of Jacob Bernt and Elisabetha, married; b 7 Nov 1782; bapt 16 Feb 1783; Wit: Doct. Henrich Schnebly and his housewife Elisabetha
Barbara of Georg Rosel and Magthalena, married; b 31 Dec 1782; bapt 30 Mar 1783; wit: Barbara
Elisabeth of --- Lang; b 1 Jan 1783; bapt 28 May
Latzarus of --- Schunbeind (or Schoenbein) b 17 Feb 1783; bapt 25 May
Jonas of David Kirschner and Elisabeth, married; b 9 May 1783; bapt 8 Jun held by same
Johannes of Martin Eschbach and mother N., married; b 22 Apr 1783; bapt 8 Jun; wit: Johannes Blottner
Susana of Peter Schwab and Catharina, married; b 18 May 1783; bapt 21 Jul; held by same
Maria Magtalena of David Tschons (ie. Johns) and Barbara, married; b 3 Dec 1782; bapt 21 Jul 1783; held by same
Susana of Johannes Marstus and Maria Matalena, married; b 1 May 1782; bapt 21 Jul 1783; wit: Sofia Kirschmaen-in
Anna Margreth of Johannes Angena and Magtalena, married; b 25 May 1783; bapt 21 Jul; wit: Adam Gerlach and his housewife Christina
Catharina of Johan George Scheckinggers(?) and Elisabeth, married; b 21 Jun 1783; bapt 17 Aug; wit: Johannes Gebhert and his housewife Margretha
Henrich of Wilhelm Tschons (ie Johns) and Elisabeth, married; b 1 Apr 1783; bapt 17 Aug; held by same

Baptismal book of 1787
Translation by Miss Electa Ziegler

John of Conrad Oster and wife Eva b Dec 17 1786; bapt Mar 17 1787; spon John Reudenauer
Samuel of Conrad Oster and wife Eva b Sep 14; bapt Sep 25 1789; spon: Mathias Reudenauer
Daniel of Conrad Oster b Feb 24; bapt May 20 1792; spon: Daniel Reudenauer
Rosina of Conrad Oster and wife Eva b Jul 27; bapt Sep 28 1794; spon: Matthias Reudenauer
Elisabetha of Daniel Kershner and wife Barbara b Dec 23 1795; bapt May 8 1796; spon: parents
Anna Maria of John Kershner and wife Magdalena b Dec 3 1795; bapt Jun 19 1796; spon: parents
Susana of Adam Schnell b Oct 17 1795; bapt Jun 19 1796; spon: Rudolf Flener and wife Magdalena
Ana Maria of Jacob Bernd and wife Elisabetha b May 30 1796; bapt Feb 26 1797; spon: David Schnebly and wife Anna Maria
Jacob of Henry Hettrich and wife Sibila b Mar 21 1796; bapt Sep 11 1796; spon: parents
Ana Margretta of John Hettridch and wife Elisabetha b Jun 28 bapt 11 1796; spon: parents

Salem Reformed Church

Georg of John Fisher and wife Catharina b Mar 19 1788; bapt Jun 7 1796; spon: father
John of John Fisher and wife Catharina b Mar 27 1791; bapt Jun 7 1796; spon: fahter
Elisabeth of John Fisher and wife Catharina b Jun 2 1793; bapt Jun 7 1796
Susana of John Fisher and wife Catharina b Sep 14 1794; bapt Jun 7 1796; spon: father
Ana Maria of John Fisher and wife Catharina b May 2; bapt Jun 7 1796; spon: father
Elisabetha of Conrad Oster and wife Eva; b Jan 27; bapt Apr 30 1797; spon: Elisabetha and Kershner
Samuel of Jacob Zoller and wife Elisabetha b Aug 6; bapt Oct 25 1797; spon: parents
Jacob of Elisabetha Deis b Jan 24 1797; bapt Oct 14 1798; spon: Mother
Ruthy of Samuel Hager and wife Catharina b Sep 11 (14?) bapt Nov 11 1798; spon: parents
Abraham of Diederich Hofman and wife Susana b Feb 18; bapt Sep 2 1798; spon: Abraham Hebeling and wife Margretta
Jacob of Leonhart Schnebely and wife Elisabetha b Oct 18 1792; bapt May 9 1793; spon: Abraham Wothring and wife Catharina
John of Leonhart Schnebely and wife Elisabetha b Sep 4; bapt Dec 13 1794; spon: parents
Peter of John Schnebely and wife Catharine b Feb 19 bapt Feb 20 1797; spon: parents.
John of William Belsch and wife Elisabeth b Oct 18 1795; bapt Apr 30 1796; spon: Anamaria Kerschner
William of William Belsch and wife Elisabetha b Jun 12; bapt Aug 19 1798; spon: John Kerschner
Elizabeth of John Schnebely and wife Catharina b Jul 31 1798; bapt Jan 17 1799; spon: parents
Rosina of Theobald Kennel and wife Elisabetha b Feb 15 ; bapt Apr 28 1799; spon: Conrad Oster and wife Eva
Anna of Jacob Stahl and wife Anamaria b apr 20; bapt Jul 24 1799; spon: parents
Elisabeth of Jacob Zoller and wife Margretta b Feb 25; bapt Jul 20 1800; spon: Martin Kershner
Anna of Jacob Birnd and wife Elisabetha b Dec 12 1798; bapt Aug 4 1799; spon: Henry Schnebely and wife Catharina
David of Conrad Oster and wife Eva b Sep 9 1799; bapt Mar 8 1800; spon: parents
Leonhart Schnebely and wife Elisabetha b Feb 9; bapt Apr 14 1800; spon: parents
Sarah of Jonas Zoller and wife Elisabetha b Mar 2; bapt Jul 20 1800; spon: Catharina Wachtel
George of Daniel Weliher and wife Veronica b Feb 4; bapt Apr 12 1801; spon: Georg Vogelsang and wife Catharina
John of Phillip Kershner and wife Christina b Sep 29 1788 bapt Mar 16 1801
Jonathan of Phillip Kershner and wife Christina b Apr 1 1791 bapt Mar 16 1801
Elisabetha of Phillip Kershner and wife Christina b Mar 31 1793 bapt Mar 16 1801
Martin of Phillip Kershner and b Jun 15 1795 bapt Mar 16 1801
Daniel of Phillip Kershner and wife Christina b Apr 21 1798; bapt Mar 16 1801
David of Phillip Kershner and wife Christina b Nov 27 1800; bapt Mar 16 1801

Salem Reformed Church

Solomon of Solomon Kerschner and Barbara Reudenauer b Jun 29 1799; bapt Mar 16 1801; spon: mother
Anna of Adam Dirn and wife Nelly b Nov 30 1800; bapt Mar 16 1801; spon: Christina Kerschner
Margretha of Jacob Zoller and wife Elisabetha b Jul 9; bapt Oct 15 1800; spon: parents
Magdalena of Christian Hager and wife b May 29; bapt Jul 19 1801
Maria Margretha of John Hebeling and wife Salome b Jul 8; bapt Nov 10 1799; spon: parents
Martin of Daniel Kerschner and wife Barbara b Nov 1; bapt Dec 12 1799; spon: parents
Anamaria of John Schnebely and wife Catharina b May 6; bapt Dec 23 1800; spon: parents
Elisabetha of Adam Alt and wife Magdalina b Apr 24 1799; bapt Jan 31 1802; spon: parents
Henry of Adam Neuman and wife Elisabeth b Oct 6 1799; bapt Nov 3 1802
Hanna of Isaac Eby and wife Margretha b Mar 27 1799; bapt Aug 8 1799; spon: parents

The Old Reformed Church, Funkstown

Translated from the original German by Mrs. Louise L. Miller and Mrs. Kurt Lande.

Births

John Frederick of Benjamin Heiskell and Anna Margaretha bapt Jan 10 1773; spon: Frederick Beyger and wife Veronica

Julia of Benedict Bowman and Catherine bapt Jan 10 1773; spon: John Leyde and wife Juliana

Jacob of Jacob Bents and Elizabeth bapt Jan 10 1773; died May 4 1773; spon: Lothar Staerr and wife Margaretha

Elizabeth of John Graff and Catharine b Jan 10 1773; spon: Nicholas Werner and wife Maria

Dorothea of Gebriel Bieler and Catharine b Jan 3 1773; spon: Michael Hoffmann and wife Dorothea

Andrew of David Shmitt and Anna Maria b Jan 6 1773; bapt Mar 7 1773; spon: Andrew Hirshmann and wife Catharine

Catharine Magdalena of Christian Seibert and Maria Barbara b Sep 1772; bapt Mar 7 1773; spon: Gabriel Beiler and wife Catharine

John Horn of Christoph Horn and Catharine bapt Apr 4 1773; spon: Nicholas Werner and wife Catharine and Peter Huyert

Anna Maria of Nicholass Reiss and Maria bapt Apr 4 1773; spon: Nicholas Werner and wife Anna Maria

Georg Schwab of Michael Schwab and Margaretha bapt Apr 4 1773; spon: George Schaerer and wife Eva

John Jacob of Jacob Reysser and Elizabeth bapt Apr 20 1773; died Jul 20 1773; spon: Jacob Loessler and wife Elizabeth

John Jacob of Christian Kessner and Anna Catharina b Mar 12 1773; spon: Jacob Loessler and wife Margaretha

John of Georg Kuslert and Anna Maria b Apr 12 1773; died Mar 30 this year; spon: Benedict Schwab Preacher and Maria Wegelin, the child's grandmother

Juliana of Conrad Korhler and Margaretha b May 2 1773; spon: parents

John Georg of Daniel Wetzstein and Maria bapt May 31 1773, age 3 weeks; spon: John Georg Hassner and wife Anna Martha

Catharine of Joseph Traeg and Margaretha bapt May 31 1773; age 3 weeks; spon: Andrew Batz and wife Catharine

John of Deidrich Bernhard and Anna bapt May 31 1773; spon: John Lauer

John of Christoph Bower and Catharine b Jun 3 1773; spon: parents

Mary Susanna of Christian Sorber and Maria Sturm bapt Jun 6, 1 mo. old; spon: John Schaerer and wife Maria Susanna

John Frederick Weil of William Weil and Sophia bapt Jul 25 1773, age 10 mo. 6 da.; spon: Frederick Koehler and wife Maria

John Ludwig Huyert of Philipp Huyert and Eva bapt Jul 25 1773; spon: Ludwig Huyert and wife Margaretha

John Augustin of George Augustin and Elisabeth bapt Jul 25 1773; age 1 mo. 11 da.; spon: Hannes (John) Augustin and wife Elisabeth

Maria Scherer of Georg Schaerer bapt Jul 25 1773, age 1(?) mo. 8 da.; spon: Sabastian Beiler and wife

John Adam Bents of Adam Bents and Margaretha bapt Dec 26 1773, age 1 mo. 14 da.; spon: Isaac Scharer

Frederick Klapper of Valentin Klapper and Juna (Johanna) bapt Jan 30 1774, 20 da. old; spon: Frederick Stahrtz and wife Anna

Elisabeth Bents of Jacob Bents and Elisabeth bapt Dec 30 1774; spon: Catharine Bundly

The Old Reformed Church, Funkstown

Elisabeth Schmitt of John Georg Schmit and Margaretha bapt Mar 20 1774, 1 mo. old; spon: Elisabeth Sturtzman
Catharina Kapp of George Michel Kapp and Catharina bapt Mar 29 1774; 4 mo. old; spon: Christina Naeph (Neff)
Catherine Schaechtely of Michel Schaechtely and Catharine b Apr 4 1774; spon: Catharine Printz
John Jacob Huyert of Peter Huyert and Magdalena bapt Apr 17 1774, age 3 mos.; spon: Jacob Loessler and wife Margaretha
Elisabeth Loessler of Jacob Loessler and Margaretha bapt Apr 17 1774; age 2 mo.; spon: parents
Eva Catharine Ruebenach of Casper Ruebenach and Catharina bapt Apr 17 1774; age 1 mo. 21 days; spon: Eva Catharina Schmitt
Maria Elisabeth Herschmann of Andreas Herschmann and Catharina bapt May 8 1774; spon: David Schmitt and wife
John Frederick Batz of Andreas Batz and Eva Catharina bapt May 8 1774, age 21 days; spon: Frederick Geiger and wife
Elizabetha Kernekam of Ludwig Kernekam and Regina bapt Aug 7 1774, age 15 mo.; spon: Elisabeth Sturtzman
John Samuel Sorwe of Christian Sorwe and Anna Maria; b Apr 2 1775; spon: Michael Keb and wife Margaretha
Elisabeth Wollenschlaeger of Vallentin Wollenschlaeger and Magdalena b Jun 25 1775; bapt 1 mo. old; spon: Elisabeth Fey
Frederick Fey of Michael Fey and Anna Eva bapt Sep 10 1774, age 21 days; spon: Frederick Geiger and wife
Anna Elisabetha Jost of Henry Jost and Anna Maria bapt May 4 1774, age weeks; spon: Anna Jost
Rebecca Jost of Henry Jost and Anna Maria bapt Sep 4 1775, age 10 days; spon: Christoph Bayer and wife Anna
John Keiss of Nicklaus Keiss and Maria bapt Sep 17 1775; spon: Baltasar Kopenhoefer
John Frederick Kernekam of Ludwig Kernekam and Regina bapt Oct 15 1775, age 1 mo. 21 days; spon: John Frederick Bauer and wife
George Frederick Haffner of Georg Haffner and Anna Martha bapt Oct 29 1775, age 1 mo. 13 days; spon: John Frederick Geiger and sister Margaretha
Elisabeth Schmitt of David Schmit and Anna Mary bapt Nov 19 1775, age 21 days; spon: Martin Steuly(?) and wife Elisabeth
Henry Schmitt of John Georg Schmit and Margaretha b Apr 19 1776; spon: John Schmitt and wife Eva Cath.
Catherine Vogelgesang of Christian Vogelgesang and Barbara b Jan 10 1777; spon: Catharina Bundel
John Roeser of Jacob Roeser and Elisabetha b Apr 4 1776; spon: Jacob Loessler
Maria Catharina Schilling of Philipp Schilling and Anna Catharina b Jan 2 1777; spon: Hanna Knochel
Elisabeth Mueller of John Mueller and wife b Jan 10 1776; spon: Elisabetha Sauter
Ludwig Kernekam of Ludwig Kernekam and Regina b Aug 19 1777; spon: Frederick Bauer and wife Catharina
Christian Zacharias of Jacob Zacharias and Elisabeth b Oct 17 1777; spon: William Fey
John Peter Gebel of Philipp Gebel and Magdalena b Sep 16 1777; spon: Peter Krieger and wife Catharina
Anna Maria Silhard of Stophel Silhard and Elisabetha b Dec 28 1777; spon: Barbara Silhard

The Old Reformed Church, Funkstown

Susanna Silhard of Stophel Silhard and Elisabetha b Aug 23 1776; spon: Susanna Erler
Cath. Margeretha Klapbach of Martin Klapbach and Cath. Margaretha b Dec 28 1777; spon: Georg Adam Haushalter and wife Cath. Margaretha
Hanna Reiss of Nicholas Reiss and Maria b Dec 4 1777; spon: Catharina Schoen
John Jacob Schilling of Philipp Schilling and Catharina b Dec 30 1778; spon: Frederick Knochel and wife Margaretha
Eva Catharine Erlewein named after her mother, b Oct 15 1778; father's name was crossed out in old record. Mother is Susannah Erlewein; spon: Eve Catharine Schmit
John Adam Henry Jeily of John Adam Jeily and Margaretha b Aug 18 1779; spon: Henry Schneider and wife Christina
Anna Cath. Silhard of Christoph Silhard and Elisabeth bapt Oct 5 1779, age 14 days; spon: Catharina Bundly
Sarah Beiler of Sabastian Beiler and Sarah bapt Jun 23 1780, age 3 yrs, 1 mo. 21 days; spon: Jacob Zacharias and wife
Christian Beiler of Sabastian Beiler and Sarah b Jan 23 1780; spon: Christian Vogelgesang and wife
Elisabetha Mueller of Georg Mueller and Judith bapt Mar 19 1780, age 19 days; spon: Jacob Bindly and wife Anna
Sophia Balmer of Peter Balmer and wife bapt Apr 16 1780, age 14 days; spon: Conrath Jacoby and wife Sophia
Catharine Seibert of Peter Seibert and Catharina bapt May 14 1780, age 8 mo. 4 days; spon: Jacob Conrath and wife Anna Maria
Catharina Lorah of Henry Lorah and Maria bapt May 28 1780, age 3 mo.; spon: Anna Maria and John Conrath
John Wollschlaeger of Vallentin Wollschlaeger and Magdalena bapt Jul 23 1780, age 17 days; spon: Adam Horn and wife Elisabeth
Frederick Jacob Beiler of Gabriel Beiler and Catharina bapt Jul 23 1780, age 20 days; spon: Frederick Locher
Eva Weydman of Mathias Weydmann and Elisabeth (Kreel) bapt Aug 20 1780, age 1 mo.; spon: Barbara Schwingel
Philipp Schilling of Philipp Schilling and Anna Catharine bapt Oct 15 1780, age 21 days; spon: Adam Wohlfarth and wife Elisabeth
Georg Schmit of Jacob Schmit and Susanna Thomasina bapt Jan 21 1781, age 1 mo. 21 days; spon: Georg Schmit and wife Margaretha
John Georg Zacharias of Jacob Zacharias and Elisabeth Fey bapt Feb 18 1781, age 21 days; spon: Christian Weisshaar and wife Margareth
Anna Maria Bentz of Jacob Bentz and Elisabeth Meyer bapt Feb 18 1781, age 5 days; spon: David Schmit and wife Anna Maria
Anna Maria Schmitt of Georg Schmit and Margaretha Sturtzmann bapt Feb 25 1781, age 21 days; spon: Anna Maria Ruevennach
Anna Barbara Burgner of Christian Burgner and Anna Maria bapt Mar 18 1781, age 14 days; spon: Anna Catharine Bund
Maria Elisabeth Wyan of Jacob Weyan and Christina Gobel bapt Apr 15 1781, age 5 days; spon: Justus Schmit and wife Elizabeth Schletz
John Vogelgesang of Christian Vogelgesang and Barbara bapt May 28 1781, age 14 days; spon: John Maninger and wife
Maria Magdalena Hoerner of Matthew Hoerner and Anna Maria bapt Jul 8 1781, age 2 mo.; spon: Daniel Conrath and wife Magdalena
John Georg Letterman of Michel Letterman and Margaretha Boeringer bapt Aug 5 1781, age 12 days; spon: Georg Hafner and wife Martha
Maria Cath. Wetzstein of Daniel Wetztein and Maria Bund bapt Sep 2 1781, age 20 days; spon: Catharine Bund, child's grandmother

The Old Reformed Church, Funkstown

Irma Maria Klein of Nicholas Klein and Margaretha Schmit bapt Sep 30 1781, age 16 days; spon: John Frederick Mittag and wife Catharine
Maria Cath. North of John North and Catharina Reichenback bapt Feb 3 1782, age 1 mo. 8 days; spon: Georg Reichart and wife Maria Barbara
John Schmitt of David Schmit and Anna Maria Bund bapt Mar 3 1782, age 1 mo. 14 days; spon: Georg Hafner and wife Martha
John Weyand of Jopst Weyand and Maria Krebs bapt Jun 16 1782, age 14 days; spon: Martin Krebs and wife Maria
John Schilling of Philipp Schilling and Anna Cath. Knochel bapt Sep 22 1782, age 23 days; spon: George Hafner and wife Martha
Benjamin Weydmann of Matthew Weydmann and Elisabeth Kried or Kriet bapt --- 29 1782, age 2 mo. 3 days; spon: Philipp Stuhn and wife Catharine
Elisabeth Wolfarth of Henry Wolfarth and Catharine Haefel bapt Sep 29 1782, age 1 mo. 24 days; spon: Adam Wolfarth and wife Elisabeth
Elisabeth Zacharias of Jacob Zacharias and Elisabeth Fey bapt Jan -- 1783, age 9 days; spon: William Fey and Maria Magdalena
John Frederick Silhart of Christoph Sillhart and Elisabeth Erlewein bapt Nov 16 1783, age 8 days; spon: John Frederick Beiger and wife Anna
John & Michel Sauer twins, of John Sauer and Margaretha Schaechtel bapt Dec 6 1783, age 2 days; spon: father, Michel Sauer, Margaretha Leddermann, Susanna Schmit
Anna Maria Loeb of John Loeb and Margaretha Conrath bapt Feb 22 1784, age 3 mo.; spon: Maria Conrath, child's mother's sister
Maria Cath. Schuhn of Philip Schuhn and Cath. Bind b Feb 26 1779; bapt Mar 14; spon: Adam Haushalter
Maria Elisabeth Schuhn of Philip Schuhn and Cath. Bind b Jul 1 1780; bapt Jul 23 1780; spon: Maria Elisabeth Negle
John Schuhn of Philip Schuhn and Cath. bind b Dec 18 1781; bapt Jan 20 1782; spon: John Maninger and wife Magdalena or Margaretha
Daniel Schuhn of Philip Schuhn and Cath. Bind b Mar 18 1784; bapt Mar 19 1784; spon: Christian Bund and wife Elisabeth
Hanna Schuhn of Philip Schuhn and Cath. Bind b Oct 18 1785; bapt Dec 11 1785; spon: Daniel Wetztein and wife Maria
Henry Schuhn of Philip Schuhn and Cath. Bind b Feb 12 1787; bapt Apr 8 1787; spon: Georg Bund and wife Eva
Susanna Schilling of Philipp Schilling and Catharine Knochel bapt Oct 17 1784, age 19 days; spon: Georg Neu and wife Magdalena
Margaretha Kehlerin of Frederick Kehler and wife Maria Elizabeth Schlegin b Mar 20 1787; bapt Apr 8 1787; spon: Margaretha Kehlerin
Eva Elisabeth Schilling of Philipp Schilling and Catharine Knochel bapt Dec 24 1786; spon: Philip Steutz and wife
John & Jacob Seibert, twin brothers of Wendel Seibert and Margaretha Maug. bapt Nov (?) 29 1784; spon: none
Catharine Seibert of Wendel Seibert and Margaretha Maug. bapt Oct 26 1786; spon: parents
Adam of Philip Schun and Catharina Bindle or Bund ... 1788 (handwriting is indistinct)
Jacob Wurtenberger of Jacob Wurtenberger and Cath Engel b Jul 8; bapt Jul 29, probably 1778; spon: Philip Stuter and wife
Susanna Groph (Groff) of Andreas Groph and Elisabeth Stather(?) b Sep 29; bapt Oct 7 1787; spon: Jacob Schmidt and wife
Eva Elisabeth Schneider of Adam Schneider and Catarine But(?) b Aug 8; bapt Oct 7 1787; spon: Daniel Guntes(?) and wife
Jacob Bens of Jacob Bens and wife b Oct 2(?) 1787; bapt 7th; spon: Frederick Koeler

The Old Reformed Church, Funkstown

Jacob Bindlie of Georg Bindlie and Petere b Dec 21 1787; bapt 30th.; spon: Jacob Petery
Annamaria Kuns of Georg Kuns and Catharina Stuter b Dec 10 1787; bapt Dec 30 1787; spon: Annamaria Stuter
Philipp Schaefer of Peter Schaefer and Elisabetha Erhardt b 1787; bapt Feb 11 1788; spon: Philipp Schilling and wife
John Philip Stuter of John Philip Stuter and Elisabetha Schweiser b Mar 19 1788; bapt Apr 20; spon: Philip Jacob Stuter and wife
Georg Schlosser of Henry Schlosser and Elisabetha Glung b Apr 6 1788; bapt Apr 25; spon: Henry Keiser and wife
Anna Elisabeth Gentes of Daniel Gentes and Eva Fogelgesang b May 2; bapt May 18; spon: Christian Fogelgesang and wife
John Bentz of Henry Bentz and Maria Conrad b Dec 26 1788; bapt Jan 25 1789; spon: Henry Printz
Anna Maria Schilling of Philip Schilling and Catharine Knockle b Feb 6 1789; bapt Mar 22; spon: David Schmidt and wife
Anna Catharine Bindle of George Bindle and Eva Petre b Apr 12; bapt May 21; spon: Philip Spon and wife
Daniel Voltz of Daniel Voltz and Anna Maria b Aug 31 1789; bapt Oct 4; spon: parents
Anna Martha Kuntz of John Georg Kuntz and Catharine b Nov 14 1789; bapt Dec 13; spon: Anna Maria Schmidt, a spinster
Jonathan Rodenfeld of John Rodenfeld and Apigael b Jul 10 1780; bapt Jan 3 1790; spon: Conrad Jacoby and wife
David Schilling of Philip Schilling and Catharine Knochel b Jul 3 1790; bapt Aug 22; spon: David Schmidt and wife
Sara Bindle of Georg Bindle and Eva Petre b Sep 28 1790; bapt Nov 14; spon: Henry Bendelin and wife
Susanna Sarah Schilling of Philip Schilling and Catharine b Mar 19 1793 and bapt; spon: Henry Beckly and wife Barbara
Jacob Weiss of Peter Weiss and Anna Maria b Sep 7 1792; bapt Jun 9 1793; spon: Henry Loens and Anna Maria
John Kisener of Andreas Kisener and wife Barbara b Dec 16 1794; bapt May 23 1795; spon: parents
Elisabeth Schyfer of Henry Schyfer and Rosina b or bapt Jan 5 1793; spon: none
Jacob Wirtemberger of John Adam Wirtemberger and Elisa b Mar 29 1795; bapt Jun 21 1795; spon: Jacob Weil and wife Susanna
Matthew Walch of George Walch and Anna Maria b Mar 25 1795; bapt Jun 21 1795; spon: Matthew Kessler and wife Eva
John Jacob of John Maninger and Magdalena b Jul 17 1795; bapt Aug 16 1795; spon: John Wagner & child's mother
John George Klein of John Klein and Barbara b May 20 1794; bapt Aug 16 1795; spon: His own mother
John Neukirch of John Neukirch and Maria b Jul 21 1795; bapt Aug 14 1795; spon: John Bindle and wife Veronica
Sara Suil(?) of Martin Suil and Elis b Jul 1 1795; bapt Aug 16 1795; spon: Susanna Silhart
Catharine Stuter of Philip Stuter and Elisabeth b Apr 15; bapt Sep 13 1795; spon: Gottlieb Grosch and wife Catharine Reiss
Maria Catharine Kepler of John Kepler and Maria Catharine b Mar 10; bapt a short time thereafter; spon: father & mother
Jacob Scherer of Christian Scherer and Magdalena b Sep 25 1795; bapt Oct 10; spon: Michel Schoeneberger and wife

The Old Reformed Church, Funkstown

girl of Michel Schoeneberger and Anna Maria b Dec 17; bapt Nov 8 1795; spon: Michel Schoeneberger the elder and wife Catharine

Daughter of Gottlieb Grosch and Catharine b Dec 20 1795; bapt Feb 2 1796; spon: Andreas Grosch the elder and wife Elisa

Jacob Knecht of Samuel Knecht (Knight) and Elisa b Mar 21 1796; bapt Mar 27 1796; spon: Jacob Bens and wife

Jospeh Baumann of Martin Baumann and wife b Jan 18 1790; bapt Mar 15 1796; spon: none

Henry Schilling of Philip Schilling and Catharine b Mar 25; bapt Jul 3 1796; spon: parents

William Morganthal of widow Hanna Morganthal b Mar 29 1785; bapt Dec 20 1796; spon: Jacob Knoth and wife M. Knoth

Sarah Morganthal of widow Hanna Morganthal b Apr 6 1786; bapt Dec 20 1796; spon: Maria Steinbrecher and Gerhard Steinbrecher

John Morganthal of widow Hanna Morganthal b Mar 8 1790; bapt Dec 20 1796; spon: Jacob Knoth and wife

George Morganthal of widow Hanna Morganthal b Jan 24 1794; bapt Dec 20 1796; spon: Jacob Knoth and wife

Jacob Klein of William Klein and Elisa b Jan 15 1792; bapt Feb 12 1797; spon: Philip Schilling and wife Catharine

Catharine Klein of William Klein and Elisa b Oct 13 1794; bapt Feb 12 1797; spon: Catharine Klein, the mother

Jacob Klein of William Klein and Elisa b May 6 1796; bapt Feb 12 1797; spon: Conrad Jacoby and wife Sofnia

Samuel Bedly of Jacob Bedly and Annamaria b Feb 21 1797; bapt Mar 12 1797; spon: father and mother

Sarah Bedley of Henry Bedley and Elisa b Sep 6 1796; bapt Mar 12 1797; spon: Conrad Knoth and wife Sara

John Gross of Gottlieb Gross and Catharine b Mar 30 1797; bapt May 7; spon: John, brother-in-law of Anna Maria

John Georg Conrad of John Conrad and Catharine b Oct 1 1796; bapt May 7; spon: Georg Adam and wife Dorothea

Catharine Arnold of Adam Arnold and Anna b Jan 30 1797; bapt May 7; spon: Christofer Schwab and wife Catharine

Catharine Kesinger of Andrew Kesinger and Barbara b Sep 16 1796; bapt May 27; spon: parents

Frederick Klein of Daniel Klein and Margareta b Jan 22 1797; bapt Aug 13; spon: Frederick Klinsck and wife Maria Magdalena

John Jacob Dritsch of Jacob Dritsch b Jul 4 1797; bapt Feb 9 1798; spon: parents

George Warth of Simon Warth and Sybilla born Schweyer; b Dec 18 1797; bapt Apr 6 1798; spon: father & mother; baptized by Rev. Smucker

Jacob Schoeneberger of Peter Schoeneberger and wife b Feb 2 1799; bapt Mar 10; spon: Jacob Bedly and wife Maria

Samuel Bauschlag of Joseph Bauschlag and Catharine b Jan 23 1799; bapt Mar 10; spon: parents

Daniel Grosch of Gottlieb Grosch and Catharine b Feb 18 1799; bapt Mar 10; spon: Andreas Grosch, Jr.

John Georg Arnold of George Arnold and Catharine b Nov 6; bapt Apr 21 1799; spon: father

Jonas of Philip Schilling and Catharine b Mar 20 17--; bapt Apr 21 1799; spon: parents

John Georg of John Arnold and Maria b Nov 8 1798; bapt Apr 21 1799; spon: parents

The Old Reformed Church, Funkstown

Jacob Vogelgesang of Christian Vogelgesang and Susanna b Mar 4; bapt Apr 21 1799; spon: parents
William Waaler of James Waaler and Maria b Jul 27 1791; bapt Feb 22 1801; spon: parents
Jeremiah Waaler of James Waaler and Maria b Apr 21 17--; bapt Feb 22 1801

St. Paul's Evangelical Lutheran and Reformed Church

Two different translations held at the Maryland Historical Society, a copy (Md. Hist. Soc. Book 13), presented by Martha L. Ankeney Foster, 1948, translated by Bertha B. Heinemann; and a second version (Md. Hist. Soc. Book 25), copied by Mrs. Warren D. Miller, Historian and presented by Mrs. Jacob Wolfinger, Chairman of Genealogical Records, Conococheague Chapter, N.S.D.A.R.

Catharina of John Muller and Juliana, married, b Dec 16 1787; christ. Jan 16 1788; wit: Rosina Graulin
Michael of Jacob Seibert and Anna Maria b Jan 30 1788; christ. May 18; wit: Selbstgezob (married)
Henry of Henry Angeni and Susanna, married, b Dec 15 1787; christ. May 1788; wit: Joseph Feury, Maria, wife
Levihard of Jacob Seibert and Elizabeth b May 30; christ. Jul 6; wit: the parents
Anna Maria of Michael Yan Est and Elizabeth b Feb 8; christ. Jul 6; wit: Henry Brua
Nicolas of Nicolas Schmidt and Catharina b Mar 25; christ. Jul 6; wit: Frederick Hirsch, Susan
Anna Maria of Jacob Hirsch and Veronica b May 11; christ. Jul 6; wit: Christina Feurfein
Jacob of Jacob Grapp and Catharina b Apr 25; christ. Jul 6; wit: George Yung
Elizabeth of George Muller and Catharina, married b Jun 28 1788; christ. Jul 27; wit: Maria Mautifna
Henry of Peter Maier and Anna Margaret, married b Jul 10 1788; christ. Jul 27; wit: Henry Maudy
Abraham of Jacob Dupie and Elizabeth b Dec 1787; christ. Aug 3; wit: Michael Burgmann
Peter of Peter Brua and his wife b Jun 8 1788; christ. Aug 3; wit: John Brua
Elizabeth b Dec 15 1792; wit: Andrew Badorg and wife
Henry of Challendin Muller and Anna Maria, married b May 6 1788; christ. Sep 28; wit: Henry Brua and Elizabeth
Challendin of Conrad Sudfort and Anna Maria, married; b Jul 20 1788; christ. Sep 28; wit: Challendin and Anna Maria Muller
Benjamin of Jacob Weidman and Margaret Eschel b Aug 1; christ. Oct 5; wit: Benjamin Schwengel
John George of Henry and Anna Maria Brua b Jul 14; christ. Aug 9; wit: Augustus Brura Dupre
Sara of Henry Hirsch and wife b May 31; wit: Frederick Hirsch Sen.
Catharina of Essau Ehli and Margaret b Mar 23; christ. Aug 9; wit: Magdalena Eichelbronn
Susanna of Caspar Schneider and Anna Maria, married; b Jul 5 1789; christ. Jul 5; wit: Susanna Frey
Jacob of Samuel Leudy and Maria, married; b Jul 8 1789; christ. Aug 16; wit: Jacob Sauer and wife
Magdalena of Abraham Lecter and Elizabeth, married; b Apr 25 1789; christ. Aug 15; wit: John Angene and wife
Christian Frederick of Peter E'lendam and Maria, wife; b Aug 20; christ. Sep 6; wit: Elizabeth Slekauer
Anna Catharine of John Angene and Magdalena, married; b Sep 11; christ. Oct 11; wit: John and Juliana Muller
Henry of George Yung and Elizabeth b Oct 15; christ. Nov 1; wit: Henry Esch
Christian of Christian Rohr and Ida b Aug 25; christ. Dec 27; wit: Jacob Hirsch and wife

St. Paul's Evangelical Lutheran and Reformed Church

John George of John Juni and Maria, married; b Sep 7 1789; christ. Jan 3 1790; wit: Selbat Gehob

Martin of Martin Speid and Elizabeth b Nov 15; christ.; wit: Jacob Hirsch and wife

Samuel of Henry Sam and Hanna; christ. Jun 13th; wit: the parents

John of Jacob Knebel and Maria Salome b Oct 27 1789; christ. Jun 13 1790; wit: John Guschwa

Segina of Jacob Trapp and Catharina b May 10; christ. May 13; wit: John Maudy and wife

George of Michael Hand and Elizabeth b Dec 4 1789; christ. Mar 25 1790; wit: Henry Brua and wife

Elizabeth of John Muller and Juliana, wife; b Jan 29; christ. Jul 11; wit: John Angene and wife

Susanna of Conrad Jones and Maria Magda b May 20 1790; christ. Jul 11 1790; wit: Jacob Hauss and wife

Jacob of Josiah [second version translates as Joseph] Wilverback and Susanna Uvon b 1789; christ. Jul 11 1790; wit: Michael Bergmann and wife

Maria of John Feyre and Sabina, wife; b Mar 19 1798; christ. Nov 24; wit: Maria Feyre

Maria of Deobald Kleockner and Elizabeth, wife; b Nov 9 1798; christ. Jan 6 1799; wit: Maria Feyre

Maria of Michael Faubel and Irma, wife; b Jun 4 1799; christ.; wit: Catharina Schneider

Jacob of Jacob Esch and Elizabeth, wife; b Sep 2 1798; christ. Mar 30 1799; wit: Frederick Hersch

Catharina of John Lefler and Anna, wife; b Sep 14 1798; christ. Apr 14; wit: Catharina Lefler

John of George Angene and Catharina, wife; b Jan 2; christ. Apr 8 1799; wit: the parents

John of Lorens Hersch and Barbara, wife; b Feb 23; christ. Apr 28 1799; wit: George Miller, Catharina, wife

Magdalena of Peter Schwob and Catharina, wife; b Feb 10; christ. Apr 28 1799; wit: the parents

Daniel of Jospeh Feyre and Magdalena, wife; b Jan 25 1799; christ. May 13; wit: Martin Kriteneis, Catharina, wife

John of Allesc Klarck and Susanna, wife; b Mar 4 1799; christ. May 13; wit: the parents

John George of Jacob Feyre and Susanna, wife; b Apr 13 1799; christ. Jun 12; wit: George Angeni, Catharina, wife

Rosina of Peter Brua and Magdalena, wife; b Mar 10 1799; christ. Jun 12; wit: the parents

daughter of John Juin and Anna Maria, wife; b Jan 14 1799; christ. Jun 12; wit: the parents

John Henry of John Seybert and Catharina, wife; b Apr 18 1799; christ. Jun 12; wit: the parents

Adam of Jacob Brua and Maria, wife; b Dec 1798; christ. Jun 12; wit: the parents

John Adam of Thomas Gillom and Elizabeth b Jun 10; christ. Jul 10; wit: Adam Schneider

Magdalena of John Angene and Magdalena b May 13; christ. Jul 10; wit: Elizabeth Angene

George of Lannard Graul and Elizabeth b Mar 2 1791; christ. Jun 9 1791; spon: the parents

David of Henry Bingem and Elizabeth b Jan 7; christ. 1790; spon: the parents

St. Paul's Evangelical Lutheran and Reformed Church

Elizabeth of George Feid and Christine Est b Mar 26 1791; christ. Jul 18 1791; wit: Seiss Freysal
Maria Elizabeth of Jacob Knebel and Maria Salome b Jun 21; christ. Aug 7; wit: George Knebel and Uscon.
Jacob of Henry Feurer and Elizabeth b Apr 14 ; christ. Aug 7; wit: Jacob Feurer
Susan of Adam Zollinger and Anna Maria b Feb 20; christ. Aug 7; spon: the parents
John of Essau Ehli and Margaret b Jun 10; christ. Aug 7; wit: Henry Feade
John Gerrich of Henry Brauer and Maria b Sep 9; christ. Oct 30; spon: the parents
Michael of Jacob Seibert and Elizabeth b Jul 11; christ. Oct 30; spon: the parents
Maria Magdalena of Jacob Toms and Catharina b Aug 9; christ. Oct 30; wit: August Ben and Uscon.
Daniel of Peter Bruart and Magdalena b May 14; christ. Oct 30; wit: Daniel Bruart
--- of Peter Schwab and Catharina Schwabin b Aug 2 1791; christ. Nov 2
--- of Henry Angene and Susanna Angene b Apr 25 1791; christ. Nov 2; wit: George Angene
Peter of Casper Schneider and Anna Maria b Sep 8 1791; christ. May 6 1792; wit: George Mauty
John of Jacob Sigmund and Susanna b Nov 4 1790; christ. May 6 1792; wit: the parents
Adam of George Hauer and Susanna b Feb 20; christ. May 6 1792; wit: Adam Gerlach
Joseph of Michael Bergmann and Susanna b Mar 20; christ. May 6 1792; wit: the parents
Maria of John Gushwah and Catharina b Dec 26 1791; christ. May 6 1792; wit: the parents
Rosina of John Mauty and Rosina b Mar 7; christ. May 6 1792; wit: Anna Maria Purg
John of Abraham Esh and Maria b Mar 29; christ. May 6 1792; wit: Catharina Esh
George Frederick of Frederick Hirsch and Catharina b Mar 21; christ. May 6 1792; wit: Frederick Hirsch, Catharina
George of Joseph Conner and Juliana b Oct 30 1791; christ. May 6 1792; wit: Peter Corber, Elizabeth, wife
John of Christian Cohr and Frances b Oct 8 1791; christ. May 6 1792; wit: Martin Mauty, Rosina, wife
Elizabeth of Elias Remmle and Catharina, wife b Jan 18 1792; christ. Apr 8 1792; wit: the parents
David of Jacob Schneider and Anna Maria, wife b Jul 24 1791; christ. Jul 28 1792; wit: the parents
William of Beal Wooden and wife b Mar 30 1789; christ. Jul 15 1792; spon: the parents
Stephen of (?Beal Wooden and wife?) b Mar 10 1791; christ. Jul 15 1792
Anamaria of John Miller and Juliana b Jul 18; christ. Oct 21 1792; wit: Peter Schwob, Catharina
John of John Hissong and Barbara b Jul 16 1792; christ. Dec 26; wit: the parents
John of Mathias Stein and Freni b Nov 27 1792; christ. Jul 20 1793; wit: John Miller, Juliana
John of John Angeni b Dec 25 1792; wit: the parents

St. Paul's Evangelical Lutheran and Reformed Church

John Christian of Christian Boby b Dec 23; christ. Nov 1792; wit: the parents
George of George Miller and Catharina b Jun 27; christ. Jul 1793; wit: Bolhar Maudy
John of David Ludy and Phillipina b Jun 6; christ. Jul 27 1793; wit: Adam Schmetzer and Margretha
John George of Henry Angne and Susanna b Jul 15; christ. Sep 29 1793; wit: George Angne, Catharina, wife
David of Casper Schneider and Anamaria, wife; b Aug 27; christ. Sep 29 1793; wit: Adam Gerlach, Christina, wife
Susanna of Elias Remle and Catharina, wife; b Sep 11; christ. Oct 27 1793; wit: Johnathan Jones, Elisabeth, wife
Elizabeth of Abraham Hebling and Margrett, wife; b Oct 11; christ. Nov 10 1793; wit: Gottfried Gremer, Margrett, wife
Henry of Conrad Graul and Elizabetha, wife; b Jun 8 1793; christ. Sep 29; wit: Henry Angne, Susanna, wife
Jacob of Peter Scheafer and Elizabeth, wife; b Jun 15; christ. Dec 1; wit: the parents
Jacob of Daniel Brua and Elizabeth, wife; b Nov 24 1793; christ. Feb 23 1794; wit: Jacob Brua
Magdalena of Henry Brua and Maria, wife; b Jul 22 1793; christ. Aug 7 1793; wit: Magdalena Bruadin
Christina of George Hauer and Susanna, wife; b Dec 27 1793; christ. Feb 22 1794; wit: Adam Gerlach, Christina, wife
Jacob of Christian Chor and Frei, wife; b Sep 23 1793; wit: Jacob Graus (note earlier names, Christian Cohr and Frances)
Jacob of Isac Ely and Margret, wife; b Oct 14 1793; christ. Mar 23 1794; wit: Jacob Hegel
Margreta of Devalt Cleckner and Elizabeth, wife; b Jan 11 1794; wit: Margret Ceafter
Peter of George Feid and Christina, wife; b Oct 1 1793; christ. May 4 1794; wit: the parents
David of Daniel Bauman and Susanna Margreth b Apr 8; christ. May 8 1794; wit: the parents
Henry of Frederick Hersch and Catharina, wife; b Mar 9; christ. May 4 1794; wit: Frederick Hersch, Christina
Elizabeth of Christophel Lieberknecht and Margretha, wife; b Jan 9; christ. May 4 1794; wit: William Jons, Anamaria
George of Peter Bruner and Catharina, wife; b Oct 21 1793; christ. Jun 8 1794; wit: the parents
Magdalena of Peter Brua and Magdalen, wife; b Feb 22; christ. Jun 8 1794; wit: John Angnes, Magdalena, wife
Anamaria of Manuel Pfeifer and Barbara, wife; b Feb 23; christ. Jun 8 1794; wit: Nicolaus Herman, Elizabeth, wife
Abraham of Peter Watring and Margaret, wife; b Apr 21; christ. Jun 8 1794; wit: the parents
Catharina of Abraham Esch and Maria, wife; b Dec 30 1793; christ. Jun 8 1794; wit: Henry Esch, Catharina, wife
John of Jacob Toms and Catharina, wife; b Nov 7 1793; christ. Jun 8 1794; wit: Conrad Toms and wife
Peter of Casper Maudy and Catharina, wife; b May 8 1794; christ. Jun 8 1794; wit: Peter Maudy
Jacob of Jacob Hersch and wife; b Jun 26 1794; christ. Jul 27 1794; wit: the parents

St. Paul's Evangelical Lutheran and Reformed Church

Anna Magdalena of John Maudy and Rosina, wife; b Jun 28 1794; christ. Jul 27 1794; wit: Casper Maudy, Catharina, wife
Catharina of Peter Lesler and Catharina, wife; b Apr 24 1794; christ. Aug 24 1794; wit: Catharina Lesler
Magdalena of John Hissang and Barbara, wife; b Jul 31 1794; christ. Aug 24 1794; wit: Magdalena Grisin
Juliana of John Miller and Juliana, wife; b Jul 11; christ. Aug 31 1794; wit: the parents
Catharina of Nicolaus Bollinan and Magdalena, wife; b Apr 17; christ. Aug 31 1794; wit: Catharina Drascehen
Elizabeth of Peter Schwob and Catharina, wife; b Sep 17; christ. Dec 28 1794; wit: the parents
Elizabeth of Peter Miller and Christina, wife; b Jan 3 1795; christ. Mar 8 1795; wit: Catharina Schwatz
Magdalena of Mathias Stein and Frehne, wife; b Oct 23 1794; christ. Mar 8 1799; wit: Henry Eill and wife C.
Jonathan of Jonathan Jons and Elizabeth, wife; b Oct 28 1794; christ. Mar 22 1795; wit: Elias Remley, Catharina Toms
Eva of Michael Bergmann and Susanna; wife b Dec 25 1794; christ. Apr 6 1799; wit: the parents
Jacob of George Angeni and Catharina, wife; b Nov 10 1794; christ. Apr 6 1799; wit: the parents
Catharina of John Juin and Anna Maria, wife; b Oct 28 1794; christ. May 3 1799; wit: Adam Schneider, Catharina, wife
Anna of Jacob Leossner and Elizabeth, wife; b Oct 24 1794; christ. Feb 24 1799; wit: Jacob Hand, Margaret, wife
--- of Jacob Beurdenberger ---
Maria of Adam Traub and Catharina, wife, b Apr 16 1779; christ. May 30 1795; wit: formerly?? wife of ?? John Brua
Jacob of John Brua and Maria, wife; b Jan 4 1792; christ. May 30 1795; wit: Jacob Brua
Susanna of John Brua and Maria, wife; b Mar 4 1794; christ. May 30 1795; wit: Susanna Brua
David of Christian Chor and Frehne, wife; b May 2 1795; christ. May 25 1795; wit: Peter Maudy
Jacob of ?? Martin(?) Sped and Elizabeth, wife; b Mar 13 1795; christ. May 31 1795; wit: the parents
Barbara of John Feorster and Elizabeth, wife; b Apr 3 1795; christ. May 31 1795; wit: the parents
Elizabeth of Daniel Eickelbrura and Catharina, wife; b Mar 22 1795; christ. May 31 1795; wit: Margaret Guschwa
Margaret of John Angene and Magdalena, wife; b Mar 31; christ. Jun 14 1795; wit: the parents
John of Peter Wolf and Magdalena, wife; b Jun 11 1795; christ. Jul 26 1795; wit: Abraham Hebling and his wife
Henry of Jacob Bechtel and Anamaria, wife; b Dec 6 1793; christ. Aug 16 1795; wit: Jacob Seibert
Elizabeth of Jacob Bechtel and Anamaria, wife; b Apr 21; christ. Aug 16 1795; wit: Elizabeth Sigmund
Anna Margaret of Christian Boby and Catharina, wife; b Mar 17 1795; christ. Nov 1; wit: the parents
Catharina of Conrad Graul and Elizabeth, wife; b Jun 15; christ. Nov 1 1795; wit: Elizabeth Feiery
Adam of Adam Schneider and Catharina, wife; b Nov 2 1795; christ. Dec 11 1795; wit: the parents

St. Paul's Evangelical Lutheran and Reformed Church

John of Jacob Feid and Susanna, wife; b Dec 13 1795; christ. Mar 20 1796; wit: John Gerlach, Margaret, wife
Jacob of Peter Bruner and Catharina, wife; b Oct 9 1795; christ. Mar 20; wit: Jacob Hens, Elizabeth, wife
Margaret of Peter Weber and Elizabeth, wife; b Dec 15 1795; christ. Apr 3 1796; wit: the parents
Jacob of Jacob Homs and Catharina, wife; b Nov 10 1795; christ. Apr 3 1796; wit: the parents
Elizabeth of Absalon Reith and Anna Maria, wife; b Feb 9 1796; christ. Apr 3; wit: Elizabeth Steorin
Salome of Peter Brua and Margaret, wife; b Aug 8 1795; christ. Apr 3 1796; wit: Susanna Brua
Jacob of David Ludi and Philipina, wife; b Sep 5; christ. May 1 1796; wit: Henry Schmelzer
Magdalena of Daniel Brua and Elizabeth, wife; b Feb 26 1796; christ. May 1 1796; wit: Susanna Brua
Bessie of Peter Leffler and Catharina, wife; b Sep 18 1795; christ. May 1 1796; wit: Catharina Bergmann
Jacob of Henry Angene and Susanna, wife; b Dec 15 1795; christ. Apr 8 1796; wit: the parents
Jacob of Deobald Gleockner and Elizabeth, wife; b Feb 24; christ. Apr 8 1796; wit: the parents
Daniel of George Miller and Catharina, wife; b Feb 29; christ. Apr 8 1796; wit: John Miller
Jacob of George Miller and Catharina, wife; b Feb 29; christ. Apr 8 1796; wit: Jacob Hersch, Veronica, wife
Barbara of John Hisson and Barbara, wife; b Mar 1; christ. Apr 8 1796; wit: the parents
John George of John Guschwa and Catharina, wife; b Jan 19; christ. May 16 1796; wit: Jacob Seibert, Anamaria, wife
Maria of Isac Eli and Margaret, wife; b Apr 14 1796; christ. Jun 12; wit: the parents
Catharina of Tobias Ritter and Eva Catharina, wife; b May 18 1796; christ. Jun 12; wit: Henry Jegle and Margaret, wife
Anna of Nicolaus Bollman and Magdalena, wife; b Dec 12 1795; christ. Jun 19 1796; wit: the parents
Michael of John Maudy and Rosina, wife; b Jul 19; christ. Aug 15 1796; wit: Michael Maudy
David of Nicolaus Frey and Barbara, wife; b May 5; christ. Sep 11 1796; wit: the parents
Maria Magdalena of Henry Feyrre and Elizabeth, wife; b Oct 24 1795; christ. Oct 29 1796; wit: the parents
George of George Angenei and Catharina, wife; b Dec 3 1796; christ. Nov 6 1797; wit: the parents
Magda of John Hand and Elizabeth, wife; b Jul 19 1796; christ. Nov 6 1796; wit: the parents

Lisabeth of John Fischer and wife Elizabeth, wife; b Oct 25 1781; christ. Aug 24 1785
Jacob b Apr 10 1785; christ. Jul 28 1785
Susanna b Aug 25 1792; christ. Oct 20 1798
Magdalena b Feb 22 1794; christ. May 6 1794
John b Jan 11 1796; christ. Feb 8 1796

St. Paul's Evangelical Lutheran and Reformed Church

Andrew of Frederick Hirsch and Catharina, wife; b Nov 13 1796; christ. Jan 22 1797; wit: Abraham Hoblin, Margaret, wife
Catharina of Henry Bruner and Elizabeth, wife; b Aug 5 1796; christ. Feb 5 1797; wit: the parents
Salome of Peter Miller and Christina, wife; b Feb 30 1797; christ. Mar 10; wit: Henry Brua, Catharina, wife
George of Wilhelm Name and Katharina, wife; b Dec 25 1796; christ. Apr 16 1797; wit: the parents
Elizabeth of Henry Yegly and Margaret, wife; b Oct 20 1796; christ. Apr 16 1797; wit: the parents
Michael of Casper Maudy and Catharina, wife; b Feb 3 1797; christ. Mar 6; wit: John Miller, Susanna, wife
Dewalt of John Angene and Magdalena, wife; b Jan 29; christ. Mar 5 1797; wit: the parents
Jonathan of John Wachtel and Elizabeth, wife; b Mar 5; christ. Apr 30 1797; wit: Jonathan Jons, Elizabeth, wife
Catharina of Jacob Zeoller and Margaret, wife; b Nov 11 1796; christ; Apr 30 1797; wit: Catharina Wachtel
John of John Brua and Maria, wife; b Mar 3 1797; christ. May 13; wit: Justanus Brua, Magdalena, wife
Jacob of George Hermann and Maria, wife; b Mar 18 1797; christ. May 14; wit: George Miller, Catharina, wife
George of Jacob Hersch and Veronica; b Apr 28 1797; christ. May 13; wit: the parents
John of John Miller and Juliana, wife; b May 28; christ. Jun 24 1797; wit: the parents
Irma Catharina of Abraham Refter and Elizabeth, wife; b Jul 24 1796; christ. Jun 24 1797; wit: John Fuyrena, Magdalena, wife
David of Peter Wolf and Magdalena, wife; b Jan 11; christ. Jul 23 1797; wit: David Esch
Elizabeth of George Brachunier and Anna Margaret, wife; b Mar 18; christ. Aug 20 1797; wit: Elizabeth Ott
Adam of Christian Boby and Catharina, wife; b Mar 25; christ. Aug 20 1797; wit: the parents
Anamaria of Joseph Gonner and Juliana, wife; b May 14; christ. Aug 20 1797; wit: John Miller, Susanna, wife
Jacob of Peter Schwob and wife; b Mar 29; christ. Apr 2 1797; wit: the parents
Frederick of George Wetstein and Elizabeth, wife; b Feb 20 1797; christ. Sep 3; wit: John Miller, Juliana, wife
George of Peter Brua and Magdalena, wife; b Jul 25 1797; christ. Sep 3; wit: the parents
Elizabeth of Henry Angene and Susanna, wife; b Aug 23; christ. Oct 15 1797; wit: the parents
Michael of Conrad Graul and Elizabeth, wife; b Aug 15; christ. Oct 15 1797; wit: Michael Boby, Barbara, wife
Elizabeth of Jacob Esch and Elizabeth, wife; b Mar 19; christ. Sep 17 1797; wit: Catharina Esch
daughter of Michael Bergman and Susanna, wife b Jun 2 1797; christ. Dec 2; wit: Catharina Bergman
daughter of Michael Faubel and Anna, wife; b Sep 30 1797; christ. Dec 26; wit: Christina Schwab
Salome of Henry Brua and Catharina, wife; b Nov 10 1797; christ. Dec 26; wit: the parents

St. Paul's Evangelical Lutheran and Reformed Church

Henry of Adam Schneider and Catharina, wife; b Oct 30 1797; christ. Jan 20 1798; wit: Henry Minich, Catharina, wife
Jonathan of Peter Lefler and Catharina, wife; b Sep 19 1797; christ. Feb 18 1798; wit: the parents
Maria of John Huber and Maria, wife; b Sep 20 1797; christ. Apr 10 1798; wit: Henry Bruner, Elizabeth, wife
Catharina of Jacob Feid and Catharina, wife; b Nov 3 1797; christ. Apr 10 1798; wit: George Knebel, Catharina, wife
Anna of John Hand and Elizabeth, wife; b Jan 6 1798; christ. May 12; wit: Joseph Feyre, Anna Maria, wife
Elizabeth of Henry Feyre and Elizabeth, wife; b Mar 19 1798; christ. Jun 10; wit: the parents
David of Jacob Sygman and Susanna, wife; b Dec 30 1797; christ. Jun 10 1798; wit: the parents
Catharina of Jacob Hehrns and Maria, wife; b Apr 22 1798; christ. Jul 8; wit: Maria Hehrns
Susanna of Jacob Hums and Catharina, wife; b May 1 1798; christ. Jul 8; wit: the parents
George of Henry Yegly and Margaret, wife; b Jun 2 1798; christ. Jul 8; wit: the parents
Elizabeth of John Klekamm and Drusilla, wife; b Apr 20 1798; christ. Sep 30; wit: the parents
Jacob of Jacob Bed and Maria, wife; b Aug 3 1798; christ. Sep 30; wit: the parents
Christina of John Angene and Magalena, wife; b Sep 19 1798; christ Oct 14; wit: the parents
William of John Juin and Anna Maria, wife; b Aug 26 1798; christ. Oct 29 1798; wit: the parents
Jacob b Nov 24 1797; christ. Oct 29 1798; wit: the parents
Anna Maria b Sep 6 1789; christ. Oct 29 1798; wit: the parents
Salome of Jacob Diprri and Elizabeth, wife; b Dec 14 1785; christ. Oct 29 1798; wit: Dorothy Bergman
George b Aug 9 1798; christ. Oct 29 1798; wit: the parents
Henry b Aug 9 1798; christ. Oct 29 1798; wit: Jacob Bergman and wife
Elizabeth of Andrew Hader and Susanna, wife; b Jun 24 1798; christ. Nov 24; wit: Jacob Stum and wife
Elizabeth of Jacob Stung and Catharina, wife; b Mar 19 1798; christ. Nov 24 1798; wit: Christian Bobe, Catharina, wife
Daniel of George Fischer and Maria b Jul 17; christ. Oct 3; spon: the parents
Catharina of Jacob Seibert and Elizabeth, wife b Nov 5 1789; christ. Jun 9 1790; spon: the parents
Henry of John Gebrel [Gerrel?] and Hanna, wife; b Jun 10 1790; spon: the parents
Catharina of John Maudi and wife; b Dec 10 1790; christ. Feb 13; spon: the parents
Jacob of Casper Maudy and Catharine b Dec 28 1790; wit: Balze Maudy
Jacob of Abraham Esst and Anna Maria b Dec 17 1790; christ. Apr 10 1791; spon: George Maudy
Sofina of George Muller and Catharina b Mar 3; christ. May 8; spon: Adam Gerlacher and wife
Margaret of John Hissong and Barbara b Jan 17; christ. Jul 10; spon: the parents
Susanna of Michael Bergmann and Eva b May 28; christ. Jul 10; spon: the parents

St. Paul's Evangelical Lutheran and Reformed Church

Catharina of Theobald Klodner and Elizabeth b Jun 15; christ. Jul 10; spon: Margaret Schmidt, wife
Jacob of John Miller and Juliana, wife; b Feb 19; christ. Apr 29 1799; wit: the parents
John of Joseph More and Elizabeth, wife; b Nov 17 1798; christ. Apr 29; wit: John Miller
George of Abraham Esch and Maria, wife; b Mar 27; christ. Jun 24 1799; wit: the parents
Eva of John Hand and Elizabeth, wife; b May 24 1799; christ. Jul 7; wit: Eva Steartzman
Thomas of Thomas Randall and Charlotte, wife; b Jun 12 1798; christ. Jul 7; wit: the parents
Isaac of Thomas Davis and Johanna, wife; b Sep 22 1797; christ. Jul 7; wit: the parents
Elizabeth of Nathaniel Niesbeth and Elizabeth, wife; b Jul 7 1799; christ. Aug 3; wit: the parents
Elizabeth of Frederick Hersch and Catharina, wife; b May 11 1799; christ. Aug 3; wit: Elizabeth Edeberger
Adam of John Brua and Maria, wife; b Jun 20 1799; christ. Aug 3; wit: the parents
Margaret of Henry Angene and Susanna, wife; b Sep 2; christ. Oct 13 1799; wit: the parents
Catharina of John Miller and Susanna, wife; b Aug 28 1799; christ. Oct 27; wit: Catharina Schneider
Sally of Philipp Schmal and Margaret, wife; b Jul 5 1799; christ. Oct 27; wit: Catharina Lefler
Susanna of Joseph Schmidt and Catharina, wife b Sep 13 1799; christ. Nov 20; wit: Eva Bergman
Margaret of Michael Bergman and Susanna, wife; b Dec 1799; christ. Apr 14 1800; wit: Catharina Schmidt
Annamaria of Jacob Beck and Anamaria, wife; b Jun 6; christ. Jun 14 1800; wit: the parents
Jacob of Henry Davis and Christina, wife; b Apr 7 1800; christ. Jul 6; wit: the parents
David of Peter Lanz and Elizabeth, wife; b Feb 9 1800; christ. Jul 6; wit: the parents
Maria of William Fadwell and Catharina, wife; b Apr 12 1800; christ. Jul 6; wit: the parents
David of Henry Brua and Catharina, wife; b Feb 7 1800; christ. May 10; wit: the parents
John of John Seybert and Catharina, wife; b Sep 13 1799; christ. Oct 26 1800; wit: the parents
Magdalena of Peter Miller and Christina, wife; b Oct 7 1800; christ. Oct 25; wit: the parents
T. George of Joseph Feyt and Magdalena, wife; b Feb 24 1800; christ. Apr 14; wit: the parents
Anna Maria of Joseph Schmidt and Catharina, wife; b Dec 8 1800; christ. Feb 15 1801; wit: Dorothy Bergman
Jacob of Michael Vaubol and Anna, wife; b Apr 1 1800; christ. Feb 15 1801; wit: Michael Bergman, Eva, wife
Veronica of Jacob Hegus and Maria, wife; b Sep 4 1800; christ. Mar 17; wit: Peter Miller and wife
Anna Maria of George Angeny and Catharina b Aug 21 1800; christ. Apr 12 1801; wit: Henry Angeny, Susanna, wife

St. Paul's Evangelical Lutheran and Reformed Church

Hanna of Tobias Ritter and Eva Catharina, wife; b Nov 24 1800; christ. May 10; wit: the parents
Catharina of Henry Feyre and Elizabeth, wife; b Nov 19 1800; christ. Jun 14 1801; wit: the parents
Maria Elizabeth of John Feyere and Sabina, wife; b Sep 3 1800; christ. Jun 14; wit: Joseph Feyere (Fiery)
daughter of Adam Zollinger and Anna Maria, wife; b Sep 13 1789; wit: the parents
son b Aug 10 1797
daughter b Jul 21 1782; christ. May 17 1801
M. Catharina of David Miller and Christina, wife; b Dec 13 1800; christ. May 17; wit: Henry Brua, Catharina, wife
Catharina of Gottfried Schmidt and Hanna, wife; b Mar 5 1798; wit: Catharina Kau
Frederick of Gottfried Schmidt and Hanna, wife; b Aug 14 1800; christ. May 17 1801
Ester of Jacob Stumpf and Catharina, wife; b Nov 20 1800; christ. May 17 1801; wit: the parents
John of John Kau and Hanna, wife; b Nov 11 1792; christ. May 17 1801; wit: the parents
Nancy b Mar 12 1798; christ. May 17 1801; wit: Conrad Schwerd, Elizabeth, wife
Hanna b Feb 8 1796; christ. May 17 1801; wit: Dirdrich Hofmann, Susanna, wife
Daniel b Jun 9 1800; christ. May 17 1801; wit: John Hofman
John of Robert Boverth and Margaret, wife; b 1796; christ. May 17 1801; wit: Henry Kau, Hanna, wife
Susanna of John Lock and Anna, wife; b Jan 1 1800; christ. May 17 1801; wit: Maria Kau
Catharina of Jacob Brakunier and Elizabeth, wife; b Aug 23 1800; christ. Jun 14 1801; wit: Dorothy Bergman
Martin of Andrew Luz and Juliana, wife; b 1799; christ. Sep 27 1801; wit: John Juen
Louisa of Christopher Arnold and Annamaria, wife; b Jul 14 1800; christ. Sep 27 1801; wit: the parents
John of Jacob Esch and Elizabeth, wife; b Nov 11 1800; christ. Nov 8 1801; wit: the parents

Jacob's Church (Lutheran)

Translated by Matilda Ripple Detrich in 1929. Copies available at A. R. Wentz Library, Lutheran Theological Seminary, Gettysburg, Pennsylvania and Maryland Historical Society.

John of Friederich Bell and wife Rosina b 29 Jun; bapt 6 Nov 1791; spon: John Bell and Margaretta Bell, both unmarried
Eva of Martin Lauman and wife Regina b 20 Oct 1791; bapt 6 Nov 1791; spon: Heinrich Jacob; Elisabeth Ledisen; both unmarried
Susanna Catharina of Andreas Leyter and wife Barbara b 3 Jul 1791; bapt 6 Nov 1791; spon: Jacob Leyter and wife Julianna
Solomon of Friederich Hauer and wife Catharina b 29 Jul 1791; bapt 6 Nov 1791; spon: the parents
Samuel of Tobias Ritter and wife Julianna b 10 Sep 1791; bapt 22 Nov 1791; spon: Henrich Sommer and wife Barbara
Jacob of Heinrich Fehr and wife Christina b 9 Feb 1791; bapt 11 Dec 1791; spon: Heinrich Fehr, Sr. and wife Catharina
Susanna of Heinrich Fehr and wife Christina b 13 Mar 1787; bapt 11 Dec 1791; spon: Martin Jacob and wife Anna Barbara
Jacob of Friederich Bühl and Catharina b Sep 9 1791; bapt Dec 11 1791; spon: Jacob Leyter, unmarried; Barbara Ritter, unmarried
John of Friederich Biehl and Catharine b Oct 6 1792; bapt Mar 17 1793; spon: John Biehl, Eva Kufer, both unmarried
Julianna of Jacob Schmidt and Dorothea b Aug 11 1792; bapt Mar 17 1793; spon: Peter Hüffner and wife Elisabeth
Barbara of Jese Hafner and Barbara b Jan 14 1793; bapt Apr 1 1793; spon: Anna Barbara Hafner
Catharina of Heinrich Vogler and Catharina b Dec 1792; bapt Mar 31 1793; spon: Hanna Spitznagel
Catharina of John Lacklen and Eva b Jan 1790; bapt Apr 21 1793; spon: Catharina Wagner, unmarried
Elisabeth of Jose Läckly and Eva b Mar 23 1791; bapt Apr 21 1793; spon: Elisabeth Ritter, wife of John Ritter
Anna Margartta of Jacob Sommer and Elisabeth b Apr 15 1793; bapt May 12 1793; spon: Anna Maria Ladis, unmarried
Elisabeth of George Läcker and Susanna b Mar 25 1793; bapt May 12 1793; spon: Anna Maria Kohler, wife of George Kohler
Absolom of Joseph Heidler and Catharina b Apr 24 1793; bapt Jun 2 1793; spon: Michael Fink and wife Elisabeth
Daniel of John Weisemann and Anna Maria b Sep 6 1792; bapt Jun 2 1793; spon: Jacob Leiter and Catharina Bell, unmarried
Ester of Peter Allbrecht and Anna Maria b Apr 7 1793; bapt Jun 2; spon: the parents
Anna Barbara of Leonhart Wiest and Elisabeth b Dec 16 1792; bapt Apr 21 1793; spon: Anna Barbara Emzfiehl, wife of George Emzfiehl
Anna Maria of Jacob Fiehl and Eva b Apr 16 1793; bapt Jun 2 1793; spon: Adam Maurer and Anna Maria Ladis, both unmarried
Barnabas of John Hays and Silana b Apr 1 1793; bapt 21 in same year; spon: mother
son of Friederich Hauer and Catharina b May 9 1793; bapt Aug 4 1793; spon: his own parents
son of Jacob Huber and Ester b Jan 31 1792; bapt Aug 4 1793; spon: John Huber
daughter of George Schmidt and Magdalena Jacob b Nov 6 1792; bapt Aug 4 1793; spon: Elisabeth Layder

Jacob's Church (Lutheran)

daughter of John Leyter and Magdalena b Apr 14 1793; bapt Aug 11 1793; spon: Andreas Leyter and wife Barbara
Elisabeth Finck of John Creafforth and Magdalena b Jun 9 1793; bapt Aug 11 1793; spon: Michael Finck and his wife Elisabeth
John of Andreas Lyter and Barbara b Jun 24 1793; bapt Aug 11 1793; spon: Martin Kiefer and wife Elisabeth
Margareda of Jacob Lauman and Margareda b Feb 9 1793; bapt Aug 11 1793; spon: Peter Shwitzer and Margareda
Anna Maria of James Raub and Appolonia b Nov 11 1792; bapt Aug 11 1793; spon: the parents themselves
Jonathan of Adam Rauhzahn and Catharina b Nov 14 1793; bapt Nov 28 1793; spon: Adam Wagener and wife Catharina
Anna Barbara of Heinrich Jacob and Anna Maria b Nov 10 1793; bapt Dec 13 1793; spon: Martin Jacob and wife Anna Barbara
Susanna of Michael Lantz and Elisabeth b Jan 13 1794; bapt Apr 21 1794; spon: godmother Elisabeth, widow
Anna Elisabeth of Matheus Reinthaler and Margareda b Feb 20 1794; bapt Apr 21; spon: John Hafner and wife Barbara
Elisabeth of Friederich Bell and Rosina b May 25 1793; bapt ---; spon: godmother Elisabeth Lentz, widow
Johe Jacob of John Botz and Christina b 17 Dec 1793; bapt May 18 1794; spon: Jacob Schweitzer and wife Magdalena
Philipp of John Pfeicker and Eva Margareda b Jan 15 1794; bapt Jun 8 1794; spon: Philipp Pfeicker, unmarried
Christina of Jacob Busch and Catharina b Jan 11; bapt Jun 8 1794; spon: the parents
Jacob of Michel Jacob and Margareda b May 17; bapt Jun 8 1794; spon: Jacob Fiehl and wife Eva Fiehl
Catharina of Matheus King and Barbara b Aug 25 1794; bapt 28, 7 tember; spon: Nicklaus Szier and wife Catharina
John of John Häfli and Annabarbara b Jul 2; bapt Sep 13 1795; spon: parents
Daniel of Andreas Augenstein and Margareda b Dec 11; bapt Dec 8 1795; spon: parents
Elisabeth of Andreas Bell and Margareda b Jun 2; bapt Dec 8 1795; spon: Peter Statler and wife Elisabeth
John George of John Geh (Gehr) and Margareda b Apr 26; bapt Dec 5 1795; spon: parents
George of George Fiel and Elisabeth b Dec 7 1795; bapt Jan 3 1796; spon: parents
Sarah of Jacob Fiel and Eva b Sep 18; bapt Jan 3 1796; spon: mother
Elisabeth of Heinrich Jacob and Annamaria b Nov 19 1795; bapt Dec 26 1795; spon: parents
Jacob of Jacob Ritter and Julianna b Jan 31; bapt Mar 27 1796; spon: David Ritter and wife; Julianna
Anton of John Della and Anna Margreda b Jan 17; bapt Mar 27 1796; spon: David Sholl and wife Saloma
Margrada of Martin Fotd(?) and Margrada b Feb 12 1796; bapt Apr 24 1796; spon: Barbara Karn
Susana of John Weinn and Annamaria b Feb 13 1796; bapt Jan 20 1797; spon: parents
Elisabeth of Adam Hison and Susana b 1796; bapt Feb 19 1797; spon: Elisabeth Lauman
Catharina of Matheias Reinthal and Margrada b Jan 1 1796; bapt Jan 28 1796; spon: parents

Jacob's Church (Lutheran)

George of Michael Jacob and Margrada b Jun 7 1796; bapt Apr 21 1797; spon: George Fiel, Elisabeth
Annamaria of David Scholl and Salome b Mar 27 1797; bapt May 14 1797; spon: Jacob Koro, and wife Catharina
John Henry of Heinrich Jacob and Anna Maria b Feb 24 1797; bapt Apr 21 1797; spon: parents
Jacob of George Sheira and Juliana b Apr 21 1797; bapt Jun 2 1797; spon: parents
Catharina of Andreas Bell and Margrada b May 12 1797; bapt Jul 30 1797; spon: John Menser and wife Catharina
Leonhart of David Ritter and Julian b Jul 26 1797; bapt Oct 15 1797; spon: Jacob Leiter and wife Juliana
John Henry of George Fihld and Elisabeth b Oct 22 1797; spon: Henrich Jacob and wife Annamaria
John Jacob of John Dolla and Anna Margrada b Sep 29 1797; spon: Martin Jacob and wife Barbara
John of Henrich Jacob b Nov 9 1798
Jacob of Andreas Bell and Margrada b Nov 28 1798; bapt Apr 6 1799; spon: parents
John of --- Schreier and wife b Dec 15 1798; bapt Jun 9 1799; spon: parents
Christian of John Gastert and Annamaria b Jan 22 1798; spon: Andreas Lieder and wife Barbara
Maria of Falantin Fehr and Elisabeth b Apr 25 1795; spon: Maria Fehr
Catharina of John Feli b Jun 28 1799; bapt Sep 22 1799; spon: Catharina Leidi
John of George Hafner and Elisabeth b Mar 9 1800; bapt May 3 1800; spon: John Hafner and Barbara
Catharina of John Mentzer and Catharina b Jun 22 1800; bapt Jul 6 1800; spon: parents
Hana of Jacob Spitznagel and Maria b Nov 15 1800; bapt Apr 15 1801; spon: Elisabeth Lauman
Jacob of Leedwic Emerich and Susana b Nov 13 1799; bapt Jul 6 1800; spon: parents
Catatina of George Schreier and Juliana b Aug 2 1800; bapt Apr 15 1801; spon: Doratha
Maria of Henrich Benner and Susana b Dec 15 1800; bapt Sep 6 1801; spon: John Hebel and Maria
Jacob of Christoph Schwitzer and Magaret b Dec 25; bapt May 20 1792; spon: Peter Schwitzer and wife
Maria Barbara of John Zentmyer and Barbara b Dec 25; bapt May 20 1792; spon: Barbara Empfiel
Leonhart of Carl Scholl and Margaretha b Apr 7 1792; bapt Jul 29 1792; spon: Christian Gilbert and wife Margretha

St. John's Parish Episcopal Church

From the Vestry Minutes (available on microfilm at the State Archives (M855)

Persons confirmed by Thomas John Clagett D.D. on 13 August 1797.
Mary Stull, Sophia Rochester, Ann Miller, Lucinda Bower, Catherine Swearingen, Matilda Stull, Elizabeth Rawlings, Rebecca Hughes, Susanna Huges, Elizabeth Hall, Margaret Taylor, Otho Williams, Joseph Williams, Holland Stull, Prudence Williams, Allice Dowlar, Phebe Grieves, Sarah Owen, and Sarah Dowlar.

Assignment of pews on 6 November 1797 at a Vestry Meeting of: Rev. George Bower, Alexr. Clagett, John Clagett, Elie Williams, Rezin Davis and William Gorden.

Pew
number To whom assigned

1	Daniel Hughes	23	William Fitzhugh
2	Igns. Taylor, Thomas Belt and Charles Carroll	9	George Bean
		10	William Gordon
3	John Clagett	11	William S. Compton
4	Samuel Ringgold	12	Edmond Rutter [gives up April 1799 which Balzer Goll takes]
5	Elie Williams		
14	Richard Pindell	13	Maurice Baker
15	Benjamin Clagett	24	William Fitzhugh
16	William Elliott	25	Peter Miller
17	Rezin Davis, Kennedy Owen	26	Perry McCoy [gives up April 1799 which Nathan Morgan takes]
18	N. Rochester, Danl. Stull		
20	John Ragan	27	John Dowlar
21	Thomas Sprigg	19	James and Griffith Henderson
22	Alexander Clagett		

Names appearing in the Vestry minutes prior to 1801: Cephas Beale, Eli Beatty, Henry Bowart, John Carr, Alexander Claggett, Hugh Claggett, John Claggett, Hezekiah Claggett, Michael Fackler, Samuel Finley, William Fitzhugh, Henry Gamwell, Turner Gor, William Gordon, Thomas Hallam, Thomas Hart, Daniel Hughes, Robert Hughes, John Lee, William Lee, Charles McCauley, Charles Ogle, Richard Pindell, Solomon Rawlings, William Reynolds, Nathaniel Rochester, Frederick Rohrer, Titus Rynhart, Henry Schryock, John Scott, Thomas Sprigg, John Stull, John Willar, Elie Williams

Reformed Church of Hagerstown

Georg of Jacob Schneider and mother, Catherina, both married people
  b. August 28, 1766, bapt. October 20, 1766 Spon: George, brother and his housewife Gertraut
Ludwig of Jacob Schneider and mother, Catharina, both married people
  b. November 23, 1768, bapt. March 12, 1769 Spon: Ludwig Stoltz
Wilhelm of Paul Christman and mother, Magthalena, both married people b.
  January 12, 1771 Spon: Wilhelm Heiser and his houswife Anna
Johannes of Christofel Boltzer and Elisabetha, both married people,
  b. May 24, 1771, bapt. June 20, 1771 Spon: Johannes Zimerman and his housewife Catha.
Georg of Christofel Boltzer and mother, Elisabetha, both married people,
  b. May 24, 1771, bapt. June 20, 1771 Spon: Martin Weber and his housewife
Elisabeth of Simon Haussholt and Elisabeth, both married people,
  b. October 18, 1774, bapt. November 18, 1774 Spon: Himself
Susana of Simon Haussholt and Elisabeth, both married people, b. October 10, 1776, bapt. November 15, 1776 Spon: Himself
Anna Elisabeth of Lorentz Frotzman and mother, Elisabeth, both married people b. October 15, 1778, bapt. November 25, 1778 Spon: Wilhelm Heiser and his housewife Anna
Anna Maria of Lorentz Frotzman and mother, Elisabeth, both married people,
  b. July 13, 1780, bapt. August 12, 1780 Spon: Jacob Weimar and his housewife Sallome
Elisabetha of Michael Fakler and mother, Helena, both married people,
  b. January 26, 1769, bapt. March 15, 1769 Spon: Henrich Schreyak and his housewife Catharina
Susana of Michael Fakler and mother, Helena, both married people, b. October 16, 1770, bapt. November 5, 1770 Spons: Lenhart Scheyak and his housewife Maria Margretha
Johannes of Rutholf Bley and mother, Anna Barbara, both married people,
  b. March 3, 1771, bapt. March 17, 1771 Spon: Jacob Teibel and his housewife Margretha
Georg of Georg Schmit and mother, Magthalena, both married people,
  b. February 13, 1771, bapt. March 1771 Spons: Peter Hoss and his housewife Salome
Adam of Jacob Wolter and mother, Anna Maria, both married people, b. January 23, 1771, bapt. March 17, 1771 Spon: Georg Frey and his housewife Anna Catharina
Rosina of Johannes Braun and mother, Sara, both married people, b. March 14, 1771, bapt. March 24, 1771 Spon: Johannes Schweitzer and Rosina Hoegerin
Anna Cathrina of Jacob Schneider and mother, Anna Elis., both married people, b. January 14, 1771, bapt. March 24, 1771 Spon: Daniel Schneider and Anna Cathrina Boyrin
Andreas of Andreas Batz and mother, Eva Catharina, both married people,
  b. January 12, 1771, bapt. March 26, 1771 Spon: Martin Stucky and his housewife Elisabetha
Christofel of Christofel Zirger and mother, Margretha, both married people,
  b. February 14, 1771, bapt. April 20, 1771 Spon: Philip Freund and his housewife Elisabetha
Margretha of Wilhelm Dackin and mother, Schin, both married people,
  b. February 4, 1769, bapt. May 8, 1771 Spon: Jonathan Herrg and his housewife Doretea
Magtalena of Conrad Eiggelberger and mother, Cathrina, both married people b. March 28, 1771, bapt. May 12, 1771 Spon: Magtalena Norfin

Reformed Church of Hagerstown

Johann Ludwig of Christian Weinman and mother, Elisabetha, both married people, b. December 2, 1771, bapt. May 12, 1771 Spon: Johannes Schehrer and his housewife Susana
Fridrich of Georg Arnolt and mother, Catharina, both married people, b. March 6, 1771, bapt. May 14, 1771 Spon: Peter Wagner and his housewife Magtalena
Elisabetha of mother Sara Dostin, unethical person, b. March 19, 1771, bapt. May 15, 1771 Spon: Elisabetha Baumenin
Eva Gretha of Philipp Schmitt and mother, both married people, b. February 17, 1770, bapt. May 15, 1771 Spons: Johannes Braun and his housewife Catharina
Margretha of Fridrich Falleto and mother, Barbara, both married people, b. February 1, 1771, bapt. May 19, 1771 Spon: Martin Seitner and his housewife Margretha
Barbara of Martin Seidner and mother, Margretha, both married people, b. 1771, bapt. May 19, 1771 Spon: Fridrich Falleto and his housewife Barbara
Doretha of Andreas Lang and mother, Fromia, both married people, b. May 23, 1771, bapt. May 23, 1771 Spon: Jonathan Harri and his housewife Doretea
Maria Elisabetha of Johannes Schneider and mother Anna Maria, both married people, b. January 2, 1771, bapt. May 26, 1771 Spon: Johan Henrich Folms and his housewife Maria Elisabetha
Henrich of Sturn Auen Lewies and mother, Anna Maria, both married people, b. March 27, 1771, bapt. May 26, 1771 Spon: Henrich Dirtz Anna - a widow Schriberin (?)
Maria Elisabetha of Fredrich Lederman and mother, Maria Catharina, both married people, b. October 5, 1766, bapt. June 6, 1771 Spon: Matheisa Feiler and his housewife Magtalena
Susanna Catharina of Fridrich Ledermann and mother, Maria Cathrine, both married people, b. October 23, 1770, bapt. June 6, 1771 Spon: Johann Peter Huelum and his housewife Susana Catharina
Samuel and Tomas Liften and mother, Anna Maria, both married people, b. March 29, 1771, bapt. May 7, 1771 Spon: Peter Crebil
Georg of Christofel Harn and mother, Catharina, both married people, b. February 17, 1771, bapt. June 9, 1771 Spon: Philipp Huit and his housewife Eva
Susana of George Winder and mother, Susana, both married people, b. November 10, 1770, bapt. June 23, 1770
Johannes of Jacob Rofel and mother Margretha, both married people, b. April 12, 1771, bapt. June 23, 1771
Johan Michael of Michael Drubel and mother, Margretha, both married people, b. June 4, 1771, bapt. 30, Spon: Rutholf Bley and his housewife Anna Barbara
Catharina of Ludwig Kernekam and mother, Regina, both married people, b. June 16, 1771, bapt. July 7, 1771 Spon: Heinrich Muller and his housewife Catharina
Catharina of Gabriel Becker and mother, Catharina, both married people, b. June 28, 1771, bapt. July 25, 1771 Spon: Daniel Dinkel and his housewife Susana
Anna Maria of Philip Eckel and mother, Catharina, both married people, b. June 2, 1771, bapt. August 2, 1771 Spon: Anna Maria Difom Perferin
Jacob of Georg Schehrer and mother, Eva Rosina, both married people, b. June 24, 1771, bapt. August 4, 1771 Spon: Jacob Schehrer and his housewife Maria Magthalena
Catharina of Peter Williart and mother, Anna Maria, both married people, b. February 29, 1771, bapt. August 18, 1771 Spon: Henrich Williart and his housewife Catharina

Reformed Church of Hagerstown

Elisabetha of Georg Troxel and mother, Margretha, both married people, b. July 10, 1771, bapt. August 25, 1771 Spon: Melchor Boltzhuber and his housewife Elisabetha

Georg and Johannes Hausshalter and mother, Margretha, both married people, b. August 2, 1771, September 15, 1771 Spon: Georg Schwengel and his housewife Margretha

George Jacob of Jacob Meyer and mother, Magtalena, both married people, b. September 8, 1771, bapt. 16, Spon: Michael Schwab and his housewife

Johan Henrich of Michael Hefele and mother, Eva Catharina, both married people, b. June 28, 1771, bapt. September 16, 1771 Spon: Henrich Stirtzman and his housewife Eva

Peter of Andreas Hirschman and mother, Cathrina, both married people, b. 1771, bapt. September 16, 1771 Spon: Peter Cusick and his housewife Eva

Johanna Georg of Wilhaelm Preiss and mother, Catharina, both married people, b. December 2, 1770, bapt. September 15, 1771 Spon: Daniel Witzstein and his housewife Anna Maria

Margretha b. April 30, 1771, bapt. September 15, 1771

Wilhelm of Wilhelm Schonefeld and mother, Maria, both married people, b. July 23, 1771, bapt. October 16, 1771 Spon: Henrich Weschenbach

Catharina of Peter Heflich and mother, Anna Maria, both married people, b. October 22, 1771, bapt. November 3, 1771 Spon: Jacob Schub and his housewife Margretha

Elisabetha Doredea of Conrath Brendlinger and mother, Anna Maria, both married people, b. August 27, 1771, bapt. November 3, 1771, Spon: Henrich Kinn and his housewife Doretra

Johann Jacob of Johannes Schuman and mother, Barbara, both married people, b. September 14, 1771, bapt. November 17, 1771 Spon: Jacob Greber and his housewife Magthalena

Henrich of Christofel Trab and mother, b. 1771, bapt. November 17, 1771 Spon: Henrich Kunn and his housewife Doretha

Eva Elisabetha of Philip Becker and mother Elisabetha, both married people, b. September 3, 1771, bapt. November 17, 1771 Spon: Ernst Becker and his housewife Eva

Margretha of Georg Frud and mother, Margretha, both married people, b. August 26, 1771, bapt. November 17, 1771 Spon: Henrich Corderman and his housewife Barbara

Johann Jacob of Peter Stiglitz and mother, Christina, both married people, b. November 5, 1771, bapt. December 1771 Spon: Jacob Kneft and his housewife Christina

Maria Magthalena of Christofel Bauman and mother, Maria, b. November 8, 1771, bapt. December 17, 1771 Spon: Jacob Bauman and his housewife Elisabetha

Elisabetha of Martin Schneider and mother, Anna Maria, both married people, b. September 8, 1771, bapt. December 1771 Spon: Martin Wehr and his housewife Elizabeth

Elisabetha of Peter Hoss and mother, Sallome, both married people, b. November 15, 1771, bapt. December 25, 1771 Spon: Georg Schmit and his housewife Magthalena

Catharina Margretha of Jacob Hausshalter and Catharina b. December 6, 1771, bapt. -25, Spon: Jacob Meirer and Margretha

Johannes of Jacob Knecht and mother, Christina, b. December 6, 1771, bapt. --25, Spon: Johannes Leydi and Susana

Susana of Valadein Schuster and mother, Doredea, both married people, b. November 20, 1771, bapt. December 27, 1771 Spon: Susana Heislin

Reformed Church of Hagerstown

Johannes of Abraham Erlenwein and Eva Catharina, both married people, b. December 1, 1771, bapt. December 27, 1771 Spon: Johannes Gross and his housewife Catharina

Johannes of Christian Jutzler and mother, Margretha, both married people, b. November 3, 1771, bapt. December 27, 1771 Spon: Michael Schuster and his housewife Margretha

Christian of Adam Huber and mother, Catharina, both married people, b. May 29, 1771, bapt. December 31, 1771 Spon: Himself

Johan Adam of Johan Tamser and mother, Susana, both married people, b. November 20, 1771, bapt. December 29, 1771 Spon: Adam Huber and his housewife Catharina

Elisabetha of Adam Aulenbach and mother, Barbara, both married people, b. October 21, 1771, bapt. January 28, 1772 Spon: Johannes Muller and his housewife Magthalena

Johan Jacob of Michael Ott and mother, Margretha, both married people, b. January 25, 1772, bapt. February 9, 1772 Spon: Joh. Jacob Greber and his housewife Margretha

Annaeta Maria of Johannes Stadler and mother, Cath. Barbara, both married people, b. February 2, 1772, bapt. February 9, 1772 Spon: Joh. Eberhart and his housewife Anna Maria

Jacobus of Aron Hack and mother, Chie, both married people, b. February 1, 1772, bapt. February 9, 1772 Spon: Himself

Susanna of Peter Flinger and mother, Catharina, both married people, b. February 19, 1772, bapt. February 23, 1772 Spon: Niclos Reidemauer and his housewife Magthalena

Anna Maria of Johannes Schreyack and mother, Anna Maria, both married people, b. February 27, 1772, bapt. on the same day Spon: Himself

Catharina of Georg Theil and mother, Fromia, both married people, b. November 30, 1772, bapt. March 13, 1772 Spon: Eugelhart Kuter and his housewife Catharina

Johannes of Tomas Keinhart and mother, Eva Elisabetha, b. October 11, 1771, bapt. March 25, 1772 Spon: Himself

Gertraut of Ehrman Bauman and mother, Herem, both married people, b. April 27, 1771, bapt. May 3, 1772 Spon: Johannes Schel and his housewife Cath.

Johan Henrich of Philip Huit and mother, Eva, both married people, b February 14, 1772, bapt. May 3, 1772 Spon: Henrich Schneiter and his housewife Margretha

Catha. of Wilhelm Kaseroth and mother, both married people, b. January 12, 1772, bapt. May 3, 1772 Spon: Jacob Schneiter and his housewife

Christofel of Baltser Gol and mother, Maria Elisabetha, both married people, b. May 9, 1772, May 12, 1772 Spon: Himself

Fridrich of Fridrich Bierzeisel and mother, Anna Maria, both married people, b. June 11, 1772, bapt. June 12, 1772 Spon: Fridrich Stades and his housewife Sibila

Fromia of Michael Fey and mother, Eva, both married people, b. January 22, 1772, bapt. June 12, 1772 Spon: Fridrich Geiger and his housewife Fromia

Johannes of Peter Breiner and mother, Catharina, both married people, b. June 9, 1772, bapt. -- 17, Spon: Johannes Stadler and his housewife Catharina

Elisabeth of Johannes Flenner and mother, Catharina, both married people, b. April 24, 1772, bapt. June 24, 1772 Spon: Henrich Deiss and his housewife Elisabeth

Susana of Johannes Taudenbusch and mother, Maria, both married people, b. May 4, 1772, bapt. May 24, 1772 Spon: Himself

Reformed Church of Hagerstown

Anna Elisabetha of Wilhelm Heiser and mother, Anna, both married people, b. May 8, 1772, bapt. June 24, 1772 Spon: Himself
Adam of Henrich Kuhnes and mother, Doretha, both married people, b. May 1, 1772, bapt. June 8, 1772 Spon: Christofel Bauman and his housewife Maria
Anna Catharina of Peter Wingert and mother, Elisabetha, both married people, b. April 4, 1772, bapt. June 8, 1772 Spon: Meister Jonathan Hoeger and Catharina Traxelsin
Cath. of Casper Huber and mother Catha., both married people, b . March 10, 1772, bapt. June 8, 1772 Spon: Lonhart Bach and his housewife Catha.
Catha. of Carl Norman and mother, Maria Clora, b. October 16, 1770, bapt. June 8, 1772 Spon: Himself
Barbara of Adam Heines and mother, Anna Maria, both married people, b. June 17, 1772, bapt. -- 8, Spon: Michael Huber and his housewife Sollome
Barbara of Johannes Giding and mother, Juliana, both married people, b. April 25, 1772, bapt. June 14, 1772 Spon: Barbara Zeichlerin
Maria Margretha of Jacob Gemberle and mother, Sara, both married people, b. February 4, 1770, bapt. July 11, 1772 Spon: Lonhart Schreyack and his housewife Margretha
Julliana of Adam Hisang and mother, Juliana, both married people, b. December 6, 1771, bapt. July 20, 1772 Spon: Himself
Anna Margretha of Martin Herdlel and mother, Susana, both married people, b. June 4, 1772, bapt. July 26, 1772 Spon: Georg Herdel and his housewife Margretha
Catharina of Melcher Beltzhuber and mother, Elisabeth, both married people, b. July 11, 1772, bapt. July 26, 1772 Spon: His sister Catharina
Fridrich of Christian Fogelgesang and mother, Barbara, both married people, b. August 15, 1772, bapt. August 17, 1772 Spon: Fridrich Geuger and his housewife Fromia
Maria Magthalena of Christian Fogelgesang and mother, Barbara, both married people, b. August 15, 1772, bapt. August 17, 1772 Spon: Jacob Schehrer and his housewife Magthalena
Catha. of Adam Wolfharth and mother, Elisabetha, both married people, b. July 24, 1772, bapt. August 24, 1772 Spon: Baltzer Gol and his housewife Elisabetha
Eva of Michael Rab, b. July 30, 1772, bapt. August 24, 1772 Spon: Eva Zertlin
Jacob of Johannes Schehrer and mother, Susana, both married people, b. May 22, 1772, bapt. September 20, 1772 Spon: Jacob Scherer and his housewife Maria Magtalena
Jacob of Jacob Wacker and mother, Elisabeth, both married people, b. December 10, 1770, bapt. September 24, 1772 Spon: Caspar Acker and his housewife Susana
Maria Eva of Jacob Stam and mother, Elisabetha, both married people, b. May 4, 1772, bapt. September 28, 1772 Spon: Henrich Jegi and his housewife Anna Margretha
Susanna of Johannes Goh and mother, Barbara, both married people, b. November 1771, bapt. October 3, 1772 Spon: Daniel Clebsadel and his housewife Catherina
Maria Salome of Daniel Teiss and mother, Cathrina, both married people, b. June 22, 1771, bapt. November 7, 1772 Spon: Maria Catharina Hauserin
Joh. Jacob of Jose Weigand and mother, Margretha, both married people, b. October 14, 1772, bapt. November 8, 1772 Spon: Jacob Wolschoeser and his housewife Catharina

Reformed Church of Hagerstown

Elisabetha of Johannes Leidi and mother, Maria Anna, both married people, b. October 19, 1772, bapt. November 8, 1772 Spon: Adam Wolfartt and his housewife Elisabetha
Elisabeth of Johannes Unsel and mother, Anna Maria, both married people, b. September 21, 1772, bapt. November 15, 1772 Spon: Elisabetha Laledi
Jacob of Georg Geiger and mother, Margretha, both married people, b. October 11, 1772, bapt. November 12, 1772 Spon: Jacob Hauser and his housewife Barbera
Elisabeth of Peter Weirich and mother, Maria, both married people, b. November 7, 1772, bapt. December 12, 1772 Spon: Johannes Oster and his housewife Elisabeth
Johannes of Georg Arnolt and mother, Catha., both married people, b. August 27, 1772, bapt. December 27, 1772 Spon: Himself
Johannes of Frantz Wagner and mother, Charlota, both married people, b. November 25, 1772, bapt. December 27, 1772 Spon: Johannes Baun
John. Fridrich of Johan Fridrick Mueller and mother, Catharina, both married people, b. December 6, 1772, bapt. January 8, 1773 Spon: Himself
Johannes of Jacob Bens and mother, Elisabetha, both married people, b. December 21, 1772, bapt. January 10, 1773 Spon: Casper Ster and his housewife Margretha
Joh. Fridrich of Benjamin Heyserl and mother, Anna Margretha, both married people, b. December 4, 1772, bapt. January 10, 1773 Spon: Johan Fridrig Geiger and his housewife Fromia
Maria Elisabetha of Johannes Grast and mother, Maria Catharina, both married people b. November 28, 1772, bapt. January 10, 1773 Spon: Nicolos Werner and his housewife Maria
Maria of Benedict Bauman and mother, Catharina, both married people, b. November 20, 1772, bapt. January 10, 1773 Spon: Johannes Leydi and his housewife Juliana
Doredea of Gabriel Becker and mother, Anna Catha., both married people, b. January 7, 1773, bapt. January 10, 1773 Spon: Michael Hostman and his housewife Doredea
Catharina Elisabeth of Rutholf Bly and mother, Barbara, both married people, b. January 11, 1773, bapt. -- 20, Spon: Fridrich Rohrer and his housewife Catha. Elisabetha
Elisabetha of Georg Schmit and mother, Magtalena, both married people, b. November 19, 1772, bapt. January 24, 1773 Spon: Georg Schmit and his housewife Christina
Carl of Carl Briderlein and mother, Elisabetha, both married people, b. December 1, 1772, bapt. February 7, 1773 Spon: Mathaus Burger and his housewife Margretha
Susanna of Johannes Broemer and mother, Margreth, both married peopel, b. January 7, 1773, bapt. February 7, 1773 Spon: Jacob Meyer and his housewife Elisabeta
Georg of Adam Theil and mother, Maria, both married people, b. December 26, 1771, bapt. February 18, 1773 Spon: Georg Theil and his housewife Fromia
Abraham of Niclos Schmit and mother, Maria Barbara, both married, b. February 5, 1773, bapt. February 20, 1773 Spon: Himself
Anna Maria of Michael Fesler and mother, Maria Catharina, both married people, b. February 7, 1773, bapt. -- 21, Spon: Michael Tomer and his housewife Anna Maria
Eva Catharina of Georg Huber and mother, Eva Elisabe, both married people, b. December 22, 1772, bapt. February 1, 1773 Spon: Catharina Beirm
Jacob of Georg Zinn and mother, Anna Maria, both married people, b. January 20, 1773, bapt. February 21, 1773 Spon: Marthin Seiller

Reformed Church of Hagerstown

Elisabetha of Johannes Steinseifer and mother, Margretha, both married people b. December 1, 1772, bapt. March 2, 1773 Spon: Elisabetha Gertraut Steinseiferin

Johannes of Michael Fackler and mother, Hoelena, both married people, b. November 10, 1772, bapt. March 23, 1773 Spon: Lenhart Schreyack and his housewife Maria Margretha

Catharina of Lenhart Schreyack and mother, Maria Marg., both married people, b. February 21, 1773, bapt. March 3, 1773 Spon: Michael Fackler and his housewife Hoelena

Catha. of Christofel Alter and mother Susana, both married people, b. March 3, 1773, bapt. ---- 7, Spon: Michael Hesler and his housewife Catharina

Johannes of Jacob Schub and mother, Christina Margretha, both married people, b. February 12, 1773, bapt. March 20, 1773 Spon: Michael Tomer and his housewife Anna Maria

Jonathan of Jacob Schneider and mother, Catharina, both married people, b. January 3, 1773, bapt. February 14, 1773 Spon: Jonathan Hager and Catharina Traxel

Johannes of Michael Denbel and Margretha, both married people, b. March 10, 1773, bapt. April 4, 1772 Spon: Dewalt Kethofn and his housewife Anna Maria

Jacob of Adam Mueller and mother, Anna, both married people, b. August 26, 1772, bapt. April 7, 1773 Spon: Jacob Hauser and his housewife

Rosina Catha. of Henrich Kres and mother, Elisabet, both married people, b. March 15, 1773, bapt. April 7, 1773 Spon: Georg Frey and his housewife Catha.

Johannes of Dsau Gnadig and mother, Elisabetha, both married people, b. February 1, 1773, bapt. April 12, 1773 Spon: Himself

Christina of Johannes Schol and mother, Catha., both married people, b. March 21, 1773, bapt. April 12, 1773 Spon: Christian Schneckberger and his housewife

Maria Magtalena and Cara of Auen Ravies and mother, Maria, both married people, b. December 1, 1772, bapt. March 2, 1773 Spon: Georg Schmit and his housewife Magtalen, Georg Frudt and his housewife Margretha

Barbara of Daniel Teiss and mother, Catha, both married people, b. March 14, 1773, bapt. May 8, 1773 Spon: Fridrich Saltete and his housewife

Magtalena of Vallentein Seftle and Anna Maria, both married people, b. March 1773, bapt. May 8, 1773 Spon: David Neidig and his housewife Magtalena

Adam of Georg Metzger and mother, Elizabeth, both married people, b. May 10, 1773, bapt. May 16, 1773 Spon: Bernhart Eberhart and his housewife Doretea

Andrew and Robert of Andrew Hecrery and mother, Jun Macall, illegitimate, b. March 26, 1773, bapt. May 16, 1773 Spon: Philip Teimel and his housewife Catharina

Johan Matheiss of Joseph Seyfrid and mother Barbera, both married people, b. May 14, 1773, bapt. ---- 30, Spon: Johan Feigli and his housewife Arsila

Anna Maria of Doreas Schuler and mother, Argretha, both married people, b. February 22, 1773, bapt. May 30, 1773 Spon: Anna Maria Womerin

Jacob of Jacob Miller and mother, Susana, both married people, b. November 1, 1772, bapt. May 30, 1773 Spon: Jacob Kirschen and his housewife Hanna

Joseph of Peter Binckel and mother, Elisabeth, both married people, b. February 30, 1773, bapt. May 30, 1773 Spon: Adam Edelman and his housewife Eva

Andrew of Philip Stark and Elisabetha, both married people, b. January 10, 1773, bapt. May 30, 1773 Spon: Joh. Andrew Simon and Anna Maria Hogein

Barbera of Jacob Hubacker and mother, Elisabetha, both married people, b. May 31, 1773, bapt. June 5, 1773 Spon: Barbera Endersein

Reformed Church of Hagerstown

Caspar of Caspar Schall and mother, Anna Catha, both married people, b. May 27, 1772, bapt. June 5, 1773 Spon: Feugli and his housewife
Gertraut of Caspar Schall and mother, Anna Catha., both married people, b. November 14, 1766, bapt. June 5, 1773 Spon: Feugli and his housewife
Magtalena of Caspar Schall and mother, Anna Catha., both married people, b. June 29, 1770, bapt. June 5, 1773 Spon: Feugli and his housewife
Cath. Elisabetha of Jacob Hubacker and mother, Elisa b. August 25, 1770, bapt. June 5, 1773 Spon: Henrich Weiss
Georg Peter of Johannes Hausshalter and mother, Maria Margreth, both married people, b. May 8, 1773, bapt. June 13, 1773 Spon: Georg Peter Ried and Elisabetha, both married people
Eva Elisabeth of Georg Hittler and mother, Maria Cath., both married people b. April 18, 1773, bapt. June 13, 1773 Spon: Martin Jacob and his housewife Barbera
Wilhelm of Johannes Deeils and mother, b. April 10, 1773, bapt. June 13, 1773 Spon: Himself
Elisabeth of William Preis and mother, Elisabeth, both married people, b. January 25, 1773, bapt. June 13, 1773 Spon: Himself
Johannes of Jacob Hoss and mother, Magtalena, both married people, b. ---, bapt. June 25, 1773 Spon: Himself
Eva of Adam Huber and mother, Catharina, both married people, b. December 26, 1772, bapt. June 27, 1773 Spon: Georg Weil and his housewife Margretha
Samuel of Georg Weil and mother, Margretha, both married people, b. March 8, 1770, bapt. June 27, 1770 Spon: Adam Huber and his housewife Cathrina
Susana of Thomas Reinhart and mother, Eva Elisabetha, both married people, b. May 4, 1773, bapt. July 4, 1773 Spon: Caspar Frisch and Susana B.
Daniel of Matheus Heckman and mother, Maria, both married people, b. June 11, 1773, bapt. July 4, 1773 Spon: Daniel Tolek and Eva Catha Reinhartin
Maria Barbera of Caspar Fritsch and mother, Susana, both married people, b. June 20, 1770, bapt. July 4, 1770 Spon: Georg Reinhart and Maria Barbera, both married people
Benjamin of Father Elitsch and mother, Sara Hostin, b. February 16, 1767, bapt. July 4, 1773 Spon: Thomas Reinhart and Eva Elisabetha
Michael of Theobalt Belhuber and mother, Anna Maria, both married people, b. June 14, 1773, bapt. July 11, 1773 Spon: Michael Deubel and his housewife Margreth
Johannes of Fridrich Horer and mother, Catharina, both married people, b. June 8, 1773, July 14, 1773 Spon: Himself
Philip of Paul Christman and mother, Magthalena, both married people, b. June 9, 1773, bapt. July 25, 1773 Spon: Wilhelm Hieser and his housewife Anna
William of Paul Christman and mother, Magthalena, b. December 12, 1770, bapt. January 26, 1771-This is recorded here, because there was no church register Spon: William Heiser and his housewife
Johannes of Michael Jeggely and mother, Catharina, b. July 1, 1773, bapt. 25 --- Spon: Christian Mautel and his housewife Barbara
Johan Henrich of Johannes Schneider and mother, Anna Maria, both married people, b. July 11, 1773, bapt. August 8, 1773 Spon: Henrich Jeger and his housewife
Anna Maria of Johannes Schoelter and mother, Anna Barbera, both married people, b. July 1, 1773, bapt. August 4, 1773 Spon: Georg Schwengel and his housewife Anna Margretha
Johannes B. of Fridrich Bitner and mother, Anna Doretra, both married people, b. July 9, 1773, bapt. August 28, 1773 Spon: Gotthart Dresel and Maria Dreselin

Reformed Church of Hagerstown

Susanna Maria of Philip Bitinger and mother Juliana Philabner, b. July 14, 1773, bapt. August 28, 1773 Spon: Gotthart Dresel and Maria Dresel
John Peter of Georg Mey and mother, Maria Christina, b. June 9, 1773, bapt. September 5, 1773 Spon: Peter Grebil and Barbera, both married people
Jacob of Georg Brecht and mother, Fromia, both married people, b. November 13, 1767, bapt. September 22, 1773 Spon: Himself
Tschi Meymy of Georg Brecht and mother, Fromia, both married people, b. October 13, 1771, bapt. September 22, 1773 Spon: Himself
Johannes of Georg Brecht and mother, Fromia, both married people, b. February 9, 1771, bapt. September 22, 1773 Spon: Himself
Elisabeth of Georg Brecht and mother, Fromia, both married people, b. September 10, 1769, bapt. September 22, 1773 Spon: Himself
Benjamin of Georg Brecht and mother, Fromia, both married people, b. August 31, 1772, bapt. September 22, 1773 Spon: Himself
Johannes of Jacob Jauer and mother, Johanna, both married people, b. July 26, 1773, bapt. September 22, 1773 Spon: Josua Schwegler and his housewife
Catharina of Henrich Fur and mother, Catharina, both married people, b. July 23, 1773, bapt. October 3, 1773 Spon: Fridrich Nicodemus and his housewife Catharina
Joseph of Jacob Reidemaner and mother, Susana, both married people, b. March 19, 1773, bapt. October 12, 1773 Spon: Henrich Stirtzman and his housewife Eva
Georg and Caspar Mefert and mother, Maria, both married people, b. September 11, 1773, bapt. October 17, 1773 Spon: Joh. Georg Meyer and his housewife Anna Elisabetha
Johannes of Johannes Morf and mother, Maria Magthalena, both married people, b. May 7, 1773, bapt. October 17, 1773 Spon: Jacob Ulm
John Fridrich of Philip Wegerlein and mother, Fromia, both married people, b. May 22, 1773, bapt. October 20, 1773 Spon: Fridrich Kraft
Peter of Jacob Wacker and Elisabetha, both married people, b. April 21, 1773, bapt. November 15, 1773 Spon: Himself
Elisabetha of Georg Schnoenefelt and Susana, both married people, b. March 25, 1773, bapt. November 15, 1773 Spon: Caspar Acker
Jacob of Jacob Beltzhuber and mother, Anna Maria, both married people, b. December 21, 1773, bapt. December 25, 1773 Spon: Melcher Beltzhuber and his housewife Elisabetha
Johannes of Johannes Keller and mother, Margretha, both married people, b. December 1, 1773, bapt. December 25, 1773 Spon: John Leydy and his wife Susana
Johannes of Johannes Oster and mother, Elisabetha, both married people, b. December 13, 1773, bapt. December 25, 1773 Spon: Himself
Susana of Martin Kirchner and mother, Susan Mueller, illegitimate, b. September 16, 1772, bapt. December 1773 Spon: Henrich Mueller and his housewife
Henrich of Henrich Bret and mother, Maria Elisabeth, both married people, b. September 1, 1773, bapt. June 9, 1774 Spon: Philip Teimel and his housewife Cathrina
Joh. Henrich of Martin Wer and mother, Elisabetha, both married people, b. February 8, 1774, bapt. March 20, 1774 Spon: Joh. Henrich Schneid and his housewife Christina
Susana of Matheis Leiser and mother, Cath., both married people, b. December 4, 1773, bapt. March 27, 1774 Spon: Susana Tamerin
Anna Maria of Baltzer Difenbach and mother, Anna Maria, both married people, b. February 11, 1773, bapt. March 30, 1774 Spon: Maria Cathrina Busmengern

Reformed Church of Hagerstown

Maria Elisabeth of Henrich Hensch and mother, Maria Elisabetha, both married people, b. August 30, 1773, bapt. April 5, 1774 Spon: Henrich Braun and his housewife Salome

Jacob and Robert Grec and mother, Johanna, both married people, b. October --, 1773, bapt. April 9, 1774 Spon: Jacob Bauman and his housewife Elisabeth

Andreas of Lenhart Schaefer and mother, Margreth, both married people, b. December 2, 1773, bapt. April 24, 1774 Spon: Andreas Bach and his housewife Margretha

Cath. Elisabeth of Jacob Katz and mother, Cath. Elizabeth, both married people, b. March 27, 1774, bapt. April 24, 1774 Spon: Himself

Catharina of Joseph Klein and mother, Anna Maria, both married people, b. March 2, 1772, bapt. May 11, 1774 Spon: Himself

Elisabetha of Christofel Beltzer and mother, Elisabetha, both married people, b. October 31, 1773, bapt. May 22, 1774 Spon: Adam Aulenbach and his housewife Anna Barbara

Elisabetha of Georg Klamport and mother, Eva Maria, both married people, b. April 2, 1774, bapt. May 22, 1774 Spon: Margretha Herdlin

Thomas of Ernst Mueller and mother, Margretha, both married people, b. March 3, 1774, bapt. May 26, 1774 Spon: Joseph Reinhart and his housewife Elisabeth

Jacob of Johan Georg Fogler and mother, Susana, both married people, b. January 1, 1774, bapt. May 30, 1774 Spon: Jacob Fogler

Anna Barbara of Georg Fogler and mother, Susana, both married people, b. January 1, 1774, bapt. May 30, 1774 Spon: Martin Hechler and his housewife Anna Barbara

Cath. of Jacob Ney and mother, Maria, both married people, b. May 21, 1774, bapt. June 15, 1774 Spon: Lorentz Dirr and Susan Amin

Anna Maria of Febes and mother, Elisabetha, both married people, b. May 12, 1774, bapt. June 15, 1774 Spon: Anna Maria Weisin

Magtalena of Niclos Feierstrein and mother, Eva Catha., both married people, b. March 2, 1774, bapt. June 16, 1774 Spon: Niclos Schneider and his housewife Catharina

Maria Cath. of Johannes Kein and mother, Anna Maria, both married people, b. May 12, 1774, bapt. June 16, 1774 Spon: Lenhart Stenes and his housewife Maria Cath.

Anna Maria of Adam Gorg and mother, Maria, both married people, b. February 1, 1774, bapt. June 16, 1774 Spon: Georg Hertzog and his housewife Jutit

Elisabeth of Georg Theil and mother, Fromia, both married people, b. October 20, 1773, bapt. June 26, 1774 Spon: Adam Theil and his housewife Maria

Elisabetha of Henrich Woppbach and mother, Elisabetha, both married people b. December 25, 1773, bapt. August 10, 1774 Spon: Elisabetha Ohrendorst in --

Elisabeth of Georg Werner and mother, Margretha, b. May 4, 1774, bapt. September 8, 1774

Anna Maria of Ernst Ditz and mother, Cathrina, both married people, b. September 15, 1774, bapt. September 24, 1774 Spon: Himself

Marianna of Christian Leider and mother, Elisabetha, both married people, b. May 29, 1774, bapt. October 9, 1774 Spon: Philip Oeter and his housewife Cath.

Elisabeth of Carl Hetrich and mother, Susana, both married people, b. September 21, 1774, bapt. dito --9, Spon: Cathrina Bechen

Catharina of Wilhelm Conrath and mother, Catharina, both married people, b. October 15, 1774, bapt. dito --29, Spon: Eustagines Jung and his housewife Margretha

Reformed Church of Hagerstown

Johan Peter of Peter Ulm and mother, Margretha, both married people,
   b. August 10, 1774, bapt. November 5, 1774   Spon: Peter Diter and his
   housewife Maria Catharina
Maria Cathrina of Frantz Wagner and mother, Charlota, both married people,
   b. October 9, 1774, bapt. November 6, 1774   Spon: Maria Catharina Buchin
Elisabeth of Simon Hausshalter and mother, Elisabetha, b. October 29, 1774,
   bapt. November 26, 1774   Spon: Himself
Daniel of Georg Arnold and mother, Cathrina, b. November 20, 1774, bapt.
   December 11, 1774   Spon: Himself
Maria Magthalena of Peter Blocher and mother, Elisabetha, b. November 23,
   1774, bapt. January 5, 1775   Spon: Jacob Hauser and his housewife
Johannes of Johannes Riel and mother, Elisabetha, both married people,
   b. September 13, 1774, bapt. January 5, 1775   Spon: Peter Diter and his
   housewife Maria Catharina
Rebeca of Jacob Roes and mother, Margretha, both married people, b. December
   2, 1772, bapt. January 5, 1775   Spon: Himself
Joseph of Jacob Roes and mother, Margretha, both married people,
   b. September 1, 1774, bapt. January 5, 1775   Spon: Himself
Conrath of Mathies Pitzer and mother, Margretha, both married people,
   b. January 6, 1775, bapt. January 24, 1775   Spon: Himself
Johan Fridrich of Ezechiel Bechtol and mother, Barbera, both married people,
   b. October 5, 1774, bapt. January 24, 1775   Spon: Fridrich Bechtol and
   his housewife Anna Cathrina
Carl Fridrich of Caspar Shell and mother, Anna Catha, both married people,
   b. November 25, 1774, bapt. February 4, 1775   Spon: Joh. Georg Carl and
   his housewife Maria Cathrina
--- of Marthin Kirschner, b. -- 1774, bapt. February 5, 1775   Spon:
   Johannes Kirschner and his housewife Maria
Elisabeth of Johan Emrich and mother, Margretha, both married people,
   b. March 3, 1775, bapt. March 3, 1775   Spon: Maria Barbara Reinhartin
Maria Magtalena of Herman Kreilich and mother, Catharina, both married
   people, b. February 9, 1775, bapt. March 5, 1775   Spon: Himself
Cath. of Jacob Holtz and mother, Cath., both married people, b. October 1,
   1773, bapt. April 2, 1775   Spon: Andani Ruf and housewife Anna Maria
--- of Rutholf Bley and mother, Barbera, both married people, b. -- 31,
   1775, bapt. April 16, 1775   Spon: ---
Georg Adams of Philip Kun and mother, Elisabetha, both married people,
   b. January 8, 1775, bapt. April 16, 1775   Spon: Georg Adam Gurangfloh and
   Christina Gurangfloh
Elisabetha of Jost Weygard and mother, Margretha, both married people,
   b. March 19, 1775, bapt. April 24, 1775   Spon: Himself
Johannes of Frantz Greilich and mother, Anna Catharina, both married people
   b. April 1, 1775, bapt. April 26, 1775   Spon: Himself
Magtalena of Christian Koenig and mother, Elisabetha, both married people,
   b. October 27, 1773, bapt. April 27, 1775   Spon: Himself
Michael of Michael Fesler and mother, Catharina, both married people, b. May
   4, 1775, bapt. May 6, 1775   Spon: Michael Tomer and his housewife Anna
   Maria
Elisabetha of Andreas Linck and mother, Anna Maria, both married people,
   b. March 27, 1775, bapt. May 7, 1775   Spon: Himself
Wiliam of Georg Breid and mother, Fromia, both married people, b. June 19,
   1774, bapt. May 17, 1775   Spon: Himself
Anna Cath. of Christian Eckel and mother, Maria Elisabetha, both married
   people, b. August 2, 1774, bapt. May 17, 1775   Spon: Himself
Michael of ---, b. February 21, 1775, bapt. ----

Reformed Church of Hagerstown

Henrich of Henrich Michael Herger and mother ---, b. February 20, 1775, bapt. August 26, 1775 Spon: Henrich Schengel
Arnedony of Philip Werner and mother, Magthalena, both married people, b. September 8, 1775, bapt. October 19, 1775 Spon: Andonny Hauer and his housewife Annamaria
Maria Catha. of Fridrich Salten and mother, Barbera, both married people, b. October 3, 1775, bapt. -- 30, Spon: Philip Kister and his housewife Maria Barbera
Maria Margretha of Adam Rigel and mother, Maria Margretha, both married people, b. October 22, 1775, November 3, 1775 Spon: Himself
Johan Adam of Joh. Georg Graeft and mother, Elisabetha, both married people, b. October 19, 1775, bapt. November 15, 1775 Spon: Johan Adam Graest
Maria Elisabeth of Peter Schneid and mother, Maria Elis., both married people, b. June 4, 1775, bapt. November 19, 1775 Spon: Lenhart Stentz and his housewife Catharina
Johan Martin of Martin Schmit and mother, Catha., both married people, b. October 13, 1775, bapt. November 19, 1775 Spon: Andang Schneid and his housewife Anna Maria
Tschin Nansi of Rabert Kreg and mother, Tschin, both married people, b. June 22, 1775, bapt. November 24, 1775 Spon: Himself
Johannes of Johannes Kann and mother, Susana, both married people, b. September 20, 1775, bapt. November 26, 1775 Spon: Himself
Johannes of Jacob Bergman and mother, Magtalena, both married people, b. September 12, 1775, bapt. November 26, 1775 Spon: Bernhart Frack and his housewife Barbera
Fridrich of Georg Bechtel and mother, Barbera, both married people, b. October 21, 1775 bapt. November 26, 1775 Spon: Fridrich Hirschhelt and his housewife Abolona
Jacob of Joh. Georg Beck and mother, Eva, both married people, b. September 22, 1775, bapt. November 26, 1775 Spon: Susana Brunnerin
Anna Margretha of Jacob Sturm and mother, Maria Margretha, both married people, b. January 10, 1775, bapt. November 29, 1775 Spon: Susana Saudern
Magthalena of Henrich Gonderman and mother, Barbera, both married people, b. November 10, 1775, bapt. December 3, 1775 Spon: Magthalena Flennerin
Elisabetha of Johnn Rabison and mother, Elisabetha, both married people, b. September 2, 1775, bapt. December 10, 1775 Spon: Himself
Catharina of Jacob Berdol and mother, Margretha, married people, b. October 25, 1774, bapt. December 10, 1774 Spon: Himself
--- of Fridrich Herdli and mother, Margretha, both married people, b. June 12, 1775, bapt. December 16, 1775 Spon: Georg Clambert and his wife Eva
Catha. of Jacob Katz and mother, Cath. Elis., both married people, b. November 2, 1775, bapt. December 24, 1775 Spon: Himself
Joh. David of Jacob Fischer and mother, Elisabetha, both married people, b. March 1, 1772, bapt. January 5, 1776 Spon: Himself
Henrich of Jacob Fischer and mother, Elisabetha, both married people, b. May 27, 1775, bapt. January 5, 1776 Spon: Himself
Elisabetha of Johnn Hert and mother, Maria, both married people, b. January 15, bapt. January 9, 1776 Spon: Himself
Susana of Isau Gnaedig and mother, Elisabetha, both married people, b. July 12, 1775, bapt. January 14, 1776 Spon: Himself
Conrath of Peter Wagner and mother, Margretha, both married people, b. November 9, 1775, bapt. January 21, 1776 Spon: Conrath Oster
Anna Elisabetha of Wilhelm Heiser and mother, Anna, both married people, b. February 24, 1776, bapt. March 10, 1776 Spon: Himself

Reformed Church of Hagerstown

Jos. Jacob of Joh. Jacob Hickl and mother, Eva, both married people, b. February 19, 1776, bapt. March 26, 1776 Spon: Himself
Anna Catharina of Peter Beck and mother, Anna Catharina, both married people, b. January 2, 1776, bapt. March 28, 1776 Spon: Fridrich Bechtel and his wife Anna Catha.
Joh. Jacob of Georg Schloser and mother, Barbera, both married people, b. January 15, 1776, bapt. March 31, 1776 Spon: Jacob Hauser and his wife
Anna Maria of Johannes Steinseifer and mother, Margretha, both married people, b. April 13, 1776, bapt. April 20, 1776 Spon: Himself
Catharina of Jacob Schup and mother, Margreta, both married people, b. May 3, 1770, bapt. May 8, 1770 Spon: Anna Barbera Schupin
Maria Elisabeta of Henrich Moll and mother, Maria Elisabetha, both married people b. ---, bapt. May 12, 1776 Spon: Himself
Maria Catha. of Henrich Moll and mother, Maria Elisabetha, both married people, b. ---, bapt. May 12, 1776 Spon: Himself
Wh. Henrich of Henrich Moll and mother, Maria Elisabetha, both married people, b. ---, bapt. May 12, 1776 Spon: Himself
Anna Catha. of Wilhelm Witzler and mother, Elisabetha, b. January 18, 1776, bapt. May 10, 1776 Spon: Henrich Schreyack and his housewife Catharina
Catha. of Jacob Schuck and mother, Ann Margreth, both married people, b. May 3, 1776, bapt. May 10, 1776 Spon: Anna Barbera
Johannes of Christofel Ber and mother, Maria Anna, both married people, b. April 16, 1776, bapt. May 10, 1776 Spon: Henrich Jost and his wife Anna Maria
Joh. Jacob of Johannes Schneid and mother, Anna Maria, both married people, b. April 6, 1776, bapt. May 26, 1776 Spon: Johannes Bricher
Anna Barbera of Peter Blecher and mother, Elisabeta, both married people, b. May 24, 1776, bapt. June 22, 1776 Spon: Jacob Hauser and his housewife Barbera
Johannes of Ernst Ditz and mother, Christina, both married people, b. May 31, 1776, bapt. June 23, 1776 Spon: Johannes Krumbach and his wife
Johann Daniel of Georg Troxel and mother, Elisabetha, both married people, b. February 11, 1776, bapt. June 25, 1776 Spon: Johan Daniel Bender
Wilhelm of Jacob Huber and mother, b. June 22, 1776, bapt. July 7, 1776 Spon: Wilhelm Heiser and his wife Anna
Christofel of Jacob Huber and mother, b. November 6, 1770, bapt. July 7, 1776 Spon: Himself
Joh. Adam of Jacob Huber and mother, b. April 6, 1773, bapt. July 7, 1776 Spon: Himself
Carl of Charl Hetrich and mother, Susana, both married people, b. July 2, 1776, bapt. -- 14 Spon: Frantz Waganer and his wife Charlotho
Johannes of Johannes Traxel and mother, Elisabetha, both married people, b. April 13, 1776, bapt. July 16, 1776 Spon: Catharina Traxelsin
Johanes of Wilhelm Conrath and mother, Catha. both married people, b. September 1, 1776, bapt. September 15, 1776 Spon: Eustragines Jung and his housewife Margretha
Johannes of Ehrhardt Bauman and mother, Hanna, both married people, b. May 16, 1775, bapt. September 22, 1776 Spon: Johannes Fuyel and his housewife Ohrfiela
Rahel of Jeremias Lenns and mother, Elisabetha, both married people, b. June 23, 1776, bapt. September 22, 1776 Spon: Anna Maria Kraemerin
Daniel of Gerhart Eydel and mother, Sozha, both married people, b. June 1, 1776, bapt. September 29, 1776 Spon: Baltaser Goll and his housewife Elisabetha

Reformed Church of Hagerstown

Elisabeth of Andreas Bothauer and mother, Anna Margret Catha., both married people, b. August 2, 1776, bapt. October 6, 1776 Spon: Ulrich Statler
Joh. Henrich of Henrich Locher and mother, Elisabeth, both married people, b. September 29, 1776, bapt. October 10, 1776 Spon: Joh. Michael Hostman and his housewife Doretea
Anna Cath. of Adam Aulenbach and mother, Anna Barbera, both married people, b. October 14, 1775, bapt. October 29, 1776 Spon: Johannes Mueller and his housewife Fromia
Joh. Jacob of Philip Kister and mother, Barbera, both married people, b. January 26, 1776, bapt. October 29, 1776 Spon: Jacob Hauser and his housewife Barbera
Georg Fridrich of Jacob Segeser and mother, Anna Maria, both married people, b. September 6, 1776, October 31, 1776 Spon: Georg Weber
Abraham of Martin Schneidt and mother, Anna Maria, both married people, b. June 10, 1773, bapt. November 4, 1776 Spon: Himself
Anna Maria of Martin Schneidt and mother, Anna Maria, both married people, b. June 16, 1775, bapt. November 4, 1776 Spon: Himself
Anna Maria of Frantz Wagner and mother, Charlota, both married people, b. October 29, 1776, bapt. November 18, 1776 Spon: Himself
Jacob of Bartun, b. February 13, 1777, bapt. March 2, 1777 Spon: Himself
Susana of Peter Seiler and mother, Barbera, both married people, b. December 26, 1776, bapt. March 23, 1777 Spon: Susana Seilerin
Janad of Samuel Back and mother, Janad, both married people, b. July 30, 1774, bapt. April 20, 1777 Spon: Himself
Jacob of Rutholph Bley and mother, Barbera, both married people, b. April 12, 1777, bapt. April 27, 1777 Spon: Ernst Ditz and his housewife Cath.
Margretha of Fridrich Hertha and mother, Cath., both married people, b. December 15, 1776, bapt. May 10, 1777 Spon: Margretha Hertlin
Susana of George Clampert and mother Eva Maria, both married people, b. December 18, 1776, bapt. May 10, 1777 Spon: Susana Hertlin
Johans of Rotholf Rust and mother, Margretha, both married people, b. May 19, 1776, bapt. May 18, 1777 Spon: Johannes Taniser and Susana
Joh. Jacob of Joh. Adam Herril and mother, Elisabeth, both married people, b. May 20, 1776, bapt. May 18, 1777 Spon: Jacob Wohlschlaeger and his housewife Cathrina
Anna Maria of Henrich Bawoth and mother, Margretha, both married people, b. June 6, 1777, bapt. --- 29, Spon: Ann Maria Bawothin
Johannes of Baltzer Tifenbach and mother, Anna Maria, both married people, b. November 3, 1776, bapt. August 17, 1777 Spon: Peter Blecher and his wife Elisabeth
Maria Barbera of Michael Fesler and mother, Maria Catha., both married people, b. September 4, 1777, bapt. --- 7, Spon: Christian Corn and his wife Maria Barbera
Juliana of Martin Wehr and mother, Elisabeth, both married people, b. ---, bapt. September 21, 1777 Spon: Johannes Krumbach and his wife Juliana
Johan Jacob of Johannes Kan and mother, Susana, both married people, b. July 7, 1777, bapt. September 21, 1777 Spon: Himself
Fridrich of Fridrich Kan and mother, Elisabeth, both married people, b. September 24, 1777, bapt. November 2, 1777 Spon: Christian Weber and Elisabeth Weberin
Jacob of Jacob Gerhart and mother, Christina, both married people, b. September 4, 1777, bapt. November 17, 1777 Spon: Niclos Opp and his housewife Hanna
Herrmanes of Herrmanes Wird and mother, Christina, b. December 24, 1777, bapt. April 19, 1778 Spon: Himself

Reformed Church of Hagerstown

Elisabeth of Christian Brannburger and mother, Magtalena, b. February 20, 1778, bapt. April 19, 1778 Spon: Peter Fluger and Elisabetha
Johannes of Henrich Schreyack and mother, Cath., both married people, b. December 25, 1777, bapt. May 18, 1778 Spon: Georg Woltz and his housewife Charlota
Anna Elisabeth b. October 15, 1778
Henrich of Henrich Wird and mother, Maria, both married people, b. May 16, 1777, bapt. June 10, 1777 Spon: Christofel Burgert and his wife Catharina
Johannes of Jacob Seiler and mother, Elisabetha, both married people, b. December 10, 1777, bapt. June 26, 1778 Spon: Georg Zinn and his housewife Anna Maria
Ester of Hermannes Wird and mother, Christina, both married people, b. May 24, 1778, bapt. August 9, 1778 Spon: Himself
Joh. Jacob of Jacob Weitman and mother, Margretha, both married people, b. July 12, 1778, bapt. August 9, 1778 Spon: Georg Schwangel and his housewife Cath.
Meril of mother Maria Kes, b. March 30, 1778, bapt. August 15, 1778 Spon: Samuel Berg and Doretea Wel
Elisabeth of Isaac Gnedig and mother, Elisabeth, both married people, b. May 11, 1778, bapt. September 6, 1778 Spon: Himself
Anna Maria of Johann Roberson and mother, Elisabeth, both married people, b. July 22, 1778, bapt. September 6, 1778 Spon: Himself
Eva Magtalena of Christian Mandel and mother, Maria Barbera, both married people, b. July 30, 1778, bapt. September 14, 1778 Spon: Abraham Bauer and his wife Eva
Cath. of Jacob Weitner and mother, Elisabeth, both married people, b. August 25, 1778, bapt. September 18, 1778 Spon: Baltzer Coll and his housewife Elisabetha
Susana of Henrich Bawat and mother, Margretha, both married people, b. October 10, 1778, bapt. November 15, 1778 Spon: Susan Brackunirem
Joseph of Joseph Georg Schorsch, b. July 7, 1778, bapt. November 28, 1778 Spon: Johanes Leidi
--- of Niclos App and mother, Hanna, both married people, b. October 31, 1778, bapt. December 27, 1778 Spon: Peter Woltz and his housewife Maria
Joh. Georg of Georg Greft and mother, Elisabeth, both married people, b. December 22, 1778, bapt. January 3, 1779 Spon: Adam Greft and his housewife Christina
Jacob of Wilhelm Conrath and mother, Cath., both married people, b. January 2, 1779, bapt. January 5, 1779 Spon: Eusaigus Jung and his housewife Margretha
Joh. Loenharth of Johannes Schoefter and mother, Barbera, both married people, b. December 23, 1778, bapt. January 19, 1779 Spon: Himself
Jacob of Frantz Greilich and mother, Anna Cathrina, both married people, b. November 20, 1778, bapt. January 24, 1779 Spon: Himself
Catha. of Simon Hausinhalter and mother, Elisabetha, both married people, b. January 7, 1779, bapt. February 7, 1779 Spon: Himself
Johannes of Johannes Schneid and mother, Anna Maria, both married people, b. January 15, 1779, bapt. February 21, 1779 Spon: Johannes Krumbach
Cath. of Ernst Ditz and mother, Catha., both married people, b. January 19, 1779, bapt. February 21, 1779 Spon: Jacob Wohlschteger and his housewife Cath.
Jacob of Jacob Katz and mother, Catharina, both married people, b. January 24, 1779, bapt. March 20, 1779

Reformed Church of Hagerstown

Jacob of Jacob Hergenroth and mother, Barbera, both married people, b. December 31, 1778, bapt. March 21, 1779 Spon: Fridrich Rohre and his wife Cath.
Joh. Georg of Johannes Loss and mother, Elisabeth, both married people, b. March 22, 1779, bapt. April 5, 1779 Spon: Henrich Hofman
Henrich of Jacob Bernt and mother, Elisabeth, both married people, b. February 26, 1779, bapt. April 15, 1779 Spon: Mr. Henrich Schnebly and his wife Elisaby
Emanuel of Jacob Stadler and mother, Anna, both married people, b. October 20, 1776, bapt. April 21, 1779 Spon: Henrich Seytz and his wife
Henrich of Jacob Stadler and mother, Anna, both married people, b. December 27, 1778, bapt. April 21, 1779 Spon: Henrich Seytz and his housewife Elisabeth
Ester of Joseph Gollenta and mother, Elisabeth, both married people, b. January 23, 1779, bapt. April 21, 1779 Spon: Himself
Henrich of Fridrich Kau and mother, Elisabeth, both married people, b. March 16, 1779, bapt. May 13, 1779 Spon: Elias Triter and his housewife Margrethe
Maria Barbera of Johannes Hauer and mother, Barbera, both married people, b. April 5, 1779, bapt. May 31, 1779 Spon: Michel Herger and his wife Doretea
Maria Cath. of Michel Herger and mother, Doretea, both married people, b. March 28, 1779, bapt. May 31, 1779 Spon: Johannes Hauer and his wife Barbera
Peter of Peter Seiler and mother, Barbera, both married people, b. August 15, 1779, bapt. November 14, 1779 Spon: Himself
Jacob of Fridrich Hertli and mother, Margretha, both married people, b. October 11, 1779, bapt. November 14, 1779 Spon: Michel Hertli and his wife Susana
Johannes of Joseph Schorsch and mother, N., both married people, b. August 1, 1779, bapt. November 21, 1779 Spon: Johanes Leidi and his wife Elisabeth
Anna Catha. of Rutholph Bley and mother, Barbera, both married people, b. November 25, 1779, bapt. December 12, 1779 Spon: Michael Teibel and his wife Margretha
Anna Catha. of Jacob Niclos and mother, Eva, both married people, b. December 21, 1779, bapt. January 19, 1780 Spon: Anna Maria Schertisin
Georg of Jost Weigant and mother, Anna Maria, both married people, b. January 11, 1780, bapt. February 20, 1780 Spon: Georg Schahl and his wife Barbera
Jacob of Johanes Oster and mother, Elisabetha, both married people, b. January 29, 1780, bapt. March 6, 1780 Spon: Jacob Greber and his housewife Magtalena
Andereas of Christian Mandel and mother, Barbera, both married people, b. February 19, 1780, bapt. March 30, 1780 Spon: Henrich Aeckret
Johannes of Martin Wehr and mother, Elisabeta, both married people, b. December 6, 1779, bapt. March 6, 1780 Spon: Johannes Schwind and his housewife Anna Maria
Catha. of Mattheis Hausshalter and mother, Eva, both married people, b. September 23, 1779, bapt. April 9, 1780 Spon: Adam Hausshalter and his wife Catharina
Johanes of Jacob Knot and mother, Margretha, both married people, b. September 12, 1779, bapt. April 15, 1780 Spon: Johannes Schefer and his wife Barbera
Maria Magtalen of Henrich Schada and mother, H., both married people, b. March 2, 1780, bapt. April 15, 1780 Spon: Matheis Knot and his wife Maria Magtalena
Anna Cath. of Daniel Heh and mother, Eva Margretha, both married people, b. March 25, 1780, bapt. June 3, 1780 Spon: Ann Cath. Steckein

Reformed Church of Hagerstown

Elisabetha of Henrich Bowat and mother, Margretha, both married people, b. April 13, 1780, bapt. June 25, 1780 Spon: Martin Jetonauer and his wife Elisabetha
Jacob of Johannes Zeit and mother, Magtalena, both married people, b. November 25, 1779, bapt. August 18, 1780 Spon: Himself
Elisabeth of Peter Windroth and mother, Anna Maria, both married people, b. December 11, 1779, bapt. August 20, 1780 Spon: Lorentz Fratzman and his housewife Elisabeth
Jacob of Georg Lampert and mother, Eva, both married people, b. July 24, 1780, bapt. September 26, 1780 Spon: Himself
Johanes of Johannes Rabesen and mother, Elisabeth, both married people, b. August 31, 1780, bapt. October 15, 1780 Spon: Himself
Adam of Ernst Ditz and mother, Catha., both married people, b. November 22, 1780, bapt. December 10, 1780 Spon: Jos. Ditz
Wilhelm of Conrad Ferri and mother, Barbera, both married people, b. October 14, 1780, bapt. November 2, 1780 Spon: Baltzer Coll and his wife Catherina
Johannes of Michael Hertly and mother, Susana, both married people, b. February 28, 1780, bapt. November 22, 1780 Spon: Martin Hertly and his housewife Susana
Jacob of Martin Hertly and mother, Susana, both married people, b. October 18, 1780, bapt. December 15, 1780 Spon: Michael Hertly and his wife Susana
Susana of Johannes Schwertzel and mother, Regina, both married people, b. September 10, 1780, bapt. December 16, 1780 Spon: Adam Wolst and his wife Susana
David of Jacob Katz and mother, Catharina, both married people, b. December 10, 1780, bapt. December 24, 1780 Spon: Himself
Jacob of Jacob Bernart and mother, Elisabetha, both married people, b. October 27, 1780, bapt. January 1, 1781 Spon: Jacob Weimer and his wife Salome
Cath. of Isau Gnedig and mother, Elisabeth, both married people, b. September 9, 1780, bapt. January 7, 1781 Spon: Christian Schak and his wife Margreth
Magtalena of Johanes Gisi and mother, Maria, both married people, b. June 3, 1780, bapt. January 24, 1781 Spon: Christian Schockei and his wife Margretha
Catha. of Fridrich Beier and mother, Anna, both married people, b. February 9, 1781, bapt. February 28, 1781 Spon: Himself
Johannes of Nicolaus Opp and mother, Anna Eva, both married people, b. May 5, 1780, bapt. February 4, 1781 Spon: George Woltz and his wife Carlota
Marianna of Henrich Schneid and mother, Susana, both married people, b. December --, 1780, bapt. April 1, 1781 Spon: Adam Schneit and his wife Marianna
Anna Elisabetha and Anna Maria of Jacob Wohlschleger and mother, Cath., both married people b. February 21, 1781, bapt. March 3, 1781 Spon: Wilhelm Heiser and his wife, Henrich Todweiler and his wife
Margretha of Martin Jetenauer, both married people, b. May 11, 1781, bapt. June 16, 1781 Spon: Henrich Bawat and Margrethe
Susana of Fridrich Herttel and mother, Gretha, both married people, b. May 5, 1781, bapt. June 24, 1781 Spon: Susana ---
Georg of Martin Crebes and mother, Magthalena, both married people, b. June 29, 1781, bapt. July 22, 1781 Spon: Jost Weigand and his housewife Maria
Susana of Johannes Kann and mother, Susana, both married people, b. June 17, 1781, bapt. July 22, 1781 Spon: Himself
David of Fridrich Eschbach and mother, Sophia, both married people, b. March 14, 1772, bapt. August 4, 1781 Spon: Himself

Reformed Church of Hagerstown

Andereas of Fridrich Eschbach and mother, Sophia, both married people, b. May 20, 1775, bapt. August 4, 1781 Spon: Himself

Catha. of Fridrich Eschbach and mother, Sophia, both married people, b. July 14, 1778, bapt. August 4, 1781 Spon: Himself

Fridrich of Fridrich Eschbach and mother, Sophia, both married people, b. --- 1781, bapt. August 4, 1781 Spon: Himself

--- of Peter Scholly and mother, Elisabeth, both married people, b. October 22, 1781, bapt. --- 23, Spon: Baltzer Golt

Rahel Fridriche was baptized on November 8, 1781 and was married to Michael Koch on November 13, 1781

Joh. Georg of Henrich Benter and mother, Elisabetha, both married people, b. September 23, 1781, bapt. November 8, 1781 Spon: Baltasar Haut and his housewife Anna Maria

David of Frantz Greilich and mother, Anna, both married people, b. --- 1781, bapt. December 23, 1781 Spon: Himself

Daniel of William Conrath and mother, Catharina, both married people, b. December 24, 1781, bapt. January 1, 1782 Spon: Eustaguis Jung and his wife

Magdalena of N. Bordun and mother, N., b. December 7, 1781, bapt. February 7, 1782 Spon: Himself

George of Simon Hausshalter and mother, Elisabetha, both married people, b. December 19, 1781, bapt. February 10, 1782 Spon: Himself

Elisabetha of Georg Schorsch and mother, N., both married people, b. December 11, 1781, bapt. February 14, 1782 Spon: Elisabeth Leidi

Henrich of Henrich Bawat and mother, Margreth, both married people, b. February 4, 1782, bapt. February 24, 1782 Spon: Henrich Weickel and his wife Susana

Gertraut Catha. of Lorentz Protzman and mother, Elisabeth, both married people, b. February 12, 1782, bapt. February 24, 1782 Spon: Peter Heflich and his wife N.

David of Georg Clambert and mother, Eva, both married people, b. February 26, 1782, bapt. June 16, 1782 Spon: Himself

Maria Catha. of Herrman Greilich and mother, Catha., both married people, b. May 11, 1782, bapt. June 29, 1782 Spon: Himself

Michael of Michael Hertli and mother, Susana, both married people, b. June 4, 1782, bapt. August 6, 1782 Spon: Himself

Johannes of Johannes Beier and mother, N., both married people, b. August 20, 1780, bapt. August 20, 1782 Spon: Johannes Steck and his wife N.

Elisabeth of Peter Simon and mother, Catha., both married people, b. May 13, 1782, bapt. September 11, 1782 Spon: Himself

Elisabetha of Jacob Niklos and mother, Eva, both married people, b. September 8, 1782, bapt. October 6, 1782 Spon: Himself

Eva of Jost Klein and mother, Anna Maria, both married people, b. March 12, 1781, bapt. October 17, 1782 Spon: Eva Schitzin

Joh. Jacob of Henrich Schneid and mother, Maria Magtalena, both married people, b. September 11, 1782, bapt. --19, Spon: Peter Tirth and his housewife Anna Catha.

Philipbina of Jacob Katz and mother, Catharina, both married people, b. October 20, 1782, bapt. January 1, 1783 Spon: Himself

Eva Catha. of Jost Engelman and mother, Catha., both married people, b. January 20, 1783, bapt. March 2, 1783 Spon: Matheis Nit and his wife Eva Cath.

Daniel of Baltzer Hess and mother, Eva, both married people, b. February 2, 1783, bapt. April 4, 1783 Spon: Peter Flieger and his wife

Barbera of Peter Seyler and mother, Barbera, both married people, b. March 11, 1783, bapt. April 18, 1783 Spon: Theobalt Schefer and his wife Rosina

Reformed Church of Hagerstown

Joh. Jacob of Jacob Kesler and mother Cath., both married people, b. March 15, 1783, bapt. April 18, 1783 Spon: Jacob Hauser and his wife Anna Maria
Johannes of George Crebach and mother, Margretha, both married people, b. April 15, 1783, bapt. May 19, 1783 Spon: Johannes Grembach and his wife Juliana
Jacob of Abraham Wotring and mother, Margretha, both married people, b. May 18, 1783, bapt. June 2, 1783 Spon: Jacob Diter and his housewife Magdalina
Anna of Henrich Schneider and mother, Susana, both married people, b. March 20, 1783, bapt. June 15, 1783 Spon: Frantz Greilich and his wife Anna
Henrich of Henrich Bender and mother, Elisabeth, both married people, b. April 26, 1783, bapt. June 15, 1783 Spon: Himself
Johannes of Conrath Hoster and mother, Margreth, both married people, b. June 2, 1783, bapt. July 14, 1783 Spon: Peter Wohlhoren and his wife Anna Cathrina
Johannes of Jonathan Dotweiler and mother, Maria Barbera, both married people, b. June 11, 1783, bapt. July 14, 1783 Spon: Himself
Susana of Joseph Schorsch and mother, N., both married people, b. March 17, 1783, bapt. August 2, 1783 Spon: Henrich Kek and his wife
Susana of Fridrich Hertle and mother, N., both married people, b. December 27, 1782, bapt. August 10, 1783 Spon: Himself
Cath. of Fridrich Bringman and mother, Anna Maria, both married people, b. November 1, 1782, bapt. August 10, 1783 Spon: Himself
Johan Georg of Martin Hertle and mother, Susana, both married people, b. May 17, 1783, bapt. August 12, 1783 Spon: Himself
Johannes of Ludwig Schmal and mother, Cath., both married people, b. January 21, 1783, bapt. August 15, 1783 Spon: Himself
Magtalena of Rutholph Bly and mother, Barbera, both married people, b. October 5, 1783, bapt. October 26, 1783 Spon: Himself
Becky of Lorentz Protzman and mother, Elizabeth, both married people, b. October 12, 1783, bapt. November 4, 1783 Spon: G. Bringman and Becky Multe
Susana of Christian Seiler and mother, Margreth, both married people, b. September 6, 1783, bapt. January 20, 1784 Spon: Peter Seiler and his housewife
Elisabeth of Ernst Ditz and mother, Cath., both married people, b. February 29, 1784, bapt. March 28, 1784 Spon: Christofel Beier and his housewife
Jacob of Peter Weberlingling and mother, Maria, both married people, b. January 25, 1784, bapt. March 28, 1784 Spon: Johannes Kausler and his wife
Johannes of Ludwig Borner and mother, Anna Gerdraut, both married people, b. January 12, 1784, bapt. April 9, 1784 Spon: Himself
David of Martin Eutenauer and mother, Elisabeth, both married people, b. December 18, 1783, bapt. April 11, 1784 Spon: David Brauner
Cath. of Henrich Bawat and mother, Margretha, both married people, b. January 30, 1784, bapt. April 18, 1784 Spon: Henrich Weikel and his wife Susana
Elisabeth of Ernst Ditz and mother, Cath., both married people, b. February 29, 1784, bapt. April 1, 1784 Spon: Christofel Beier and his wife Anna
Maria of Daniel Fenner and mother, Elisabetha, both married people, b. December 21, 1783, bapt. April 25, 1784 Spon: Caspar Schneid and his wife Elisabet
Johannes of Georg Carle and mother, Elisabet, b. October 28, 1783, bapt. May 16, 1784 Spon: Henrich Schned and his wife N.
William of William McDasch and mother, Sarah, b. December 8, 1783, bapt. May 23, 1784 Spon: Georg Reinhart and his wife Barbera

Reformed Church of Hagerstown

William of William McDasch and mother, Sarah, b. August 21, 1783, bapt. May
   23, 1784 Spon: Georg Reinhart and his wife Barbera
Catha. of Henrich Zimerman and mother, Barbera, both married people, b. ----
   1784, bapt. May 30, 1784 Spon: Jost Zimerman and his housewife Charlotha
Susan of Sebastian Herdly and mother Barbera, both married people, b. April
   14, 1784, bapt. August 7, 1784 Spon: Himself
Anna Maria of Jonathan Dotweiler and mother, Barbera, both married people,
   b. August 30, 1784, bapt. September 12, 1784 Spon: Himself
Johan Michael of Michel Schnit and mother, Susana, both married people,
   b. September 23, 1784, bapt. December 5, 1784 Spon: Conrath Hosterand
   his wife
Magtalena of Philip Wipel and mother, Engel, b. February 29, 1784, bapt.
   December 26, 1784 Spon: Himself
Anna Maria of Georg Kilmer and mother, Eva, both married people,
   b. September 1, 1784, bapt. December 26, 1784 Spon: Anna Maria Bucherin
Rebecka of Jacob Katz and mother, Cath. Elis., both married people,
   b. September 2, 1784, bapt. December 26, 1784 Spon: Himself
Joh. Henrich of Philip Reblogel and mother, Maria, both married people,
   b. February --, 1784, bapt. December 26, 1784 Spon: Himself
Jacob of Martin Crebes and mother, Magtalena, both married people, b. August
   23, 1784, bapt. October 17, 1784 Spon: Himself
Anna Elisabeth of Thomas Rith and mother, Fromia, both married people,
   b. July 30, 1784, bapt. January 23, 1785 Spon: Jost Zimerman and Carline
Anna Maria of Thomas Rith and mother, Fromia, both married people,
   b. November 25, 1783, bapt. January 23, 1785 Spon: Peter Werking and his
   wife Anna Elisabeth
Elisabeth of Wilhelm Conrath and mother, Cath. both married people, b. March
   1, 1785, bapt. March 6, 1785 Spon: Anna Margretha Yungling
Elisabeth of Jost Engleman and mother, Cath., both married people,
   b. September 26, 1784, bapt. March 27, 1785 Spon: Moritz Bauer and his
   wife Cath.
Elisabeth of Herrman Dick and mother, Anna Maria, both married people,
   b. January 23, 1785, bapt. May 7, 1785 Spon: Himself
N. of Fridrich Hertly and mother, N., both married people, b. October 7,
   1784, bapt. May 1, 1785 Spon: Himself
Joh. Fridrich of Johannes Dibor and mother, Elisabeth, both married people,
   b. September 20, 1784, bapt. May 14, 1785 Spon: Joh. Fridrich Seidner
   and his wife Margretha
Henrich of Adam Hirschberger and mother, Catha., both married people,
   b. March 17, bapt. May 15, 1785 Spon: Henrich Hirschberger and Barbera
   Hirschberger
Anna of Johannes Mueller and mother, Anna, both married people, b. April 11,
   1785, bapt. June 14, 1785 Spon: Himself
Johannes of Johannes Schein and mother, Magtalena, both married people, b.
   December 21, 1784, bapt. June 20, 1785 Spon: Christian Luntz and his
   wife Maria Elisabeth
Johanes of Michael Hertly and mother, N., both married people, b. April 4,
   1785, bapt. July 12, 1785 Spon: Himself
Barbera of Martin Crasis and mother, Barbera, both married people, b. June
   14, 1783, bapt. September 4, 1785 Spon: Georg Balt and his Barbera
Peter of Martin Crasis and mother, Barbera, both married people, b. July 15,
   1785, bapt. September 4, 1785 Spon: Peter Geiger and his wife Barbera
Georg of Johan Peter Herr and mother, Susana, b. August 12, 1784, bapt.
   September 15, 1784 Spon: Joh. George Weis and his wife

Reformed Church of Hagerstown

Johan Fridrich of Fridrich Seitner and mother, Margretha, both married
   people, b. November 8, 1784, bapt. September 10, 1785 Spon: Adam
   Auerbach and his wife Maria Barbera
---- of Nicolaus Opp and mother, Anna Eva, both married people, b. ----,
   bapt. September 4, 1785 Spon: Himself
Elisabeth of Georg Lambert and mother, Eva, both married people, b. August
   24, 1785, bapt. September 28, 1785 Spon: Himself
Elisabetha of Jonatha Hager and mother, Maria Magtalena, both married
   people, b. August 1, 1785, bapt. October 1, 1785 Spon: Christofel
   Ohrendorf and his wife Elisabeth
Johan Georg of Peter Brecht and mother, Barbra, both married people,
   b. December 2, 1784, bapt. October 1, 1785 Spon: Joseph Deboi and his
   wife Christina
Jacob of Johannes Hann and mother, Catharina, both married people, b.
   September 24, 1784, bapt. October 9, 1785 Spon: Himself
Catharina of Abraham Mueller and mother, Elisabeth, both married people,
   b. August 15, 1785, bapt. November 5, 1785 Spon: Simon Hastner and his
   wife Catharina
Sara of Paul Werner and mother, Maria, both married people, b. August 30,
   1785, bapt. November 13, 1785 Spon: David Reutenauer and his wife Sara
David of Jacob Kesler and mother, Cath., both married people, b. July 29,
   1785, bapt. November 13, 1785 Spon: Himself
Jacob of Peter Kesler and mother, Cath., both married people, b. July 10,
   1785, bapt. November 13, 1785 Spon: Jacob Schitz ans his wife Cath.
Schmal-George of Henrich Deringer and mother, Rebecca, both married people,
   b. November 21, 1785, bapt. December 26, 1785 Spon: Himself
Wilhelm of Parents: see number 33, b. January 1, 1786, bapt. January 8,
   1786 Spon: Christian Schop
David of Jonathan Dotweiler and mother, Doretea, both married people, b.
   December 3, 1785, bapt. January 8, 1786 Spon: David Reutemann and his
   wife Sara
Henrich of Johannes Ytneier and mother, Doretea, both married people,
   b. November 11, 1785, bapt. January 18, 1786 Spon: Himself
James of James Grams and mother, Anna, both married people, b. December 20,
   1785, bapt. January 22, 1786 Spon: Himself
Elisabeth of Daniel Becher and mother, Elisabeth, both married people,
   b. February 1, 1785, bapt. February 20, 1785 Spon: Rosina Rebei
Samuel of Joh. Peter Herr and mother, Susana, b. February 16, 1786, bapt.
   March 5, 1786 Spon: Himself
Daniel of Henrich Schnebly, the young one, mother, Catha., both married
   people, b. February 13, 1786, bapt. April 2, 1786 Spon: Henrich
   Schnebly, the old one
Wilhelm of Johannes Woller and mother, N., both married people, b. March 23,
   1786, bapt. April 3, 1786 Spon: Wilhelm Conrath and his wife Catharina
Johannes of Henrich Bawath and mother, Margretha, both married people,
   b. April 7, 1786, bapt. April 17, 1786 Spon: Henrich Weikel and his
   housewife Susanna
Jacob of Georg Weiss and mother, Catha., both married people, b. April 21,
   1786, bapt. June 3, 1786 Spon: Jacob Weimer and his wife Salome
Anna Margretha of Jost Zimerman and mother, Margretha, both married people,
   b. April 13, 1786, bapt. June 4, 1786 Spon: Michael Deibelhies and his
   housewife N.
Wilhelm of Wilhelm Brux and mother, Maria, both married people, b. May 10,
   bapt. -- 22, Spon: Himself

Reformed Church of Hagerstown

Margretha of Henrich Schneider and mother, Susana, both married people, b. January 9, 1786, bapt. June 25, 1786 Spon: Margretha Jungin
Henrich of Christophel Beier and mother, Anna, both married people, b. July 18, 1786, bapt. July 21, 1786 Spon: Ernst Ditz and his wife
Abraham of Jacob Weitman and mother, Margretha Elis., both married people, b. July 7, 1786, bapt. August 21, 1786 Spon: Michael Hofteli
Johannes of Conrath Caffereth and mother, Magtalena, both married people, b. July 22, 1786, bapt. August 27, 1786 Spon: Johannes Frener
Sara of Adam Leidy and mother, Rosina, both married people, b. -- 20, 1785, bapt. September 24, 1786 Spon: Himself
Barbera of Daniel Buche and mother, Elisabeth, both married people, b. October 17, 1786, bapt. November 5, 1786 Spon: Susana Batzin
Nathanael of Lorentz Protzman and mother, Elisabeth, both married people, b. June 24, 1786, bapt. December 25, 1786 Spon: Nathanael Protzman
Elisabeth of Martin Krebes and mother, Magtalena, both married people, b. December 31, 1786, bapt. February 18, 1787 Spon: Nicolaus Hagi and his wife Elisabeth
Margretha of Georg Krebes and mother, Margretha, both married people, b. February 4, 1787, bapt. March 18, 1787 Spon: Georg Schall and his housewife Margretha
Elisabetha of Frantz Reinhart and mother, Margretha, both married people, b. February 2, 1787, bapt. March 18, 1787 Spon: Elisabetha Osterin
Anna of Peter Seiler and mother, Barbera, both married people, b. January 8, 1787, bapt. February 18, 1787 Spon: Georg Neu and his housewife Magtalena
Samuel of Emanuel Trexler and mother Catha., both married people, b. June 19, 1786, bapt. April 31, 1787 Spon: Himself
Ester of William Piet and mother, Dorethea, both married people, b. September 4, 1786, bapt. April 31, 1787 Spon: Himself
Hanna of John Wicher and mother, Hanna, both married people, September 27, 1786, bapt. April 15, 1787 Spon: Himself
Johan Georg of Johannes Eitenauer and mother, Dorethea, both married, b. March 1, 1787, bapt. April 25, 1787 Spon: Georg Schaefer
Anna of Jacob Katz and mother, Elisabetha, b. February 11, 1787, bapt. April 29, 1787 Spon: Himself
Susana of Jost Engelman and mother, Cath., both married people, b. March 28, 1787, bapt. May 19, 1787 Spon: Margreth Elisabeth Weitmaenin
--- of Fridrich Hertly and mother, Margretha, both married people, b. November 5, 1786, bapt. May 27, 1787 Spon: Wilhelm Schenenfeltes' Daughter
Georg of Jacob Nikel and mother, Eva, both married people, b. May 16, 1787, bapt. May 25, 1787 Spon: Himself
Anna Margretha of Wilhelm Conrath and mother, Catha., both married people, b. July 13, 1787, bapt. July 19, 1787 Spon: Johannes Dewies and his wife Anna Margretha
Johannes of Michael Kelchner and mother, Anna Margretha, both married people, b. June 11, 1787, bapt. July 22, 1787 Spon: Henrich Riblet
Maria of Jeams Bery and mother, Elisabeth, both married people, b. May 30, 1787, bapt. July 22, 1787 Spon: Anna Maria Schopin
Elisabetha of Martin Eschbach and mother, Eva Elisa., both married people, b. June 2, 1787, bapt. August 5, 1787 Spon: Johannes Platte and his housewife Anna Elisabetha
Anna Christina of Michel Conrath and mother, Anna Margreta, both married people, b. April 21, 1787, bapt. August 5, 1787 Spon: Anna Christina
Joh. Jacob of Michael Nikel and mother, Catharina, both married people, b. May 16, 1787, bapt. August 12, 1787 Spon: Jacob Nikel and his wife Eva

Reformed Church of Hagerstown

Hanna of Ernst Ditz and mother, Cath., both married people, b. June 27, 1787, bapt. September 2, 1787 Spon: Henrich Wolter and his wife Anna Christina

Vallentien of Peter Scholley and mother, Elisabeth, both married people, b. August 28, 1787, bapt. September 9, 1787 Spon: Fridrich Roth and his wife Anna Maria

Georg of Jacob Kesler and mother, Cath., both married people, b. May 19, 1787, bapt. September 17, 1787 Spon: Georg Schloser and his wife Barbera

Johannes of Johannes Frener and mother, Susana, both married people, b. August 20, 1787, bapt. October 2, 1787 Spon: Abraham Bauer and his housewife

Johannes of Christian Weinbrenner and mother, Anna Maria, both married people, bapt. October 9, 1787 Spon: Christian Weinbrenner and his wife Christina

Peter of Jacob Flikinger and mother, Susana, both married people, b. October 12, 1787, bapt. October 23, 1787 Spon: Peter Wotring

Elisabeth of Sebastian Hertli and mother, Catharina, both married people, b. February 12, 1787, bapt. November 11, 1787 Spon: Himself

Wilhelm of Conrad Ferri and mother, Barbera, both married people, b. October 14, 1787, bapt. November 2, 1787 Spon: Baltzer Goll and his housewife Catharina

Elisabeth of Frantz Eltzroth and mother, Cath., both married people, b. November 24, 1787, bapt. January 1, 1788 Spon: Himself

Jacob of Henrich Graf and mother, Maria, both married people, b. March 2, 1787, bapt. January 14, 1788 Spon: Peter Krieger and his wife Barbera

Jonathan of Jacob Becker and mother, Anna, both married people, b. December 25, 1787, bapt. January 20, 1788 Spon: Jonathan Heger and his housewife Anna

Susana of Johannes Mueller and mother, Anna Maria, both married people, b. January 2, 1788, bapt. February 9, 1788 Spon: Himself

Johan Henrich of Nicolaus Huiet and mother, N., both married people, b. February 6, 1788, bapt. March 22, 1788 Spon: Gerhart Eitel and his wife

Elisabetha of Jacob Baum and mother, Catha., both married people, b. June 11, 1787, bapt. March 22, 1788 Spon: Himself

Jonathan of Johannes Woller and mother, N., both married people, b. March 3, 1788, bapt. April 1, 1788 Spon: Himself

Abraham of Abraham Mueller and mother, Elisabeth, both married people, b. January 22, 1787, bapt. March 15, 1788 Spon: Himself

Elisabeth of Henrich Bawath and mother, Margretha, both married people, b. November 7, 1787, bapt. April 1, 1788 Spon: Barbera Brockgunierin

Johannes of Martin Bringman and mother, Margretha, both married people, b. February 9, 1788, bapt. April 27, 1788 Spon: Himself

Cath. of Henrich Becker and mother, Margretha, both married people, b. March 26, 1788, bapt. April 11, 1788 Spon: Martinus Ott and his wife Cath.

Anna Maria of Joh. Peter Herr and mother, Susana, both married people, b. May 13, 1788, bapt. May 25, 1788 Spon: Anna Maria Weisin

Susana of Georg Carl and mother, Elisabeth, both married people, b. March 16, 1788, bapt. July 6, 1788 Spon: Henrich Schneid and his wife Susana

Samuel of David Bramier and mother, Cath., both married people, b. May 30, 1788, bapt. August 17, 1788 Spon: Henrich Bawat and his wife Margretha

Jacob of David Wolf and mother, Nentzi, both married people, b. February 20, 1788, bapt. August 17, 1788 Spon: Peter Web and his wife Elisabeth

Anna Maria of Daniel Renol and mother, Anna Maria, both married people, b. July 11, 1788, bapt. August 21, 1788 Spon: Peter Renol and his housewife

Reformed Church of Hagerstown

Margretha of Daniel Renol and mother, Anna Maria, both married people, b. July 11, 1788, bapt. August 21, 1788   Spon: Ludwig Huiet and his housewife Margretha

Georg of Jost Zimerman and mother, Cath. Marg., both married people, b. July 12, 1788, bapt. August 31, 1788   Spon: Georg Bald and his wife Maria Barbera

Cath. of Peter Wotring and mother, Margretha, both married people, b. October 1, 1788, bapt. November 9, 1788   Spon: Abraham Wothring and his wife Cath.

Maria Magtalena of Conrad Cafferoth and mother, Magtalena, both married people, b. October 3, 1788, bapt. November 9, 1788   Spon: Anna Maria Baurin

Anna Elisabeth of Georg Schloser and mother, Barbera, both married people, b. July 24, 1788, bapt. -- 15, Spon: Jacob Kesler and his wife Catharina

Elisabeth of Frantz Greilich and mother, Anna, both married people, b. Septemter 24, 1788, bapt. November 16, 1788   Spon: Himself

Margreth of Johannes Schenefelt and mother, N., both married people, b. ---- 1788, bapt. November 16, 1788   Spon: Jacob Lekron ahd his wife N.

Elisabeth of Jacob Lekron and mother, N., both married people, b. --- 1788, bapt. November 16, 1788   Spon: Johannes Schenfelt and his wife N.

William of Rudolf Rust and mother, Margreth, both married people, b. June 3, 1788, bapt. December 7, 1788   Spon: Conrad Tempel and his wife Margretha

Maria of Jahn McGurt and mother, Hanna, both married people, b. August 21, 1788, bapt. December 13, 1788   Spon: Himself

Margretha of Peter Seiller and mother, Barbra, both married people, b. September 28, 1788, bapt. January 1, 1789   Spon: Johannes Herti and his housewife Elisabetha

Anna Margretha of Johannes Ochs and mother, Anna Maria, both married people, b. January 7, 1789, bapt. February 9, 1789   Spon: Christian Schopfer and his housewife Margretha

Johannes of Henrich Wingert and mother, Cath., both married people, b. January 17, 1789, bapt. January 28, 1789   Spon: Johannes Weiss and his wife Christina

Johan of Peter Reser and mother, Cath., both married people, b. October 8, 1788, bapt. February 22, 1789   Spon: Michael Kapp and his wife Catha.

Johannes of Johannes Grumbach and mother, Anna, both married people, b. January 29, 1789, bapt. March 4, 1789   Spon: Johannes Grumbach and his wife

--- of Johannes Rohrer and mother, N., both married people, b. ----, bapt. ----   Spon: ----

Elisabeth of Conrad Grumbach and mother, Catharina, both married people, b. March 1, 1789, bapt. March 15, 1789   Spon: Johannes Grumbach, the young one, and his, Anna

Johannes of Johannes Schneid and mother, Cath., both married people, b. February 15, 1789, bapt. April 13, 1789   Spon: John Beltz

Magtalena of Georg Krebes and mother, Margretha, both married people, b. March 29, 1789, bapt. April 28, 1789   Spon: Martin Krebes and his housewife Magtalena

Susana of Jacob Nickel and mother, Eva, both married people, b. April 6, 1789, bapt. May 3, 1789   Spon: Himself

Jacob of Christophel Heier and mother, Anna, both married people, b. March 13, 1789, bapt. May 30, 1789   Spon: Johannes Beier and his wife Estor

Barbera of Fridrich Hertel and mother, Margretha, both married people, b. April 10, 1789, bapt. June 28, 1789   Spon: ----

Anna Catha. of Jacob Bieckel and mother, Catharina, both married people, b. June 22, 1789, bapt. July 12, 1789   Spon: Johannes Annawoll and his wife Susana

Reformed Church of Hagerstown

Anna Maria of Georg Mandel and mother, Elisabeth, both married people, b. March 16, 1789, bapt. July 12, 1789 Spon: Henrich Huber and his housewife Anna Maria
Daniel of Henrich Schnel and mother, Christine, both married people, b. March 22, 1788, bapt. July 12, 1789 Spon: Himself
Jacob of Jacob Weigand and mother, Elisabeth, both married people, b. March 21, 1789, bapt. July 24, 1789 Spon: Himself
Georg of Peter Seiler and mother, Anna Maria, b. May 27, 1789, bapt. July 26, 1789 Spon: Georg Feg and his wife Margretha
Elisabeth of Henrich Becker and mother, Margretha, both married people, b. June 19, 1789, bapt. August 9, 1789 Spon: Simon Kisaker and his wife Elisabetha
Elisabeth Barbera of Johannes Mueller and mother, Elisabetha, both married people, b. July 6, 1789, bapt. September 6, 1789 Spon: Jacob Burgert and his wife Catharina
Elisabeth of Fridrich Eschbach and mother, Sofia, both married people, b. August 3, 1789, bapt. October 18, 1789 Spon: Henrich Bawath and his wife Margretha
Judith of Wilhelm Conrad and mother, Cath., both married people, b. October 11, 1789, bapt. October 25, 1789 Spon: Margretha Junin
Georg of Carl Olwein and mother, Doretea, both married people, b. September 5, 1789, bapt. November 8, 1789 Spon: Georg Krebes and his wife
Daniel and Jacob Katz and mother, Catharina, both married people, b. April 31, 1789, bapt. December 27, 1789 Spon: Himself
Peterus of Nicolaus Huiet and mother, Elisabeth, both married people, b. November 15, 1789, bapt. January 2, 1790 Spon: Himself
Susana of Martin Bringman and mother, Margretha, both married people, b. December 12, 1789, bapt. January 30, 1790 Spon: Susana Fakler
---- of Philip Weller and mother, ----, b. ----, bapt. ----, Spon: ----
Georg of Johannes Weller and mother, Magtalena, both married people, b. February 8, 1790, bapt. March 4, 1790 Spon: Fridrich Alter and his wife
Elisabeth of Jacob Weinbrener and mother, Margretha, both married people, b. December 26, 1789, bapt. March 6, 1790 Spon: Ad. Stirtzman and his wife Elisabeth
Georg of Martin Krebes and mother, Magtalena, both married people, b. February 22, 1790, bapt. April 4, 1790 Spon: Georg Schall and his wife N.
Wilhelm of Ernst Dietz and mother, Maria, married people, b. April 13, 1790, bapt. July 2, 1790 Spon: The parents
Elisabetha of Jacob Stahl and mother, Anna Maria, both married people, b. December 31, 1789, bapt. July 2, 1790 Spon: The parents
Henrich of Michael Weitner and mother, Barbera, married people, b. April 11, 1790, bapt. August 9, 1790 Spon: Henrich Schneider and Susana
Maria Magdalena of Patrick McClary and mother, Elisabeth, married people, b. July 13, 1790, bapt. August 9, 1790 Spon: The mother
Elisabeth of Nico. Nunnemacher and mother, Esther, married people, b. ---, bapt. August 14, 1790 Spon: Baptized grown-up
Susanna of Joh. Wohlgemuth and mother, Maria, married people, b. July 15, 1771, bapt. August 14, 1790 Spon: Baptized as grown-up
Maria of Joh. Wohlgemuth and mother, Maria, married people, b. February 15, 1773, bapt. August 14, 1790 Spon: Baptized as grown-up
Anna of Martin Kirschner and mother, Elisabeth, married people, b. February 3, 1790, bapt. August 14, 1790 Spon: The parents
Joseph of Geo. Bradschaw and mother, Anne Uxor, b. April 25, 1789, bapt. August 14, 1790 Spon: The parents

Reformed Church of Hagerstown

Georg of Henrich Schnell and Christina, married people, b. May 4, 1790, bapt. August 15, 1790 Spon: The parents
Catharina of Joseph Straub and Cat., married people, b. November 28, 1789, bapt. August 15, 1790 Spon: Magd. Conradt (single)
Adam of Peter Klein and Elisabeth, married people, b. September 12, 1790, bapt. October 18, 1790 Spon: The parents themselves
Adam of Jacob Becker and Anna Martha, married people, b. August 22, 1790, bapt. October 18, 1790 Sponosrs: Adam Boraft and Elisabeth (married)
Elisabetha of Henrich Bergman and Cat., married people, b. October 7, 1790, bapt. October 18, 1790 Spon: Elis. Schneiderin (single)
Georg Wilhelm of Conrad Kasteroth and Magdalena, married people, b. September 10, 1790, bapt. October 18, 1790 Spon: Martin Krebes and Magdalena (married)
Metilda of Peter Woltz and Maria, married people, b. September 8, 1790, bapt. October 18, 1790 Spon: Georg Woltz and Charlotta (married)
Rahel of Lorentz Protzman and Elisabeth, b. November 3, 1790, bapt. December 8, 1790 Spon: The parents
Elias of Theodor and Marg, married people, b. January 21, 1791, bapt. February 14, 1791 Spon: Jacob Baeger and Anna (married)
Anna Maria of Jacob Nicol and Eva, married people, b. January 26, 1791, bapt. February 14, 1791 Spon: The parents
Anna Maria of Carl Setzer and Maria Cat., married people, b. March 7, 1790, bapt. February 16, 1791 Spon: The parents
Johannes of Nicolaus Hachin and Dorothea, married people, b. February 2, 1791, bapt. ---- 17, 1791 Spon: The parents
Georg of Christ. Mertz and Barbara, married people, b. December 3, 1789, bapt. April 4, 1791 Spon: The parents
Jacob of Mark Beatty and Barbara, married people, b. January 29, 1791, bapt. May 4, 1791 Spon: Joh. Weller (single)
Jacob of Joh. Bayer and Ester, married people, b. April 2, 1791, bapt. May 5, 1791 Spon: Jacob Duenschman
Michael of Jacob Nicol and his wife, Eva, b. October 20, 1777, bapt. ---- 29, Spon: The parents
Petrus & Johannes of Jacob Nicol and his wife, Eva, b. August 6, ----, bapt. September 4, 1792 Spon: The parents
Anna Maria of Ernst Ditz and wife, Anna Maria, b. January 8, ----, bapt. March 26, 1792 Spon: Margeretha Runter
Johanes of Daniel Renhit and wife, Elisabetha, b. August 28, 1791, bapt. shortly afterwards by Mr. Gueting - 1791 Spon: The parents
Henrich Wilhelm of Johannes Frener and wife, Susana, b. September 18, 1792, bapt. ---- Spon: Henrich Middelrauf
Friderich of Henrich Baumwart and wife, Margretha, b. June 13, 1790, bapt. ---- Spon: Fridrich Ehenbach and Sophia
Margretha of Johan Conrad Schoen and wife, Margretha, b. May 16, ----, bapt. June 4, 1792 Spon: The parents
Johanes of Peter Richter and wife, Catharina, b. August 25, 1791, bapt. by Mr. Goering Spon: Johanes Bezman and wife Anamaria
Johannes of Johanes Wolfersperger and wife, Elisabetha, b. March 9, 1788, bapt. March 15, 1788 Spon: The parents
Ana of Johannes Wolfersperger and Elisabetha, b. February 14, ----, bapt. April 14, 1790 Spon: The parents
Michael of Michael Weitner and wife, Barbara, b. December 15, 1793, bapt. May 9, 1794 Spon: Melchor Wickert and wife Maria Barbara
Wilhelm of David Kuck and wife, Catharina, b. January 25, 1793, bapt. May 10, 1794 Spon: Jacob Dutweiler and wife Catharina

Reformed Church of Hagerstown

Elisabetha of Nicolaus Hachen and wife, Dorothea, b. June 1, 1793, bapt.
April 27, 1794 Spon: Magdalena Reudenauerin
Thomas of Thomas Reight and wife, Elisabetha, b. August 6, 1793, bapt. April
27, 1794 Spon: Peter Krieger and wife Barbara
Johanes of Samuel Bieler and wife, Anamaria, b. December 6, 1792, bapt.
January 4, 1793
Magdalena of Wiliam Lewis and wife, Magdalena, b. December 22, 1791, bapt.
October 26, 1794 Spon: Mother
Elisabetha of Jacob Borghart and wife, Catharina, b. December 19, 1793,
bapt. April 18, 1794 Spon: Wilhelm Storn and wife Elisabetha
Johannes of Georg Leiby and wife, Catharina, b. December 16, 1793, bapt.
September 7, 1794 Spon: The parents
Catharina of Peter Richter and wife, Catharina, b. January 27, ----, bapt.
June 1, 17-- Spon: Peter Rufer and wife Catharina
Anamaria of Bez, b. July 2, 1793, bapt. October 6, 1793 Spon: Ana Bezin
Susana of Johannes Wolfersperger and wife, Elisabetha, b. November 12, 1791,
bapt. April 16, 1795 Spon: Father
Catharina of Johannes Wolfersperger and wife, Elisabetha, b. January 17,
1794, bapt. April 16, 1795 Spon: Father
Henrich of Martz Rueckenbach and Ana, b. December 24, ----, bapt. November
1792 Spon: Parents
Juliana of Conrad Cafferoth and Magdalena, b. July 17, 1792, bapt. October
28, 1792 Spon: Juliana Cafferothin
Samuel of Michael Heffele and wife, N., b. September 20, 1792, bapt. January
1, 1793 Spon: Mathias Reitenauer
Henrich of Henrich Schnell and mother, Christina, b. April 12, 1792, bapt.
December 25, 1792 Spon: Parents
Anamaria of Benjamin Reudenauer and housewife, Anamaria, b. February 9,
----, bapt. March 18, 1793 Spon: Parents
Elisabeth of Thomas Bern and Christina, b. January 4, ----, bapt. January
27, 1793 Spon: Rudolff Bley and wife Barbara
Johanes of Mathias Berntheuser and wife, Christina, b. December 11, 1792,
bapt. March 31, 1793 Spon: Christian Weinbrenner and wife, Christina
Georg of Georg Goranflauer and wife, Catharina, b. June 22, 1791, bapt.
April 6, 1793 Spon: Parents
Catharina of Adam Schneider and wife, Catharina, b. March 16, ----, bapt.
April 8, 1793 Spon: Henrich Muentze and wife Catharina
Henrich of Georg Biegler and wife, Elisabetha, b. March 30, ----, bapt.
April 16, 1793 Spon: Parents
Anamaria of George Koehler and wife, Anamaria, b. March 9, ----, bapt. May
5, 1793 Spon: Jacob Bindeby and wife Catharina
Johanes of Henrich Keiper and wife, Margretha, b. February 17, ----, bapt.
May 5, 1793 Spon: Johanes Riplet and wife Catharina
Jacobus of Leonhart Schnebely and mother, Elisabetha, b. October 18, 1792,
bapt. May 9, 1793 Spon: Abraham Wotring and Catharina
Martin of Martin Ruekebach and mother, Ana, b. April 3, ----, bapt. May 9,
1793 Spon: Parents
Johanes of Abraham Shneider and mother, Anamaria, b. December 22, 1792,
bapt. May 11, 1793 Spon: Parents
Jacob Herry of Johanes Geiger and wife, Susana, b. April 1, bapt. June 12,
1793 Spon: Jacob Herry and wife Maria Elisabetha
Johannes of Joseph Dauny and wife, Catharina, b. June 7, bapt. June 27, 1793
Spon: Parents
Anamaria of Christian Fischer and Catharina, b. May 8, bapt. June 30, 1793
Spon: Eva Hethen

Reformed Church of Hagerstown

Juliana of Ludwig Wisman and Elisabetha, b. April 7, bapt. July 7, 1793
   Spon: Parents
Johanes of Johanes Reb and wife, Elisabeth, b. March 8, bapt. July 28, 1793
   Spon: Henrich Bergman and Catharina
Catharina of Henrich Bergman and Catharina, b. June 23, bapt. July 28, 1793
   Spon: Catharina Conradin
Henrich of Georg Reiper and mother, Ana, b. June 18, bapt. August 13, 1793
   Spon: Henrich Reiper and Margretha
Simson of Henrich Orendorf and Margretha, b. June 17, bapt. August 22, 1793
   Spon: Jacob Brosim and Catharina
Samuel of Georg Schenck and wife, Catharina, b. March 5, bapt. March 23,
   1793 Spon: Abraham Leider and wife, Chorina
Henrich and Barbara of George Schlosser and wife, Barbara, b. August 22,
   bapt. August 27, 1793 Spon: Christophel Kern and wife Catharina
Georg of Jacob Schneider and wife, Juliana, b. August 18, bapt. October 27,
   1793 Spon: Georg Schem and wife, Catharina
Elisabetha of Nicolaus Kern and wife, Christina, b. September 5, bapt.
   October 27, 1793 Spon: Parents
Samuel of Philip Krieger and wife, Barbara, b. September 26, bapt. October
   27, 1793 Spon: Parents
Joseph of Philip Weller and wife, Magdalena, b. September 20, bapt. November
   17, 1793 Spon: Parents
Conrad of Conrad Tempel and wife, Margreth, b. September 22, bapt. November
   18, 1793 Spon: William Biaben and Sussana
Elisabetha of Friederich Koehler and wife, Magdalena, b. October 6, bapt.
   November 30, 1795 Spon: Maria Margreth Koehlerin
Andreas of Johannes Wein and wife, Elisabetha, b. November 7, bapt. December
   1, 1793 Spon: Andreas Bietterfield and wife Elisabeth
Johan Henrich of Johan Paulus Wegelein and Margretha, b. December 9, bapt.
   December 15, 1793 Spon: Parents
Johannes of Michael Rob and wife, Elisabetha, b. November 21, bapt. December
   25, 1793 Spon: Stephan Schleifer and wife, Magdalena
Rafael of John McLure and wife, Hana, b. November 16, bapt. December 28,
   1793 Spon: Parents
Elisabetha of Henrich Rener and wife, Sara, b. February 10, 1793, bapt.
   January 4, 1794 Spon: Mother
Sara of Johanes Miller and wife, Anamaria, b. February 19, 1793, bapt.
   January 19, 1794 Spon: Parents
Elisabetha of Johan Peter Herr and wife, Sussana, b. December 17, 1793,
   bapt. January 19, 1794 Spon: Johanes Geiger and wife Sussana
Johanes of Johanes Crumbach and wife, Anna, b. January 11, bapt. January 25,
   1794 Spon: Child's father and Juliana Grumbachin
Johannes of Christophel Hes and wife, Magdalena, b. May 10, 1793, bapt.
   January 26, 1794 Spon: Conrad Noll
Adam of Carl Selzer and wife, Catharina, b. October 5, bapt. October 13,
   1793 Spon: Henrich Adam and wife Susana
Margretha of Carl Selzer and wife, Catharina, b. October 15, bapt. ---- 13,
   1793 Spon: Toris Dayel and Margretha
Catharina of Daneil Rensch and wife, Elisabetha, b. October 25, 1793, bapt.
   February 15, 1794 Spon: Parents
Elisabetha of Peter Roeser and wife, Catharina, b. October 24, 1793, bapt.
   February 2, 1794 Spon: Adam Miller and wife Ana Catharina
Samuel of Johanes Han and wife, Catharina, b. December 29, 1793, bapt.
   February 10, 1794 Spon: The parents

Reformed Church of Hagerstown

Margreth of Conrad Noll and wife, Catharina, b. September 30, 1793, bapt. February 16, 1794 Spon: Conrad Tempel and Margreth
Samuel of Johanes Frener and Susana, b. February 14, bapt. ---- 15, 1794 Spon: Parents
Jacob of Ernst Dietz and wife, Anamaria, b. February 13, bapt. April 6, 1794 Spon: Parents
Ana Mary of John Lee and wife, Ana, b. February 22, 1793, bapt. March 27, 1794 Spon: Parents
Christina Margareth of Johanes Kausler and wife Christina Margaretha, b. February 25, bapt. March 23, 1794 Spon: Lenhart Streit and wife Barbara
Johannes of Jonathan Rahauser and wife, Anamaria, b. February 23, bapt. March 30, 1794 Spon: Johannes Schaefer and wife An Elisa
Johanes of unknown, found by Simsen on March 18, bapt. ---- 30, 1794 Spon: Conrad Tempel and wife, Magdalena
Anamaria of William Klein and wife, Elisabetha, b. March 18, bapt. April 17, Spon: Jost Klein and wife Anamaria
Susana of Jacob Bauer and wife, Catharina, b. January 27, bapt. June 1794 Spon: Martin Krebes and wife Magdalena
Jacob of David Bracunier and wife, Catharina, b. October 28, 1793, bapt. April 20, 1794 Spon: Jacob Braunier
Catharina of Mathias Schafner and wife, Elisabetha, b. March 26, bapt. June 1, 1794 Spon: Parents
Catharina of Johannes Odruwald and wife, Elisabetha, b. April 26, bapt. June 15, 1794 Spon: Abraham Leder and Catharina
Henrich of Henrich Baumwart and wife, Margretha, b. October 31, 1793, bapt. September 7, 1794 Spon: Henrich Weizel and Susana
Catharina of Henrich Klein and wife, Magdalena, b. April 18, bapt. June 16, 1794 Spon: Balzar Goll and wife Catharina
Catharina of Christian Vogler and wife, Susana, b. November 20, 1793, bapt. May 11, 1794 Spon: Parents
Christian of Henrich Hettrich and wife, Sibila, b. February 24, bapt. March 30, 1794 Spon: Christian Hettrich
Jonathan of Johanes Schaefer and wife, Anelika, b. April 14, bapt. May 8, 1794 Spon: Jonathan Rahauser and wife Anamaria
Elisabetha of Johanes Weller and wife, Magdalena, b. May 18, bapt. June 15, 1794 Spon: Parents
Johannes of Simeon Lecron and wife, Elisabetha, b. February 7, bapt. May 11, 1794 Spon: Parents
Maria Barbara of Jacob Pril and wife, Maria, b. July 12, 1793, bapt. August 24, 1794 Spon: Wilhelm Ezeika and wife Maria Barbara
Petrus of Nicolaus Becker and wife, Salome, b. March 26, bapt. August 13, 1794 Spon: Parents
Catharina of Philip Sprecher and wife, Magdalena, b. June 22, bapt. July 13, 1794 Spon: Parents
Johanes of Georg Leiby and wife, Catharina, b. October 16, 1793, bapt. July 7, 1794 Spon: Parents:
Johannes of Robert McCaul and wife, Catharina, b. August 4, bapt. September 7, 1794 Spon: Parents
Johanes of Michael Comfer and wife, Hana, b. April 5, bapt. April 27, 1794 Spon: Georg Comfer and Elisabetha Knaufel
Georg of Georg Schindelbauer and wife, Ana, b. March 14, bapt. April 22, 1794 Spon: Parents
Elisabetha of Marcus Betty and wife, Barbara, b. January 12, bapt. May 1, 1794 Spon: Johanes Scheider and wife Anamaria

Reformed Church of Hagerstown

Catharina of Martin Bringman and wife, Margretha, b. August 11, bapt. October 26, 1794 Spon: Parents
Barbara of Samuel Bieler and wife, Anamaria, b. October 8, bapt. November 9, 1794 Spon: Parents
Wilhelm of Johanes Schleich and wife, Anamaria, b. August 23, bapt. October 5, 1794 Spon: Parents
Catharina of Daniel Rauser and wife, Sophia, b. August 10, bapt. October 12, 1794 Spon: Parents
Henrich of Johanes Long and wife, Elisabetha, b. March 8, bapt. September 27, 1794 Spon: Parents
Henrich of Peter Kemmerer and wife, Sara, b. July 8, bapt. September 27, 1794 Spon: Parents
Rosina of Conrad Oster and wife, Eva, b. July 27, bapt. September 28, 1794 Spon: Eva Reudenauern
Johanes of Leonhart Schnebly and wife, Elisabetha, b. September 4, bapt. December 13, 1794 Spon: Parents
Susana of Jacob Ritter and wife, Maria, b. July 8, bapt. December 14, 1794 Spon: Juthit Ritterin
Friederich of Georg Knad and wife, Catharina, b. October 7, bapt. December 14, 1794 Spon: Michael Kapp and wife Catharina
Anmargreth of Jacob Zoeler and wife, Anmargretha, b. November 11, bapt. December 14, 1794 Spon: Peter Sterzman and wife Margretha
Susana of Georg Schall and wife, Margretha, b. November 18, 1794, bapt. January 11, 1795 Spon: Martin Bringman and wife Margretha
Henrich of Jost Zimerman and wife, Catharina Margretha, b. December 16, 1794, bapt. January 10, 1795 Spon: Georg Nue and wife Magdalena
Georg of Peter Richter and wife, Catharina, b. August 29, 1794, bapt. January 15, 1795 Spon: Devalt Eichelberner and wife Barbara
Wilhelm of Johan Conrad Schoen and wife, Margretha, b. December 8, bapt. December 25, 1795 Spon: Parents
Georg of Johanes Biel and wife, Eva, b. December 1, 1794, bapt. January 17, 1795 Spon: Catharina Kiefern
Catharina of Conrad Cafferoth and wife, Magdalena, b. December 14, 1794, bapt. January 24, 1795 Spon: Parents
Wilhelm of Conrad Crumbach and wife Catharina, b. December 17, 1794, bapt. February 1, 1795 Spon: Parents
Samuel of Joseph Downy and wife, Catharina, b. January 9, bapt. January 28, 1795 Spon: Parents
Ana Juthit of Joseph Renolds and wife, Elisabetha, b. September 6, 1794, bapt. February 2, 1795 Spon: Parents
Juthit Ana of Jacob Heyser and wife, Catharina, b. November 23, 1794, bapt. February 2, 1795 Spon: Ana Heysern
Daniel of Jonathan Rohauser and wife, Anamaria, b. October 3, bapt. November 11, 1795 Spon: Henrich Schnebely
Daniel of Ludwig Wisman and wife, Elisabetha, b. March 16, bapt. April 6, 1795 Spon: Henrich Werley and wife Anamaria
Elisabetha of Henrich Alt and wife, Christina, b. October 8, 1794, bapt. April 5, 1795 Spon: Elisabetha Gnaedig
Elisabetha of Johan Hums and wife, Margratha, b. October 28, 1794, bapt. April 19, 1795 Spon: Johannes Weller and wife Magdalena
Henrich of Peter Binckely and wife, Catharina, b. February 16, bapt. April 16, 1795 Spon: Jacob Binckely and wife Catharina
Maria of Zacharias Schucker and wife, Eva, b. January 31, bapt. April 19, 1795 Spon: Parents

Reformed Church of Hagerstown

Samuel of Henrich Middelkauf and wife, Barbara, b. April 14, bapt. April 19, 1795 Spon: Parents

Johannes of Abraham Koenig and wife, Magdalena, b. February 4, bapt. April 19, 1795 Spon: Jacob Koenig and wife Elisabetha

Samuel of Martin Rickenbach and wife, Ana, b. April 28, bapt. May 17, 1795 Spon: Parents

Johanes of Friederich Betz and wife, Ana Catharina, b. January 31, bapt. May 17, 1795 Spon: Parents

Johan Henrich of Henrich Schmitt and wife, Catharina, b. January 7, bapt. May 17, 1794 Spon: Jacob Urban and wife Maria Eva

Barbara of Henrich Sommer and wife, Barbara, b. January 26, bapt. May 18, 1795 Spon: Parents

Catharina of Jacob Stephan and wife, Tilly, b. November 9, 1794, bapt. May 19, 1795 Spon: Scharlotta Hes

Adam of Georg Han and wife, Margretha, b. March 5, bapt. May 24, 1795 Spon: Friederich Hertel and wife Margretha

Jonas of Georg Lambert and wife, Eva, b. August 5, 1794, bapt. May 24, 1795 Spon: Parents

Elisabetha of Carl Ohlwein and wife, Elisabetha, b. April 4, bapt. May 24, 1795 Spon: Parents

Susana of Valentin Wagner and wife, Magdalena, b. January 26, bapt. May 25, 1795 Spon: Susana Gnaedig

Ester of Bastian Hertel and wife, Catharina, b. October 3, 1794, bapt. June 28, 1795 Spon: Nicolaus Hess and wife, Scharlotta

Johannes of Henrich Gnaedig and wife, Elisabetha, b. April 12, bapt. June 29, 1795 Spon: Christian Hachen and wife, Juliana

Maria Magdalena of Friederich Koesler and wife, Maria Magdalena, b. May 27, bapt. July 20, 1795 Spon: Martin Steck and wife Catharina

Barbara of Thomas Perry and wife, Christina, b. September 28, 1794, bapt. July 26, 1795 Spon: Rudolf Bley and wife Barbara

Susana of Henrich Schneider and wife, Anamaria, b. June 20, bapt. August 30, 1795 Spon: Johanes Frener and wife Susana

Elisabetha of Johanes Odenwald and wife, Elisabetha, b. June 18, bapt. September 6, 1795 Spon: Parents

Catharina of Johannes Schaeffer and wife, Anelika, b. August 19, bapt. October 4, 1795 Spon: Peter Hoeflich and wife Barbara

Elisabetha of Jacob Binckely and wife, Catharina, b. September 20, bapt. October 18, 1795 Spon: Friederich Fischach and wife Catharina

Johan Georg of Anthony Procupein and wife, Catharina, b. August 9, bapt. October 27, 1795 Spon: Matheias Armeschary

Salome of Abraham Neukirch and wife, Sibila, b. April 10, bapt. November 8, 1795 Spon: Parents

Elis. of Matheias Schaper and wife, Elisabetha, b. October 25, bapt. November 22, 1795 Spon: Parents

Sara of Martin Krebes and wife, Magdalena, b. August 25, bapt. November 29, 1795 Spon: David Reudenauer and wife Sarah

Catharina of Daniel Klein and wife, Margretha, b. October 11, bapt. November 30, 1795 Spon: Johanes Grumbach and wife Juliana

Jacob of ----, b. November 14, bapt. December 25, 1795

Barbara of Samuel Fried and wife, Maria, b. November 9, bapt. December 25, 1795 Spon: Michael Strohm and wife Elisabetha

Barbara of Nicolaus Kern and wife, Christina, b. February 16, bapt. April 4, 1795 Spon: Parents

Henrich of Daniel Volck and wife, Anamaria, b. September 23, bapt. December 13, 1795 Spon: Jacob Binckely and wife Catharina

Reformed Church of Hagerstown

Maria Magdalena of Nicolaus Huert and wife, Elisabetha, b. February 8, bapt. November 17, 1795 Spon: Parents
Wilhelm of John Holand and wife, Catharina, b. ---- 1794, bapt. April 5, 1795 Spon: Conrad Noll and wife Maria Elisabetha
Friederich and Jacob Lecron and wife, Margretha, b. August 21, 1794, bapt. January 1, 1796 Spon: Parents
Ana of Simeon Lecron and wife, Elisabetha, b. November 5, 1795, bapt. January 1, 1796 Spon: Catharina Leidy
Johannes of Jacob Orendorf and wife, Susana, b. June 22, 1795, bapt. January 4, 1796 Spon: Henrich Orendorf and wife Margretha
William of Henrich Orendorf and wife, Margretha, b. August 28, bapt. January 4, 1796 Spon: Jacob Orendorf and wife Susana
Daniel of Johan Peter Herr and wife, Susana, b. December 14, 1795, bapt. January 24, 1796 Spon: Parents
Ana Margretha of Michael Oxt and wife, Elisabetha, b. November 3, 1795, bapt. January 31, 1796 Spon: Jost Zimmermann and wife Carolina Margretha
Daniel of Johannes Beier and wife, Ehester, b. June 17, 1795, bapt. January 24, 1796 Spon: Henrich Orendorf and wife Margretha
Elisabetha of Johannes Wolf and wife Maria, b. December 28, 1795, bapt. March 5, 1796 Spon: Johannes Deis and wife Elisabetha
Jacob of Jacob Koenig and wife, Elisabetha, b. February 5, bapt. March 6, 1796 Spon: Abraham Koenig and wife Magdalena
Catharina of Friederich Kau and wife, Elisabetha, September 26, 1795, bapt. March 30, 1796 Spon: Anamaria
Sara of Georg Confer and wife, Eva, b. September 2, 1795, bapt. April 23, 1796 Spon: Michael Confer and wife Ana
Jacob of Johanes Kolt and wife, Barbara, b. December 26, 1795, bapt. April 4, 1796 Spon: Daniel Reudenauer and wife Elisabetha
Anamaria of Henrich Maniger and wife, Elisabetha, April 20, 1794, bapt. April 7, 1796 Spon: Parents
Johannes of Henrich Zimmermann and wife, Barbara, b. October 18, 1795, bapt. April 19, 1796 Spon: Michael Oxt and wife Elisabetha
Johannes of William Belsch and wife, Elisabetha, b. April 16, bapt. April 30, 1796 Spon: Anamaria Kerschner
Jesse of Phillip Meyer and wife, Catharina, b. March 24, bapt. May 1, 1796 Spon: Carl Gelwichs and wife Barbara
Samuel of Matheias Knod and wife, Magdalena, b. January 15, bapt. May 7, 1796 Spon: Johannes Protzmann and wife Anamaria
Johannes of Phillip Kriger and wife, Barbara, b. March 18, bapt. May 16, 1796 Spon: Parents
Elisabetha of Abraham Kornman and wife, Maria, b. December 19, 1795, bapt. May 20, 1796 Spon: Elisabetha Ritter
Johannes of Jacob Braeunier and wife, Margretha, b. March 29, bapt. May 22, 1796 Spon: Parents
Nancy of Friederich Hertel and wife, Margretha, b. August 24, 1795, bapt. May 21, 1796 Spon: Jonathan Rohauser and wife Anamaria
Maria Henrietta of Henrich Dillman and wife, Catharina, b. August 30, 1795, bapt. May 22, 1796 Spon: Parents
Johanes of Joseph Reynolds and wife, Elisabetha, b. June 15, bapt. June 29, 1796 Spon: Mother
Anamaria of Georg Krebs and wife, Margretha, b. March 29, bapt. July 12, 1796 Spon: Parents
Maria Eva of Henrich Schmitt and wife, Catharina, b. July 17, bapt. August 14, 1796 Spon: Catharina Urban

Reformed Church of Hagerstown

Johannes of James More and wife, Susana, b. May 18, bapt. September 3, 1796 Spon: Parents
Daniel of Nicolaus Hachen and wife, Dorethea, b. June 16, bapt. September 4, 1796 Spon: Parents
Henrich of Johan Conrad Schoen and wife, Margretha, b. September 6, bapt. September 10, 1796 Spon: Parents
Sarah of Adam Fischer and wife, Catharina, b. July 1, bapt. September 14, 1796 Spon: Henrich Schneider and wife Margretha
Elisabetha of Jacob Rensch and wife, Margretha, b. August 27, bapt. September 18, 1796 Spon: Parents
Johan Daniel of Daniel Jungman and wife, Catharina, b. July 18, bapt. September 15, 1796 Spon: Parents
Elisabetha of Tobias Bretheg and wife, Nancy, b. August 9, bapt. September 25, 1796 Spon: William Ratter and wife Sarah
Johannes of Friederich Beck and wife, Juliana, b. June 24, bapt. October 20, 1796 Spon: Parents
Isau of Johannes Gnaedig and wife, Margretha, b. September 12, bapt. October 20, 1796 Spon: Friederich Beck and wife Juliana
Johanes of Peter Wottring and wife, Margretha, b. October 8, bapt. November 4, 1796 Spon: Parents
David of Ludwig Jung and wife, Catharina, b. September 27, bapt. November 4, 1796 Spon: Parents
Elisabetha of Ludwig Edkhart and wife, Ana Elisabetha, b. June 24, bapt. November 4, 1796 Spon: Parents
Daniel of Nicolaus Schmahl and wife, Elisabetha, b. October 15, bapt. November 4, 1796 Spon: Parents
Anamaria of Henrich Middelkauf and wife, Barbara, b. August 2, bapt. November 6, 1796 Spon: Parents
Johanes of Henrich Weis and wife, Catharina, b. October 16, bapt. November 20, 1796 Spon: Parents
Ana Magdalena of John Hallman and wife, Maria Catharina, b. September 1, bapt. November 20, 1796 Spon: Ana Magdalena Hallman
Wilhelm of Jacob Heyser and wife, Catharina, b. October 6, bapt. November 27, 1796 Spon: Ana Heyser
Johannes of Michael Strohm and wife, Elisabetha, b. October 30, bapt. November 27, 1796 Spon: Jacob Trab and wife Catharina
Anamaria of Jacob Trab and wife, Catharina, b. November 9, bapt. November 27, 1796 Spon: Michael Strohm and wife Elisabetha
Elisabetha of Henrich Klein and wife, Magdalena, b. August 29, bapt. November 30, 1796 Spon: Teobald Eichelberner and wife Barbara
Henrich of Samuel Dorf and wife, Maria, b. May 15, 1795, bapt. January 1, 1797 Spon: Henrich Schneider and wife Ana Maria
Anamaria of Daniel Rensch and wife, Elisabetha, b. November 25, 1795, bapt. January 6, 1797 Spon: Father
ELisabetha of Michael Confer and wife, Hanna, b. November 22, 1796, bapt. January 12, 1797 Spon: Parents
Elisabetha of Johanes Oxt and wife, Anamaria, b. November 29, 1796, bapt. January 24, 1797 Spon: Michael Oxt and wife Elisabetha
Sem of Georg Lambert and wife, Eva, b. July 4, 1796, bapt. February 9, 1797 Spon: Parents
Daniel of Robert McCaul and wife, Catharina, b. December 7, 1796, bapt. February 12, 1797 Spon: Daniel Klebsattel and wife Ana
Jacob of Henrich Schreiber and wife, Anamaria, b. October 2, 1796, bapt. February 16, 1797 Spon: Parents

Reformed Church of Hagerstown

Peter of Johannes Schnebily and wife, Catharina, b. February 19, bapt. February 20, 1797 Spon: Parents

Anamaria of Jacob Derr and wife, Catharina, b. October 4, bapt. February 20, 1797 Spon: Parents

Daniel of Abraham Koenig and wife, Magdalena, b. February 6, bapt. February 26, 1797 Spon: Georg Martiny and wife Susana

Wilhelm Michael of William Krebs and wife, Ana, b. February 5, bapt. March 5, 1797 Spon: Martin Krebs and wife Magdalena

Wilhelm of Phillip Keller and wife, Barbara, b. December 26, 1796, bapt. March 12, 1797 Spon: Wilhelm Hes and wife Magdalena

Wilhelm of Samuel Bieler and wife, Maria, b. December 23, 1796, bapt. March 19, 1797 Spon: Parents

Jacob of Matheas Schaffner and wife, Elisabetha, b. February 5, bapt. March 26, 1797 Spon: Parents

Petrus of Johannes Lang and wife, Elisabetha, January 8, bapt. April 1, 1797 Spon: Parents

Catharina of Jacob Lecron and wife, Margretha, b. August 8, 1796, bapt. April 14, 1797 Spon: Catharina Arzt

Amalia of Jonathan Rohauser and wife, Anamaria, b. March 31, bapt. April 23, 1797 Spon: Georg Miller and wife Christina

Henrich of Henrich Alt and wife, Christina, b. November 8, 1796, bapt. May 7, 1797 Spon: Phillip Weiant and wife Margretha

Barbara of Phillip Weiant and wife, Margretha, b. August 15, 1796, bapt. May 7, 1797 Spon: Henrich Alt and wife Christina

Sarah of Carl Ohlwein and wife, Elisabetha, b. December 7, 1796, bapt. May 7, 1797 Spon: Parents

Wiliam of Johanes Reb and wife, Elisabetha, b. December 15, 1796, bapt. May 21, 1797 Spon: Parents

Samuel of Conrad Grumbach and wife, Catharina, b. April 27, bapt. May 25, 1797 Spon: Parents

Elisabetha of Georg Meiper and wife, Anna, b. May 10, bapt. May 31, 1797 Spon: Simeon Kisecker and wife Elisabetha

Friederich of Friederich Bez and wife, Ana Catharina, b. March 8, bapt. June 4, 1797 Spon: Parents

Jacob of Bastian Hertel and wife, Catharina, b. November 3, 1796, bapt. June 4, 1797 Spon: Parents

Johanes of Johanes Schleich and wife, Anamaria, b. February 27, bapt. June 4, 1797 Spon: Johanes Kausler and wife Christina

Elisabetha of Georg Jegel and wife, Anamaria, b. December 19, 1796, bapt. June 10, 1797 Spon: Gerhart Eidel and wife Sophia

Henrich of Daniel Reinoll and wife, Anamaria, b. April 13, bapt. June 11, 1797 Spon: Carl Gelwicks and wife Barbara

Margretha of Christian Middelkauf and wife, Rossina, b. November 29, 1796, bapt. June 11, 1797 Spon: Maria Elisabetha Middelkauf

Catharina of Devalt Kennel and wife, Elisabetha, b. November 11, 1796, bapt. June 11, 1797 Spon: George Kerschner and wife Maria

Susana of Robert Higins and wife, Catharina, b. September 6, 1796, bapt. June 16, ---- Spon: Parents

Susana of John Wolf and wife, Ana, b. March 29, bapt. July 29, 1797 Spon: Elisabetha Reb

Jacob of Phillip Schaffner and wife, Elisabetha, b. November 17, 1796, bapt. August 6, 1797 Spon: Johanes Reb and wife Elisabetha

Elisabetha of Samuel Forder and wife, Margretha, b. September 23, 1796, bapt. August 9, 1797 Spon: Parents

Reformed Church of Hagerstown

Susana of David Reudenauer and wife, Catharina, b. July 16, bapt. August 13, 1797 Spon: Daniel Reudenauer and wife Elisabetha
Ana Barbara of Georg Confer and wife, Eva, b. December --, 1796, bapt. August 27, 1797 Spon: Parents
Maria Catharina of Peter Storm and wife, Susanna Maria, b. January 29, bapt. September 22, 1797 Spon: Parents
Sophia of Zacharias Schuckers and wife, Eva, b. July 7, bapt. October 10, 1797 Spon: Parents
Amalia of Thomas Schley and wife, Catharina, b. January 1, 1796, bapt. October 19, 1797 Spon: Parents
Wilhelm of Conrad Cafferoth and wife, Magdalena, b. May 23, bapt. October 23, 1797 Spon: Samuel Bieler and wife Ana Maria
Samuel of Friederich Koehler and wife, Anamaria, b. August 25, bapt. October 24, 1797 Spon: Martin Steck and wife Catharina
Sarah of Tobias Bretneg and wife, Nancy, b. November 7, bapt. November 16, 1797 Spon: Parents
Anamaria of Johannes Han and wife, Catharina, b. March 6, bapt. November 19, 1797 Spon: Teobald Eichelberner and wife Barbara
Johanes of Jonas Kramer and wife, Catharina, b. October 13, bapt. November 26, 1797 Spon: Parents
Margretha of Jacob Balzel and wife, Anna, b. August 11, bapt. December 16, 1797 Spon: Teobald Eichelberner and wife Barbara
Conrad of Johan Peter Herr and wife, Susanna, b. November 26, 1797, bapt. January 1, 1798 Spon: Parents
Salome of Phillip Maier and wife, Catharina, b. December 12, 1797, bapt. January 4, 1798 Spon: Catharina Hartman
Samuel of Georg Miller and wife, Catharina, October 10, 1797, bapt. January 7, 1798 Spon: Peter Miller and wife Anamaria
Jacob of Martin Ruackenbach and wife, Anna, b. December 10, 1797, bapt. January 14, 1798 Spon: Parents
Amelia of Johan Conrad Schoen and wife, Margretha, b. January 31, bapt. February 8, 1798 Spon: Parents
Anamaria of Simeon Lecron and wife, Elisabetha, b. October 13, 1797, bapt. February 18, 1798 Spon: Andreas Bard and wife Anamaria
Johanes of Georg Klein and wife, Elisabetha, b. December 7, 1797, bapt. March 17, 1798 Spon: Johanes Wolfarth
Daniel of David Bracunier and wife, Catharina, b. November 6, 1797, bapt. March 25, 1798 Spon: Parents
Barbara of Matheas Eberts and wife, Catharina, b. March 3, bapt. March 25, 1798 Spon: Rudolf Bley and wife Barbara
Magdalena Hagern of Johannes Rohrer and wife, Catharina, b. August 25, 1797, bapt. April 4, 1798 Spon: Jonathan Hager and wife Magdalena
Sarah of Friederich Arnold and wife, Barbara, b. December 25, 1797, bapt. April 8, 1798 Spon: Parents
Johannes of Leonhart Rillmeier and wife, Catharina, b. March 20, bapt. April 8, 1798 Spon: Parents
Magdalena Hagern of Johanes Wolf and wife, ----, b. September 11, 1797, bapt. April 13, 1798 Spon: Johanes Hager and wife, Magdalena
Jacob of Johanes Ox and wife, Catharina, b. February 27, bapt. April 10, 1798 Spon: Christian Kugel and wife Elisabetha
Johannes of Thomas Reight and wife, Elisabetha, b. January 25, bapt. April 23, 1798 Spon: Peter Hose and wife Susana
Maria of Michael Lawman and wife, Rosina, b. February 4, 1769, bapt. April 10, 1798 Spon: Parents

Reformed Church of Hagerstown

Isabela of Johanes Flenner and wife, Agnes, b. November 14, 1796, bapt. May 6, 1798 Spon: Parents
Anna of Johanes Flenner and wife, Agnes, b. February 21, bapt. May 6, 1798 Spon: Parents
Susana of Jacob Bracunier and wife, Elisabetha, b. February 21, bapt. May 9, 1798 Spon: Susana Baumwart
Julianna of Michael Haucks and wife, Anamaria, b. April 20, bapt. April 21, 1798 Spon: Catharina Leisinger
Sarah of Michael Haucks and wife, Anamaria, b. April 20, bapt. April 21, 1798 Spon: Margretha Schoen
Wiliam of Nicolaus Hachen and wife, Dorethea, b. October 1, 1797, bapt. May 20, 1798 Spon: Parents
Joseph of Christian Arzt and wife, Catharina, b. September 23, 1797, bapt. May 27, 1798 Spon: Jacob Lecron and wife Margretha
Henrich of John Schup and wife, Elisabetha, b. May 7, bapt. June 4, 1798 Spon: Henrich Schup
Elisabetha of Joseph Reinels and wife, Elisabetha, b. May 26, bapt. June 10, 1798 Spon: Parents
David of Philip Weiant and wife, Margretha, b. March 1, 1793, bapt. June 13, 1798 Spon: Parents
Margretha of Christian Heterich and Elisabetha Reudenauer, illegitimate, b. February 10, 1797, bapt. June 14, 1798 Spon: Mother
Manduall of Friederich Miller and wife, Catharina, b. January 6, bapt. June 24, 1798 Spon: Parents
Georg of Jacob Binckly and wife, Catharina, b. June 2, bapt. July 21, 1798 Spon: George Binckly and wife Eva
Edmund of Michaem Stolz and wife, Catharina, b. May 14, bapt. July 30, 1798 Spon: Abraham Esch and wife Maria
Sarah of Philipp Krieger and wife, Barbara, b. January 12, bapt. August 12, 1798 Spon: Parents
Catharina of Thomas Parry and wife, Christina, b. November 29, 1797, bapt. August 12, 1798 Spon: Matheas Eberts and wife Catharina
Wilhelm of Wiliam Belsch and wife, Elisabetha, b. June 12, bapt. August 19, 1798 Spon: John Kerschner
Susana of Johannes Kerschner and wife, Magdalena, b. March 18, bapt. August 19, 1798 Spon: Parents
Maria of Matheas -itsch and wife, Elisabetha, b. July 8, bapt. August 25, 1798 Spon: Peter Kraut and wife Elisabetha
Georg of Georg Ludwig Eckhart and wife, Ana Elisabetha, b. November 27, 1797, bapt. August 26, 1798 Spon: Parents
Samuel of Henrich Weis and wife, Catharina, b. August 10, bapt. September 2, 1798 Spon: Parents
Anna Elisabetha of Jacob Heyser and wife, Catharina, b. June 10, bapt. September 14, 1798 Spon: Parents
Johannes of Johannes Gnaedig and wife, Margretha, b. June 26, bapt. September 8, 1798 Spon: Peter Hose and wife Susana
Susanna Lomfort of David Little and wife, Elisabetha, b. May 27, bapt. October 9, 1798 Spon: Parents
Anamaria Magdalena of Philipp Keller and wife, Barbara, b. July 21, bapt. October 7, 1798 Spon: Wilhelm Hes and wife Magdalena
George Vortne of Wilhelm Krebs and wife, Anna, b. October 10, bapt. November 11, 1798 Spon: Georg Schall and wife Margetha
Lidia of Georg Krebs and wife, Margretha, b. September 23, bapt. November 25, 1798 Spon: Herman Lohrshach and wife Elisabetha

Reformed Church of Hagerstown

Johannes of Matheas Schaffner and wife, Elisabetha, b. October 13, bapt. November 25, 1798 Spon: Parents

Samuel of Philipp Walter and wife, Maria, b. August 18, bapt. December 9, 1798 Spon: Jacob Kraft and wife Susana

Susana of Zacharias Mihls and wife, Susanna, b. November 7, bapt. December 12, 1798 Spon: Parents

Hanna of John Meier and wife, Hanna, b. August 14, bapt. December 23, 1798 Spon: Parents

Seth of Johannes Beier and wife, Ester, b. December 23, 1797, bapt. December 29, 1798 Spon: Jonathan Rahauser

Margretha of Jacob Kremer and wife, Rachael, b. February 4, bapt. September 29, 1797 Spon: Parents

Samuel of Jonas Zoeller and wife, Elisabetha, b. September 26, 1798, bapt. January 1, 1799 Spon: Isau Jones and wife Margretha

Elisabetha of Peter Umrichhauser and wife, Maria, b. September 2, 1798, bapt. January 13, 1799 Spon: Parents

Margretha of Jacob Rensch and wife, Margretha, b. September 30, 1798, bapt. January 17, 1799 Spon: Parents

Elisabetha of Johann Schnebily and wife, Catharina, b. July 31, 1798, bapt. January 17, 1799 Spon: Parents

Maria of Johnn Halan and wife, Catharina, b. December 13, bapt. January 20, 1799 Spon: Martin Ferber and wife, Maria

Johan Carl Bernhart of Carl Ohlwein and wife, Elisabetha, b. January 7, bapt. January 20, 1799 Spon: Bernhard Ohlwein and wife Anamaria

Maria Christina of Johan Jacob Werner and wife, Elisabetha, b. October 28, 1794, bapt. January 22, 1799 Spon: Rebecca Schmitt

Eva Juthit of Martin Krebs and wife, Magdalena, b. December 10, 1798, bapt. February 22, 1799 Spon: Wilhelm Krebs and wife Anna

Henrich Jonathan of Jonathan Rohauser and wife, Anamaria, b. February 6, bapt. February 26, 1799 Spon: Henrich Schnebely and wife Catharina

Marty of Abraham Koenig and wife, Magdalena, b. January 13, bapt. March 10, 1799 Spon: Parents

Ana of Robert McCaul and wife, Catharina, b. December 19, 1798, bapt. March 24, 1799 Spon: Daniel Klebsattel and wife Anna

Susana of Joseph Boyd and wife, Susana, b. January 18, bapt. March 24, 1799 Spon: Susana Baumwart

Michael of Michael Confer and wife, Anna, b. November 30, 1798, bapt. March 24, 1799 Spon: Albrecht Peter and wife Anamaria

Anamaria of Nicolaus Hachen and wife, Dorethea, b. April 12, bapt. April 13, 1799 Spon: Anamaria Belzhuber

Jacob of Ezechiel Ehenry and wife, Maria, b. April 23, 1797, bapt. April 17, 1799 Spon: Parents

Anamaria of Johannes Schleich and wife, Anamaria, b. February 20, bapt. April 21, 1799 Spon: Friederich Koehler and wife Maria Magdalena

Rosina of Teobald Kennel and wife, Elisabetha, b. February 15, bapt. April 28, 1799 Spon: Conrad Oster and wife Eva

Anamaria of Jacob Koenig and wife, Elisabetha, b. March 23, bapt. April 28, 1799 Spon: Abraham Koenig and wife Magdalena

Daniel of David Flenner and wife, Susana, b. November 11, 1798, bapt. May 4, 1799 Spon: Parents

Christina of Joseph Grafert and wife, Margretha, b. April 10, 1793, bapt. May 8, 1799 Spon: Christina Hann

Johan Jacob of Joseph Grafert and wife, Margretha, b. May 1, 1797, bapt. May 8, 1799 Spon: Mother

Reformed Church of Hagerstown

Salome of Jacob Lecron and wife, Anmargretha, b. October 19, 1798, bapt. May 10, 1799 Spon: Elisabetha Moz
Elisabetha of Conrad Noll and wife, Maria Elisabetha, b. March 24, bapt. May 12, 1799 Spon: Henrich Blum and wife Catharina Elisabetha
Michael of Michael Strohm and wife, Elisabetha, b. March 20, bapt. May 12, 1799 Spon: Jacob -rab and wife Catharina
Valentin of Valentin Wagener and wife, Magdalena, b. February 13, bapt. May 13, 1799 Spon: Peter Hose and wife Susana
Anamaria of Henrich Han and wife, Christina, b. March 5, 1798, bapt. June 2, 1799 Spon: Anamaria Han
Adam of Henrich Alt and wife, Christina, b. November 7, 1798, bapt. June 9, 1799 Spon: Parents
Jacob of Henrich Christ and wife, Catharina, b. September 25, 1798, bapt. June 11, 1799 Spon: Parents
Elina of Samuel Bieler and wife, Ana Maria, b. March 4, bapt. June 16, 1799 Spon: Parents
Elisabetha of Joseph Beier and wife, Margretha, b. April 23, bapt. June 17, 1799 Spon: Johannes Beier and wife Esther
Maria of Johan Henrich Klein and wife Ana Magdalena, b. October 20, 1798, bapt. June 7, 1799 Spon: Parents
Maria of George Guety and wife, Catharina, b. March 1, bapt. July 14, 1799 Spon: Parents
Johan Jacob of Henrich Schmitt and wife, Catharina, b. July 10, 1798, bapt. July 28, 1799 Spon: Jacob Urban
Maria Magdalena of Abraham Walter and wife, Elisabetha, b. May 15, bapt. August 4, 1799 Spon: Peter Renner and wife Magdalena
Elisabetha of Johannes Dunckel and wife, Magedalena, b. May 1, bapt. August 4, 1799 Spon: Samuel Bieler and wife Anamaria
Peter of Johan Peter Herr and wife, Susana, b. June 18, 1799, bapt. August 11, 1799 Spon: Gottlieb Clasbrener and wife Margretha
Margretha of Henrich Reunauer and wife, Susana, b. June 14, bapt. August 11, 1799 Spon: Catharina Heinsmann
Henrich of Henrich Schneider and wife, Anamaria, b. October 4, 1797, bapt. August 12, 1799 Spon: Parents
Friederich Koehler of Friederich Koehler and wife, Maria Magdalena, b. August 14, bapt. August 25, 1799 Spon: Parents
Daniel of Tobias Bretney and wife, Ana, b. July 31, bapt. September 1, 1799 Spon: Parents
Henrich of Johanes Frener and wife, Susana, b. February 14, 1798, bapt. September 8, 1799 Spon: Parents
Johanes of Christian Bez and wife, Eva, b. July 19, bapt. September 21, 1799 Spon: Parents
Michel Hager of Johanes Wolf and wife, Anamaria, b. August 18, bapt. September 25, 1799 Spon: Parents
Susana of Daniel Klein and wife, Margretha, of August 17, bapt. September 26, 1799 Spon: Parents
Daniel of Friederich Arnold and wife, Barbara, b. September 25, bapt. November 3, 1799 Spon: Parents
Johenas Johanes of Johannes Schafer and wife, Anelika, b. September 15, 1799, bapt. November 18, 1799 Spon: Parents
Magdalena of Johanes Huet and wife, Elisabetha, b. December 8, 1798, bapt. November 19, 1799 Spon: Elisabetha Huet
David of Martin Rickenbach and wife, Ana, b. December 9, bapt. December 20, 1799 Spon: Parents

Reformed Church of Hagerstown

Johann Georg of Georg Confer and wife, Eva, b. October 18, bapt. December 25, 1799 Spon: Parents
Salamina of Bastian Hertel and wife, Catharina, b. March 24, bapt. December 25, 1799 Spon: Catharina Reisenger
Henrich of Conrad Cafferoth and wife, Magdalena, b. December 19, 1799, bapt. February 6, 1800 Spon: Parents
Jese of Zacharias Schuker and wife, Eva, b. December 18, 1799, bapt. February 11, 1800 Spon: Parents
Nancy of Johannes Hofman and wife, Susana, b. September 7, 1798, bapt. February 16, 1800 Spon: Parents
William Heyser of Joseph Reinolds and wife, Elisabetha, b. March 10, 1799, bapt. March 11, 1800 Spon: Ana Heyser
Lidia of Johannes Reb and wife, Elisabetha, b. October 20, 1799, bapt. April 13, 1800 Spon: Catharina Weis
Abraham of Nicolaus Hachen and wife, Dorethea, b. April 15, bapt. April 15, 1800 Spon: Parents
Elias of Jsim Scheimer and wife, Sarah, b. December 6, 1798, bapt. April 16, 1800 Spon: Ana Krebs
Samuel of Wilhelm Bauer and wife, Catharina Sophia, b. February 2, bapt. April 26, 1800 Spon: Barbara Drab
Joseph of Georg Reschey and wife, Christina, b. September 25, 1799, bapt. May 1, 1800 Spon: Parents
Samuel of Jacob Binckley and wife, Catharina, b. February 3, bapt. May 3, 1800 Spon: Parents
Anamaria of Henrich Renner and wife, Sophia, b. March 3, bapt. May 9, 1800 Spon: Parents
Jacob of Friederich Bez and wife, Ana Catharina, b. December --, 1799, bapt. June 1, 1800 Spon: Parents
Benjamin of Adam Oswald and wife, Maria, b. April 15, bapt. June 15, 1800 Spon: Henrich Zimmermann and wife Barbara
Samuel of Henrich Gnaedig and wife, Elisabetha, b. November 3, 1799, bapt. June 20, 1800 Spon: Parents
Elisabetha of Simeon Leckron and wife, Elisabetha, b. March 8, bapt. June 29, 1800 Spon: Parents
Henrich of Henrich Klapper and wife, Barbara, b. April 4, bapt. June 29, 1800 Spon: Parents
Nancy of Jacob B--zel and wife, Anna, b. November 10, 1799, bapt. June 30, 1800 Spon: Parents
Jacob of Peter Miller and wife, Nancy, b. May 22, 1797, bapt. July 20, 1800 Spon: Parents
Oliver of Peter Miller and wife, Nancy, b. November 18, 1798, bapt. July 20, 1800 Spon: Parents
Sarah of Jacob Reudenauer and wife, Susana Anamaria, b. March 27, bapt. August 2, 1800 Spon: Parents
Anamaria of Ludwig Eckhart and wife, Anna Elisabetha, b. October 25, 1799, bapt. August 2, 1800 Spon: Parents
Daniel of Henrich Middelkauf and wife, Barbara, b. May 14, bapt. August 24, 1800 Spon: Parents
Susana Malvina of Friederich Miller and wife, Catharina, b. May 29, Spon: Parents
Elisa of William Krebs and wife, Anna, b. July 18, bapt. September 21, 1800 Spon: Georg Krebs and wife Margretha
Georg of Matheias Schaffner and wife, Elisabetha, b. July 31, bapt. October 8, 1800 Spon: Parents

Reformed Church of Hagerstown

Jacob of Henrich Bergmann and wife, Catharina, b. July 9, bapt. October 19, 1800 Spon: Parents
Johanes of Johannes Dollinger and wife, Elisabetha, b. December 23, 1798, bapt. October 19, 1800 Spon: Carl August Monschuld and wife Eva
Abraham of Jonnes Frener and wife, Susana, b. March 8, bapt. October 20, 1800 Spon: Abraham Bauer and wife Eva
Catharina of Philip Krieger and wife, Barbara, b. April 20, bapt. October 29, 1800 Spon: Parents
Henrich of Georg Klein and wife, Elisabetha, b. October 14, bapt. October 30, 1800 Spon: Henrich Wohlfort
Eva of Robert Higins of wife, Catharina, b. February 8, 1798, bapt. October 8, 1800 Spon: Parents
Elisabetha of Christian Vogeler and wife, Susana, b. November 20, 1799, bapt. November 30, 1800 Spon: Parents
Salomon of Michael Confer and wife, Hanna, b. October 22, bapt. November 30, 1800 Spon: Parents
Sophia of Abraham Koenig and wife, Magdalena, b. October 24, bapt. November 30, 1800 Spon: Jacob Koenig and wife Elisabetha
Anamaria of Christian Arzt and wife, Catharina, b. August 31, 1799, bapt. December 10, 1800 Spon: Parents
William of William Has and wife, Elisabetha, b. August 27, bapt. December 21, 1800 Spon: Parents
William of Georg Getty and wife, Catharina, b. September 13, 1800, bapt. January 1, 1801 Spon: Parents
Johan Heinrich of Jacob Stamm and wife, Maria Magdalena, b. December 7, 1800, bapt. January 10, 1801 Spon: Mother
Sarah of Phillip Keller and wife, Barbara, b. November 21, 1799, bapt. January 18, 1801 Spon: William Hes and wife Magdalena
Maria Magdalena of Weizel -- Johanes Weisel and wife, Eva, b. December 18, 1800, bapt. January 18, 1801 Spon: William Hes and wife Magdalena
Wilhelm of Johanes Hofman and wife, Susana, b. November 8, 1800, bapt. January 18, 1801 Spon: Thomas Schley and wife Catharina
Catharina of Jacob Feger and wife, Magdalena, b. January 7, bapt. February 2, 1801 Spon: Parents
Johanes of Peter Wild and wife, Catharina, b. November 30, 1800, bapt. February 15, 1801 Spon: Parents
Jacob of Johan Peter Herr and wife, Susana, b. January 17, 1801, bapt. February 22, 1801 Spon: Parents
Daniel of Henrich Gerhart and wife, Magdalena, b. November 17, 1800, bapt. March 25, 1801 Spon: Daniel Reinoll
Salomon of Tobias Bretneg and wife, Anna, b. January 4, bapt. February 26, 1801 Spon: Parents
Petrus of Jacob Rensch and wife, Margretha, b. December 31, 1800, bapt. March 9, 1801 Spon: Parents
Catharina of Georg Dunn and wife, Susana, b. ----, bapt. March 9, 1801 Spon: Margretha Rensch
Georg of Felix Reck and wife, Annamaria, b. November 3, 1800, bapt. March 27, 1801 Spon: Georg Beck and wife Catharina
Georg of Henrich Bernhard and wife, Catharina, b. October 2, 1800, bapt. March 27, 1801 Spon: Felix Beck and wife Anamaria
Daniel of Johanes Schup and wife, Elisabetha, b. August 2, 1800, bapt. April 13, 1801 Spon: Parents
Elisabetha of Abraham Walter and wife, Elisabetha, b. December 21, 1800, bapt. April 18, 1801 Spon: Abraham Becker

Reformed Church of Hagerstown

Elisabetha of William Belsch and wife, Elisabetha, b. April 20, 1801, bapt. April 24, 1801 Spon: John Kerschner, Sr.
Benjamin of David Guschwa and wife, Catharina, b. April 12, bapt. April 28, 1801 Spon: Parents
Elisabetha of Johanes Brandstaeter and wife, Margretha, b. November 29, 1800, bapt. May 2, 1801 Spon: Margretha Keiper
Julialia of Johan Gnaedig and wife, Margretha, b. October 20, 1800, bapt. May 2, 1801 Spon: Maria Reight
William Fransis of John Finley and wife, Margretha, b. March 18, 1799, bapt. May 6, 1801 Spon: Parents
Samuel Johanes of John Finley and wife, Margretha, b. August 19, 1800, bapt. May 6, 1801 Spon: Parents
Johan Jacob of Jacob Kuhn and wife, Elisabetha, b. April 26, 1799, bapt. May 14, 1801 Spon: Parents
Milial of Jacob Kuhn and wife, Elisabetha, b. February 21, bapt. May 14, 1801 Spon: Reinhard Domer and wife Anamaria
Eli of William Warner and wife, Elisabetha, b. September 10, 1799, bapt. May 21, 1801 Spon: Georg Krebs and wife Margretha
Elisabetha of Jacob Bracunier and wife, Elisabetha, b. June 10, 1800, bapt. May 24, 1801 Spon: David Bracunerier and wife Catharina
Josia of Elias Kerschner and Catharina Wachtel, illegitimate, b. February 5, bapt. May 25, 1801 Spon: Mother
Elisabetha of Daniel Schneider and wife, Sibila, b. February 26, bapt. June 1, 1801 Spon: Elisabetha Urban
Elisabetha of Jacob Nicol and wife, Susanna, b. December 7, 1800, bapt. May 31, 1801 Spon: Elisabetha Nicol
Nathan of David Littel and wife, Elisabetha, b. April 9, bapt. June 13, 1801 Spon: Parents
William of Daniel Riblet and wife, Christian, b. February 8, bapt. July 1, 1801 Spon: Parents
Samuel of William Jansen and wife, Magdalena, b. June 7, bapt. July 1801 Spon: Samuel Jansen
Anamaria of Georg Beck and wife, Catharina, b. April 3, bapt. August 1, 1801 Spon: Parents
Anamaria of Henrich Schneider and wife, Anamaria, b. March 9, bapt. August 3, 1801 Spon: Georg Krebs and wife Margretha
Sarah of Henrich Klein and wife, Magdalena, b. November 9, 1800, bapt. August 8, 1801 Spon: Catharina Grissenger
Johan Abraham of Samuel Eberts and wife, Anamaria, b. July 10, bapt. August 22, 1801 Spon: Parents
Sophia of Carl Ohlwein and wife, Elisabetha, b. July 15, bapt. August 30, 1801 Spon: Parents
Samuel of Daniel Bracunier and wife, Barbara, b. April 5, bapt. August 30, 1801 Spon: Parents
Christian of Jacob Miller and wife, Elisabetha, b. July 1, bapt. August 30, 1801 Spon: Parents
Catharina of Johanes Conrad and wife, Sarah, b. August 11, bapt. September 6, 1801 Spon: Henrich Gieser and wife Margretha
Rebecca b. January 19, 1800, bapt. October 18, 1801 of Georg Han and wife, Margretha Spon: Susana Lambert
Samuel b. June 7, 1799, bapt. October 22, 1801 of Samuel Gray and wife, Catharina Spon: Peter Reinoll
Georg b. June 7, 1800, bapt. October 22, 1801 of Samuel Gray and wife, Catharina Spon: Daniel Reinoll

Reformed Church of Hagerstown

Joseph b. August 3, 1800, bapt. November 6, 1801 of Henrich Deis and wife Susanna Spon: Parents
Margretha b. December 16, 1800, bapt. November 9, 1801 of Friederich Koehler and wife, Magdalena Spon: Eberhart Ringer and wife Juliana
Othia Holland Stull b. September 29, 1800, bapt. November 4, 1801 of Peter Miller and wife, Nancy Spon: Susana Miller
Johan Peter b. January 31, 1798, bapt. May 6, 1802 of Johanes Wolfensperger and wife Susana Spon: Parents
Elisabetha b. February 16, 1800, bapt. May 6, 1802 of Johanes Wolfensperger and wife, Susana Spon: Parents
Jenet b. January 13, 1800, bapt. August 12, 1802 of Samuel Ros and wife, Catharina Spon: Parents
Christian b. February 1, 1800, bapt. November 6, 1802 of Christian Aryt and wife, Catharina Spon: Parents
Johan Georg b. April 12, 1800, bapt. November 6, 1802 of Henrich Han and wife, Christina Spon: Father
Elisabetha b. December 20, 1784, bapt. April 25, 1801 of Georg Dun and wife, Susana
Catharina b. March 7, 1800, bapt. December 10, 1802 of Henrich Han and wife, Maria Amweg Spon: Parents
Salamina b. December 6, 1795, bapt. February 4, 1803 of Johannes Goll and wife Catharina Spon: Parents
Susana b. April 16, 1798, bapt. February 4, 1803 of Johannes Goll and wife Catharina Spon: Parents
Elisabetha b. May 3, 1800, bapt. February 4, 1803 of Christian Wagener and wife, Catharina Spon: Parents
Jacob b. August 15, 1797, bapt. October 23, 1803 of Samuel Kromer and wife, Maria Spon: Jacob Leider
Scharlotta b. September 4, 1795, bapt. April 16, 1804 of Johannes Gruber and wife, Catharina Spon: Parents
Rebecca b. December 28, 1796, bapt. April 16, 1804 of Johannes Gruber and wife, Catharina Spon: Parents
Keresia b. July 17, 1799, bapt. April 16, 1804 of Johannes Gruber and wife, Catharina Spon: Parents
Elisabetha b. March 27, 1795, bapt. June 21, 1805 of Mattheas Klapper and wife, Annamaria Spon: Parents
Annamaria b. September 1, 1798, bapt. June 21, 1805 of Matthea Klapper and wife, Annamaria Spon: Parents
Elisabetha b. September 9, 1800, bapt. August 8, 1805 of Johan Kerschner and wife, Magdalena Spon: Parents
Jonathan Hager b. October 22, 1800, bapt. August 21, 1805 of Joseph Brunner and wife, Elisabetha Spon: Elisabetha Lowrens
Hanna b. July 27, 1798, bapt. December 31, 1805 of Henrich Dillman and wife Catharina Spon: Parents
Andreas b. August 8, 1799, bapt. March 21, 1806 of Daniel Rensch and wife, Elisabetha Spon: Parents
Eleischa b. June 1, 1800, bapt. March 21, 1806 of Daniel Miller and wife, Catharina Spon: Parents
Elisabetha b. December 29, 1799, bapt. March 21, 1806 of Henrich Brumbach and wife, Margretha Spon: Parents
Elisabetha b. August 12, 1800, bapt. March 23, 1806 of Mattheas Berenger and wife Magdalena Spon: Parents
Petrus b. February 22, 1800, bapt. June 15, 1807 of Henrich Schoenfeld and wife, Susan Spon: Parents
Mary b. July 6, 1800, bapt. June 23, 1807 of Johannes Long and wife, Elisabetha Spon: Father

Zion Lutheran Church, Williamsport

Anna Maria of John Schupp and wife Catherine (nee Brachlerlen) b. April 19, 1791, bapt. May 15, 1791 Godparents: Jacob South and wife Christina
John George of Richard Lichtweiler and wife Ada (nee Lichtweiler) b. April 11, 1791, bapt. May 15, 1791 Godparents: Richard Zeitenaues and wife Catherine
Ludwig of Christian Entwenger and wife Margaretha (nee Zolleerird) b. April 19, 1791, bapt. May 15, 1791 Godparents: Ludwig Entwenger and wife Anna Eva
Anna of Richard Davis and wife Catherine b. February 14, 1790 Godparents: were the parents themselves
John Peter of George Lichtweiler and wife Catherine b. July 25, 1791, bapt. August 7, 1791 Godparents: John Peter Sampsel and wife Catherine
John of John George Frey and wife Juliana b. June 13, 1791, bapt. August 7, 1791 Godparents: John Miller and wife Anna Maria
John of Martin Justes and wife Maria b. March 10, 1791, bapt. August 7, 1791 Godfather: Mr. Bauer
John Jacob of Matthias Behley and wife Juliana (nee Gittingarin) b. January 25, 1792, bapt. April 22, 1792 Godparents: John George Gittinger and wife Elizabeth
John of John Engelhart and wife Magdalena (nee Bauschlagin) b. February 8, 1791 Godfather: John Bauschlag
Mary Ann Elizabeth of John Henry Bingen and wife Mary Shearer b. March 16, 1791, bapt. April 1, 1792 Godparents: Parents
John of David Zoller and wife Catherine (nee Hublen) b. February 11, 1791, bapt. March 18, 1792 Godparents: Peter Hoh and wife Catherine
Mary Magdalene of Ludwig Entwenger and wife Ella (nee Hauserin) b. April 1792, bapt. June 17, 1792 Godparents: Christian Entwenger and wife Margaretha
George of David Thomas and wife Susanna b. March 19, 1792, bapt. September 30, 1792 Witness: George Schindel
Maria Magdalena of John Schugg and wife Catherine b. September 20, 1792, bapt. October 21, 1792 Witnesses: Hyind Dellinger and his wife
Barbara of Richard Davis and wife Catherine b. October 7, 1792, bapt. March 17, 1793 Witnesses: Jacob Ard and wife
Joseph Peter of John Gast and wife Maria Barbara b. November 11, 1792, bapt. March 17, 17?? Witnesses: Anton Hurd and wife Catherine
Elizabeth of John Thor and wife Margaretha b. July 2, 1793, bapt. August 4, 1793 Witnesses: John Kugel and wife Catherine
William of George Miller and Catherine b. September 19, 1793, bapt. October 14, 1793 Godparents: Fortfardt Hann and Magdalena
George of George Ekerts and wife Evah b. July 1, 1793, bapt. October 14, 1793 Witnesses: Parents
John Peter of John Engelhardt and wife Magdalena b. October 3, 1793, bapt. November 18, 1793 Godfather: John Peter Klein
Elizabeth of Henry Fyster and wife Catherine bapt. April 21, 1794 Godparents: George Gittingen and wife
Anna Maria of Christian Entsminger and wife Eva Margaretha b. April 21, 1793, bapt. April 21, 1794 Godparents: Jacob Entsminger and wife Anna
Jacob of Jacob Miller and wife Christina b. February 15, 1794, bapt. May 2, 1794 Witnesses: John Story and wife Catherine
Catherine of John Wetzel and wife Barbara b. March 26, 1794 Witnesses: Peter Sensel and wife Catherine
John George of Michael Maurer and wife Catherine b. February 27, 1794 Witnesses: John George Gittinger and wife Elizabeth
Anna Maria of David Zeller and wife Catherine b. July 8, 1794, bapt. August 24, 1794 Godparents: Christian Ensminger and wife Eva Margaretha

Zion Lutheran Church, Williamsport

Elizabeth of John Hauer and wife Catherine b. June 12, 1794, bapt. September 22, 1794 Godparents: Elizabeth Hauer
Daniel of John Baushlag and wife Catherine b. July 25, 1794, bapt. September 29, 1794 Godparents: His parents
Lena of Nicolaus Reydenauer and wife Catherine b. November 19, 1793, bapt. November 16, 1794 Godparents: Mathias Reydenauer and wife Magdalena
Jacob of Jacob Loy and wife Anna Barbara b. December 18, 1794[sic], bapt. November 16, 1794[sic] Godfather: Jacob Schack
Cath. daughter of George Fey and wife Magaretha b. December 19, 1794[sic], bapt. November 16, 1794[sic] Godparents: Peter Heck and wife Catherine
Magdalena of John Kugel and wife Catherine b. December 28, 1794, bapt. January 11, 1795 Godparents: Peter Heck and wife Catherine
Daniel of George Michael Householder and wife Susanna b. November 28, 1794, bapt. February 8, 1795 Godparents: Benjamin Schwengel and wife Eva
Elizabeth of William Hebler and wife Christina b. January 17, 1795, bapt. February 8, 1795 Godmother: Christina Martin
Joseph of Henry Zeller and wife Catherine b. July 25, 1794, bapt. February 17, 1795 Godparents: His own parents
Elizabeth Magdalena of Philip Klein and wife Anna Maria b. October 15, 1794, bapt. March 8, 1795 Godparents: Valentine Marden and wife Susanna
Son of Conrad Speiglar and wife Christina b. January 8, 1794, bapt. April 4, 1795 Godparents: John Heck and wife Elizabeth
George of Daniel Meister and wife Catherine b. January 30, 1795, bapt. April 4, 1795 Godparents: His Parents
Jacob of Michael Foutz and wife b. November 1794, bapt. April 24, 1795 Godparents: Peter Foutz and wife
Kezia daughter of Richard Davis and wife b. December 27, 1794, bapt. April 24, 1795 Godmother: Barbara Scheid
Samuel of Roger Barnes and wife Betzy b. January 11, 1795, bapt. April 1795 Godparents: Parents
Elias of Henry Maundy and wife Annie b. January 5, 1794, bapt. May 3, 1795 Godfather: Jacob Hager
Samuel of Philip Ammaman and wife Mary b. January 17, 1795, bapt. June 7, 1795 Godparents: Parents
Susana of Herman Hornbecker and wife Elena b. May 17, 1794, bapt. June 17, 1795 Godparents: Parents
Anna Maria of George Klein and wife Anna Maria b. January 17, 1795, bapt. June 7, 1795 Godmother: Anna Margaret Rehnir
Maria Eva of Ludwig Ensminger and wife Eva b. June 8, 1794, bapt. June 7, 1795 Godparents: Peter Foutz and wife Anna Maria
John Michael of Michael Beyroth and wife Margaret b. December 17, 1794, bapt. June 7, 1795 Godparents: George Klein and wife Anna Maria
Catherine of Lantz Heutzel and wife Barbara b. July 18, 1795[sic], bapt. June 26, 1795[sic] Godparents: John Kugel and wife Catherine
Susana of John Derr and wife Margaret b. April 23, 1795, bapt. September 6, 1795 Godparents: Parents
John of Henry Seister and wife Catherine b. December 5, 1795, bapt. December 10, 1795 Godparents: Parents
Catherine of John Hurd and wife Susan b. October 13, 1795, bapt. December 26, 1795 Godmother: Catherine Deris
Anmaria of John Engelhard and wife Mary b. November 3, 1795, bapt. December 26, 1795 Godmother: Anna Maria Kleinin
Elizabeth of George Miller and wife Catherine b. October 12, 1795, bapt. December 26, 1795 Godparents: Christian Ardinger and wife Ana Maria

Zion Lutheran Church, Williamsport

Lydia of Matheus Reydenauer and wife Ana Maria b. November 23, 1795, bapt. January 13, 1796 Godparents: Valentine Marten, wife Susana
John of Nicolaus Becker and wife Salome b. December 15, 1795, bapt. March 6, 1796 Godparents: Parents
Elizabeth of Ludwig Deliner and wife Anna Maria b. February 7, 1796, bapt. April 9, 1796 Godparents: Parents
Anna Maria of George Kittinger and wife Elizabeth b. December 5, 1795, bapt. December 14, 1795 Witness: Barbara Wethmauer
John of Jacob Zuck and wife Elizabeth b. February 2, 1790, bapt. May 1, 1796 Witnesses: Valentine Marten and wife
David of Mathias Konig and wife Elizabeth b. March 2, 1796, bapt. May 1, 1796 Witnesses: Peter Heck and wife Catherine
Elizabeth of John Nizel and wife Barbara b. March 25, 1796, bapt. May 1, 1796 Witnesses: Conrad Oster and wife Eva
John of George Fermer and wife Christina b. April 2, 1796, bapt. May 1, 1796 Witnesses: Jacob Jungber and wife Maria
Elizabeth of Peter Huck and wife Barbara b. February 6, 1796, bapt. May 1, 1796 Witnesses: Henry Zeller and wife Catherine
Anna Maria of John Hauer and wife Catherine b. February 20, 1796, bapt. May 1, 1796 Witnesses: Ludwig Ensminger and wife Eva
Henry of John M. Prinz and wife Catherine b. February 4, 1796, bapt. June 12, 1796 Witnesses: Henry Schilkomp and wife Eva
Catherine of Fred Drosmer and wife Catherine b. February 22, 1796, bapt. June 12, 1796 Witnesses: Parents
[Twins], Jacob and John of George Lingscreiber and wife Elizabeth b. April 8, 1796, bapt. April 24, 1796 Witnesses: Peter Sensel and wife Catherine
William of Valentine Marder and wife Sus. b. June 29, 1796, bapt. July 10, 1796 Witnesses: Parents
Jacob of John George Klein and wife Anna Maria b. March 13, 1796, bapt. July 10, 1796 Witnesses: Jacob Ensminger
Sara of George Oin and wife Susana b. August 25, 1796, bapt. September 4, 1796 Witnesses: Parents
David of John Banschlag and wife Catherine b. June 22, 1796, bapt. September 4, 1796 Witnesses: Philip Sprecher and wife Magdalena
Anna Maria of Michael Basel and wife Dorrothea b. July 15, 1796, bapt. September 4, 1796 Witnesses: Michael Fouz and wife A. Maria
John George of Jacob Ley and wife Barbara b. October 7, 1796, bapt. February 19, 1797 Witnesses: John Kugel and wife Catherine
Maria of Jacob Boyer and wife Elizabeth b. January 22, 1797, bapt. February 19, 1797 Witnesses: Parents
Susana of Daniel Bauman and wife Susana Margaretha b. September 2, 1796, bapt. November 27, 1796 Witnesses: Parents
Maria of Peter Sensel and wife Catherine b. September 11, 1796, bapt. October 2, 1796 Witnesses: Matheus Reidenauer and wife A. Maria
Ana Maria of John Koss and wife Maria Barbara b. January 3, 1797, bapt. March 19, 1797 Witnesses: Parents
A. Maria of Lorenz Heuzel and wife Barbara b. January 6, 1797, bapt. March 19, 1797 Witnesses: John Kugel and wife Catherine
Jacob of Henry Philipi and wife A. Maria b. September 15, 1796, bapt. April 17, 1797 Witnesses: Parents
Othi of William Phen and wife Athe b. August 24, 1796, bapt. April 17, 1797 Witnesses: Henry Philip and wife A. Maria
Maria Elizabeth of George Kittinger and wife Elizabeth b. May 10, 1797, bapt. May 14, 1797 Witnesses: George Kershner and wife Maria

Zion Lutheran Church, Williamsport

Mary Elizabeth of George Maudi and wife Catherine b. April 3, 1797, bapt. May 14, 1797 Witnesses: Valentine Marder and wife Susana
George of John Haushalter and wife Hanna b. January 21, 1797, bapt. May 14, 1797 Witnesses: George Fry and wife Catherine
Sara of Daniel Weisel and wife Margaretha b. March 10, 1797, bapt. May 14, 1797 Witness: Juliana Startzman
Anna of Henry Zell and wife Maria Catherine b. February 25, 1797, bapt. May 14, 1797 Witnesses: Christian Ensminger and wife Catherine
Eva Dorothea of Michael Foutz and wife Dally b. April 24, 1797, bapt. May 8, 1797 Witnesses: Peter Foutz and wife A. Maria
Margaretha of Peter Ekeberger and wife Maria b. November 26, 1796, bapt. June 5, 1797 Witnesses: Michel Maurer and wife Catherine
William of Adam Schreider and wife Dolly b. October 9, 1796, bapt. June 5, 1797 Witnesses: Thomas Meking and wife Susana
Andenas of John Bauman and wife Catherine b. May 16, 1797, bapt. August 6, 1797 Witnesses: Parents
Catherine of John Skeyls and wife Christina b. January 1, 1797, bapt. August 4, 1797 Witnesses: John Kugel and wife Catherine
John George of Martin Zeller and wife Anna b. April 16, 1797, bapt. August 4, 1797 Witnesses: Christina Zeller
Brudius daughter of Henry Maudi and wife Anna Cugel b. July 1, 1797, bapt. September 3, 1797 Witnesses: George Miller and wife Catherine
Elizabeth of Michel Besel and wife Dorrothea b. December 25, 1797, bapt. February 18, 1798 Witnesses: Peter Foutz and wife Anna Maria
Catherine of Emanuel Pfeifer and wife Barbara b. September 23, 1797, bapt. February 18, 1798 Witnesses: George Miller and wife Catherine
Jacob of Nicolaus Bekar and wife Salome b. November 12, 1797, bapt. December 28, 1797 Witnesses: Parents
Anna Maria of John Haunet and wife Catherine b. October 4, 1797, bapt. April 6, 1898 Witnesses: Anna Maria Maudy
Peter of Peter Seenzel and wife Catherine b. March 31, 1798, bapt. May 27, 1798 Witnesses: John Nizel and wife Barbara
Frederick of George Linxweiler and wife Catherine b. April 20, 1798, bapt. May 27, 1798 Witnesses: Peter Foutz and wife Maria
Solomon of Solomon Tyle and wife Christina b. February 7, 1798, bapt. May 27, 1798 Witnesses: James Schlecter
Joseph of Jacob Hauk and wife Christina b. April 27, 1798, bapt. July 7, 1798 Witnesses: Parents
Valentine of Frederick Kau and wife Elizabeth b. January 26, 1798, bapt. July 7, 1798 Witnesses: George Reiss and wife Barbara
Eva of Martin Schafer and wife Catherine b. July 30, 1798, bapt. September 31, 1798 Witnesses: Henry Sclulknecht and wife Eva
John of Michel Bizer and wife Maria b. May 1, 1798, bapt. September 31, 1798 Witnesses: John Scheser and wife Fibia
Elizabeth of Jacob Boyer and wife Elizabeth b. August 28, 1798, bapt. September 31, 1798 Witnesses: Parents
Peter of Peter Lesher and wife Elizabeth b. April 30, 1798, bapt. September 31, 1798 Witnesses: Andros Kieseker and wife A. Maria
Elizabeth of Jacob Paulus and wife Elizabeth b. December 26, 1798, bapt. January 20, 1799 Witnesses: Valentine Marder and wife Susana
Rosina of Martin Maudi and wife Rosina b. October 28, 1798, bapt. January 20, 1799 Witnesses: Parents
Henry of John Bouman and wife Catherine b. December 20 or 27, 1798, bapt. January 20, 1799 Witnesses: Parents

Zion Lutheran Church, Williamsport

John of David Thomas and wife Susana b. November 10, 1798, bapt. January 20, 1799 Witnesses: John Schussell and wife Savina
Maria of Adam Haushalter and wife Catherine b. December 20, 1798, bapt. February 17, 1799 Witness: Catherine Davis
Jacob of John Engelhard and wife Magdalene b. November 29, 1798, bapt. March 17, 1799 Witnesses: Nicolaus Beker and wife Salome
David of George Maudi and wife Margaretha b. February 7, 1799, bapt. April 4, 1799 Witnesses: Christian Ensminger and wife Catherine
Sara of David Zeller and wife Catherine b. October 30, 1798[sic], bapt. April 14, 1798[sic] Witnesses: George Albert and wife Catherine
William of John Geissinger and wife Susana b. December 31, 1798, bapt. April 14, 1799 Witnesses: George Maudi and wife Margaretha
John of Jacob Loy and wife Barbara b. February 29, 1799, bapt. May 13, 1799 Witnesses: Christian Diel and wife Maria
Sally of John Haushalter and wife Hanna b. January 3, 1799, bapt. May 13, 1799 Witnesses: Andreas Tys and wife Catherine
Mary Susana of Peter Schus and wife Barbara b. January 11, 1799, bapt. May 13, 1799 Witnesses: John Hurd and wife Susana
John of Jonas Skeals and wife Christina b. February 16, 1799, bapt. May 13, 1799 Witnesses: John Kugel and wife Catherine
Maria of Michael Maurer and wife Catherine b. April 18, 1799, bapt. May 13, 1799 Witnesses: Henry Reitenauer and wife Eva
Adam of John Kugel and wife Catherine b. May 13, 1799, bapt. June 9, 1799 Witnesses: John Kugel and wife Catherine
Magdalena of Philip Sprecher and wife Magdalena b. January 17, 1799, bapt. June 9, 1799 Witnesses: Parents
John of John Kro and wife Susana b. March 29, 1799, bapt. June 9, 1799 Witnesses: Jacob Stek and wife Peggy
Sarah of Theodore Milts and wife Catherine b. February 19, 1798, bapt. June 9, 1799 Witness: Catherine Kro
Daniel of Daniel Bauman and wife Susana b. March 11, 1799, bapt. July 7, 1799 Witnesses: Parents
Daniel of Nicolaus Reitenauer and wife Catherine b. March 24, 1799, bapt. July 7, 1799 Witnesses: Parents
Jacob of Martin Zeller and wife Anna b. February 13, 1799, bapt. July 7, 1799 Witnesses: Parents
Daughter of William Siegman and wife Catherine b. July 26, 1799, bapt. August 4, 1799 Witnesses: Benjamin Schlauger and wife Eva
Sara of James Sleter and wife Maria b. May 24, 1799, bapt. September 1, 1799 Witnesses: Parents
Solomon of Nicolaus Beker and wife Salome b. August 26, 1799, bapt. September 27, 1799 Witnesses: Parents
Orth of James Walles and wife Susana b. August 6, 1799, bapt. December 22, 1799 Witnesses: Wilhelm Stek
Peter of Jacob Stek and wife Margaretha b. November 4, 1799, bapt. December 22, 1799 Witnesses: Peter Sentzel and wife Catherine
Michael of Michael Foutz and wife Catherine bapt. December 22 1799 Witnesses: Parents
Daughter Christina of George Linxweiler and wife Catherine b. January 25, 1800, bapt. March 16, 1800 Witnesses: Christian Erdinger and wife A. Maria
Dorothea of Michael Haushalter and wife Susana b. January 11, 1800, bapt. March 16, 1800 Witnesses: Philip Kieseker and wife Dorothea
A. Maria of Daniel Weisel and wife A. Margaret b. December 6, 1799, bapt. March 16, 1800 Witness: Eva Startzman

Zion Lutheran Church, Williamsport

Nanzi of Wilhelm Stek and wife Ester b. March 29, 1800, bapt. May 11, 1800 Witnesses Jacob Boyer and wife
Magdalena of John Nizel and wife Barbara b. April 30, 1800, bapt. July 6, 1800 Witnesses: Jacob Boyer and wife Elizabeth
Peter Sentzel, wife Catherine (Rest of entry is illegible)
Jacob of Christian Seussmuer and wife Catherine bapt. August 3, 1800 Witnesses: Jacob Baulus and wife Elizabetha
Jacob of Jacob Boyer and wife Elizabeth b. August 6, 1800, bapt. August 31, 1800 Witnesses: Parents
M. Catherine of Philip Sprecher and wife Magdalena b. May 21, 1800, bapt. August 31, 1800 Witnesses: Abras Hebling and wife M. Catherine
Elias of Henry Maudy and wife Hanipe b. February 13, 1800, bapt. August 31, 1800 Witnesses: Parents
Catherine of John Hauerd and wife Catherine b. June 23, 1800, bapt. September 28, 1800 Witness: Catherine Schmidt
Samuel of Jacob Baulus and wife Elizabeth b. February 12, 1801, bapt. March 15, 1801 Witnesses: Parents
Catherine of Michael Maurer and wife Catherine b. February 12, 1801, bapt. March 15, 1801 Witnesses: Philippina Reitenauer
Elizabeth of Casper Maudy and wife Catherine b. January 16, 1801, bapt. March 15, 1801 Witnesses: George Miller and wife Catherine
Philip of George Kittinger and wife Elizabeth b. March 24, 1801, bapt. April 12, 1801 Witnesses: Philip Schwengel and wife
Elizabeth of Christian Diel and wife A. Maria b. February 7, 1801, bapt. March 12, 1801 Witnesses: Jacob Hirsh and wife Fronia

INDEX

The use of N. indicates that the name was not known. Note that the feminine endings, -in and -n, were frequently used in the church registers. These endings are omitted in the compilation of the index except when doubt exists as to the correct surname.

In this index various spellings of the same family name have been grouped together and cross referenced. Christian names are generally listed with a preferred spelling with other spellings in parentheses. In searching for names consider a wide range of possible spellings, remembering that the following letters were often used interchangeably: B and P; C, G and K; D and T; F and V; and, J and Y. Note that the same name may appear more than once on the same page. CHECK THE ENTIRE PAGE.

INDEX

--- Jacob 95
--- Johanes 93
--- Michael 75
--- Simsen 93
--- Susana 81
-ITSCH Elisabetha 100; Maria 100; Matheas 100
-RAB Catharina 102; Jacob 102
ABOLD Bally 19; George Nic. 19; Maria 19
ACKER Caspar 69, 73; Susana 69
ADAM Dorothea 49; Georg 49; Henrich 92; Susana 92
ADAMS Fanny 26
AECKRET Henrich 80
AGUSTIN (See Augenstein, Augustin) Cath. 17; Elisabeth 17; Philip 17
ALBERT Catherine 111; George 111
ALBREITH Cath. 30
ALLBRECHT Anna Maria 61; Ester 61; Peter 61
ALLENDER Richan 27
ALT Adam 19, 43, 102; Bally 19; Christina 94, 98, 102; Elisabetha 43, 94; Henrich 94, 98, 102; Magdalina 19, 43
ALTER Ann Mary 2; Catha. 71; Christine Margareth 3; Christofel 71; Christoph 2, 3, 5, 6, 7, 14, 19; Daniel 8; Elisabeth (Eliz.) 1, 26; Eva 5; Fenrich 7, 8; Frederic (Friderich, Friederich, etc.) 1, 3, 5, 11, 15, 19, 21, 89; George 6; Gustav 2; Johanna 2, 5; Magdalene (Magd.) 3, 28; Margaretha (Marg., Margareth, Margarethe) 1, 2, 3, 5, 7, 11, 15; Maria Marg. 19, 21; Maria Sara 5; Rebecca 26; Samuel 7; Sarah 30; Stophel 21; Susanna 2, 3, 6, 7, 14, 19, 21, 71
ALTVATER Anna Maria 34; Fridrich 34; Magthalena 34
AMEN Polly L. 27
AMMAMAN Mary 108; Philip 108; Samuel 108
ANDERSON (See Enderson) Barb. 27; Elisabeth 22; Johannes 22
ANGENA (See Angene, Angenei/Angeni/ Angeny, Angenor) Anna Margreth 41; Christian 33; Elisabetha 33; Georg 33; Johannes 41; Margretha 37; Maria 37; Theobald (Theobalt) 34, 37
ANGENE (See Angena, Angenei/Angeni/ Angeny, Angenor) Anna Catharine 51; Catharina 52; Christina 58; Dewalt 57; Elizabeth 52, 57; George 52, 53; Henry 53, 56, 57, 59; Jacob 56; John 51, 52, 55, 57, 58; Magdalena 51, 52, 55, 57, 58; Margaret 59; Susanna 53, 56, 57, 59
ANGENEI/ANGENI/ANGENY (See Angena, Angeni, Angenor) Anna Maria 59; Catharina 52, 55, 56, 59; George 52, 55, 56, 59; Henry 51, 59; Jacob 55; John 53; Susanna 51, 59
ANGENOR (See Angena, Angeni, Angenei/Angeni/Angeny) Elisabetha 34; Theobald 34
ANGLE Cath. 27; Mary 27
ANGNE/ANGNEA/ANGNES Catharina 54; George 54; Henry 54; John 54; John George 54; Magdalena 41, 54; Susanna 54
ANNAWOLL/ANNEWALD Cath. 13; Johannes 13, 88; Susana 13, 88
ANSELT Anna Maria 31; Henrich 31; Johannes 31
ANTBEBBROZGEZ Susy 27
APP Hanna 79; Niclos 79
ARBAN Jacob 12
ARD Jacob 107
ARDINGER Anna Maria 108; Christian 108
ARMESCHARY Matheias 95
ARNOLD/ARNOLT Adam 11, 49; Anna 11, 49; Annamaria 60; Bally 22; Barbara 99, 102; Bridrich 66; Catharine (Cathrina) 49, 66, 70, 75; Christopher 60; Daniel 75, 102; Elisabeth 22; Friederich 99, 102; George 49, 70, 75; Henrich (Henry) 22, 23, 28; John 49; Johannes 70; John Georg 49; Louisa 60; Maria 49; Polly 23; Sara 23, 99; Susana 28
ARTZ/ARZ A. Maria 23; Anna Maria (Anamaria) 12, 104; Catharina 98, 100, 104; Christian 100, 104; David 12; Joseph 100; Maria 12, 13, 18; Peter 12, 13, 18, 23; Sara 13; Sofia 18
ARYT Catharina 106; Christian 106
AUERBACH Adam 85; Maria Barbera 85
AUGENSTEIN (See Agustin, Augustin) Andreas 62; Daniel 62; Margareda 62
AUGUSTIN (See Agustin, Augenstein) Elisabeth 44; George 44; Hannes 44; John 44
AULENBACH Adam 68, 74, 78; Anna Barbara 74, 78; Anna Cath. 78; Barbara 68; Elisabetha 68

INDEX

AX Elis. 26

B--ZEL Anna 103; Jacob 103; Nancy 103
BACH (See Back) Andreas 74; Catha. 69; Lonhart 69; Margretha 74
BACK (See Bach) Janad 78; Samuel 78
BACKER Christian 27
BADORG Andrew 51; Elizabeth 51
BAECKER/BAEGER (See Baker) Anna 90; Gabriel 31; Jacob 90; Maria Catharina 31
BAER (See Baur, Bauer, Ber)
BAILEY (See Behly)
BAKER (See Baecker/Baeger) Manrall 26; Maurice 64; Michael 26
BALD Georg 88; Maria Barbera 88
BALMER (See Palmer) Peter 46; Sophia 46
BALT Barbera 84; Georg 84
BALZEL Anna 99; Jacob 99; Margretha 99
BANART (BAUART?) Anna Maria 4; Margaretha 4; Michael 4
BAND Gottfried 40; Margretha 40
BANSCHLAG Catherine 109; David 109; John 109
BAR Cath. 29; Hennerich 16; Marg. 16; Martin 16
BARCKDALL (See Barkdull, Berckdoll, Bergdoll) Peter 29
BARD A. Maria 17; Anamaria 99; Andreas 99; Cath. 17; Elisabeth 17; Georg 17; Johannes 17; Maria 17; Michael 17; Sally 17; Sus. 17; Zacharias 17
BARKDULL (See Barckdall, Berckdoll, Bergdoll) Cath. 27
BARNER Anna Maria 40; Gertraut 40; Ludwig 40
BARNES Betzy 108; Roger 108; Samuel 108
BARON Catharina 33, 36; Joh. Adam 36; Niclos 33, 36
BARRIT --- 36
BARTUN Jacob 78
BASEL Anna Maria 109; Dorrothea 12, 109; Michael 12, 109
BATARF Henrich 35
BATORFF Georg 39; Maria Barbara 39; Martin 39
BATZ (See Bautz, Botz) Andreas 45, 65; Andrew 44; Catharine 44; Eva Catharina 45, 65; John Frederick 45; Susana 86

BAUART (See Banart, Bowart/Bowat) A. Marg. 20; Andreas 14; Anna Margaretha 7; George 6; Marg. 11, 14; Margaretha 6, 7; Michael 6, 7, 11, 14, 20; Sarah 20
BAUDER A. Maria 17; Georg 21; Johannes 17; Marg. 21; Melcher 17; Samuel 21
BAUER (See Baur, Bower) Abraham 79, 87, 104; Adam 6, 14; Anna 24; Catharina (Cath.) 16, 21, 24, 45, 84, 93; Catharina Sophia 103; Christina Elisabeth 5; Elis. 30; Eva 79, 104; Frederick 5, 45; Hanna 18; Jacob 6, 7, 16, 21, 24, 93; Johannes (Joh.) 18, 21; John Frederick 45; Katharina 5, 6, 7; Magdalena 6; Moritz 84; Mr. 107; Rosina 6, 14; Salome 16; Samuel 103; Sovia 15; Susanna 14, 93; Wilhelm 15,103
BAULUS (See Paulus) Elizabeth(a) 112; Jacob 112; Samuel 112
BAUM (See Baun) Catha. 87; Elisabetha 87; Jacob 87
BAUMAN/BAUMANN/BAUMEN Andenas 110; Anna Maria 12; Balzer 20; Benedict 70; Catharina 70, 110; Christofel 67, 69; Daniel 54,109, 111; David 54; Ehrhardt 77; Ehrman 68; Elisabeth 66, 67, 74; Gertraut 68; Hanna 77; Herem 68; Jacob 12, 67, 74; Johannes 77; John 110; Joseph 49; Katharina 7, Magdalena (Magd.) 5, 7, 15, 22; Maria 5, 67, 69, 70; Maria Magthalena 67; Martin 49; Sabina 20; Simon 5, 7, 15, 22; Susana 109, 111; Susana Margaretha (Margreth) 54, 109
BAUMWART Friderich 90; Henrich 90, 93; Margretha 90, 93; Susana 100, 101
BAUN (See Baum) Johannes 70
BAUR (See Bauer, Bower) Anna Maria 88
BAUSCHLAG/BAUSHLAG Catharine 49, 108; Daniel 108; John 107, 108; Joseph 49; Magdalena 107; Samuel 49
BAUSER Cath. 21; Elis. 27; Joh. 21; magd. 21
BAUTZ (See Batz, Botz) Anna Elisabeth 31; Catharina 31; Jacob 31
BAWAT/BAWATH/BAWOTH (See Bauart, Bowart/Bowat) Anna Maria 78; Cath. 83; Elisabeth 87; Henrich 78, 79, 81, 82, 83, 85, 87, 89; Johannes 85; Margretha (Margreth,

114

INDEX

Margrethe) 78, 79, 81, 82, 83, 85, 87, 89; Susana 79
BAYER (See Beier) Anna 45; Cath. 28; Christolph 45; David 17; Elisabeth 22, 25, 16, 17 (Elis.) ; Ester 90; Jacob 90; Joh. 16, 17, 22, 26, 27, 90; Magdalena (Magd.) 16, 27; Peter 30; Susana 22
BEALE Cephas 64
BEAN George 64
BEARD Michael 26
BEATTY (See Betty) Barbara 90; Eli 64; Jacob 90; Mark 90
BECHEN (See Beck) Cathrina 74
BECHER (See Becker, Bekar/Beker) Anna Maria 12; Christian 12; Daniel 85; Elisabeth 85; Peter 12
BECHTEL/BECHTOL Anamaria 55; Anna Catharina 75, 77; Barbera 75, 76; Elizabeth 55; Esechiel 75; Fridrich 75, 76, 77; Georg 76; Henry 55; Jacob 55; Johan Fridrich 75
BECK (See Reck, Bechen) Anna Catharina 77; Anna Maria 59, 104, 105; Barbara 12; Catharina 104, 105; Elisabeth 12; Eva 76; Felix 104; Friderick (Friederich) 11, 97; Georg 12, 104, 105; Jacob 59, 76; Joh. Georg 76; Johannes 97; Juliana 11, 97; Peter 77; Wilhelm 11
BECKER (See Becher, Bekar/Beker) Abraham 104; Adam 90; Anna 87; Anna Catha. 70; Anna Martha 90; Catharina 66, 87; Christian 12; Doredea 70; Elisabeth(a) 67, 89; Ernst 67; Eva 67; Eva Elisabetha 67; Gabriel 66, 70; Henrich 87, 89; Jacob 87, 90; John 109; Jonathan 87; Margretha 87, 89; Nicolaus 93, 109; Petrus 93; Philip 67; Salome 93, 109; Sarah 28
BECKEY Joh. 30
BECKLY Barbara 48; Henry 48
BED Jacob 58; Maria 58
BEDLY Annamaria 49; Elisa 49; Henry 49; Jacob 49; Maria 49; Samuel 49; Sarah 49
BEHLEY John Jacob 107; Juliana 107; Matthias 107
BEIER (See Bayer) Anna 81, 83, 86; Catha. 81; Christofel (Christophel) 83, 86; Daniel 96; Ehester 96; Elisabetha 102; Esther (Ester, Estor) 88, 101, 102; Fridrich 81; Henrich 86; Johannes 82, 88, 96, 101, 102; Joseph 102; Margretha 102; N. 82; Seth 101
BEIGER Anna 47; John Frederick 47
BEIGLER (See Bugler) Elisabeth (Elis.) 10, 12, 17, 19; Georg 10, 12, 17; Johannes 12
BEIKMAN Doretea 41; Eva 41; Michael 41
BEILER Catharina 46; Christian 46; Frederick Jacob 46; Gabriel 44, 46; Sabastian 44, 46; Sarah 46
BEIRM (BEHM, BOEHM?) Catharina 70
BEKAR/BEKER (See Becher, Becker) Jacob 110; Nicolaus 110, 111; Salome 110, 111; Solomon 111
BELHUBER (See Belzhuber)
BELL Andreas 62, 63; Ann 3; Anton(y) 1, 3; Catharina 61, 63; Daniel 3; Elisabeth 1, 62; Friederich 61, 62; Jacob 1, 63; John 61; Margaretta (Marg., Margareda, Margrada) 25, 61, 62, 63; Mary 1, 3; Mary Elisbeth 3; Mary Margaratha 1; Nancy 30; Peter 1, 3; Rosina 61, 62
BELSCH Elisabeth(a) 42, 96, 100, 105; Johannes 96; John 42; Wilhelm 100; William 42, 96, 100, 105
BELT Thomas 64
BELTZ Johnn 88
BELTZER Christofel 74; Elisabetha 74
BELZHUBER/BELTZHUBER/BELHUBER/BOLTZHU- BER) Anna Maria 72, 73, 101; Catharina 69; Elisabeth(a) 2, 15, 67, 69, 73; Henry 2; Jacob 2, 73; Magdalena 2; Melcher (Melchior) 2, 67, 69, 73; Michael 72; Theobalt 72
BEN (See Bens/Benns, Bents, Bentz) August 53; Uscon. 53
BENDELIN Henry 48
BENDER Anna Elisabetha 31; Anna Maria 10, 35; Elisabeth 83; Georg 19; Gotfrid (Gottrit) 32, 38; Henrich 83; Johan Daniel 77; Johann Georg 32; Johannes 38; Margretha (Marg.) 14, 19, 32, 38; Melder 10; Niclos 31, 35; Susanna 31, 35; Wilhelm 14
BENNER Henrich 63; Maria 63; Susana 63
BENS/BENNS (See Ben, Bents, Bentz) Elisabetha (Elis.) 26, 70; Jacob 47, 49, 70; Johannes 70
BENTER Elisabetha 82; Henrich 82; Joh. Georg 82; John 27

115

INDEX

BENTS (See Ben, Bens/Benns, Bentz) Adam 44; Elisabeth 44; Jacob 44; John Adam 44; Margaretha 44
BENTZ (See Ben, Bens/Benns, Bents) Anna Maria 46; Elisabeth Meyer 46; Henry 48; Jacob 46; John 48; Maria Conrad 48
BER Christofel 77; Johannes 77; Maria Anna 77
BERCKDOLL (See Barckdall, Barkdull, Bergdoll) Jacob 30
BERDOL Catharina 76; Jacob 76; Margretha 76
BERENGER Elisabetha 106; Magdalena 106; Mattheas 106
BERG Samuel 79
BERGAMANN (See Bergman, etc.) Michael 52
BERGDOLL (See Barckdall, Barkdull, Berckdoll) Elis. 27
BERGMAN/BERGMANN/BERGAMANN Catharina (Cat.) 56, 57, 90, 92, 104; Dorothy 58, 59, 60; Elisabetha 90; Eva 55, 59; Henrich 90, 92, 104; Jacob 27, 58, 76, 104; Johannes 76; Joseph 53; Magtalena 76; Margaret 59; Michael 52, 53, 55, 57, 58, 59; Susanna 53, 55, 57, 58, 59
BERLIN Anna Margaretha 2; Jacob 1, 2; John Jacob 1; Magdalene 1, 2
BERN/BERND/BERNT (See Birnd) Ana Maria 41; Elisabetha 41, 80, 91; Henrich 80; Jacob 41, 80; Thomas 91
BERNART/BERNHARD/BERNHART Anna 44; Catharina 104; Deidrich 44; Elisabetha 81; Frantzcisca Appolonia 32; George 32, 104; Henrich 104; John 44; Maria Elisabetha 32; Peter 30; Thomas 91
BERNT (See Bern/etc., Birnd)
BERNTHEUSER Christina 91; Johanes 91; Mathias 91
BERY Elisabeth 86; Jeams 86; Maria 86
BESEL Dorrothea 110; Elizabeth 110; Michel 110
BETHELE Katharina 6; Magdalena 6; Philip 6
BETTY (See Beatty) Barbara 93; Elisabetha 93; Marcus 93
BETZ Ana Catharina 95; Friederich 95; Johanes 95
BEUCKLE Jacob 32; Margretha 32
BEURDENBERGER Jacob 55
BEX Ana Catharina 98
BEYERLY Barbara 21; Johannes 21
BEYGER Frederick 44; Veronica 44
BEYROTH John Michael 108; Margaret 108; Michael 108
BEZ Ana 91; Ana Catharina 103; Anamaria 91; Christian 26, 102; Eva 102; Friederich 98, 103; Jacob 103; Johanes 102
BEZMAN Anamaria 90; Johanes 90
BEZMAR Elis 26
BIABEN Sussana 92; William 92
BIARD Cath. 26
BIDINGER Johannes 12; Mag. 12
BIECKEL Anna Catha. 88; Catharina 88; Jacob 88
BIEGLER Cath. 14; Elisabeth(a) 14, 19, 23, 91; Georg(e) 14, 19, 23, 91; Henrich 91; Sovia 23
BIEHL/BIEL Catharine 61; Eva 10, 94; Friederich 61; George 94; Johannes 10, 94; John 10, 61
BIELER Anamaria (Ana Maria) 91, 94, 99, 102; Barbara 94; Catharine 44; Dorothea 44; Elina 102; Gebriel 44; Johanes 91; Maria 98; Samuel 91, 94, 98, 99, 102; Wilhelm 98
BIENKKE Cath. 22; Jacob 22
BIERZEISEL Anna Maria 68; Fridrich 68
BIETTERFIELD Andreas 92; Elisabeth 92
BIGINGER Georg 12
BINCKEL/BINCKELE/BINCKLE Cath. 13; Elisabeth 71; Eva 16, 24; Georg 24; Jacob 13, 16; Joseph 71; Peter 71
BINCKELY/BINCKLEY/BINCKLY Amalia 17; Catharina 94, 95, 100, 103; Elisabetha 95; Eva 17, 100; Georg 17, 100; Henrich 94; Jacob 94, 95, 100, 103; Peter 94; Samuel 103
BIND Cath. 47
BINDEBY Catharina 91; Jacob 91
BINDLE Anna Catharine 48; Catharina 47; Eva Petre 48; George 48; John 48; Sara 48; Veronica 48
BINDLIE/BINDLY Anna 46; Georg 48; Jacob 46, 48; Petere 48
BINGEM David 52; Elizabeth 52; Henry 52
BINGEN John Henry 107; Mary Ann Elizabeth 107; Mary Shearer 107
BIRND Anna 42; Elisabetha 42; Jacob 42
BISHOF/BISHOFF 19; Anna Maria 12; Elisabeth 19; Georg 19
BITINGER Juliana Philabner 73; Philip 73; Susanna Maria 73

116

INDEX

BITNER Anna Doretra 72; Fridrich 72; Johannes B. 72
BIZER John 110; Maria 110; Michel 110
BLACKITON Jams 30
BLECHER/BLACHER (See Blocher) Anna Marbera 77; Elisabetha 77, 78; Peter 77, 78
BLENDLINGER Anna 21; Conrad 11, 18, 21; Dorrothea 11, 18, 21; Friderick 18
BLEY Anna Barbara 65, 66, 80; Anna Catha. 80; Barbara (Barbera) 75, 78, 80, 91, 95, 99; Jacob 78; Johannes 65; Rudolf (Rutholf, Rutholph, etc.) 65, 66, 75, 78, 80, 91, 95, 99
BLOCHER (See Blecher/etc.) Elisabetha 75; Maria Magthalena 75; Peter 75
BLOTTNER Johannes 41
BLUM Catharina Elisabetha 102; Henrich 102
BLY Barbara 70, 83; Catharina Elisabeth 70; Magtalena 83; Rutholf (Rutholph) 70, 83
BOBE (See Boby) Catharina 58; Christian 58
BOBY (See Bobe) Adam 57; Anna Margaret 55; Barbara 57; Catharina 55, 57; Christian 54, 55, 57; John Christian 54; Michael 57
BOERSON Joh. 26
BOLLIAN Nicolaus 55
BOLLINAN Catharina 55; Magdalena 55
BOLLMAN Anna 56; Magdalena 56; Nicolaus 56
BOLTZER Christofel 65; Elisabeth(a) 65; Georg 65; Johannes 65
BOLTZHUBER (See Belzhuber)
BONDER Anna Maria 8; Melchior 8; Michael 8
BONDLE Eva Petre 48
BONEBRAKE George 27
BOPE Katharine 3; Mary 3; William 3
BORAF/BORAFT/BORAHF Adam 13, 90; Elisabeth 13, 18, 90; Maria 13; Sara 18
BORCKEL Jacob 29
BORDUN Magdalena 82; N. 82
BORGHART (See Bernart/etc.) Catharina 91; Elisabetha 91; Jacob 91
BORNER Anna Gerdraut 83; Johannes 83; Ludwig 83
BORSTLER Christian 17; Dorrothea 17
BOTHAUER Andreas 78; Anna Margret Catha. 78; Elisabeth 78

BOTZ (See Batz, Bautz) Christina 62; Johe Jacob 62; John 62
BOUGHMAN (See Bouman, Bowman) Andrew 27
BOUMAN (See Boughman, Bowman) Catherine 110; Henry 110; John 110
BOUYRER (See Boyer) Joh. 27
BOVERTH John 60; Margaret 60; Robert 60
BOWART/BOWAT (See Bawat/etc., Bauart) Elisabetha 80; Henrich (Henry) 64, 81; Margretha 81
BOWER Catharine 44; Christoph 44; George 64; John 44; Lucinda 64
BOWMAN (See Boughman, Bouman) Benedict 44; Catharine 44; Julia 44; Mary 28
BOWSER Maria 30
BOWSLER George 27
BOXE Katharine 3; Mary 3; William 3
BOYD Anna 20; Joseph 101; Mickella 20; Nelly 30; Susana 101; Walter 20
BOYER (See Bouyrer, Boyrin) Elizabeth(a) 109, 110, 112; Jacob 27, 109, 110, 112; Maria 109
BOYRIN (See Boyer) Anna Cathrina 65
BRACHLERLEN Catherine 107
BRACHUNIER/BRACKGUMIER/BRACKUNIREM/BRACUMIER/BRACUNERIER/BRACUNIER/BROCKGUNIER/BRAEUNIER/BRAKUNIER Anna Margaret 57; Barbara 87, 105; Catharina 60, 93, 99, 105; Daniel 99, 105; David 93, 99, 105; Doretea 41; Elisabeth(a) 57, 60, 100, 105; George 57; Jacob 60, 93, 96, 100, 105; Johannes 96; Margretha 96; Samuel 105; Susana (Susan) 79, 100
BRADSCHAW George 89; Joseph 89
BRAMIER Cath. 87; David 87; Samuel 87
BRANDSTAETER/BRADSTATER Elisabetha 105; Johanes 105; John 29; Margretha 105
BRANNBURGER Christian 79; Elisabeth 79; Magtalena 79
BRAUER Abraham 33; Gerrich John 53; Henry 53; Maria 33, 53; Rahel 33; Sara 33; Sofia 33
BRAUN Catharina 66; Henrich 34, 74; Johannes 65; John 2; John George 2; Johnnes 66; Katharina 2; Magd. 16; Maria Salome 34; Polly 28; Rosina 65; Salome 74; Sara 65
BRAUNER/BRAUNIER David 83; Jacob 93
BRECHT Barbra 85; Benjamin 73; Elisabeth 73; Fromia 73; Georg 73;

INDEX

Johan Georg 85; Johannes 73; Peter 85; Tschi Meymy 73
BREID Fromia 75; Georg 75; William 75
BREINER Catharina 68; Johannes 68; Peter 68
BRENDEL/BRENDLE (See Brindel) Barbara 28; Cath. 24; Georg 30
BRENDLINGER Anna Maria 67; Conrath 67; Dorothea 7; Elisabetha Doredea 67; Fenrich 7; Judit 22; Konrad 7; Sus. 27
BRENDNER Susana 14
BRET Henrich 73; Maria Elisabeth 73
BRETHEG/BRETNEG/BRETNEY Anna 102, 104; Daniel 102; Elisabetha 97; Nancy 97, 99; Salomon 104; Sarah 99; Tobias 97, 99, 102; 104
BRICHER Johannes 77
BRIDERLEIN Carl 70; Elisabetha 70
BRIETINSTEIN Dorrothea 16; Jacob 16
BRINDEL (See Brendel/Brendle) Cath. 26
BRINGMAN Anna Maria 83; Catharina (Cath.) 83, 94; Fridrich 83; G. 83; Johannes 87; Margretha 87, 89, 94; Martin 87, 89, 94; Susana 89
BRISCOE Mary 26
BROCKGUNIER (See Bracunier, etc.) Barbera 87
BROEMER Johannes 70; Margreth 70; Susanna 70
BROSIM Catharina 92; Jacob 92
BROTZMAN/BROTZMANN (See Protzman/Protzmann) A. Maria 18; Anna Maria 6; Joh. 18; John 6
BROWN Joh. 29
BRUA (See Prua) Adam 52, 59; Anna Maria 51; Catharina (Cath.) 20, 57, 59, 60; Daniel 54, 56; David 59; Elizabeth 51, 54, 56; George 57; Henry (Hennerich) 20, 51, 52, 54, 57, 59, 60; Imanuel 20; Jacob 52, 54, 55; John 51, 55, 57, 59; John George 51; Justanus 57; Magdalen(a) 52, 54, 56, 57; Margaret 56; Maria 52, 54, 55, 57, 59; Peter 51, 52, 54, 56, 57; Rosina 52; Salome 56, 57; Susanna 55, 56
BRUAD Magdalena 54
BRUART Magdalena 53; Daniel 53; Peter 53
BRUMBACH Elisabetha 106; Henrich 106; Johannes 88; Margretha 106
BRUNER (See Brunner) Catharina 54, 56, 57; Charlota 39; Elisabeth 39, 57, 58; George 54; Henry 57, 58; Hn. Lenhart 39; Jacob 56; Peter 54, 56
BRUNNER (See Bruner) Elisabetha (Eliz.) 27, 106; Jonathan Hager 106; Joh. 28; Joseph 106; Nancy 30; Susana 76
BRUVA Jacob 27; Susana 27
BRUX Maria 85; Wilhelm 85
BUCH (See Buche) Christina 62; Maria Catharina 75
BUCHE (See Buch) Barbera 86; Daniel 86; Elisabeth 86
BUCHER Anna Maria 84
BUECHLI/BUECKLE Conrath 32, 33; Elisabeth 33; Margretha 33
BUGLER(See Biegler, Beigler) Georg 10
BUHL Catharina 61; Friederich 61; Jacob 61
BULER Magd. 21; Samuel 21
BUNCKELE Cath. 12; Jacob 12
BUND Anna Catharine 46; Anna Maria 47; Catharina (Catharine) 46, 47; Christian 47; Elisabeth 47; Eva 47; Georg 47
BUNDEL Catharina 45
BUNDLY Catharina (Catharine) 44, 46
BURCHHARDT/BURGERT Catharina 24, 79, 89; Christofel 79; Jacob 24, 89; Joh. Georg 24
BURGER Margretha 70; Mathaus 70
BURGMANN (See Bergman/etc) Michael 51
BURGNER Anna Barbara 46; Anna Maria 46; Christian 46
BURKART Sus. 28
BURKE James 27
BUSCH Catharina 62; Jacob 62
BUSMENGERN Maria Cathrina 73
BUT Catarine 47
BUTTERBACH Cath. 26
BUZZARD Cath. 28
BYERLY Joh. 28

CAFFERETH COFFEROTH Catharina 94; Conrad (Conrath) 86, 91, 94, 99, 103; Johannes 86; Juliana 91; Magdalena (Magtalena) 86, 91, 94, 99, 103; Maria 88; Wilhelm 99
CALL (See Coll, Goll) Elisabetha 34; Georg 34
CANDERMAN/CANTERMAN (See Conterman, Gonderman) Barbara 32; Georg 32; Henrich 32; Johan Georg 32; Martin 32
CARL/CARLE Andreas 24, 30; Christ. 23; Elisabeth (Elisabet) 83, 87;

INDEX

Georg 83, 87; Jacob 23; Johannes 83; Joh. Georg 75; Maria Cathrina 75; Nanzi 24; Samuel 24; Susana 87
CARR John 64
CARROLL Charles 64
CARTER Feni 28; Joh. 27
CAU (See Cow, Kau) Barbara 39; Cath. 26; Christian 39
CAYWOOD Thomas 28
CEAFTER Margret 54
CHARLES Andrew 28
CHOR Christian 54, 55; David 55; Frances 54; Frehne 55; Frei 54; Jacob 54
CHRIST Catharina 102; Henrich 102; Jacob 102
CHRISTMAN/CHRISTMANN Georg Paulus 31; Johan Wilhelm 31; John 3; John Adam 7; Magthalena (Magdalena) 3, 5, 31, 65, 72; Michael 29; Paul 3, 5, 7, 65, 72; Philip 72; Susana 5; Wilhelm 65; William 72
CITMAN Margretha 39; Philibina 39; Vallentin 39
CLAESNER Catharina 32; Catharina Elisabetha 32; Jacob 32
CLAGETT/CLAGGETT Alexander 64; Benjamin 64; Hezekiah 64; Hugh 64; John 64; Thomas John 64
CLAMBERT/CLAMPERT (See Clembert) David 82; Eva 76; Eva Maria 78; Georg 76, 78, 82; Susana 78
CLAPSADDLE (See Clebsadel, Klebsattel)
CLARCH Alex. 28
CLASBRENER (See Glasbrener) Gottleib 102; Margretha 102
CLEBSADEL (See Klebsattel) Catherina 69; Daniel 69
CLECKNER Devalt 54; Elizabeth 54; Margreta 54
CLEMBERT (See Clambert/Clampert) Eva 82
CLETY Georg 32; Magdalena 32; Wilhelm 32
CLOPPER Friederich 28
COFFEROTH Magtalena 88
COFMAN Caspar 34; Margretha 34
COHR Ana Catharina 35; Barbara 35; Christian 35, 53; Frances 53; John 53
COLDMAN Nathan 30
COLL (See Goll) Baltzer 79, 81; Catherina 81; Elisabetha 79
COLP Phil 30
COMFER Georg 93; Hana 93; Johanes 93; Michael 93
COMPTON William S. 64
CONFAIR George 26
CONFER Anna (Ana) 96, 101; Ana Barbara 99; Elisabetha 97; Eva 96, 99, 103; Georg 96, 99, 103; Hanna 97, 104; Johann Georg 103; Michael 96, 97, 101, 104; Salomon 104; Sara 96
CONNER George 53; Joseph 53; Juliana 53, 57
CONRAD/CONRADT (See Conrath) Catharina (Catharine, Cath.) 49, 89, 92, 105; Daniel 26; Eliz. 28; Johanes 105; John 49; John Georg 49; Judith 89; Magd. 90; Sarah 105; Wilhelm 89
CONRATH (See Conrad/Conradt) Anna Christina 86; Anna Margret(h)a 86; Anna Maria 46; Catharina (Cath.) 74, 77, 79, 82, 84, 85, 86; Daniel 46, 82; Elisabeth 84; Jacob 46, 79; Johanes 77; John 46; Magdalena 46; Margaretha 47; Maria 47; Michel 86; Wilhelm 74, 77, 79, 84, 85, 86; William 82
CONTERMAN (See Canterman/Canderman) Barbara 37; Georg 34; Henrich 37; Magthalena 37; Rahel 34
COOCK Hennry 28; Peggy 28
COOK Cath. 27
COOKERLY Peter 29
COON Marg. 28
COR Barbara 37, 38; Christian 37, 38; Rosina 37
CORBER Elizabeth 53; Peter 53
CORDERMAN Barbara 67; Henrich 67
CORN (See Karn) Christian 78; Maria Barbera 78
COROY Mary 26
COW (See Cau, Kau) Elis. 29; Henry 28; Sus. 28
COWIN Elisabeth 18; Susana 18; Tomas 18
CRAMER Elis 30
CRASIS Barbera 84; Martin 84; Peter 84
CREAFFORTH Elisabeth Finck 62; John 62; Magdalena 62
CREBACH George 83; Johannes 83; Margretha 83
CREBES Georg 81; Jacob 84; Magt(h)alena 81, 84; Martin 81, 84
CREBIL Peter 66
CRESAP Tomas 26
CRISINGER Sus. 29

INDEX

CRUIST Jacob 29
CRUMBACH (See Grembach, Grumbach, Krumbach) Anna 92; Catharina 94; Conrad 94; Johanes 92; Wilhelm 94
CUNNINGHAM Francis 28; James 28
CURNICAM Maria 29
CUSICK Peter 67

DACKIN Margretha 65; Schin 65; Wilhelm 65
DAILY Cath. 26
DAMM Barbara 1; Jacob 1
DANNER Cath. 19; Eva Mayer 19; Jacob 19
DANY Anna Christina 34; Elisabeth 34; Georg 34
DAUBEIN Ewin 37; Margretha 37; Mary 37
DAUNY (See Downy) Catharina 91; Johannes 91; Joseph 91
DAVIS Anna 107; Baggy 29; Barbara 107; Catherine (Cath.) 28, 107, 111; Christina 59; Henry 59; Isaac 59; Jacob 59; Johanna 59; Kezia 108; Rezin 64; Richard 107, 108; Thomas 59
DAVISON Robert 28
DAYEL Margaretha 92; Toris 92
DEAL(See Deeils, Deil, Deyl, Deyle, Diel) Christ. 29; Eliz. 26
DEBOI Christina 85; Joseph 85
DEEILS (See Deal, Deil, Deyl, Deyle, Diel) Johannes 72; Wilhelm 72
DEFERN Fridricch 34; Maria Barbara 34
DEIBELBIESS/DEIBELBISS/DEIBELHIES (See Devilbiess) George 7; Jacob 4; Margaretha 4, 7; Michael 4, 7, 85; N. 85
DEIBELE/DEIBLE Ann 2; Ann Mary 1; Anna 4; Christine 2; Frederic 1; Jacob 1, 2, 4; John 4
DEIL (See Deal, Deeils, Deyl, Deyle, Diel) Elisabeth 22; Georg 22; Rebecca 22
DEIS/DEISS Elisabetha 35, 37, 42, 68, 96; Henrich 35, 37, 68, 106; Jacob 42; Johnes 96; Joseph 106; Susanna 35, 106
DEISZSCHNUG Joh. 38; Margretha 38; N. 38
DELINER Anna Maria 109; Elizabeth 109; Ludwig 109
DELLA (See Dolla) Anton 62; John 62; Zanna Margreda 62
DELLINGER Hyind 107
DEMPSTER Elis. 30

DENBEL Johannes 71; Margretha 71; Michael 71
DENGLER/DENLER (See Dingler) Anna Maria 4, 36; George 4, 36; Jacob 4; Sus. 28
DERINGER Henrich 85; Rebecca 85
DERIS Catherine 108
DERR (See Dirr) Anamaria 98; Catharina 98; Jacob 98; John 108; Margaret 108; Susana 108
DEUBEL Margreth 72; Michael 72
DEVILBIESS (See Deibelbiss, etc.) Ann Katharina 2; Margaretha 2; Michael 2
DEWIES Anna Margretha 86; Johannes 86
DEYL Christina 30
DEYLE Adam 26
DIBOR Elisabeth 84; Joh. Fridrich 84; Johannes 84
DICK Anna Maria 84; Elisabeth 84; Herrman 84
DICT Cath. 78
DIEL (See Deal, Deeils, Deil, Deyl, Deyle) A. Maria 112; Cath. 29; Christian 111, 112; Elizabeth 112; Maria 111
DIETER Ana Elisabetha 31; Catharina 31; Detrich 31; Margaretha 31
DIETZ Anamaria 93; Ernst 89, 93; Jacob 93; Maria 89; Wilhelm 89
DIFENBACH Anna Maria 73; Baltzer 73
DILLMAN Catharina 96, 106; Hanna 106; Henrich 96, 106; Maria Henrietta 96
DIM Cath. 28
DINGLER (See Dengler/Denler) Ann Mary 2; George 2; Katharina 2
DINKEL Daniel 66; Susana 66
DIPRRI Elizabeth 58; George 58; Henry 58; Jacob 58; Salome 58
DIRN Adam 43; Anna 43; Nelly 43
DIRR (See Derr) Lorentz 36, 74; Susan Amin 74
DIRTZ Henrich 66
DITER Jacob 83; Magdalina 83; Maria Catharina 75; Peter 75
DITZ Adam 81; Anna Maria 74, 90; Cathrina (Cath.) 74, 79, 81, 83, 87; Christina 77; Elisabeth 83; Ernst 74, 77, 78, 79, 81, 83, 86, 87, 90; Hanna 87; Johannes 77; Jos. 81
DOHMER Ann Mary 2; John Frederic 2; Michael 2
DOLLA (See Della) Anna Margrada 63; John 63; John Jacob 63
DOLLINGER Elisabetha 104; Johanes 104
DOLWAR (Dowlar?) Peggy 26

120

INDEX

DOMER Anamaria 105; Reinhard 105
DORF Henrich 97; Maria 97; Samuel 97
DORFIN Barbara 10; Christoph 10; Rebeca 10
DORMAN Nanzi 29
DOSTIN Elisabetha 66; Sara 66
DOTWEILER (See Dutweiler, Todweiler) Anna Maria 84; Barbera 84; David 85; Doretea 85; Johannes 83, 84, 85; Maria Barbera 83
DOWLAR Allice 64; John 64; Sarah 64
DOWNY Catharina 94; Joseph 94; Samuel 94
DOYL George 27
DRAB Barbara 103
DRABER William 29
DRASCEHEN Catharina 55
DRESEL Gotthart 72, 73; Maria 72, 73
DRILL Elisabeth 18; Georg 18; Hennerich 18
DRITSCH Jacob 49; John Jacob 49
DROSMER Catherine 109; Fred 109
DRUBEL Johan Michael 66; Margretha 66; Michael 66
DUENSCHMAN Jacob 90
DUER Lorentz 36
DUN/DUNN Catharina 104; Elisabetha 106; Georg 104, 106; Susana 104, 106
DUNCKEL Elisabetha 102; Johannes 102; Magedalena 102
DUPIE Abraham 51; Elizabeth 51; Jacob 51
DUPRE (See Dipprri) Augustus Brura 51
DUSALER Barb. 29
DUSING Adam 28
DUSINGER Elis. 28
DUSSING Ann Mary 2, 3; Anna Maria 6, 7; Elisabeth 7; John 6; Philip 2, 3, 6, 7; Susanna 3
DUTWEILER (See Dotweiler, Todweiler) Catharina 90; Jacob 90

E'LENDAM Christian Frederick 51; Maria 51; Peter 51
EAKLE Sarah 30
EARHART (See Ehrhart) John 26
EBBERT/EBERT/EBERTS Anna Maria 68, 105; Barbara 99; Bernhart 71; Catharina 99, 100; Doretea 71; Joh. 68; Dietrich 5; Elisabeth 3, 4, 5; Johan Abraham 105; Katharine 3; Maria 4; Matheas 99, 100; Samuel 105; Valentin 3, 4
EBY Hanna 43; Isaac 43; Margretha 43

ECKAHRT (See Eckhart) Georg Ludwig 100
ECKEBERGER Rosina 13; Valentin 13
ECKEL Anna Cath. 75; Anna Maria 66; Catharina 66, 75; Maria Elisabetha 75; Philip 66
ECKHART (See Eckahrt, Edkhart) Anna Elisabetha 100, 103; Georg 100; Ludwig 103
EDANBERGER/EDEBERGER/EDENBERGER Adam 4; Dorothea 4; Elisabeth 4, 59; Eva 4; Jacob 4
EDELMAN (See Etelman, Edermann) Adam 71; Eva 71
EDERMANN Maria Cathrine 66
EDKHART (See Eckhart) Ana Elisabetha 97; Anamaria 103; Elisabetha 97; Ludwig 97
EHENBACH Fridrich 90; Sophia 90
EHENRY Ezechiel 101; Jacob 101; Maria 101
EHLI Catharina 51; Essau 51, 53; John 53; Margaret 51, 53
EHRET Chirstopher 1; Katharina 1; Michael 1
EHRHART Cath. 24; Jacob 19; Joh. 24; Maria 19; Sally 24; Samuel 19
EICHELBERGER/EICHELBERNER/EIGGELBERGER/EIKEBERGER/EKEBERGER Barbara 13, 15, 94, 97, 99; Cathrina 65; Conrad 65; Devalt (Dewald) 13, 15, 23, 94; Lora 23; Magtalena 65; Margaretha 110; Maria 110; Peter 110; Teobald 97, 99; Walter 25
EICHELBRONN Magdalena 51
EICKELBRUA/EICKELBRURA Catharina 55; Daniel 55; Elizabeth 55
EIDEL Gerhart 98; Sophia 98
EILL C. 55; Henry 55
EITEL Gerhart 87
EITENAUER Dorethea 86; Johan Georg 86; Johannes 86; Susana 7
EKERTS Evah 107; George 107
ELI (See Ely) Isac 56; Margaret 56; Maria 56
ELITSCH Benjamin 72; Sara Hostin 72
ELLINGER John George 1; Katharina 1; Matias 1
ELLIOTT William 64
ELTZRINTH Frantz 8; James 8
ELTZROTH Cath. 87; Elisabeth 87; Frantz 87
ELY (See Eli) Isac 54; Jacob 54; Margret 54

INDEX

EMERICH/EMMERICH/EMRICH Anna
  Margaretha 13; Elisabeth 75; Eve
  Katharina 5; Jacob 63; Johan 75;
  John Hennerich 13; Jonas 5, 6, 13;
  Leedwic 63; Margareth(a) 5, 6, 75;
  Rosina 6; Susana 63
EMPIG Juliana 13; Philip 13;
  Scharlotta 13
EMPFIEL/EMSFIEHL Anna Barbara 61;
  Barbara 63; George 61
ENDERNS Barbara 1; George Peter 1;
  Nicolas 1
ENDERSEIN/ENDERSON (See Anderson)
  Barbera 71; Eva 28
ENGEL Cath. 47
ENGELHARD/ENGELHARDT/ENGELHART
  Anmaria 108; Jacob 111; John 107,
  108, 111; John Peter 107; Magdalena
  107, 111; Mary 108
ENGELMAN/ENGLEMAN Cath. 82, 84, 86;
  Elisabeth 84; Eva Catha. 82; Jost
  82, 84, 86; Susana 86
ENGLISH Bab 38; Catharina 38; William
  38
ENNEREIS Anna Katharina 4; Anna
  Margaret 4; Jonas 4
ENSCH Elisabeth(a) 92, 97
ENSMINGER/ENTSMINGER/ENTZMINGER (See
  Entwenger, Ersminger) Anna 107;
  Anna Maria 107; Catherine 110, 111;
  Christian 107, 110, 111; Eva 108,
  109; Eva Margaretha 107; Henry 29;
  Jacob 107, 109; John 4; Katharina
  4; Ludwig 108, 109; Maria Eva 108;
  Nicolaus 4
ENTWENGER (See Ensminger, etc.,
  Ersminger) Anna Eva 107; Christian
  107; Ella 107; Ludwig 107;
  Margaretha 107; Mary Magdalena 107
EOLLER Henrich 35; Magtalena 35;
  Margretha 35
ERDINGER A. Maria 111; Christian 111
ERICH Elis. 27
ERLENBACH Anna Maria 33; Henrich 33;
  Joh. Peter 33
ERLENWEIN Abraham 68; Eva Catharina
  68; Johannes 68
ERLER Susanna 46
ERLEWEIN Elisabeth 47; Eva Catharine
  46; Susannah 46
ERN Christina 91
ERSMINGER (See Ensminger, etc.,
  Entwenger) Ludwig 30
ESBHSCHI Joh. Jacob 36

ESCH (See Esh) Abraham 54, 59, 100;
  Adam 35; Catharina 31, 35, 37, 54,
  57; David 57; Elizabeth 52, 57, 60;
  George 59; Henrich 31, 35, 36, 37;
  Henry 51, 54; Jacob 52, 57, 60;
  Johannes 36; John 60; Maria 54, 59,
  100
ESCHBACH Andereas 82; Catha. 82;
  David 81; Elisabeth(a) 86, 89; Eva
  Elisa. 86; Fridrich 81, 82, 89;
  Johannes 41; Martin 41, 86; N. 41;
  Sophia (Sofia) 81, 82, 89
ESCHHEL Margaret 51
ESCHER Geo.Gabriel 26
ESCHI Catharina 33
ESH (See Esch) Abraham 53; Catharina
  53; John 53; Maria 53
ESHER Elisabeth 5; George 5; William
  5
ESRON Catharina 34; Christophel 34
ESST/EST Abraham 58; Anna Maria 51,
  58; Christine 53; Elizabeth 51, 52;
  Jacob 58; Michael Yan 51
ESTER Conrad 5; Eva 5; John 5
ETELMAN Adam 32; Eva 32; Joh. Adam 32
EUDENAUER/EUTENAUER Anamaria 91;
  David 83; Elisabeth 83; Martin 83
EYBERT Catharina 59
EYDEL Daniel 77; Gerhart 77; Sozha 77
EZEIKA Maria Barbara 93; Wilhelm 93

FABER Cath. 22; George 22
FACH Elisabeth 3; Magdalene 3;
  Nicholas 3
FACHI Elisabeth 4; Juliana 4;
  Nicolaus 4
FACHY Christian 5, 8; Elisabeth 6;
  George 6; John George 5; Juliana 5,
  8; Margareth 8; Nicolaus 6
FACKLER Hoelena 71; Johannes 71;
  Michael 64, 71
FAD Berhard 2; Margaretha 2; Zanna 2
FADEL Katharina 3; Magdalene 3;
  Mickel 3
FADELE Christoph 2; Katharine 2;
  Michael 2
FADLER Eve 4; John 2, 4; Maria Eva 4;
  Mary Eva 2; Mary Helen 2; Susanna 4
FADWELL Catharina 59; Maria 59;
  William 59
FAERER Ann Mary 1; Joseph 1; Mary
  Elisabeth 1
FAGER Jacob 4; Jonathan 4; Mary 4
FAKLER Elisabetha 65; Helena 65;
  Michael 65; Susana 65, 89

122

INDEX

FALLETO Barbara 66; Fridrich 66; Margretha 66
FARMAR George 26
FARMER Christina 27
FASENACHT/FASNACHT/FASSNACHT/FASTENACHT Adam 16, 21, 23; Barbara 16, 21, 23; Bernard (Bernhart) 23, 29; Cath. 27; Elis. 23; Juliana 29; Polly 23
FASSEL/FASSELE Anna Maria 7; Carl 7; Charles 6; John Jacob 6; Katharina 6, 7; Peter 8; Salome 8
FAUBEL Anna 57; Irma 52; Maria 52; Michael 52, 57
FEABRAN Rebecca 27
FEADE Henry 53
FEBES Anna Maria 74; Elisabetha 74
FECHTIG Christ. 25; Christian 11, 25; Georg 25; Jacob 25; Johannes 25; Margaretha 11; Sus. 11; Sus. 25; Susanna 11
FEG Georg 89; Margretha 89
FEGER Catharina 104; Jacob 104; Magdalena 104
FEHR Christina 61; Elisabeth 63; Falantin 63; Heinrich 61; Jacob 61; Maria 63; Susanna 61
FEID Catharina 58; Christina 54; Christine Est 53; Elizabeth 53; George 53, 54; Jacob 56, 58; John 56; Peter 54; Susanna 56
FEIERSTREIN Eva Catha. 74; Magtalena 74; Niclos 74
FEIGELE/FEIGELI/FEIGLI Anna Maria 10; Anna Maria Cath. 10; Arsila 71; Cath. 14, 18; Fenrich 6, 8; George 2; Johan 71; Jonathan 18; Katharina 6, 7; Martin 2; Peter 6, 7, 8, 10, 14, 18; Samuel 14; Sophronia 2
FEIGHT Jacob 27
FEILER Magtalena 66; Matheisa 66
FEISKEL/FEISSKEL Anna Margaretha 4; Anna Maria 4; Benjamin 4; Frederick 4; George Frederick 4; Katharina 4
FELI Catharina 63; John 63
FELLETO Barbara 66
FENICK Albin 30
FENNER Daniel 83; Elisabetha 83; Maria 83
FENTZ Anna Rebeca 5; Christina 4, 5; Jacob 4, 5; John 6
FEORSTER Barbara 55; Elizabeth 55; John 55
FEQUE Barbara 11
FERBER Maria 101; Martin 101

FERIN Anna Margaretha 5; David 5; John Jacob 5; Marg. 19; Mary 19; William 19
FERMER Christina 109; George 109; John 109
FERN John 5; Martin 5; Susana 5
FERRALL/FERREL Elis. 27; John 26
FERRE (See Ferri, Feyre/Feyrre) Anna Margaretha 6, 7; Anna Maria 8; David 6, 7; Elisabeth 6, 7, 8; George 7; Jacob 6, 7, 8; John 6, 7, 8; Maria Elisabeth 6, 7, 8; Martin 6, 7, 8; Peter 8; Samuel 6; Susana 6, 7, 8
FERRI (See Ferre, Feyre/Feyrre) Barbera 81, 87; Conrad 81, 87; Wilhelm 81, 87
FERRJANIOR Jacob 4; Martin 4; Susana 4
FESLER/FESSLER (See Fisler) Anna Maria 70; Catharina 75; Jacob 29; Maria Barbera 78; Maria Catha. 70, 78; Michael 70, 75, 78; Sus. 30
FESS John Fenrich 7; Magdalena 7; William 7
FETH Henrich 35; Tam 35
FETZMINGER Christian 6; John David 6; Margaretha 6
FEUCHT Anna Maria 5; John 5; Maria 5
FEUER/FEURER Anna Maria 39; Elizabeth 53; Eva 39; Henry 53; Jacob 53; Joseph 39
FEUN Anna Margaretha 5; David 5; John Jacob 5
FEURFEIN Christina 51
FEURY Joseph 51; Maria 51
FEY Anna Eva 45; Cath. 108; Elisabeth 45, 47; Eva 68; Frances Michael 31; Frederick 45; Fromia 68; George 108; Margaretha 108; Maria Eva 31; Maria Magdalena 47; Michael 45, 68; William 45, 47
FEYGELE Cath. 12, 23; Peter 12, 23
FEYERE/FEYRE/FEYRRE (See Ferre, Ferri) Anna Maria 58; Catharina 60; Daniel 52; Elizabeth 56, 58, 60; Henry 56, 58, 60; Jacob 52; John 52, 60; John George 52; Joseph 52, 58, 60; Magdalena 52; Maria 52; Maria Elizabeth 60; Maria Magdalena 56; Sabina 52, 60; Susanna 52
FEYT Joseph 59; Magdalena 59; T. George 59
FICHY Christian 6; John 6; Juliana 6
FIEHL/FIEL/FIHLD Anna Maria 61; Elisabeth 62, 63; Eva 61, 62;

INDEX

George 63; Jacob 61, 62; John Henry 63; Sarah 62
FIERE/FIERY Elis. 27; Jacob 28; Joseph 27
FILSON Elisabeth 16; Samuel 16
FINCK/FINK Elisabeth 61, 62; Michael 61, 62
FINLEY John 105; Margretha 105; Samuel 64; Samuel Johanes 105; William Fransis 105
FISBACH Maria 30
FISCHACH Catharina 95; Friederich 95
FISCHER (See Fisher) Adam 39, 97; Anamaria 91; Anna 33; Anna Margretha 39; Anna Maria 33, 35; Bally 18; Catharina 18, 21, 24, 25, 91, 97; Christian (Christ.) 18, 91; Daniel 58; Elisabetha 56, 76; George 58; Henrich 76; Jacob 21, 24, 25, 33, 35, 56, 76; Joh. David 76; Joh. Georg 18; John 56; Lisabeth 56; Magdalena 56; Maria 58; Sara(h) 21, 97; Susanna 39, 56
FISCUS Cath. 27
FISHER (See Fischer) Ana Maria 42; Catharina 42; Elisabeth 42; Georg 42; John 42; Price 30; Susana 42
FISLER (See Fesler/Fessler) Jacob 29
FITZHUGH William 64
FLAGER Cath. 19; Jacob 19, 21, 27; Joh. Jacob 21; Marg. 19, 21
FLENER/FLENNER Agnes 100; Anna 100; Anna Magthalena 36; Catharina 35, 37, 40, 68; Daniel 34, 38, 101; David 27, 31, 101; Elisabeth 28, 38, 68; Isabela 100; Johannes 32, 34, 35, 37, 38, 40, 68, 100; Jonathan 37; Magdalena 31, 34, 36, 37, 38, 41, 76; Margreth 38; Rudolf (Rutholf) 31, 34, 36, 38, 41; Susana 101
FLIDINGER/FLINDINGER Christian 8; Peter 8; Taborah 8
FLIEGER (See Fluger) Elisabeth 2, 3, 5; Jacob 5; John 2; Katharina 3; Peter 2, 3, 5, 82
FLIKINGER Jacob 87; Peter 87; Susana 87
FLINGER Catharina 26, 68; Peter 68; Susanna 68
FLORI Eva 28; Georg 28
FLUGER (See Flieger) Elisabeth 6, 79; John Peter 6; Peter 6, 79
FOCKLER Adam 23
FOESSLICH Ann Mary 1; John 1; Peter 1

FOGELGESANG (See Vogelgasang, etc.) Barbara 69; Cath. 21; Christian 28, 31, 48, 69; Fridrich 69; Maria Barbara 31; Maria Eva 31; Maria Magthalena 69
FOGLER (See Vogler) Anna Barbara 74; Christian 19; Jacob 74; Johan Georg 74; Sara 19; Susana 19, 74
FOLMS Johan Henrich 66; Maria Elisabetha 66
FOLTZ Marg. 27
FORBES Tom 30
FORDER Elisabetha 98; Margretha 98; Samuel 98
FORMAR Mary 26
FORREST Charity 27
FORTER Bezy 25
FOSS Anna Maria 4; Christina 2; George 3; Jacob 3; John 4; Katharina 4; Magdalene 3; Mary 3; Michel 2; Peter 3; Salome 3
FOSTER Martha L. Ankeney 51
FOTD Margrada 62; Martin 62
FOUTZ/FOUZ A. Maria 109, 110; Anna Maria 110; Catherine 111; Dally 110; Eva Dorothea 110; Jacob 108; Maria 110; Michael 108, 109, 110, 111; Peter 108, 110
FRACK Barbera 76; Bernhart 76
FRANCKEBERGER/FRENCKEBERGER Conrad 30; Hennerich 15; Ludwig 15; Marg. 15
FRAND Philip 7
FRATZMAN Elisabeth 81; Lorentz 81
FREEBORN Ellender 26
FREILICH Frantz 79, 82, 88
FRENER Abraham 104; Henrich 102; Henrich Wilhelm 90; Johanes 86, 87, 90, 93, 95, 102; Jonnes 104; Samuel 93; Susana 87, 90, 93, 95, 102, 104
FREUND Ann Mary 2; Elisabetha 4, 65; George 2; Margareth 4; Mary 2; Philip 65; Tobias 4
FREY (See Fry) Abraham 25; Anna Catharina 65; Barbara 56; Catha. 15, 71; David 56; Elisabeth 15; Georg 65, 71; Johannes 15, 26, 107; John George 107; Juliana 107; Nicolaus 56; Susanna 51
FREYBERGER (See Fryberger) Andrew 2, 3; Ann Katharina 2, 3; Jacob 2
FREYSAL Seiss 53
FRIDRICHE Rahel 82
FRIED Abraham 10; Barbara 95; Maria 10, 95; Samuel 10, 95

INDEX

FRISCH/FRITSCH/FRITZ Caspar 72; Maria Barbera 72; Elisabeth 35; Johannes 35; Susana 72; Susana B. 72
FROTZMAN Anna Elisabeth 65; Anna Maria 65; Elisabeth 65; Lorentz 65
FRUCHT John 6; Magdalena 6; Maria 6
FRUD/FRUDT Georg 71; Margretha 67, 71
FRY (See Frey) Catherine 110; George 110
FRYBERGER (See Freyberger) Andreas 7; Anna Katharina 7; Christina 7
FUHROHR Anna Maria 12; Hennerich 12
FUNCK Jacob 26
FUR Catharina 73; Henrich 73
FUYEL Johannes 77; Ohrfiela 77
FUYRENA John 57; Magdalena 57
FYE Cath 29
FYSTER Catherine 107; Elizabeth 107; Henry 107

GADER Anna Maria 9; John 9
GALL --- 37; Elisabeth 37; Georg 37; Michael 37
GAMWELL Henry 64
GANDER Anna Maria 10; Elis Susanna 10; Georg Peter 13; Johannes 10, 12, 13; Jung Magd. 12; Magd. 12; Maria 13
GANNER Jacob 34; Johannes 34; Susanna 34
GANTER Joh. 20; Maria 20; Susana Lidia 20
GANTZ Jacob 29
GARIER Cath. 16; Johannes 16; Nicolaus 16
GASSER Anna Maria 10; Joh. 10
GAST John 107; Joseph Peter 107; Maria Barbara 107
GASTERT Annamaria 63; Christian 63; John 63
GAUER (See Gayer, Gehr, Geyer) Cath. 16; Johannes 16; Nicolaus 16
GAVER Easter 27
GAYER (See Gauer, Gehr, Geyer) Dorroth. 13; Jacob 13
GEBEL Abraham 37; John Peter 45; Magdalena 45; Margreth 37; Philipp 45; Rebecca 37
GEBHART/GEBHERT Johannes 41; Margretha 41; Maria 27
GEBL.IDS Carl 7; John 7; Maria Barbara 7
GEBREL Hanna 58; Henry 58; John 58
GECK Cath. 24; Georg 24; Lidia 24
GEED Fenrich 7; Katharina 7
GEGNER Margretha 40; Theobal 40

GEHOB Selbat 52
GEHR (See Gauer, Gayer, Geyer) John 62; John George 62; Margareda 62
GEIGER (See Geuger) Anna Maria 6; Barbera 84; Elisabeth 6; Ellenora 22; Fenrich 6, 7; Franida 6; Frederick (Fridrich) 45, 68; Fromia 68, 70; Fronia (Feronica) 5, 17; Fronida 8; Georg 7, 70; Jacob 7, 70; Jacob Herry 91; Johan Fridrig 70; Johanes 12, 17, 19, 20, 22, 92; John 5, 6, 8; John Frederick 45; Katharina 6, 7; Margaretha 5, 45, 70; Peter 8, 84; Susana 12, 17, 19, 20, 22, 91, 92
GEISSER Cath. 29
GEISSINGER John 111; Susana 111; William 111
GELBERT Catharina 33; Joh. Adam 33; Johannes 33
GELLOIDS/GELLUDS Barbara 8; Carl 7, 8; John 7; Maria Barbara 7; Susanah 8
GELWICHS/GELWICKS Barbara 96, 98; Carl 20, 96, 98; Carl Fried. 20; M. Barbara 20; Maria 20
GEMBERLE Jacob 69; Maria Margretha 69; Sara 69
GENANT Conrad 12
GENTES Anna Elisabeth 48; Daniel 48; Eva Fogelgesang 48
GEORGE Johannes 39; Joseph 39
GERHARD Eitel 11; Sovia 11
GERHART Christina 20, 78; Daniel 104; Eutel 33, 35; Henrich 35, 104; Jacob 20, 78; Magdalena 104; Sovia (Sofia) 33, 35; Susana 33
GERHARTH Eutol 40; Sophia 40
GERLACH/GERLACHER Adam 37, 40, 41, 53, 54, 58; Christian 40; Christiana 37; Christina 40, 41, 54; Henrich 32; John 56; Magthalena 32; Margaret 56; Susana 37
GERREL Hanna 58; Henry 58; John 58
GETTY Catharina 104; Georg 104; William 104
GEUGER (See Geiger) Fridrich 69; Fromia 69
GEYER (See Gauer, Gayer, Gehr) Cath. 12; Dorrothea 8, 14, 19, 23; Elisabeth 8; Friderich 12; Georg 23; Hennerich 12; Jacob 8, 14, 19, 23; Susana 19
GIDING Barbara 69; Johannes 69; Juliana 69
GIESER Henrich 105; Margretha 105

INDEX

GILBERT Catharina 35; Christian 63; Johannes 35; Margretha 63; Maria Margretha 35
GILLAM/GILLOM Elizabeth 52; John Adam 52; Thomas 52
GISI Johanes 81; Magtalena 81; Maria 81
GITTINGEN George 107
GITTINGAR/GITTINGER Elizabeth 107; John George 107; Juliana 107
GLASBRENNER/GLASSBRENNER (See Clasbrener) Christina 25; Era Christina 1; Georg 13; Gottlieb 1, 15, 16, 19; Margaretha 1, 15, 19
GLEOCKNER Deobald 56; Elizabeth 56; Jacob 56
GNADIG/GNAEDIG/GNEDIG Cath. 81; Dsau 71; Elisabetha 18, 22, 71, 76, 79, 81, 94, 95, 103; Georg 18; Henrich 18, 95, 103; Isaac 79; Isau 76, 81, 97; Johannes 71, 95, 97, 100, 105; Juliana 105; Margretha 97, 100, 105; Samuel 103; Susana 76, 95
GOERING Bezi 13; Jacob 13; Mr. 90
GOH Barbara 69; Johannes 69; Susanna 69
GOL (See Coll, Goll) Baltzer 31, 68, 69; Christofel 68; Elisabetha 69; Jacob 31; Maria Elisabetha 31, 68
GOLBERT Catharina 37; Elisabeth 37; Johannes 37
GOLL (See Coll, Gol, Golt) Anna Maria Cath. 11; Baltasar (Baltzer, Balzar, Bazer, etc.) 2, 11, 13, 17, 64, 77, 87, 93; Catharina 11, 13, 17, 87, 93, 106; Elisabetha 77; Georg 37; Jacob Goring 13; Johannes 106; Mary Elisabeth 2; Rebeca 17; Salamina 106; Susana 106
GOLLENTA Elisabeth 80; Ester 80; Joseph 80
GOLT (See Coll, Gol) Baltzer 82
GONDERMAN (See Canderman/Canterman, Conterman) Barbera 76; Henrich 76; Magthalena 76
GONNER Annamaria 57; Joseph 57
GOR Turner 64
GORANFLAUER Catharina 91; Georg 91
GORDEN William 64
GORG Adam 74; Anna Maria 74; Maria 74
GOYER Dorrothea 10; Jacob 10
GRABER A. Maria 18; George 9; Jacob 9, 18; John 9; Katharina 9; Magdalena 9; Samuel 9

GRAEFT (See Graf/Graff, Greft, Groff/Groph) Elisabetha 76; Johan Adam 76; Joh. Georg 76
GRAEST Johan Adam 76
GRAFERT/GRAFFORT Christina 101; Joh. 27; Johan Jacob 101; Joseph 101; Margretha 101
GRAF/GRAFF (See Graeft, Greft, Groff/Groph) Catharine 44; Elizabeth 44; Henrich 87; Jacob 87; John 44; Maria 87
GRAMLICH David 7; Fenrich 7
GRAMS Anna 85; James 85
GRAPP Catharina 51; Jacob 51
GRAST Johannes 70; Maria Catharina 70; Maria Elisabetha 70
GRAU/GRAUL Catharina 55; Conrad 54, 55, 57; Elizabeth(a) 54, 55, 57; Elizabeth Est 52; George 52; Henry 54; Joh. 29; Lannard 52; Michael 57; Rosina 51
GRAY Catharina 105; Georg 105; Samuel 105
GREBER Anna Maria 6; George 6; Jacob 6, 67, 80; Joh. Jacob 68; Magtalena 67, 80; Margretha 68
GREBIL Barbera 73; Peter 73
GREC Jacob 74; Johanna 74; Robert 74
GREEN William 30
GREFT (See Graf/Graff, Graeft, Groff/Groph) Adam 79; Christina 79; Elisabeth 79; Georg 79; Joh. Georg 79
GREILICH Anna 82, 83, 88; Anna Catharina 75, 79; Catha. 82; David 82; Elisabeth 88; Frantz 75, 83; Herrman 82; Jacob 79; Johannes 75; Maria Catha. 82
GREMBACH (See Grumbach) Johannes 83; Juliana 83
GREMER Gottfried 54; Margrett 54
GRIEGER Anna Maria 9; Daniel 9; George 9; Henry 9; John 9; William 9
GRIESSMAN (See Grissman) Cath. 11; Joh. Christian 11; Joh. Georg 11
GRIEVES Phebe 64
GRIFFER Cath. 29
GRISIN Magdalena 55
GRISINGER Cath. 11; Georg 11
GRISSENGER Catharina 105
GRISSMAN (See Griessman) Bally 17; Cath. 17; Georg 17
GROFF/GROPH (See Graf/Graff, Graeft, Greft) Andreas 47; Elisabeth Stather 47; Susanna 47

INDEX

GROSCH Andreas 49; Andreas, Jr. 49; Catharine 49; Daniel 49; Elisa 49; Gottlieb 48, 49
GROSS Betty 24; Catharina 49, 68; Elisabeth 15, 21; Gottlieb 49; Hennerich 15; Johannes 68; John 49; Marg. 15; Samuel 21
GROSSKOPF Margaretha 21
GROVE Elis. 30; Sus. 30
GRUB Elisabetha 32; Jacob 32
GRUBER Catharina 106; Johannes 106; Keresia 106; Rebeccas 106; Scharlotta 106
GRUF Georg 67
GRUMBACH (See Crumbach, Grembach, Krumbach) Anna 88; Catharina 88, 98; Conrad 88, 98; Elisabeth 88; Johannes 88, 95; Juliana 92, 95; Samuel 98
GUETING Mr. 90
GUETY Catharina 102; George 102; Maria 102
GULSEN Isaac 21; Magd. 21; Marg. 21
GUNTES Daniel 47
GURANGFLOH Christina 75; Georg Adam 75
GUSCHWA/GUSHCHWA Benjamin 105; Catharina 53, 56, 105; David 105; John 52, 53, 56; John George 56; Margaret 55; Maria 53

HABLITZEL Adam 3; Christine 3; Magdalene 3
HACHEN/HACHIN/HACKEN/HACKIN Abraham 103; Anamaria 101; Christian 11, 95; Daniel 97; Dorethea 90, 91, 97, 100, 101, 103; Elisabeta 91; Johannes 90; Juliana 11, 25, 95; Nicolaus 90, 91, 97, 100, 101, 103; Samuel 11; William 100
HACK Aron 68; Chie 68; Jacobus 68
HACKMAN Matheus 72
HACKMEYER Cath. 13, 23; Conrad 12, 16, 23; Jonas 13, 20; Maria 12; Maria Magd. 16; Mary Magd. 12; Rebecca 20; Samuel 12, 22, 23; Susana 13, 20
HADER Andrew 58; Elizabeth 58; Susanna 58
HADLEY Richard 28
HAEFEL Catharine 47
HAFFNER (See Hafner/Haffner)
HAFLI Annabarbara 62; John 62

HAFNER/HAFFNER Anna Barbra 61; Anna Martha 45; Barbara 61, 62, 63; Elisabeth 63; Eva 39; Georg 45, 46, 47, 63; George Frederick 45; Jese 61; John 62, 63; Martha 46, 47
HAGAR (See Heger, Hoeger) Anna 11; Barbara 37; Catharina 42; Christian 43; Elisabetha 85; Henrich 37; Jacob 108; Johannes 37, 99; Jonathan (Jonadan) 11, 71, 85, 99; Magdalena 43, 99; Maria Magtalena 85; Ruthy 42; Samuel 42
HAGI Elisabeth 86; Nicolaus 86
HALAN Catharina 101; Johnn 101; Maria 101
HALL Elizabeth 64
HALLAM Thomas 64
HALLE Georg 30
HALLMAN Ana Magdalena 97; John 97; Maria Catharina 97
HAM Conrath 31, 36; Joh. Jacob 36; Maria Catharina 31; Maria Gertraud 31, 36
HAMEL Joh. 24, 29; Maria 24
HAMER Cath. 16, 22; Georg 16, 22; Maria 22
HAMILTON Bally 22; Barbara 22; Joseph 22
HAMNINGER Elisabeth 4
HAN (See Hann, Hans) Adam 95; Anamaria 99, 102; Catharina 92, 99, 106; Christina 102, 106; Georg 95, 105; Henrich 102, 106; Johan Georg 106; Johannes 92, 99; Margretha 95, 105; Maria Amweg 106; Rebecca 105; Samuel 92
HAND (See Han, Han) Anna 58; Elizabeth 52, 56, 58, 59; Eva 59; George 52; Jacob 55; John 56, 58, 59; Maga 56; Margaret 55; Michael 52
HANES William 27
HANKER Jacob 26
HANLY Christoph 21
HANN (See Han, Hans, Hand) Catharina 85; Christina 101; Eva 28; Fortfardt 107; Jacob 85; Johannes 85; Magdalena 107
HANS (See Han, Hann) Jacob 33; Margretha 33
HARDMAN (See Hartman) Joh. 11
HARN Catharina 66; Christofel 66; Georg 66
HARRI Doretea 66; Johnathan 66
HART Thomas 64
HARTMAN (See Hardman) Catharina 99

INDEX

HAS Abraham 37; Agnes 36; Anna 37; Christina 36; Elisabetha 104; Jacob 36; Peter 36, 37; William 104
HASLICH Anna Maria 7; Rebeca 7; Valentin 7
HASON Elis. 28
HASSNER Anna Martha 44; John Georg 44
HASTNER Catharina 85; Simon 85
HATFIEL Joh.Georg 28
HATTE Georg 30
HAUCK/HAUCKS/HAUK Anamaria 100; Christina 110; Elisabetha 35; Jacob 35, 110; Jacobina 26; Johannes 35; Joseph 110; Julianna 100; Michael 35, 100; Sarah 100
HAUER/HAUERD Adam 32, 53; Anna Maria 32, 35, 76, 109; Anthony (Andonny, Andani) 35, 76; Barbera 80; Catharina 61, 108, 109, 112; Christina 54; Elizabeth 108; Friederich 61; George 53, 54; Johannes 80; John 108, 109, 112; Maria Barbera 80; Solomon 61; Susanna 53, 54
HAUN Anna Maria 14; Michael 14
HAUNET Anna Maria 110; Catherine 110; John 110
HAURET Andoni 16; Anthony 12, 21; Jonadan 12; Maria 12, 16, 21; Martini 16; Rosina 21
HAUS Anna 21; Bezi 21; Wilhelm 21
HAUSER Anna Maria 83; Barbara 33, 70, 77, 78; Elisabeth 33; Ella 107; Jacob 70, 71, 75, 77, 78, 83; Maria Catharina 69
HAUSHALTER/HAUSLATER/HAUSHOLTER/ HAUSINHALTER/HAUSSHALTER/ HOUSEHOLDER/HUSSHALTER Adam 28, 47, 80, 111; Catherine (Cath.) 17, 28, 67, 79, 80, 111; Cath. Margaretha 46, 67; Christ. 30; Daniel 108; David 8; Dorothea 111; Elisabetha 17, 75, 79, 82; Eva 80; Fried. 29; George 67, 82, 110; Georg Adam 4, 46; George M. 5, 8; Georg Michel 4, 8, 17, 40, 108; Georg Peter 72; George W. 8; Hanna 110, 111; Jacob 27, 67; Johannes 26, 67, 72; John 110, 111; Margaretha 4, 67; Maria 111; Maria Margreth 72; Mattheis 80; Michael 111; Philip 5; Sally 111; Simon 75, 79, 82; Susana 5, 8, 40, 111, 108
HAUSLER Cath. 22
HAUSS Jacob 52

HAUT Anna Maria 82; Baltasar 82
HAWZ (See Haus, Hoss) Haty 26
HAYNES (See Heines) Jacob 27
HAYS Barnabas 61; John 61; Silana 61
HAYSONI Nicholas 28
HEBEL John 63; Maria 63
HEBELING Abraham 42; John 43; Margretta 42; Maria Margretha 43; Salome 43
HEBLER Christina 108; Elizabeth 108; William 108
HEBLING Abraham 54, 55; Abras 112; Elizabeth 54; M. Catherina 112; Margrett 54
HECHLER Anna Barbara 74; Martin 74
HECK Catherine 108, 109; Elizabeth 108; John 108; Peter 108, 109
HECKMAN Daniel 72; Maria 24, 72; Math. 24
HECRERY Andrew 71; Robert 71
HEDINGER Bethina 16; Joh. 16; Sally 16
HEFELE Eva Catharina 67; Johan Henrich 67; Michael 67
HEFFELE A. Maria 25; Catharina 15; Elias 25; Elis. 25; Hennerich (Henrich) 11, 15, 16, 19, 24, 25; Jacob 19, 25; Marg. 11; Michael 25, 91; N. 91; Samuel 91; Susana (Sus., Susanna, Susann) 11, 15, 16, 19, 24
HEFFLICH Barbara 14; Joh. Peter 14; Johann 28
HEFFNER Benjamin 26
HEFLICH Anna Maria 67; Catharina 67; N. 82; Peter 67, 82
HEGEL Jacob 54
HEGER (See Hager, Hoeger) Anna 87; Christian 38; David 40; Elisabetha 38,40; Johannes 38, 40; Jonathan 35, 87
HEGUS Jacob 59; Maria 59; Veronica 59
HEH Anna Cath. 80; Daniel 80; Eva Margretha 80
HEHRNS Catharina 58; Jacob 58; Maria 58
HEIDLER Absolom 61; Catharina 61; Joseph 61
HEIER Anna 88; Christophel 88; Jacob 88
HEIK Cath. 29
HEIMS Philipine 34; Wendel 34
HEINEMANN Bertha B. 51
HEINES (See Haynes) Adam 69; Anna Maria 69; Barbara 69

INDEX

HEINISCH Henrich 32; Maria Elisabeth 32; Maria Susana 32
HEINSMANN Catharina 102
HEISER (See Heyser, Heysern, Hieser) Anna 65, 69, 76, 77; Anna Elisabetha 69, 76; Wilhelm 65, 69, 76, 77, 81; William 72
HEISKELL/HEISKKELL/HEISTKELL Anna Margaretha 44; Benjamin 44; Friedrich (Frederic) 2, 7; John 2; John Frederick 44; Katharina 2, 7; Samuel Stedinger 7
HEISLIN Susana 67
HEISS Cath. 30
HELLMAN Anna 5; Anna 5; Herrman 5; Magdalen 5
HELMS Anna Maria 34
HELSER Anna 65; Wilhelm 65
HEMEL Cath. 24; Georg 24; Johannes 24
HEMS Anna Maria 38; Elisabetha 38; Jacob 38
HEMTON Mary 26
HENAVEL Cath. 27
HENDERSON Griffith 64; James 64
HENOP N.Pastor 31
HENRY Elis. 30
HENS Elisabetha 36, 56; Jacob 36, 56
HENSCH Henrich 74; Maria Elisabeth 74
HENTZ Elisabeth 39; Jacob 39
HERDEL Georg 69; Margretha 69
HERDLEL Martin 69; Susana 69
HERDLI Fridrich 76; Margretha 74, 76
HERDLY Barbera 84; Sebastian 84; Susan 84
HERFLEL Anna Margretha 69
HERGENROTH Barbera 80; Jacob 80
HERGER Doretea 80; Henrich 76; Henrich Michael 76; Maria Cath. 80; Michel 80
HERGERT Peter 38; Susana 38
HERIOT Elisabetha 39; Ludwig 39; M. Marg. 39
HERMAN/HERMANN Anna Maria 5; Elizabeth 54; George 57; Jacob 57; Johanna 5; John 5; Maria 57; Nicolaus 54
HERR (See Herre) Anna Maria 87; Conrad 99; Daniel 96; Elisabetha 92; Georg 84; Jacob 104; Johan Peter 84, 85, 87, 92, 96, 99, 102, 104; Peter 102; Samuel 85; Susana 84, 85, 87, 92, 96, 99, 102, 104
HERRE (See Herr) Anna Maria 12; David 10, 12; Elisabeth Maria 12; Hanna 16; Jacob 12, 13, 16, 22; M.

Elisabeth 22; Margaretha (Marg.) 10, 12; Maria Elisabeth 13, 16; Samuel 12; Susana 22
HERRG Doretea 65; Johnathan 65
HERRIL Elisabeth 78; Joh. Adam 78; Joh. Jacob 78
HERRIS Dina 18; Tomas 18
HERRY Jacob 91; Maria Elisabeth 91
HERSCH (See Hirsch/Hirsh) Barbara 52; Catharina 54, 59; Christina 54; Elizabeth 59; Frederick 52, 54, 59; George 57; Henry 54; Jacob 54, 56, 57; John 52; Lorens 52; Veronica 56, 57
HERSCHMANN (See Hirshman) Andreas 45; Catharina 45; Maria Elisabeth 45
HERT Elisabetha 76; Johnn 76; Maria 76
HERTEL Barbera 88; Bastian 95, 98, 103; Catharina 95, 98, 103; Ester 95; Friederich (Fridrich) 88, 95, 96; Jacob 98; Margretha 88, 95, 96; Nancy 96; Salimina 103
HERTHA Cath. 78; Fridrich 78; Margretha 78
HERTI Elisabetha 88; Johannes 88
HERTLE Fridrich 83; Johan Georg 83; Martin 83; N. 83; Susana 83
HERTLI Catharina 87; Elisabeth 87; Fridrich 80; Jacob 80; Margretha 80; Michael 80, 82; Sebastian 87; Susana 80, 82
HERTLIN Margretha 78; Susana 78
HERTLY Fridrich 84, 86; Jacob 81; Johannes 81, 84; Margretha 86; Martin 81; Michael 81, 84; N. 84; Susana 81
HERTTEL Fridrich 81; Gretha 81; Susana 81
HERTZOG Georg 36, 74; Hanna 36; Juthit (Jutit) 36, 74
HES (See Hess) Christophel 92; Johannes 92; Magdalena 92, 98, 100, 104; Scharlotta 95; Wilhelm 98, 100; William 104
HESLER Catharina 71; Michael 71
HESS (See Hes) Anna Maria Barbara 10; Baltzer 82; Christoph 15; Daniel 82; Elisabeth 15; Eva 82; Magdalena 14, 15; Marg. 15; Nicolaus 95; Scharlotta 95; Wilhelm 14, 15
HETERICH/HETRICH/HETTRICH/HETTRIDCH Ana Margretta 41; Carl 74, 77; Charl 77; Christian 93, 100; Elisabeth(a) 41, 74; Henrich (Henry) 41, 93; Jacob

INDEX

41; John 41; Margretha 100; Sibila 41, 93; Susana 74, 77
HETHEN Eva 91
HETTINGER Betyna 20; Joh. 20
HEUTZEL/HEUZEL A. Maria 109; Barbara 108, 109; Catherine 108; Lantz 108; Lorenz 109
HEYBERGER Conrad 26
HEYSER (See Heiser, Heysern, Hieser) Anna 31, 94, 97, 103; Anna Elisabetha 100; Catharina 94, 97, 100; Jacob 94, 97, 100; Juthit Ana 94; Wilhelm 31, 97
HEYSERL Anna Margretha 70; Benjamin 70; Joh. Fridrich 70
HEYSERN Ana 94
HICKL Eva 77; Joh. Jacob 77; Jos. Jacob 77
HIESER (See Heiser, Heyser, Heysern) Anna 72; Wilhelm 72
HIGHSHO Elis. 30
HIGINS Catharina 98, 104; Eva 104; Robert 98, 104; Susana 98
HIPSCH Eva 31
HIRSCH/HIRSH (See Hersch) Andrew 57; Anna Maria 51; Catharina 53, 57; Christina 35, 40; Frederick (Fridrich) 35, 40, 51, 53, 57; Fronia 112; George Frederick 53; Henry 51; Jacob 51, 52, 112; Sara 5; Susan 51; Veronica 51
HIRSCHBERGER Adam 84; Barbera 84; Catha. 84; Henrich 84
HIRSCHHELT Abolna 76; Fridrich 76
HIRSCHMAN/HIRSHMAN (See Herschmann) Andreas 67; Andrew 44; Catharina (Catharine) 44, 67; Peter 67
HIRSH (See Hersch, Hirsch) Jacob 112
HISANG/HISON/HISSANG/HISSON/HISSONG Adam 62, 69; Barbara 21, 53, 55, 56, 58; Elisabeth 62; John 53, 56, 58; Julliana 69; Magdalena 55; Margaret 58; Peter 21; Susana 62
HISTER Daniel 34, 37; Rosina 34, 37
HITTLER Eva Elisabeth 72; Georg 72; Maria Cath. 72
HIX Ann Maria 31; Anna Maria 37; Barbara 36, 40; Jacob 36, 37, 40; Sarah 40; Susana 37
HOBLIN Abraham 57; Margaret 57
HOCKER Andrew 28
HOECH Maria 36; Michael 36; Simon 36
HOEFLICH (See Hoflich) Barbara 95; Peter 95

HOEGER (See Hager, Heger) Catharina 36; Johannes 36; Jonathan 37; Meister Jonathan 69; Rosina 65; Susana 36
HOEHLER Friederich 92
HOENISCH Anna Catharina 39; Henrich 39; Maria Elisabetha 39
HOERNER Anna Maria 46; Maria Magdalena 46; Matthew 46
HOFER Catharina 38, 40; Elisabet 40; Maria Catharina 40; Rutholf 38, 40; Susana 38
HOFFMAN (See Hofman/Hofmann) Barbara 11; Dorothea 44; Johannes 11, 30; Michael 44
HOFLICH (See Hoeflich) Jacob 8; Margaretha 8; Peter 8
HOFMAN/HOFMANN (See Hoffman) Abraham 42; Diederich (Dirdrich) 42, 60; Doratea 31; Friedrick 5; Henrich 80; Johannes 103, 104; John 5, 60; John George 1; Jonathan 31; Kaspar 1; Margareth 1; Maria Rebeca 5; Martin 31; Nancy 103; Rutolf 31; Susana 42, 60, 103, 104; Wilhelm 104
HOFTELI Michael 86
HOGEIN Anna Maria 71
HOH Catherine 107; Peter 107
HOISE Eva 28
HOLAND Catharina 96; John 96; Wilhelm 96
HOLTZ Cath. 75; Jacob 75
HOMS Catharina 56; Jacob 56
HOOSS Elisabeth 22; Peter 22; Sus. 22
HORER Catharina 72; Fridrich 72; Johannes 72
HORN Adam 46; Catharine 44; Christoph 44; Elisabeth 46; John 44
HORNBECKER Elena 108; Herman 108; Susana 108
HORNISH Cath. 16, 23; Philip 16, 23; Salome 16; Willhelm 23
HOSE Hanna 26; Mollena 26; Peter 99, 100, 102; Susana 99, 100, 102
HOSLICH Anna Maria 8; Margaretha 8; Peter 8
HOSS (See Haus, Hauss) Catharina 14, 22; Elisabetha 67; Friderich (Fried.) 14, 17, 22; Jacob 1, 17, 21, 72; Johannes 72; Magdalene 1, 17, 21, 72; Marg. 14, 17, 22; Peter 1, 2, 18, 65, 67; Salome 2, 18, 65, 67; Sus. 18
HOSTER Ablonia 33; Conrath 83, 84; Jacob 33; Johannes 33, 83; Margreth 83

INDEX

HOSTMAN Doredea 70, 78; Joh. Michael 78; Michael 70
HOUK (See Hauk/Hauks) Joh. 27
HOUSEHOLDER (See Haushalter/etc.)
HOUSLEY Levi 29
HUBACKER Barbera 71; Cath. Elisabetha 72; Elisa 72; Elisabetha 71; Jacob 71, 72
HUBER Adam 1, 68, 72; Anna Maria 11, 89; Casper 69; Catharina 24, 68, 69, 72; Christian 68; Christofel 77; David 24; Elis. 24; Ester 61; Eva 72; Eva Catharina 70; Eva Elisabe 70; Georg 70; George Adam 1; Henrich 11, 89; Jacob 61, 77; John 58, 61; Katharina 1; Maria 58; Michael 69; Nanzi 24; Samuel 24; Sollome 69; Wilhelm 77
HUBLEN Catherine 107
HUCK Barbara 109; Elizabeth 109; Peter 109
HUDSON Tom 30
HUELUM Johann Peter 66; Susana Catharina 66
HUERSCH Fridrich 35
HUERT Elisabetha 96; Maria Magdalena 96; Nicolaus 96
HUET (See Huiet)
HUFFNER Elisabeth 61; Peter 61
HUGES/HUGHES Daniel 64; Margaret 28; Rebecca 64; Robert 64; Susanna 64
HUIET/HUET Elisabeth(a) 89, 96; Eva 66, 68; Johanes 102; Johan Henrich 68, 87; Ludwig 88; Magdalena 102; Margretha 88; N. 87; Nicolaus 87, 89; Peterus 89; Philip 66, 68
HUIEZ Elis. 26
HUKENS Cath. 12; Rabert 12; William 12
HUMBET Christ. 29
HUMS Catharina 58; Elisabetha 94; Jacob 58; Johan 94; Margratha 94; Susanna 58
HUNGBER Jacob 109
HURD Anton 107; Catherine 107, 108; John 108, 111; Susan 108; Susana 111
HURSCMAN Jacob 27
HUSSHALTER (See Haushalter/etc.) Johannes 72
HUTFELD/HUTFELT Catharina 33; Georg 33; Johannes 33
HUYERT Eva 44; John Jacob 45; John Ludwig 44; Ludwig 44; Magdalena 45; Margaretha 44; Peter 44, 45; Philipp 44

IRIG Cath. 14; Eva 14; Jacob 14

JABSON (See Jobson) Jonathan 26
JACKEL Jacob 11
JACKSON Nathan 26
JACOB Anna Barbara 61, 62; Anna Maria 62, 63; Barbara 63, 72; Elisabeth 62; George 63; Heinrich 61, 62, 63; Jacob 62; John 63; John Henry 63; Magdalena 61; Margareda 62, 63; Martin 61, 62, 63, 72; Michael 62, 63
JACOBY Conrad (Conrath) 46, 48, 49; Sophia (Sofia) 46, 49
JADEL Magdalene 5; Michael 5
JAEGER Ann Sophie 3; John 3; Jonathan 3
JANS Jane 27
JANSEN (See Jensen) Samuel 105; William 105
JAUER Jacob 73; Johannes 73
JEGEL Anamaria 98; Elisabetha 98; Georg 98
JEGER Henrich 72
JEGGELY (See Jegle, Jegly) Catharina 72; Johannes 72; Michael 72
JEGI Anna Margretha 69; Henrich 69
JEGLE (See Jeggely, Jegly) Henry 56; Margaret 56
JEGLY (See Jeggely, Jegle) Andres 22; Cath. 21, 22; Elisabeth 21; Hennerich 26; Jacob 21, 28; Joh. 22, 30; Sus. 22
JEILY John Adam 46; John Adam Henry 46; Margaretha 46
JENANEIN/JENAWEIN Christiana 8; Maria Magdalena 8; Peter 8
JENSEN (See Jansen) Magdalena 105
JETENAUER/JETONAUER Elisabetha 81; Margretha 81; Martin 81
JOBSON (See Jabson) Sarah 28
JOHNS (See Schons, Tschons) Anna Maria 34, 35, 38; Barbara 41; David 33, 41; Elisabeth 37, 38, 41; Elisabeth B. 40; Henrich 41; Jacob 38, 40; Johannes 38, 40; Jonathan 37, 38, 40; Magtalena 38, 40; Margretha 33; Maria Magtalena 41; Susana 35, 36; Thomas 38, 40; Wilhelm 34, 35, 38, 39, 40, 41
JONES Conrad 52; Elisabeth 23, 54; Isaac 23; Isau 101; Jonathan 54; Margretha 23, 101; Maria Magda 52; Susanna 52

INDEX

JONS (See Jones) Anamaria 54; Elizabeth 55, 57; Jonathan 55, 57; William 54
JOPSELE Elisabeth 6; John Christoph 6
JOST Anna 45; Anna Elisabetha 45; Anna Maria 45, 77; Henrich 77; Henry 45; Rebecca 45
JUIN Anna Maria 52, 55, 58; Catharina 55; Jacob 58; John 52, 55, 58; Margretha 89; William 58
JUNG (See Young, Yung) Adam 32; Anna Catharina 38; Anna Maria 11, 38; Atthilia 12; Catharina 11, 20, 97; David 97; Elisabeth 2, 36, 38; Eustagines (Eustaguis, Eustragines) 74, 77, 79, 82; Georg 2, 4, 36; Jacob 12, 13, 15, 20; Joh.Georg 38; John 2; Litia 15; Ludwig 11, 97; Margaretha (Margreth) 2, 4, 74, 77, 79, 86; Maria Elisabeth 32; Otilia 13, 15, 20; Samuel 4; Wilhelm 32
JUNGBER Maria 109
JUNGMAN Catharina 97; Daniel 97; Johan Daniel 97
JUNI John 52; John George 52; Maria 52
JUQUES Sus. 29
JUSTES John 107; Maria 107; Martin 107
JUTZLER Christian 68 Johannes 68; Margretha 68

KAAR Francis 29
KADEMANN Elisabeth 4; Michael 4; Simon 4
KAFFROTH (See Caffereth, Cafferoth, Cofferoth) Conrad 11; Magd. 11
KAIPP Catha. 88
KAN/KANN Elisabeth 78; Fridrich 78; Johan Jacob 78; Johannes 76, 78, 81; Susana 76, 78, 81
KAPP Catharina 19, 45, 94; George Michel 45; Michael 19, 88, 94
KARN (See Corn) Barbara 62
KASEROTH Catha. 68; Wilhelm 68
KASTEROTH Conrad 90; Georg Wilhelm 90; Magdalena 90
KATZ Anna 86; Catharina 79, 81, 82, 89; Cath. Elisabeth 74, 76, 84;Daniel 89; David 81; Elisabetha 86; Jacob 74, 76, 79, 81, 82, 84, 86, 89; Philipbina 82; Rebecka 84
KAU (See Caw, Cow) Catharina 60, 96; Daniel 60; Elisabetha 5, 36, 80, 96, 110; Fenrich 7; Friederich (Fridrich, Frederick) 80, 96, 110; Hanna 60; Henrich (Henry) 60, 80; John 60; Maria 7, 60; Nancy 60; Nicolaus 36; Peterus 36; Susanna 5; Theobold 5; Valentine 110
KAUFMAN Adam 32, 35; Catharina 35
KAUSLER/KAUSSLER A. Maria 18; Christina 5, 6, 7, 18, 98; Christina Margareth 93; Jacob 6; Johannes 11, 18, 83, 93, 98; John 5, 6, 7; Rosina 5; Sarah 7
KEB Margaretha 45; Michael 45
KECK Anna Cath. 14; Georg 14; Loisa Fredericka 14
KEFER Martin 30
KEHLER (See Keohler) Frederick 47; Margaretha 47; Maria Elizabeth Schlegin 47
KEHLHOFER Ann Mary 3; Elisabeth 3; Theobold 3
KEICKERLE Elisabeth 16; Jacob 16; Philip 16
KEIN Anna Maria 74; Johannes 74; Maria Cath. 74
KEINHART Eva Elisabetha 68; Johannes 68; Tomas 68
KEIPER Henrich 91; Johanes 91; Margretha 91, 105
KEISER Henry 48
KEISS John 45; Maria 45; Nicklaus 45
KEISSKELL Friedrick 6; Katharina 6; Sally 6
KEK Henrich 83
KELCHNER Anna Margretha 86; Johannes 86; Michael 86
KELHOFER A. Maria 18, 22; Dewald (Dewalt) 18, 22; Elisabeth 22; Hennerich 29; Maria 22
KELHOOVER/KELHOVER Eliz. 27; Hennerich 22
KELLER Anamaria Magdalena 100; Barbara 98, 100, 104; Christina 21; Johannes 73; Margretha 73; Molly 28; Philipp 98, 100, 104; Sarah 104; Wilhelm 98
KELLY Mary 29
KEMMERER Henrich 94; Peter 94; Sara 94
KEMS Elisabetha 39; Georg 39
KENNEDY William 26
KENNEL Catharina 98; Devalt (Duwalt) 12, 98; Elisabeth 12, 42, 98, 101; Magdalena 12; Rosina 42, 101; Teobald (Theobold) 42, 101
KENSINGER Elis. 26

INDEX

KEOHLER (See Kehler) Maria Magdalena 101
KEPLER John 48; Maria Catharine 48
KEPLING Polly 29
KEPLINGER Jacob 30
KERN Barbara 95; Catharina 92; Christina 92, 95; Christophel 92; Elisabetha 92; Nicolaus 92, 95
KERNEKAM/KERNKAUM Catharina 66; Elisabetha 45; Jacob 5; John Frederick 45; Ludwig 5, 45, 66; Maria 22; Regina 5, 45, 66
KERNETAM/KERTENAM Cath. 23; Ludwick 19, 23; Magd. 23; Marg. 23; Regina 19
KERSCHNER/KERSHNER (See Kirschner) Anamaria 42, 96; Barbara 28, 43; Christina 42, 43; Daniel 41, 42, 43; David 42; Elias 105; Elisabetha 41, 42, 106; George 21, 98, 109; Johannes 100, 106; John 42, 100, 105; Jonathan 42; Josia 105; Magdalena 41, 100, 106; Maria 21, 98, 109; Martin 16, 42, 43; Phillip 42; Solomon 43; Susana 100
KES Maria 79; Meril 79
KESINGER Andrew 49; Barbara 49; Catharine 49
KESLER/KESSLER (See Koesler) Andreas 24; Catharina (Cath.) 18, 83, 85, 87, 88; David 24, 85; Eva 12, 14, 18, 19, 20, 24, 48; Georg 87; Jacob 83, 85, 87, 88; Joh. Jacob 83; Matheus 12, 14, 18, 20; Mathias 18, 19, 24; Matthew 48; Peter 85; Samuel 12; Susanna 24
KESSNER Anna Catharina 44; Christian 44; John Jacob 44
KETHOFN Anna Maria 71; Dewalt 71
KIEFER/KIEFERN Catharina 94; Elisabeth 62; Martin 62
KIESECKER/KIESEKER/KIESSECKER/KISAKER /KISECKER A. Maria 110; Andros 110; Dorrothea 10, 13, 111; Elisabeth(a) 10, 14, 25, 89, 98; Joh. Jacob 10; Johannes 11, 13, 27; Philip 10, 13, 111; Simon (Simeon) 10, 14, 21, 89, 98
KIESIEDER/KISSEDER Anna Margaretha 5; Elisabetha 9, 10; Johanes 10; John Jacob 10; Maria Elisabeth 5; Nicholaus 9; Philip 9; Simon 5, 9, 10
KIESSMAN Elisabeth 3; Georg 3; Johanna 3
KIFER Marg. 29

KILMER Anna Maria 84; Eva 84; Georg 84
KINCKEL Casper 30
KING Barbara 62; Catharina 62; Matheus 62
KINN Doretra 67; Henrich 67
KIRCHNER Martin 73; Susana 73
KIRSCH David 40; Johannes 36; Maria 36
KIRSCHEN Hanna 71; Jacob 71
KIRSCHMAEN (See Kirschmann) Sofia 41
KIRSCHNER (See Kerschner/Kershner) Anna 89; Anna Maria 31, 33, 36, 37, 40; Barbara 36; Catharina 35; Christiana 37; Conrath 32; David 32, 34, 35, 37, 41; Elias 34; Elisabeth 31, 32, 34, 35, 36, 37, 40, 41, 89; Eva 34; Eva Elisabetha 31; Georg 31, 33, 34, 37, 38, 40; Hanna 32; Jacob 40, 41; Joh. Georg 38; Johannes 31, 33, 35, 36, 38, 40, 75; John 37; Jonas 41; M. 40; Margaretha Angener 40; Margretha 40; Maria 35, 38, 75; Marthin 36, 75; Martin 37, 40, 41, 89; N. 40; Rosina 32, 34; Salomon 38
KIRSHMANN (See Kirschmaen) Elisabeth 5; George 5; Maria 5
KISAKER, KISECKER (See Kiesecker, etc.)
KISENER Andreas 48; Barbara 48; John 48
KISSEDER (See Kiesieder)
KISTER Barbera 78; Joh. Jacob 78; Maria Barbera 76; Philip 76, 78
KITCHEN John 27
KITSMILLER/KITSMULLER/KIZMILLER Adam 26; Jacob 27; Joh. 30
KITTINGER Anna Maria 109; Elizabeth 109, 112; George 109, 112; Maria Elizabeth 109; Philip 112
KLAMPORT Elisabetha 74; Eva Maria 74; Georg 74
KLAPBACH Cath. Margeretha 46; Martin 46
KLAPPER Annamaria 106; Barbara 103; Elisabetha 106; Fraderick 44; Henrich 103; Johanna 44; Juna 44; Mattheas 106; Valentin 44
KLARCK/KLARK Allesc 52; John 52; Joseph 14; Margaretha 14; Sally 29; Susanna 52; William 14
KLEBSATTEL Ana 97; Anna 101; Daniel 97, 101
KLECAN Elisabet 39

INDEX

KLEIN Adam 90; Ana Magdalena 102; Anna Maria 74, 82, 93, 108, 109; Barbra 48; Catharina 49, 74, 93, 95; Daniel 13, 49, 95, 102, 104; Elisabetha (Elisa, Elisabeth) 14, 49, 90, 93, 97, 99, 104; Elizabeth Magdalena 108; Eva 82; Frederick 49; Georg 14, 99, 104, 108; Henrich 93, 97, 104, 105; Irma Maria 47; Jacob 49, 109; Joh. Georg 14; Johan Henrich 102; Johannes 16, 99; John 6, 48; John George 48, 109; John Peter 107; Joseph 74; Jost 82, 93; Katharina 6; Magdalena 16, 93, 97, 105; Margareta 49; Margaretha Schmit 47; Margretha 95, 102; Maria 102; Nicholas 47; Peter 16, 90; Philip 108; Sarah 105; Susana 102; William 49, 93
KLEINSCHMIDT/KLEINSMIDT/KLENSCMIDT Andreas 4, 14; Barbara 14; John 4; Margaretha 4; Maria 14; Rebeca 4
KLEKAM/KLEKAMM Drusilla 17, 58; Elizabeth 58; Joh. 17; John 58; Georg 17; Joh. 17
KLEOCKER Deobald 52; Elizabeth 52; Maria 52
KLEPPER Friederich 21; Johannes 21; Sarah 21
KLINSCK Frederick 49; Maria Magdalena 49
KLODNER Catharina 59; Elizabeth 59; Theobald 59
KNAD (See Knod/Knode) Catharina 94; Friederich 94; Georg 94
KNAUFEL Elisabetha 93
KNEBEL Catharina 58; George 53, 58; Jacob 52, 53; John 52; Leonhard 29; Maria Elizabeth 53; Maria Salome 52, 53; Uscon. 53
KNEBERGER Nenzi 26
KNECHT Christina 67; Elisa 49; Jacob 49, 67; Johannes 67; Samuel 49
KNEFT Christina 67; Jacob 67
KNIGHT Elisa 49; Samuel 49; Jacob 49
KNOCHEL Anna Cath. 47; Frederick 46; Hanna 45; Margaretha 46
KNOD/KNODE (See Knad) Cath. 15, 20; Georg 15; Joh. 13; Jonathan 13; Magdalena 96; Matheias 96; Michael 15; Samuel 96
KNODEL Elisabeth 13; Jacob 29; Joh. 13; Jonathan 13
KNOT Jacob 80; Johanes 80; Margretha 80; Maria Magtalena 80; Matheis 80

KNOTH Conrad 49; Jacob 49; M. 49; Sara 49
KOCH Anna Katharina 5; Anna Maria 7; Catharina 5, 23; David 5, 6, 7; Elis. 23; Joh. 23, 29; Katharina 5, 6, 7; Magdalena 5; Maria Margaretha 6; Michael 82
KOEHLER/KOELER (See Kohler, Kohrler, Koler) Anamaria 91, 99; Elisabetha 92; Friederich (Frederick) 44, 47, 99, 101, 102, 106; George 91; Magdalena 92, 106; Margretha 106; Maria Magdalena 102; Maria Margreth 92; Samuel 99
KOENIG (See Konig) Abraham 95, 96, 98, 101, 104; Anamaria 101; Christian 75; Daniel 98; Elisabetha 75, 95, 96, 101, 104; Jacob 95, 96, 101, 104; Johannes 95; Magdalena 75, 95, 96, 98, 101, 104; Marty 101; Sophia 104
KOESLER Friederich 95; Maria Magdalena 95
KOHLER/KOHRLER/KOLER (See Kohler, etc.) Anna Maria 61; Christ. 29; Conrad 44; George 61; Juliana 44
KOLT Barbara 96; Jacob 96; Johanes 96
KONIG (See Koenig) Abraham 18; David 109; Elizabeth 109; Magd. 18; Mathias 109
KOOGLE (Kugel) Benjamin 27
KOPENHOEFER Baltasar 45
KOR (See Cor) Barbara 38; Christian 38
KORHLER Margaretha 44
KORNMAN Abraham 96; Elisabetha 96; Maria 96
KORO Catharina 63; Jacob 63
KOSS Ana Maria 109; John 109; Maria Barbara 109
KRAEMER Anna Maria 77
KRAFT Eva 11, 14; Fridrich 73; Jacob 11, 14, 101; Katharina 8; Margaretha 11; Peter 8; Susana 101
KRAMER Catharina 99; Elisabeth 12; Johanes 99; Jonas 99
KRAUT Elisbetha 100; Jacob 38; Magtalena 38; Peter 38, 100
KREB/KREBES/KREBS (See Krebs) Anamaria 96; Anna 15, 98, 100, 101, 103; Elisa 103; Elisabeth 86; Eva Juthit 101; Georg 86, 88, 89, 96, 100, 103, 105; George Vortne 100; Katharina 6; Lidia 100; Magdalena 6, 86, 88, 89, 90, 93, 95, 98, 101; Margretha 86, 88, 96, 100, 103,

INDEX

105; Maria 47; Martin 6, 47, 86, 88, 89, 90, 93, 95, 98, 101; Rabert 76; Sara 95; Wilhelm 100, 101; Wilhelm Michael 98; William 15, 98, 103
KREG Tschin 76; Tschin Nansi 76
KREILICH Catharina 75; Herman 75; Maria Magtalena 75
KREMER Jacob 101; Margretha 101; Rachael 101
KREPS Wil. 26
KRES Elisabet 71; Henrich 71; Rosina Catha. 71
KRIED Elisabeth 47
KRIEG Katharina 2; Nicholas 2; Philip 2
KRIEGER/KRIGER A. Maria 19, 23; Anna Maria 13; Barbara 13, 20, 87, 91, 92, 96, 100, 104; Catharina 45, 104; Hennerich 19, 23; Johannes 96; Joh. Hennerich 13; Peter 45, 87, 91; Philip 13, 92, 96, 100, 104; Samuel 19, 92; Sarah 100; Susanna 23
KRIET Elisabeth 47
KRIM Philip 38
KRING Elisabeth 3; Mary 3; Philipp 3
KRITENEIS Catharina 52; Martin 52
KRO Catherine 111; John 111; Susana 111
KROKERLY Elena 20
KROMER Jacob 106; Maria 106; Samuel 106
KROUT Elis. 23; Johannes 23; Peter 23
KRUMBACH (See Crumbach) Johannes 77, 78, 79; Juliana 78
KRUP Henrich 31; Jacob 31
KUCK Catharina 90; David 90; Wilhelm 90
KUEBLER Ann Margaretha 2; Jacob 2; John George 2
KUFER Eva 61; Martin 21
KUGEL Adam 111; Benjamin 19, 23; Catherine 107, 108, 109, 110, 111; Christian 99; Dorrathea 19, 23; Elisabetha 99; John 107, 108, 109, 110, 111; Jonathan 23; Lidia 19; Magdalena 108
KUHN/KUHNES/KUN/KUNN/KUNS (See Kuntz) Adam 69; Anamaria 48; Catharina Stuter 48; Doretha 67, 69; Elisabeth(a) 15, 19, 75, 105; Georg 48; Georg Adams 75; Henrich 67, 69; Jacob 105; Johan Jacob 105; Leonhard (Leonhart) 15, 19, 26;

Littia 15; Maria Dorrothea 19; Milial 105; Philip 75
KUKER Elis. 29
KUNTZ (See Kuhn, etc.) Anna Martha 48; Catharine 48; John Georg 48
KURBEL Catharina 37, 39; Georg 37, 39; Georg Lenhart 37
KURTZ Cath. Clem. 18; Jacob 18; Sus. 18
KUSLERT Anna Maria 44; Georg 44; John 44
KUTER Catharina 68; Eugelhart 68

LACKER Elisabeth 61; George 61; Susanna 61
LACKLEN Catharina 61; Eva 61; John 61
LACKLY Elisabeth 61; Eva 61; Jose 61
LADIS Anna Maria 61
LALEDI Elisabetha 70
LAMBERT/LAMPERT Elisabeth 85; Eva 81, 85, 95, 97; Georg 81, 85, 95, 97; Jacob 81; Jonas 95; Sem 97; Susana 105
LAMS Jacob 37; Regina 37
LANDE Kurt 44
LANE Rebecca 301 Seth 28
LANG (See Long) Andreas 66; Angnes 33; Canrath 40; Catharina 40; Doretha 66; Elisabeth 41, 98; Fromia 66; Georg 40; Johannes 98; Maria 40; Martin 33; Peter 40; Petrus 98
LANGBERGER Andreas 5; Anna Katharina 5; Elisabeth 5
LANGENADER Anna Margaretha 8; Christian 8; Rebeca 8
LANGENECKER Abraham 26; Anna Marg. 12; Cath. 27; Christian 12; Sus. 29
LANGRENDER Christian 9; David 9; Elisabeth 9; Margaretha 9
LANIA William 7
LANTZ/LANZ David 59; Elisabeth 18, 59, 62; Michael 62; Peter 18, 26, 59; Susanna 62
LAUER John 44
LAUMAN --- 25; Elisabeth 62, 63; Eva 61; Jacob 62; Margareda 62; Martin 61; Regina 61
LAURI/LAURY Barbara 16, 20; Cath. 20; Michael 16, 20; Susana 16
LAUT Eva 35; Jacob 35; Maria 35
LAWMAN Maria 99; Michael 99; Rosina 99
LAYDER Elisabeth 61

INDEX

LECKRON/LECRON (See Lekron) Ana 96; Anamaria 99; Anmargretha 102; Catharina 98; Elisabetha 93, 96, 99, 103; Friederich 96; Jacob 96, 98, 100, 102; Johannes 93; Margretha 96, 98, 100; Salome 102; Simeon 93, 96, 99, 103
LECTER Abraham 51; Elizabeth 51; Magdalena 51
LEDER Abraham 93; Catharina 93
LEDDERMANN/LEDERMAN/LEDERMANN Caspar 36; Caspar 38; Fredrich/Fridrich 66; Margaretha 47; Maria Catharina 66; Maria Elisabetha 66; Susanna Catharina 66
LEDISEN Elisabeth 61
LEE Ana 93; Ana Mary 93; John 64, 93; William 64
LEFEBRE/LEFEVER David 23, 29; Elis. 23; Sus. 23
LEFFLER/LEFLER Anna 52; Bessie 56; Catharina 52, 58, 59; John 52; Jonathan 58; Peter 58
LEFNER Cath. 29
LEH Anna 10; Jacob 10; Samuel 10
LEIBY Catharina 91, 93; Georg 91, 93; Johannes 91, 93
LEICHT Cath. 16
LEID Adam 37; Joh. Georg 37; Rosina 37
LEIDER (See Leiter/Leitert, Leyter, Lyter) Abraham 92; Chorina 92; Christian 74; Elisabetha 74; Jacob 106; Marianna 74
LEIDI/LEIDY Adam 35, 36, 37, 40, 86; Anna 40; Barbara 35; Catharina 63, 96; Elisabeth 70, 80, 82; Fridrich 35; Georg 37; Henrich 40; Johannes 70, 80; Maria Anna 70; Rosina 35, 36, 37, 40, 86; Sara 86
LEIGHTER (See Leiter) Abraham 28; Eva 27
LEINBACH Bally 18; Elisabeth 18; Hanna 18; Joseph 18; Maria Berry 18
LEISE Cath. 30
LEISER Cath. 73; Matheis 73; Susana 73
LEISINGER/LEISSINGER Anna Maria 14; Catharina 14, 100; Dewald 14; Fenrick 7; Jacob 7; Margaretha 7
LEITER/LEITERT (See Leighter, Leyter, Lieder, Lyter) Abraham 2, 3, 4, 23; Christian 1; Elisabeth 1, 23; Eve 3; Jacob (Jakob) 1, 2, 3, 4, 61, 63; Johanna Katharine 3; John 4;
Juliana 1, 4, 63; Katharina 2, 4; Mary Ann 3; Peter 3
LEKRON (See Leckron/Lecron) Elisabeth 88; Jacob 88; N. 88
LENNS/LENTZ Elisabetha 62, 77; Jeremias 77; Rahel 77
LEOSSNER Anna 55; Elizabeth 55; Jacob 55
LEPTEN Sarah 29
LESCHURR/LESHER Elizabeth 110; Friederich 28; Peter 110
LESIG Marg. 26
LESLER Catharina 55; Peter 55
LETHURMAN Mary 27
LETTERMAN John Georg 46; Margaretha Boeringer 46; Michel 46
LEUDY Jacob 51; Maria 51; Samuel 51
LEWIES Anna Maria 66; Henrich 66; Sturn Auren 66
LEWIS Magdalena 91; William 91
LEY Barbara 109; Jacob 109; John George 109
LEYDE/LEYDI/LEYDY/LEYTE (See Lidi) Adam 33, 40; Barbara 61; Johannes (Johnn.) 67, 70, 73; John 44; Juliana 44, 70; Margretha 33; Rosina 33, 40, 67; Susana 73
LEYSINGER Cath. 19, 23; Daniel 19; Dewald 19, 23; Jacob 23
LEYTER (See Leider, Leiter/Leitert, Lieder, Lyter) Andreas 61, 62; Barbara 62; Jacob 61; John 62; Julianna 61; Magdalena 62; Susanna Catharina 61
LFFLER Catharina 56; Peter 56
LICHTWEILER Ada 107; Catherine 107; George 107; John George 107; John Peter 107; Richard 107
LIDI (See Leyde/ etc.) Johanes 79
LIDMAN Catharina 31; Vellendin 31
LIEBERKNECHT Christophel 54; Elizabeth 54; Margretha 54
LIEDER (See Leider, Leiter/Leitert, Leyter) Andreas 63; Barbara 63
LIFLER Joh. 30
LIFTEN Anna Maria 66; Samuel 66; Tomas 66
LILENDLINGER Dorodea 9; Henry 9; Jacob 9; John George 9; Konrad 9
LILLICH Christ. 19; Elisabeth 19; Hennerich 19
LILLIG Christiana 22; Hennerich 22; Samuel 22
LINCK Andreas 75; Anna Maria 75; Elisabetha 75

136

INDEX

LIND Andreas 9; Elisabeth 9; Magdalena 9; Peter 9
LINEBACH Joseph 26
LINGSCREIBER Elizabeth 109; George 109; Jacob 109; John 109
LINXWEILER Catherine 110, 111; Christina 111; Frederick 110; George 110, 111
LITTEL/LITTLE David 26, 100, 105; Elisabetha 100, 105; Nathan 105; Samuel 27; Susanna Lomfort 100
LOCH (See Lock) Daniel 13; Jacob 13; Nenzi 13
LOCHER Elisabeth 78; Frederick 46; Henrich 78; Joh. Henrich 78
LOCK (See Loch) Anna 60; John 60; Susanna 60
LOEB Anna Maria 47; John 47; Margaretha Conrath 47
LOEHLER Maria 44
LOENS Anna Maria 48; Henry 48
LOESSLER Elisabeth 44, 45; Jacob 44, 45; Margaretha 44, 45
LOGNE Joh. 29
LOHRSHACH (See Lorshbach) Elisabetha 100; Herman 100
LONG (See Lang) Elisabetha 94, 106; Henrich 94; Johannes 94, 106; Mary 106
LORA/LORAH Catharina 29, 46; Henry 46; Maria 46
LORSHBACH (See Lohrshach) Elisabeth 15, 20; George 15; Hennerich 12; Herman 12, 15, 20; William 20
LOSS Elisabeth 80; Joh. Georg 80; Johannes 80
LOWMAN Martha 27
LOWRENS Elisabetha 106
LOY Anna Barbara 108; Barbara 111; Jacob 108, 111; John 111
LUDI/LUDY David 54, 56; Jacob 56; John 54; Philipina 54, 56
LUNTZ Christian 84; Maria Elisabeth 84
LUZ Andreas 12; Andrew 60; Cath. 12; Juliana 12, 60; Martin 60
LYTER (See Leider, Leiter/Leiter, Leyter, Lieder) Andreas 62; Barbara 62; John 62

M'DONNOL Polly 22; Reinherd 22
MACALL Jun 71
MAGFETSCHRIN Magthalena 33
MAGGIN Elis. 28

MAHNINGER Ann Margarethe 3; Elisabeth 3; Fenrick 4; Henry 3
MAIER Anna Margaret 51; Catharina 99; Henry 51; Peter 51; Phillip 99; Salome 99
MANAN Elisabeth 40; Stephan 40
MANDEL Andereas 80; Anna Maria 89; Barbera 80; Christian 79, 80; Elisabeth 89; Eva Magtalena 79; Georg 89; Maria Barbera 79
MANDI Ann Mary 2; Balthasar 2; Elisabeth 19; Jacob 2; Joh. 19; Rosina 19
MANE Anna Maria 36
MANEN Lenhart 36; Stefan 36
MANGARD George 26
MANIGER Anamaria 96; Elisabetha 96; Henrich 96
MANINGER John 46, 47, 48; John Jacob 48; Magdalena 47, 48; Margaretha 47
MANN Georg 27
MANTEL Anna Susanna 31; Barbara 31; Christian 31; Maria Barbara 5; Martha 5
MANTI Baltzer 36; Johan Peter 36; N--- 36
MARDEN Susanna 108; Valentine 108
MARDER Susana 109, 110; Valentine 109, 110; William 109
MARGANTHAL George 49
MARS Alexander 37; Elisabetha 37; John 37
MARSTELLER Benjamin 12; Elis. 12; Maria 12
MARSTUS Johannes 41; Maria Matalena 41; Susana 41
MARTEN Susana 109; Valentine 109
MARTIN Ana 29; Christina 108
MARTINI A. Maria 16; Georg 16, 21; Margaretha 21; Sus. 21
MARTINY Georg 98; Susana 98
MASTALLEN Sarah 28
MATINY Georg 23
MATTICK Gottfried 29
MAUDI/MAUDY (See Mauti/Mauty) Anna Cugel 110; Anna Magdalena 55; Anna Maria 6, 110, ; Balthasar 6; Balze 58; Bolhar 54; Brudius 110; Casper 54, 55, 57, 58, 112; Catharina 54, 55, 57, 58, 110, 112; David 111; Elias 112; Elizabeth 112; George 58, 110, 111; Hanipe 112; Henry 51, 112, 110; Jacob 6, 58; John 52, 55, 56, 58; Margaretha 111; Martin 110;

INDEX

Mary Elizabeth 110; Michael 56, 57; Peter 54, 55; Rosina 55, 56, 110
MAUNDY Annie 108; Elias 108; Henry 108
MAUERER/MAURER Adam 61; Catherine 107, 110, 111, 112; George 1; John George 107; John Henry 1; Magdalene 1; Margareth 1; Maria 111; Mich(a)el 107, 110, 111, 112
MAUTEL Barbara 72; Christian 72
MAUTI/MAUTY (See Maudi/Maudy) Anna Maria 40; Balthasar (Baltzer) 31, 32, 34, 40; Elisabeth 31, 32, 34; George 53; Joh. Adam 32; John 53; Martin 53; Rosina 53
MAUTIFNA Ana Maria 51
MAYER (See Meier, Meyer, Myers) Cath. 15; Elisabeth 12, 15, 20; Hennerich 12; Jacob 12, 15, 20, 25; Margaretha 19; Samuel 20; Susanna 25
McCANEDY Sarah 27
McCAUL Ana 101; Catharina 93, 97, 101; Daniel 97; Johannes 93; Robert 93, 97, 101
McCAULEY Charles 64
McCLARY Elisabeth 89; Maria Magdalena 89; Patrick 89
McCORMICK (See McKormick, McOrmick)Joh. 25
McCOY Perry 64
McCULLOUGH Mary 27
McDASCH Sarah 83, 84; William 83, 84
McEVON Elis. 26
McFERIN Anna Leidi 40; Johannes 40; William 40
McGURT Hanna 88; Jahn 88; Maria 88
McHARRY Hanna 26
McINTIRE Rachel 29
McKINLY Joh. 30
McKORMICK (See McCormick, McOrmick) Elis. 25; Marg. 11; William 11
McLURE Hana 92; John 92; Rafael 92
McORMICK (See McCormick, McKormick) Cath. 15; Joh. Georg 15; William 15
MECKLU Hanna 24; Joh. 24; Johannes 24
MEFERT Caspar 73; Georg 73; Maria 73
MEIER (See Meyer, Mayer, Myers) Elisabetha 40; Emanuel 40; Hanna 101; John 101; Jonathan 40
MEIPER Anna 98; Elisabetha 98; Georg 98
MEIRER Jacob 67; Margretha 67
MEISTER Catherine 108; Daniel 108; George 108
MEKING Susana 110; Thomas 110

MENSER/MENTZER/MENZER Barbara 26; Catharina 63; John 63
MERCKEL Cath. 18; Georg 18; Magd. 18
MERTZ Barbara 90; Christ. 90; Georg 90
METTY Motlaka 27
METZ Barb. 30; Christ 27
METZGER Adam 71; Elisabeth 71; Georg 71
MEY Georg 73; John Peter 73; Maria Christina 73
MEYER/MEYERS (See Mayer, Meier, Myers) Anna Elisabetha 73; Elisabeta 70; George Jacob 67; Jacob 67, 70; Jesse 96; Joh. 30; Joh. Georg 73; Magtalena 67; Martin 27; Phillip ; Catharina 96
MICHAEL/MICHEL Anna Maria 41; George 6; Joh. Eberhart 41; Johannes 39; Simon 6; Susana 6
MIDDELKAUF/MIDDELRAUF Anamaria 97; Barbara 95, 97, 103; Christian 98; Daniel 103; Henrich 90, 95, 97, 103; Margretha 98; Maria Elisabetha 98; Rossina 98; Samuel 95
MIHLS Susana 101; Zacharias 101
MILLER A. Maria 13, 17, 20, 21; Adam 92; Ana Catharina 92; Anamaria (An. Maria, Anna Maria) 10, 13, 14, 16, 53, 92, 99, 107; Andreas 14, 15; Ann 64; Bolly 20; Catharina 13, 21, 22, 27, 52, 54, 56, 57, 59, 99, 100, 103, 106, 107, 108, 110, 112; Christian 105; Christina 4, 11, 14, 16, 20, 55, 57, 59, 60, 98, 107; Daniel 56, 106; David 60; Eleischa 106; Elias 24; Elisabeth (Elis., Elisabetha) 20, 22, 26, 55, 105, 108; Eva 17, 21, 39; Friederich 100, 103; Georg 16, 52, 54, 56, 57, 98, 99, 107, 108, 110, 112; Georg Matheus 21; Hennerich 11, 15; Hesekiel 20; Isaac 17, 21; Jacob 4, 22, 56, 59, 71, 103, 105, 107; Johanes 10, 13, 17, 19, 20, 24, 29, 30, 92; John 53, 55, 56, 57, 59, 107; Julian 53; Juliana 55, 57, 59; Lana 11; Lidia 16; Louise 44; M. Catharina 60; Magdalena 59; Maria 24; Mary 26; Mauduall 100; Michael 11, 27; Mrs. Warren D. 51; Nancy 103, 106; Oliver 103; Othia Holland Stull 106; Peter 11, 13, 14, 16, 20, 21, 55, 57, 59, 64, 99, 103, 106; Philip 4; Rebecca 20; Rosina 11, 15; Sallomon 39; Salome 57; Samuel 17, 99; Sara 92;

138

INDEX

Susana 10, 11, 29, 30, 57, 59, 71, 106; Susana Malvina 103; William 107
MILTS Catherine 111; Sarah 111; Theodore 111
MINICH Catharina 58; Henry 58
MIRKER Daniel 27
MITTAG Catharine 47; John Frederick 47
MOHLS Samuel 7; Susana 7; Zacharias 7
MOLL Henrich 77; Maria Catha. 77; Maria Elisabetha 77; Wh. Henrich 77
MOLLOTH Rebecca 26
MOLLS Daniel 15; Prudens 22; Sus. 15, 22; Zacharias 15, 22
MONG Barbara 16; Georg 16; Jacob 16
MONSCHULD Carl August 104; Eva 104
MONTGOMERY Eva 7; Huen (Kuen?) 7; Mary 7
MOON Samuel 29
MOOREHEAD --- 29
MORE Elizabeth 59; James 97; Johannes 97; John 59; Joseph 59; Susana 97
MORF Johannes 73; Maria Magthalena 73
MORGAN/MORGON Judith 21; Magdalena 4; Margaretha (Marg.) 4, 26; Nathan 8, 64; Nathanael 4, 21
MORGANTHAL Hanna 49; John 49; Sarah 49; William 49
MORRIS Nancy 30
MOSER Benjamin 27; Elisabetha 32; Eva Barbara 38; Jacob 36; Johan Peter 33; Johann Jacob 32; Margreth(a) 33, 36, 38; Peter 33, 38; Samuel 32
MOTZ Martin 27
MOYER Cath. 23; Philip 23
MOZ Elisabetha 102
MU..AR Henry 28
MUELLER (See Muller) Abraham 37, 85, 87; Adam 71; Andrew 1; Ann Mary 1; Anna 71, 84; Anna Maria 37, 39, 87; Catharina 31, 36, 70, 85; Conrad 31; Daniel 39, 40; David 40; Elisabeth(a) 39, 45, 46, 85, 87, 89; Elisabeth Barbera 89; Ernst 74; Eva 36, 38; Fridrich 38; Fromia 78; Fronica 1; Georg 35, 36, 46; Henrich 31, 73; Jacob 1, 31, 71; Joh. Sallomon 38, 39; Johan Fridrick 70; Johannes 35, 36, 37, 39, 78, 84, 87, 89; John 1, 45; John George 1; John. Fridrich 70; Judith 46; Juliana 39, 40; Magtalena 35; Margretha 74; Maria Eva 39; Peter 39; Susan(a) 73, 87; Thomas 74
MUENTZE Catharina 91; Henrich 91

MULLER (See Mueller) Adam 7; Anna Maria 51; Catharina 51, 58, 66; Challendin 51; Elisabeth 7, 51, 52; Ester 7; Fenrich 7; George 51, 58; Heinrich (Henry) 51, 66; Johannes 68; John 7, 51, 52; Juliana 51, 52; Katharina 7; Magthalena 68; Sofina 58
MULTE Becky 83
MUNCH Elisabeth 7; Katharina 7; Philip 7
MUNDUS Casper 11; Elisabeth 11
MUNTSH John 27
MURRY Elias 26
MUSELMAN/MUSSELMAN Mary 29; Sus. 30
MYERS (See Mayer, Meier, Meyer, Jacob 30

NAEPH (See Nef/Neff, Neph) Christina 45
NAME George 57; Katharina 57; Wilhelm 57
NEF/NEFF (See Naeph, Nepf) Anna Maria 4; Christina 45; Elisabeth 6, 9, 15, 24; George 6, 9, 15, 24; Jacob 4; John 6; Rebeca 4; Sovia 15
NEGLE Maria Elisabeth 47
NEID (See Nied) John 6; Katharina 6
NEIDIG David 71; Magtalena 71
NEIG Andreas 6
NEITH Samuel 26
NEMMINGER Andrew 2; Ann Mary 2; Frederic 2
NEPF (See Naeph, Nef/Neff) Barbara 5; Jacob 5; Margaretha 5
NEST Elisabeth 8; Katharina 8; Leonhard 8
NETZ Elisabeth 7; George 7
NEU (See New, Nue) Adam 13; Christina 38; Elisabeth 5; Georg(e) 5, 6, 7, 8, 13, 16, 17, 24, 47, 86; John George 5; Katharina 8; M. Magd. 16; Magdalen(a) (Magtalena, etc.) 5, 6, 7, 8, 13, 17, 24, 47, 86; Maria Magdalena 7; Michael 7; Susana 6
NEUKIRCH Abraham 95; John 48; Maria 48; Salome 95; Sibila 95
NEUMAN Adam 43; Elisabeth 43; Henry 43
NEW (See Neu, Nue) George 3; Magdalene 3
NEY Cath. 74; Jacob 74; Maria 74
NICKEL (See Nicol, Nikel) Eva 88; Jacob 88; Susana 88
NICLOS (See Niklos) Anna Catha. 80; Eva 80; Jacob 80

INDEX

NICODEMUS Catharina 73; Fridrich 73; Pastor 31
NICOL (See Nickel, Nikel) Anna Maria 90; Elisabetha 105; Eva 90; Jacob 90, 105; Johannes 90; Michael 90; Petrus 90; Susanna 105
NIED A. Maria 20; Anna Maria 13, 14; Daniel 13, 14, 20; Jacob 20; Johann Peter 14; John Jacob 1; Katharine 1; Matias 1
NIESBERT Elizabeth 59
NIESBETH Elizabeth 59; Nathaniel 59
NIKEL (See Nickel, Nicol) Catharina 86; Eva 86; Georg 86; Jacob 86; Joh. Jacob 86; Michael 86
NIKLOS (See Niclos) Elisabetha 82; Eva 82; Jacob 82
NIT Eva Cath. 82; Mattheis 82
NIZEL Barbara 109, 110, 112; Elizabeth 109; John 109, 110, 112; Magdalena 112
NOLL Catharina 93; Conrad 92, 93, 96, 102; Elisabetha 102; Margreth 93; Maria Elisabetha 96, 102
NORFIN Magtalena 65
NORMAN Carl 69; Catha. 69; Maria Clora 69
NORTH Catharina Reichenback 47; John 47; Maria Cath. 47
NOUSE Eva 26
NUE (See Neu, New) Georg 94; Magdalena 94
NUNNEMACHER Elisabeth 89; Esther 89; Nico. 89

OBERMEYER Joh. 28
OCHS/OCKS Andreas 30; Anna Margretha 88; Anna Maria 88; Johannes 88
ODENWALD/ODRUWALD Catharina 93; Elisabetha 93, 95; Johanes 93, 95
OETER Cath. 74; Philip 74
OFF Adam 11, 15; Bally 17; Cath. 18; Jacob 18; Juliana 11, 15, 18
OGLE Charles 64
OHARROUGH John 26
OHLWEIN/OLWEIN Anamaria 101; Bernhard 101; Carl 89, 95, 98, 105; Doretea 89; Elisabetha 95, 98, 101, 105; Georg 89; Johan Carl Bernhart 101; Sarah 98; Sophia 105
OHRENDORF (See Orendorf) Christofel 85; Elisabeth 85
OHRENDORST Elisabetha 74
OIN (See Owen) George 109; Sara 109; Susana 109

OISSEDER Dorothea 3; Elisabeth 3; Philipp 3
OLLINGER David 32; Elisabetha 32; Juliana 32
OLWEIN (See Ohlwein)
OPP Anna Eva 81, 85' Hanna 78; Johannes 81; Nicolaus (Niclos) 78, 81, 85
ORENDORF (See Ohrendorf) Henrich 92, 96; Jacob 96; Johannes 96; Margretha 92, 96; Simson 92; Susana 96; William 96
OSS Joh. 23; Johannes 23
OSTER Anna 39; Anna Elisabetha 40; Conrad (Conrath) 41, 42, 76, 94, 101, 109; Daniel 41; David 35, 42; Elisabeth(a) 34, 40, 42, 70, 73, 80, 86; Eva 41, 42, 94, 101, 109; Georg 39; Georg Jacob 31; Jacob 35, 80; Joh. Peter 34; Johan Georg 31; Johannes 40, 70, 73, 80; John 41; Juliana 31, 32, 35; Maria 32; Maria Elisabeth 36; Peter ; Johannes 40; Rosina 41, 94; Samuel 41; Susana 36, 39; Vallentin 32, 34, 36
OSSWALD/OSWALD Adam 18, 103; Benjamin 103; Eva 18; M. Eva 18; Maria 18, 103
OT/OTT Adam 4; Anna Maria 4; Cath. 87; Elisabetha 9, 39, 57; Friedrich 4; George 9; Jacob 4, 9; Johan Jacob 68; John 9; Juliana 4, 9; Katharina 4, 9; Maggretha 2, 9, 68; Martinus 87; Matheis 39; Michael 2, 68
OWEN (See Oin) Kennedy 64; Sarah 64
OX/OXX/OXT Ana Margretha 96; Anamaria 97; Catharina 30, 99; Elisabeth 13, 96, 97; Jacob 99; Johanes 97, 99; Michael 13, 96, 97; Sus. 30
OYER Francis 28; Wendel 27

PALMER (See Balmer) Christ. 29
PAREKEE Elisabeth 18; Mary 18; Samuel 18; Tomas 18
PARRY Catharina 100; Christina 100; Thomas 100
PAULUS (See Baulus) Elizabeth 110; Jacob 110
PECK Joh. 26
PENDER Georg 26
PENNERICH John 3; Jonas 3; Margaretha 3
PERFERIN Anna Maria Difom 66
PERRY Barbara 95; Christina 95; Thomas 95

INDEX

PETER Abraham 13, 17; Albrecht 101; Anamaria 101; Anna 13; Cath. 13, 17, 22; Sara 17; Sus. 22
PETERY (See Pitri) Jacob 48
PFAD Barbara 36; Jacob 36
PFEICKER Eva Margareda 62; John 62; Philipp 62
PFEIFER/PFEIFFER Anamaria 54; Barbara 54, 110; Catherine 15, 110; Christian 38; Christina 38; Doretea 38; Emanuel 110; Manuel 54
PFEISTER Anna Maria 4; Elisabeth 6; Jacob 6; Katharina 4; Leonhard 4, 6
PFLATZGRAF Joh.Georg 26
PHEIFER Leonhard 4; Mariana 4; Martin 4
PHEN Athe 109; Othi 109; William 109
PHILIP A. Maria 109; Henry 109
PHILIPI A. Maria 109; Frantz 33; Henry 109; Jacob 109; Margretha 33
PIET Dorethea 86; Ester 86; William 86
PINDEL Richard 64
PIPER Jacob 27
PISBET Mary 27
PITRI (See Petery) Barbara 17; Jacob 6, 17
PITZER Conrath 75; Margretha 75; Mathies 75
PLATTE Anna Elisabetha 86; Johannes 86
POL Caspar 36; Catharina 36; Johan Henrich 36
PREIS/PREISS (See Price) Catharina 67; Elisabeth 72; Johanna Georg 67; Margretha 67; Wilhaelm 67; William 72
PRICE (See Preis/Preiss) Elina Boyd 29; Georg 20
PRIL/PRILL Jacob 93; Maria 93; Maria Barbara 93
PRINTZ/PRINZ Catherine 45, 109; Henry 48, 109; John M. 109
PROCUPEIN Anthony 95; Catharina 95; Johan Georg 95
PROTZMAN/PROTZMANN (See Brotzman) Anamaria 96; Becky 83; Elisabeth 82, 83, 86, 90; Gertraut Catha. 82; Johannes 96; Lorentz 82, 83, 86, 90; Nathanael 86; Rahel 90
PRUA (See Brua) David 37; Joseph 38; Jost 37, 39; Magthalena 37, 39; Margretha 38; Susana 39
PRYER Elis. 30

PSEISER/PSEISTER Anna Maria 4; Elisabeth 6; Jacob 6; Katharina 4; Leonhard 4, 6; Mariana 4; Martin 4
PURDGARD Robert 26
PURG Anna Maria 53
PURMAN Cath. 22, 23; Hennerich 22, 23
PURSEL Joseph 27

QUICKEL Fronica 32; Georg 32; Michael 32

RAB Eva 69; Michael 69
RABESEN/RABISON Elisabeth(a) 76, 81; Johannes (Johnn.) 76, 81
RAGAN John 64
RAHAUSER (See Rohauser) Anamaria 93; Johannes 93; Jonathan 93, 101
RANDALL Charlotte 59; Thomas 59
RAP/RAPP Christina 33; Jacob 33; John 1; Mary Margareth 1; Mathaeus (Mathes) 1, 33
RATTER Sarah 97; William 97
RAU Catharina 36, 39; Elisabeth 4, 35, 40; Henrich 35; Johannes 36; Katharina 4; Nicolaus 35; Theobold 4
RAUB Anna Maria 62; Appolonia 62; James 62
RAUCH Elisabeth 3; George 3; Johann Georg 32; John 3
RAUDENAUER (See Reitenauer/etc.)
RAUHZAHN Adam 62; Catharina 62; Jonathan 62
RAUK George Henry 2; Henry 2; Mary 2
RAUSER Catharina 94; Daniel 94; Sophia 94
RAVIES Auen 71; Cara 71; Maria 71; Maria Magtalena 71
RAWLINGS Elizabeth 64; Solomon 64
READENAUER (See Reitenauer/etc.)
REB Anna Maria 6; Elisabeth 3, 5, 6, 7, 8, 92, 98, 103; Hanna 8; Johanes 92, 98, 103; Johanna 3; John 3, 5, 6, 7, 8; John Fenrick 5; Katharina 5, 7; Lidia 103; William 98
REBEI Rosina 85
REBER Wilhelm 32
REBLOGEL Anna Maria 35; Anna Maria Margretha 35; Barbara 32, 35; Daniel 35; Jacob 32; Joh. Henrich 84; Maria 84; Philip 35, 84; Reinhart 32, 35
RECK Annamaria 104; Felix 104; Georg 104
REED James 25; Margaret 27; Samuel 25; Tomas 12; Vronica 12

INDEX

REFSCHNEIDER Andreas 12; Elisabeth 12; Sara 12
REFTER Abraham 57; Elizabeth 57; Irma Catharina 57
REGEN Elisabeth 8; George 8; John 8; Lilia 8; Maria 8; William 8
REHNIR Anna Margaret 108
REICHART Georg 47; Maria Barbara 47
REICHENBACK Catharina 47
REIDANAUER (See Reitenauer/etc.)
REIDEMANER Jacob 73; Joseph 73; Susana 73
REIDEMAUER Magthalena 68; Niclos 68;
REIDENAUER (See Reitenauer/etc.)
REIDENAUR (See Reitenauer/etc.)
REIDER Cath. 22; Georg 22
REIGHT Elisabetha 91, 99; Johannes 99; Maria 105; Thomas 91, 99
REINELS (See Reinolds, Reinels, Renol, Reynolds) Elisabetha 100; Joseph 100
REINHARD/REINHARDT/REINHART Ann Mary 2; Barbera 83, 84; Elisabeth(a) 4, 74, 86; Eva Catha. 72; Eva Elisabeth(a) 2, 3, 72; Frantz 86; Georg(e) 24, 72, 83, 84; John 2; Joseph 74; Margretha 86; Maria Barbara 72, 75; Maria Elisabeth 4, 8; Susanna 3, 72; Thomas 3, 4, 8, 72
REINOLDS (See Reinoll, Reinels, Renol, Reynolds) Elisabetha 103; Joseph 103; William Heyser 103
REINOLL (See Reinolds, Reinels, Renol, Reynolds) Anamaria 98; Daniel 98, 104, 105; Henrich 98; Peter 105
REINTHAL Catharina 62; Margrada 62; Matheias 62
REINTHALER Anna Elisabeth 62; Margareda 62; Matheus 62
REIPER Ana 92; Georg 92; Henrich 92; Margretha 92
REISENGER Catharina 103
REIS/REISS Anna Maria 44; Barbara 11, 16, 110; Catharine 16, 48; Elisabeth 11; Georg 11, 16, 110; Hanna 46; Maria 31, 44, 46; Maria Sara 31; Nicholas (Niclos) 31, 44, 46
REISER/REISSER David 20; Elisabeth 7; Joh. 20, 22; John 7; Magdalena 7, 22; Maria Magd. 20
REITEMANN Elisabeth 8; Fenrick 8; Margaretha 8

READENAUER/REIDEMANER/REIDEMAUER/ REIDENAUER/REITENAUER/REIDANAUER/ REIDENAUER/REITENAUER/REUDENAUER/ REUNAUER/REUTENAUER/REYDENAUER/RIDENAUER/ RUDENAUER A. Cath. 16; A. Maria 21, 109; Adam 3, 28; Agatha 12, 27; Anamaria (Anna Maria) 12, 91, 109; Anna 24; Barbara 43; Benjamin 12, 21, 91; Catherin(a) 11, 15, 33, 99, 108, 111; Christina 9; Christoph 30; Conrad 6; Daniel 1, 15, 28, 41, 99, 111; David 5, 6, 7, 8, 16, 27, 33, 85, 95, 99; Dorly 27; Elisabeth(a) 2, 4, 6, 8, 15, 21, 96, 99, 100; Eva 1, 4, 5, 6, 9, 12, 13, 15, 94, 111; Eve Katharina 5; Fenrick (Fenrich) 5, 6; Friedrick 2, 6; George 6; Henrich (Henry) 1, 3, 4, 15, 31, 33, 102, 111; Jacob 1, 4, 5, 6, 7, 73, 103; Johannes (Joh.) 12, 15, 24; John 1, 5, 8, 9, 41; John George 6; John Nichlas 1; Jonas 15; Joseph 24, 73; Katharina 2, 3, 4, 5, 6, 7, 8; Lena 108; Lewis 1, 3; Ludwig 4, 5, 6; Lydia 109; Magdalen(a) 4, 27, 68, 91, 108; Margarethe (Margretha) 3, 33, 102; Maria 12; Martin 1, 2, 33; Martin Jacob 6; Mathias (Mathes, Matheiss, Matheus, Mathews, Mathis) 1, 5, 8, 9, 11, 12, 41, 91, 108, 109; Michael 7; Nicolaus (Nicholaus) 4, 5, 6, 7, 16, 68, 108, 111; Philippina 6, 112; Rebeca 4, 5; Rosina 1, 2, 3, 4, 5, 6, 7; Sara(h) 1, 4, 6, 7, 16, 85, 95, 103; Susan(a) 6, 73, 99, 102; Susana Anamaria 103
REITENAUR (See Reitenauer/etc.)
REITH Absalon 56; Anna Maria 56; Elizabeth 56
REMER Friderich (Fridrich) 35, 38; Margreth 38; Maria Margretha 35
REMLE/REMLEY/REMMLE Catharina 53, 54; Elias 53, 54, 55; Elizabeth 53; Susanna 54
RENHIT Daniel 90; Elisabetha 90; Johanes 90
RENER/RENNER Anamaria 103; Elisabetha 92; Henrich 92; Magdalena 102; Peter 102; Sara 92; Sophia 103
RENOL Anna Maria 87, 88; Daniel 87, 88; Margretha 88; Peter 87
RENOLDS Ana Juthit 94; Elisabetha 94; Joseph 94
RENSCH Anamaria 97; Andreas 33, 35, 105; Catharina 92; Daniel 92, 97, 106; Elisabetha 33, 35, 97, 106;

INDEX

Jacob 97, 101, 104; Margretha 33, 97, 101, 104; Petrus 104
RESCHEY Christina 103; Georg 103; Joseph 103
RESER Cath. 88; Johan 88; Peter 88
REUDENAUER (See Reitenauer/etc.)
REUNAUER (See Reitenauer/etc.)
REUNNER Henrich 103
REUSSER John 8; Katharina 8; Magdalena 8
REUTEMANN David 85; Sara 85
REUTENAUER (See Reitenauer/etc.)
REYDENAUER (See Reitenauer/etc.)
REYNOLDS (See Reinels, Reinolds, Reinoll, Renol, Renolds) Elisabetha 96; Johanes 96; Joseph 96; William 27, 64
REYSSER Elizabeth 44; Jacob 44; John Jacob 44
RIBLET Christian 105; Daniel 105; Henrich 86; William 105
RICHTER Abraham 32; Catharina 90, 91, 94; George 94; Johanes 90; Maria Catharina 32; Peter 32, 90, 91, 94
RICKENBACH Ana 95, 102; David 102; Martin 95, 102; Samuel 95
RIDENAUER (See Reitenauer/etc.)
RIED Ann Katharina 1; Elisabetha 72; Georg Peter 72; Peter 1
RIEL Elisabetha 75; Johannes 75
RIGEL Adam 76; Maria Margretha 76
RIGERAIN Magd. 10; Samuel 10
RILLMEIER Catharina 99; Johannes 99; Leonhart 99
RINCKE Georg 33; Magtalena 33
RINGER Cath. 25; Eberhart 106; Juliana 106; Philip 25
RINGGOLD Samuel 64
RIPLET Catharina 91; Johanes 91
RIPEL/RIPPEL Angelica 2; Catharina 38; Engel 35; Johan Philip 35; Katharina 2; Philipp 2, 38
RITH Anna Elisabeth 84; Anna Maria 84; Fromia 84; Thomas 84
RITER/RITTER Abraham 1, 16, 28, 33, 38; Barbara 61; Catharina 16, 56; David 62, 63; Elisabetha 61, 96; Eva 11; Eva Anna 20; Eva Catharina 20, 56, 60; Hanna 60; Jacob 62, 94; Johannes 16, 33; John 61; Julian 63; Juliana 61, 62; Juthit 94; Leonhart 63; Margretha 1, 38; Maria 94; Samuel 11; Sara 33; Susana 94; Tobias 11, 20, 56, 60, 61; William 1

ROADS George 27
ROB Elisabetha 92; Johannes 92; Michael 92
ROBARS Amotia 26
ROBERSON Anna Maria 79; Elisabeth 79; Johann 79
ROBERTS Lyday 27
ROBEY Mary 30
ROCHEL Jacob 9; John 9; Susana 9
ROCHESTER N. 64; Nathaniel 64; Sophia 64
RODENFELD Apigael 48; John 48; Jonathan 48
ROE John 5; Margaretha 5
ROED Margretha 75
ROEMER Fridrich 36; Johannes 36; Margretha 36, 38
ROES Jacob 75; Joseph 75; Rebeca 75
ROESER Catharina 92; Elisabetha 45, 92; Jacob 45; Peter 92; John 45
ROFEL Jacob 66; Johannes 66; Margretha 66
ROHAUSER Amalia 98; Anamaria 94, 96, 98, 101; Daniel 94; Henrich Jonathan 101; Jonathan 94, 96, 98, 101
ROHER/ROHR/ROHRE/ROHRER Catharina 80, 99; Christian 51; Elisabetha 70; Fridrich (Frederick) 64, 70, 80; Ida 51; Johannes 88, 99; Magdalena Hagern 99
ROLLI Johannes 34; Margretha 34; Maria 34
RONK Sus. 26
RONALS/RONNELS Joh. 26; John. 18; Maria 18
RONNOLD Joh. 20; Magd. 20; Matilda 20
ROS Catharina 106; Jenet 106; Samuel 106
ROSEL/ROSSEL Barbara 41; Georg 41; Joh. 21, 24; Magthalena 41; Sus. 21, 24
ROTH Anna Maria 87; Catharina 16, 19, 22, 34; Fridrich 87; Georg 16, 19, 22; Johannes 16, 34; Juliana 22, 34; Regina 19
ROTTER Elias 13; Elisabeth 13; Marg. 13; Mihle 20; Sara 20, 24; Sus. 24; Willhelm 20, 24
ROTZMAN Eva 4; Henry 4
ROYNOLDS Charlotta 22; Johannes 22
RUACKENBACH (See Rueckenbach/etc.)
RUCH Georg 37
RUDENAUER (See Reitenauer/etc.)
RUEBENACH (See Rueckenbach/etc.)

INDEX

RUECKENBACH/RUEKEBACH/RUEVANNACH/
  RUACKENBACH/RUEBENACH Ana 91; Anna
  99; Anna Maria 46; Casper 45;
  Catharine 45; Eva Catharine 45;
  Henrich 91; Jacob 99; Martin 91,
  99; Martz 91
RUF Andani 75; Anna Maria 75;
  Catharina 34; Elisabeth 34;
  Nicolaus 34
RUFER Catharina 91; Peter 91
RUNTER Margeretha 90
RUS/RUSS Andoni 32; Ann Katharina 1;
  Anna Maria 32; Elisabetha 1, 32;
  Katharina 2; Maria Elisabetha 32;
  Michael 2, 32; Nicholas (Nicolas)
  1, 2
RUSSEL Cath. 13; James 29; Joh. 13;
  Katharine 1; Lewis 1; Mary 1;
  Susana 13
RUST Johans 78; Margretha 78, 88;
  Rotholf 78; Rudolf 88; William 88
RUTH Easter 26
RUTTER Edmond 64
RYLE Nanzi 19; Reger 19
RYNHART Titus 64

SACHY Christian 9; Elisabeth 9; John
  Jacob 9; Juliana 9
SACKMAN A. Maria 15; Hennerich 15
SALLATE Frederic 1; John Henry 1;
  Regina 1
SALTEN Barbera 76; Fridrich 76; Maria
  Catha. 76
SALTETE Fridrich 71
SAM Anna Maria 34; Conrath 34;
  Gertraut 34; Hanna 52; Henry 52;
  Samuel 52
SAMPSEL Catherine 107; John Peter 107
SATTLES Henry 1; John 1; Mary Barbara
  1
SAUER Jaocb 51; John 47; Margaretha
  Schaechtel 47; Michel 47
SAUDERN/SAUTER Elisabetha 45; Susana
  76
SCHAAL Amilia 15; Georg 15; Marg. 15,
  21
SCHACK Jacob 108
SCHAD Christian 3; Juliana 3;
  Magdalene 3; Margarethe 3; Mary
  Elisabeth 3
SCHADA H. 80; Henrich 80; Maria
  Magtalen 80
SCHAECHTEL Margaretha 47
SCHAECHTELY Catharine 45; Michel 45
SCHAEFER/SCHAEFFER/SCHAFER/SCHAFFER
  An Elisa 93; Andreas 74; Anelika
  93, 102; Anna Maria 32; Catharina
  39, 95, 110; Cath. Elisabetha 34;
  Christina 31, 34; Elisabetha 31,
  34, 54; Elisabetha Erhardt 48; Eva
  39, 110; Georg 31, 32, 33, 34, 36,
  38, 39, 86; Hann Nicolaus 31; Jacob
  54; Johannes 11, 31, 93, 95, 102;
  Johenas Johanes 102; Jonathan 93;
  Lenhart 74; Margretha 34, 36, 74;
  Maria 31; Martin 110; Michael 39;
  Peter 48, 54; Philipp 48; Sussanna
  31
SCHAERER (See Scharer/Schauer,
  Schehrer, Scherer) Eva 44; Georg
  44; John 44; Maria 44; Maria
  Susanna 44
SCHAF David 34; Fronica 34; Johanes
  34
SCHAFFNER/SCHAFNER Catharina 93;
  Elisabetha 93, 98, 101, 103; Georg
  103; Jacob 98; Johannes 101;
  Matheas 93, 98, 101, 103; Phillip
  98
SCHAHL (See Schall/etc.)
SCHAK Christian 81; Margreth 81
SCHAHL/SCHALL Anna Catha. Feugli ---
  72; Barbara 80; Caspar 72; Georg
  21, 80, 86, 89, 94, 100; Gertraut
  72; Magtalena 72; Margretha 86, 94,
  100; N. 89; Susana 94
SCHALLE/SCHALLI/SCHALLY Johannes 38;
  Johan Georg 33; Lucas 33, 38, 39;
  Margretha 33, 38
SCHAPER Elisabetha 95; Matheias 95
SCHAPP Hennerich 12
SCHARER/SCHAUER (See Schaerer,
  Schehrer, Scherer) Harvy 27; Isaac
  44
SCHAUMA Michael 29
SCHAUNCKER Cath. 15, 16; Georg 16;
  Martin 15; William 15
SCHAW Maria 26
SCHECKINGGER/SCHECKINGGERS Catharina
  41; Elisabeth 41; Johan Georg 41
SCHEFER/SCHEFFER A. Maria 19; And.
  19; Anelika 95; Barbera 80; Daniel
  19; Dewalt 14, 16; Franz 26; Georg
  35; Johannes 80; Magtalena 34;
  Niclos 34; Rosina 14, 16, 82;
  Theobalt 82
SCHEFFNER Cassper 12; Cath. 12; Jacob
  Salede 12
SCHEHRER (See Schaerer,
  Scharer/Schauer, Scherer) Eva
  Rosina 66; Georg 66; Jacob 66, 69;
  Johannes 66, 69; Magthalena 69;
  Maria Magthalena 66; Susana 66, 69
SCHEID Barbara 108; Catharina 33

INDEX

SCHEIDER Anamaria 93; Johanes 93
SCHEIMER Elias 103; Jsim 103; Sarah 103
SCHEIN Johannes 84; Magtalena 84
SCHEL Cath. 68; Johannes 68
SCHEM Catharina 92; Georg 92
SCHENCK Catharina 13, 14, 15, 19, 21, 23, 36, 92; Elisabeth 13, 14; Georg 13, 14, 15, 19, 21, 23, 92; Jacob 36; Johannes 23; Marg. 19; Samuel 92
SCHENEFELT/SCHENENFELTES/SCHENFELT Johannes 88; Margreth 88; N. 88; Wilhelm 86
SCHENGEL Henrich 76
SCHERAH Joseph 26
SCHERER (See Schaerer, Schar/Schauer, Schehrer) Christian 48; Jacob 48, 69; Magdalena 48; Maria Magtalena 69
SCHERTISIN Anna Maria 80
SCHESER Fibia 110; John 110
SCHEYAK Lenhart 65; Maria Margretha 65
SCHICH/SCHICK Loren(t)z 25, 30
SCHILKOMP Eva 109; Henry 109
SCHILLING Anna Catharina 45, 46; Anna Maria 48; Catharina 46, 48, 49; Catharine Knochel 47, 48; David 48; Eva Elisabeth 47; Henry 47; John 47; John Jacob 46; Jonas 49; Maria Catharina 45; Philip 45, 47, 48, 49; Susanna 47; Susanna Sarah 48
SCHINDEL George 107
SCHINDELBAUER Ana 93; Georg 93
SCHITZ Cath. 85; Jacob 85
SCHITZIN Eva 82
SCHLAUGER Benjamin 111; Eva 111
SCHLECTER James 110
SCHLEGEL Joh. 30
SCHLEGIN Maria Elizabeth 47
SCHLEICH A. Maria 18; Anamaria 94, 98, 101; Johanes 18, 94, 98, 101; Wilhelm 94
SCHLEIFER Magdalena 92; Stephan 92
SCHLEISS A. Maria 25; Anna Maria 10; Cath. 13; Elisabeth 13; Peter 10, 13, 25; Samuel 25
SCHLEY Amalia 99; Catharina 99, 104; Elis. 26; Thomas 99, 104
SCHLIMMER Elis. 26
SCHLIUS Anna Maria 10; Peter 10
SCHLOSER/SCHLOSSER Anna Elisabeth 88; Barbera 77, 87, 88, 92; Elisabetha Glung 48; Georg 48, 77, 87, 88, 92; Henrich (Henry) 48, 92; Joh. Jacob 77

SCHLULKNECHT (SCHILDKNECHT?) Eva 110; Henry 110
SCHMAHL/SCHMAL/SCHMALS Daniel 97; Cath. 83; Elisabetha 97; Johannes 83; John 18; Ludwig 83; Margaret (Marg.) 18, 59; Nicolaus 97; Philipp 59; Rubin 18; Sally 59; Sara 18
SCHMALZER Nedren 26
SCHMEISER/SCHMEISSERN --- 36; Anna Engel 39; Johannes 39; Marg. 25; Matheis 39
SCHMELZER Henry 56
SCHMETZ Abraham 29
SCHMETZER Adam 54; Margretha 54
SCHMIDT/SCHMIT/SCHMITT/SCMITT/SHMID/ SHMIDT/SHMITT Abraham 70; Adam 2, 3, 4; Andrew 44; Anna Maria 44, 46; 48, 59; Anna Maria Bund 47; Anna Mary 45; Barbara 16, 18, 20; Catharina 16, 20, 22, 24, 51, 59, 60, 76, 95, 96, 102, 112; Christ. 24, 28; Christina 70; David 44, 45, 46, 47, 48; Dorothea 5, 61; Elisabeth(a) 22, 45, 70; Elizabeth Schletz 46; Eva 25; Eve (Eva) Catharine 45, 46; Eva Gretha 66; Frederick 60; Georg 2, 3, 5, 8, 17, 24, 46, 61, 65, 67, 70, 71; Gottfried 60; Hanna 60; Henrich (Henry) 45, 95, 102; Jacob 4, 46, 47, 61; Joh. 17, 29, 30; Johan Henrich 95; Johan Jacob 102; Johan Martin 76; John 3, 45, 47; John Georg 45; Joseph 59; Julianna 61; Justus 46; Katharina 8; Magdalena (Magdalane, Magthalena) 2, 3, 5, 40, 65, 67, 70, 71; Magdalena Jacob 61; Margaret(ha) 28, 45, 46, 47, 59; Margaretha Sturtzmann 46; Maria 17; Maria Anna 4; Maria Barbara 70; Maria Eva 96; Martin 76; Mary 3; Mary Magdalene 2; Michael 28; Nic(h)olaus (Niclos) 16, 20, 22, 51, 70; Philipp 66; Rebecca 101; Salome 2; Samuel 8; Simon 3; Susanna 47, 59; Susanna Thomasina 46
SCHMUCKER Catharina 13, 14, 21; Ferdinand 13; Georg 13, 14, 21; J. Georg 25; Samuel Simon 21
SCHNEBELI/SCHNEBELY/SCHNEBILY/SCHNEBLY Anna Maria 41, 43; Barbara 39; Catharina 42, 43, 85, 98, 101; Christina Magthelena 40; Daniel 34, 85; David 31, 41; Doct. Henrich 41; Dr. 34; Elisabetha 34, 41, 42, 91, 94, 101; Elisaby 80; Henrich (Henry) 31, 42, 80, 85, 94, 101;

INDEX

Jacob 42; Jacobus 91; Johannes 39, 40, 94, 98, 101; John 42, 43; Leonhart 42, 91, 94; M. 34; M. Henrich 34; Maria Sabina 39; N. 40; Peter 42, 98
SCHNECKBERGER Christian 71
SCHNED/SCHNEID/SCHNEIDT/SCHNEIT Abraham 78; Adam 81; Andang 76; Anna 34, 35, 36, 38; Anna Maria 34, 35, 39, 76, 77, 78, 79; Caspar 35, 36, 39, 83; Catharina 40, 73, 88; Daniel 33, 34, 35, 36, 38, 40; David 40; Elisabet 83; Hanna 38; Henrich 81, 82, 83; Henry 87; Jacob 38; Joh. Henrich 34, 73; Joh. Jacob 77, 82; Johannes 34, 35, 39, 77, 79, 88; Maria Elisabeth 76; Maria Magtalena 82; Marianna 81; N. 39, 83; Martin 78; Peter 76; Susana 81, 87
SCHNEIDER/SCHNEITER/SHNEIDER Abraham 91; Adam 22, 47, 52, 55, 58, 91; Anna 83; Anna Cathrina 65; Anna Elisabeth 65; Anna Margretha 40; Anna Maria (Anamaria) 33, 35, 36, 51, 53, 54, 66, 67, 72, 91, 95, 97, 102, 105; Barbara 29; Caspar 36, 51, 53, 54; Catarine But 47; Catharina 22, 32, 52, 55, 58, 59, 65, 71, 74, 91; Catharina Elisabetha 35; Christina 46; Cooper 18; Daniel 65, 105; David 53, 54; Elisabeth 18, 67, 90, 105; Eva Elisabeth 47; Georg 18, 65, 92; Henrich (Henry) 46, 58, 68, 83, 86, 89, 95, 97, 102, 105; Jacob 32, 53, 65, 68, 71, 92; Joh. Jacob 33; Johan Georg 36; Johan Henrich 72; Johannes 33, 35, 40, 66, 72, 91; John Georg 35; Jonathan 71; Juliana 92; Ludwig 65; Margretha 68, 86, 97; Maria Elisabetha 66; Martin 67; Nichlos 74; Peter 53; Philipp 22; Sibila 105; Susana 25, 51, 83, 86, 89, 95
SCHNEL/SCHNELL Adam 41; Christina (Christine) 89, 90, 91; Daniel 89; Georg 26, 90; Henrich 89, 90, 91; Susana 41
SCHNIT Johan Michael 84; Michel 84; Susana 84
SCHNOENEFELT Elisabetha 73; Georg 73; Susana 73
SCHOCK Jacob 26
SCHOCKEI Christian 81; Margretha 81
SCHOEFER Elisabeth 35; Georg 35

SCHOEFTER Barbera 79; Joh. Loenharth (Leonhart) 79; Johannes 79
SCHOELTER Anna Barbera 72; Anna Maria 72; Johannes 72
SCHOEN Amelia 99; Catharina 46; Henrich 97; Johan Conrad 90, 94, 97, 99; Margretha 90, 94, 97, 99, 100; Wilhelm 94
SCHOENBEIN Latzarus 41
SCHOENEBERGER Anna Maria 49; Catharine 49; Jacob 49; Michel 48, 49; Peter 49
SCHOENENFELT Fridrich 34; Georg Michael 34; Magdalena 34
SCHOENFELD Henrich 106; Petrus 106; Susan 106
SCHOENGEL Anna Katharina 4; Christina 4; George 4; Katharina 4; Maria Rebeca 4
SCHOL/SCHOLL Annamaria 63; Carl 63; Catha. 71; Christina 71; David 63; Johannes 71; Leonhart 63; Margaretha 30, 63; Salome 63
SCHOLLEY/SCHOLLY Elisabeth 82, 87; Peter 82, 87; Vallentien 87
SCHON/SCHONS (See Tschons) Anmaria 18, 33; Catharina 14, 18, 23, 24, 33; Daniel 23; David D. 32; George 14; Hennerich 18, 23, 24; Peter 32; Susana 24, 32; Wilhelm 33
SCHONEFELD/SCHONEFELT Elisabeth 12; Jacob 12; Maria 67; Mary 30; Susana 12; Wilhelm 67
SCHOP Anna Maria 86; Christian 85
SCHOPFER Christian 88; Margretha 88
SCHORSCH Elisabetha 82; Georg 82; Johannes 80; Joseph 79, 80, 83; Joseph Georg 79; N. 80, 82, 83; Susana 83
SCHOURCKER Cath. 23; Johannes 23; Martin 23
SCHRADER Cath. 17; Hennerich 17; Johannes 17, 30
SCHRAM Georg 30
SCHREIBER/SCHRIBER Anamaria 97; Anna 66; Beggy 29; Henrich 97; Jacob 97
SCHREIDER Adam 110; Dolly 110; William 110
SCHREIER Catatina 63; George 63; John 63; Juliana 63
SCHREYACK/SCHREYAK/SCHRUYACK/SCHRYOCK Anna Elisabeth 79; Anna Maria 10, 68; Catharina 31, 36, 65, 71, 77, 79; Christiana 15; Henrich (Henry) 31, 36, 64, 65, 77, 79; Johannes 10, 68, 79; Lenhart (Lonhart) 69,

INDEX

71; Margretha 69; Maria Margretha 71; Samuel 10
SCHROB John 5
SCHUANDER Catharina 31; Jacob 31; Maria 31
SCHUB Christina Margretha 71; Jacob 67, 71; Johannes 71; Margretha 67
SCHUCK Ann Margreth 77; Catharina 39, 77; Georg 39; Jacob 77; Susana 39
SCHUCKER/SCHUCKERS/SCHUKER Ese 103; Eva 94, 99, 103; Maria 94; Sophia 99; Zacharia(s) 94, 99, 103
SCHUGG Catherine 107; John 107; Maria Magdalena 107
SCHUHN Cath. Bind 47; Daniel 47; Hanna 47; Henry 47; John 47; Maria Cath. 47; Maria Elisabeth 47; Philip 47
SCHUIN Elis. 26
SCHULER Anna Maria 71; Argretha 71; Doreas 71
SCHULTZ/SCHULTZE Anna Maria 37; Elisabeth 34; Georg 33
SCHUMAN Barbara 67; Bezie 10; George 9; James 9; Johann Jacob 67; Johannes 67; John 7; Samuel 15; Sarah 8; Susana(h) 7, 8, 9, 10, 13, 15, 19, 23; Thomas (Tomas) 7, 8, 10, 13, 15, 19, 23
SCHUMFELD Joh. 29
SCHUN Adam 47; Catharina Bindle 47; Catharina Bund 47; Philip 47
SCHUNBEIND Latzarus 41
SCHUP/SCHUPP (See Shupp) Anna 10, 13, 20, 24, 25; Anna Barbera 77; Anna Maria 107; Catherine (Catharina) 77, 107; Christ. Marg. 10; Christina Margaret 1; Daniel 25, 104; David 10, 25; Elisabeth(a) 24, 25, 100, 104; Eva 10; Frederic 1, 10; Hanna 24; Henrich 25, 100; Jacob 1, 10, 13, 20, 24, 25, 77; Joh. Jacob 25; Johannes 25, 100, 104; John 107; John Jacob 1; Jonathan 25; Margreta 77; Peter 24; Samuel 10, 25; Simon Peter 25; Susana 13, 25
SCHUS Barbara 111; Mary Susana 111; Peter 111
SCHUSSELL John 111; Savina 111
SCHUSTER Doredea 67; Margretha 68; Michael 68; Susana 67; Valadein 67
SCHUTZ Johannes 11; Maria 11; Martin 11; Mary 28
SCHWAB (See Schwob) Benedict 44; Catharina (Catherine) 11, 24, 49, 53; Christ. 24; Christina 57; Christofer 49; Christoph 11; Georg 44; Margaretha 44; Michael 28, 44, 67; Peter 53
SCHWANGEL Cath. 79; Georg 79
SCHWATZ (Swartz) Catharina 55
SCHWEGLER Josua 73
SCHWEITZER/SCHWITZER/SHWITZER Anna 33, 37, 39, 40; Anna Maria 34; Christoph 63; Elisabeth 39; Jacob 62, 63; Joh. Jacob 40; Johannes 33, 34, 37, 39, 40, 65; Magdalena 62; Margaret (Margareda) 62, 63; Peter 62, 63
SCHWENGEL Anna Margretha 72; Benjamin 16, 25, 51, 108; Eva 15, 16, 108; Friderick 15; Georg 67, 72; Jacob 16; Margretha 67; Philip 15, 112
SCHWERD/SCHWERT Anna Elisabeth 41; Conrad 60; Elizabeth 60; Georg 41; Joh. Jacob 41
SCHWERTZEL/SCHWERTZOL Abraham 35; Christina Barbara 35; Johannes 81; Mathaus 35; Regina 81; Susana 81
SCHWEYER/SCHWEYERE Anna Maria 14; Sybilla 49
SCHWIEDER Elisabeth 32; Michael 32
SCHWIND Anna Maria 80; Johannes 80
SCHWINGEL Barbara 46
SCHWITZER (See Schweitzer)
SCHWOB (See Schwab) Catharina 52, 53, 55; Elizabeth 55; Jacob 57; Magdalena 52; Peter 52, 53, 55, 57
SCHWOEGTER Christina 34; Josua 34
SCHYFER Elisabeth 48; Henry 48; Rosina 48
SCMITT (See Schmidt, Schmit, Schmitt) Henrich 96
SCOT/SCOTT John 25, 64; Ra(c)hel 25
SCWEPSER Johannes 32
SCWIEDER Peter 32
SEENZEL Catherine 110; Peter 110
SEFTLE Anna Maria 71; Magtalena 71; Vallentein 71
SEGESER Anna Maria 78; Georg Fridrich 78; Jacob 78
SEIBERT Anamaria (Anna Maria) 38, 51, 56; Catharina 46, 47, 58; Catharine Magdalena 44; Christian 44; Elisabeth 35, 36, 51, 53, 58; Jacob 36, 38, 51, 53, 55, 56, 58; Joh. Jacob 35, 38; Johannes 36; John 47; Levihard 51; Margaretha Maug. 47; Maria Barbara 44; Michael 51, 53; Peter 46; Wendel 47

INDEX

SEIDNER Anna Maria 8; Barbara 66; Friedrich 8; Joh. Fridrich 84; Margareth Barbara 2; Margaretha 2, 66, 84; Maria 8; Martin 2, 66
SEILER/SEILLER (See Seyler) Barbera (Barbra) 80, 88; Anna 86; Anna Maria 89; Barbera 78, 86; Christian 83; Christina 38; Elisabetha 79; Georg 89; Jacob 38, 79; Johannes 38, 79; Margreth(a) 83, 88; Marthin 70; Peter 78, 80, 83, 86, 88, 89; Susana 78, 83
SEISTER Catherine 108; Henry 108; John 108
SEITNER Fridrich 85; Johan Fridrich 85; Margretha 66, 85; Martin 66
SEITZ (See Seytz) Anna 34; Henrich 34; Johannes 34
SELBSTGEZOB Mrs. 51
SELSER/SELZER Adam 92; Carl 92; Catharina 30, 92; Margretha 92
SENSEL/SENTZEL Catherine 107, 109, 111, 112; Maria 109; Peter 107, 109, 111, 112
SETZER Anna Maria 90; Carl 90; Maria Cat. 90
SEUSSMUER Catherine 112; Christian 112; Jacob 112
SEYBERT Catharina 52; John 52, 59; John Henry 52
SEYFRID Barbera 71; Johan Matheiss 71; Joseph 71
SEYLER (See Seiler/Seiller) Barbera 82; Peter 82
SEYTZ (See Seitz) Anna 36; Elisabeth 80; Henrich 36, 80; Jacob 36
SHACKS Elis. 30
SHAFAL Georg 4; Katharina 4; Rebeca 4
SHAL Georg 6, 7; Margaretha 6, 7
SHAPP Felix 7; Jacob 7; Maria 7
SHEIRA George 63; Jacob 63; Juliana 63
SHELL Anna Catha 75; Carl Fridrich 75; Caspar 75
SHEND Anna Maria 8; George 8; Katharina 8
SHERRICK Joh. 28
SHMID/SHMIDT/SHMITT (See Schmidt/etc.)
SHNEIDER (See Schneider)
SHNELL Fenrich 6; John 6; Margaretha 6
SHNENGEL Elisabeth 5; Michael 5; Nicolaus 5
SHOLL David 62; Saloma 62
SHROB Christop 5; Dorothea 5

SHRYOCK/SHRYOK/SHRYOTZ Amilia 9; Anna Barbara 9; Henry 5, 9; July 9; Katharine 5, 9; Liberty 5; Samuel 9
SHULL Peter 30
SHUMAN/SHUMANN (See Schuman)
SHUNKIN Cathrina 35
SHUPP (See Schup/Schupp) Chris. Marg. 10; Daniel 10; Elisabeth 10; Emmerich 10; Eva 10; Friedrich 10; George 10; Jacob 10; John 10, 28; John Jonathan 10; Katharina 10
SHWITZER (See Schweitzer)
SICHRIST Joh.Georg 38; Susana 38; Vallentein 38
SICHWALT Catharina Elisabetha 35
SIEGMAN/SIGMOND/SIGMUND Catherine 111; Elizabeth 27, 55; Jacob 53; John 53; Susanna 53; William 111
SILHARD/SILHART/SILLHART Anna Cath. 46; Anna Maria 45; Barbara 45; Christoph 46, 47; Elisabetha 45, 46; Elisabeth Erlewein 47; John Frederick 47; Stophel 45, 46; Susanna 46, 48
SILLINGER Andru 26
SIMON Catha. 82; Elisabeth 82; Joh. Andrew 71; Peter 82
SITZLER Elisabetha 32; Nansi 32; Wilhelm 32
SKEALS/SKEYLS/SKILS Catherine 110; Christina 110, 111; Joh. 26; John 110, 111; Jonas 111
SLATER James 26
SLEKAUER Elizabeth 51
SLETER James 111; Maria 111; Sara 111
SLOHN Samuel 28
SMITH Eliz. 27; William 27
SMUCKER Rev. 49
SNAVELY Jacob 29
SOMMER Anna Margartta 61; Barbara 61, 95; Elisabeth 61; Henrich 61, 95; Jacob 61
SORBER Christian 44; Mary Susanna 44
SORWE Anna Maria 45; Christian 45; John Samuel 45
SOUTH Christina 107; Jacob 107
SPA---YS George 30
SPED/SPEID Elizabeth 52, 55; Jacob 55; Martin 52, 55
SPEIGLAR/SPIEGLER Christina 108; Conrad 108; Frederick 15; Maria 15; Salome 15; Samuel 15
SPESSARD David 28
SPICKLER Elisabeth 20; Joh. Nicolaus 18; Nicholas 20; Samuel 20

INDEX

SPITZNAGEL Hana 63; Hanna 61; Jacob 63; Maria 63
SPON Philip 48
SPRECHER Catharina 93; M. Catherine 112; Mag. 15; Magdalena 93, 109, 111, 112; Philip 15, 93, 109, 111, 112
SPRIGG Thomas 64
SPRINGER Christina 19; Magd. 19; Philip 19
STACK Jacob 29; Sus. 29; Willhelm 29
STADES Fridrich 68; Sibila 68
STADLER (See Statler) Anna 36, 80; Annaeta Maria 68; Catharina 68; Catharina Barbara 39, 68; Emanuel 80; Eva 1; Henrich 80; Jacob 36, 80; Johannes 39, 68; John 1; Michael 1
STAERR Lothar 44; Margraretha 44
STAHL/STAL/STALL Anna 33, 35, 42; Anna Maria (Anamaria) 42, 89; Elisabetha 89; Henrich 33, 35, 37, 40; Jacob 42, 89; Lenhart 36; Rosina 40
STAHRTZ Anna 44; Frederick 44
STAL/STLL (See Stahl)
STAM/STAMM Adam 15; Clara 17; Elisabetha 69; Georg 14, 17; Glora 14; Jacob 15, 17, 69, 104; Johan Heinrich 104; Johannes 14; M. Magd. 17; Magd. 15; Maria Eva 69; Maria Magdalena 104
STANTZ Lenhart 76
STARK Andrew 71; Elisabetha 71; Philip 71
STARR Cath. 11; Elisabetha 11; William 11
STARTZMAN/STARZMAN/STEARTZMAN (See Sterzman, Stortzman, Sturtzman) Daniel 23; David 16; Elisabeth 16; Eva 14, 23, 31, 59, 111; Fanny 28; Henrich 14, 16, 23, 31; Jacob 21; Johan Henrich 14, 31; Juliana 14, 110; Magd. 21, 23; Marg. 14, 16, 21; Martin 14, 21, 23, 28; Peter 14, 16, 21; Sara 14, Susana 14, 16, 21, 28
STATHER Elisabeth 47, 62
STATLER/STATTLER (See Stadler) Cath. 22; Johannes 41; Josoha (Joshua?) 41; Maria Barbara 41; Peter 62; Ulrich 78
STATS Fridrich 31; Sibila 31
STECK/STECKEIN (See Stek) Ann Cath. 80; Catharina 95, 99; Johannes 82; Martin 95, 99; N. 82
STED John 4; Katharina 4
STEHR Kaspar 1; Katharina 1; Mary 1

STEIN Eve Elisabeth 5; Eve Katharina 5; Frehne 55; Freni 53; John 53; Magdalena 55; Mathias 53, 55; Michael 5
STEINBACK Anna Maria 4; Gerhard 4
STEINBRECHER Gerhard 49; Maria 49
STEINSEIFER Anna Maria 77; Elisabetha 71; Elisabetha Gertraut 71; Johannes 71, 77; Margretha 71, 77
STEK (See Steck/Steckein) Ester 112; Jacob 111; Margaretha 111; Nanzi 112; Peggy 111; Peter 111; Wilhelm 111, 112
STEMPEL/STEMPFEL/STEMPFLE (See Stempel) Anna Maria 35; Christian 7, 8; David 8; Elizabeth 8; Eva Katharina 8; Gotfried 3, 32, 35; John 3; Katharina 7; Magdalena 7, 8; Margaretha 32, 35; Maria Magdalena 8; Martin 32; Mary Margareth 3
STENES Lenhart 74; Maria Cath. 74
STENTZ Catharina 76
STEORIN Elizabeth 56
STEPHAN Catharina 95; Jacob 95; Tilly 95
STER Casper 70; Margretha 70
STERZMAN (See Startzman/etc., Stirtzman, Stortzman, Sturtzman) Margretha 94; Peter 94
STEULY Elisabeth 45; Martin 45
STEUTZ Philip 47
STIGLITZ Christina 67; Johann Jacob 67; Peter 67
STIHELADER Peter 27
STIRTZMAN (See Startzman/etc., Sterzman, Stortzman, Sturtzman) Ad. 89; Elisabeth 89; Eva 67, 73; Henrich 67, 73
STOLL Anna 33, 34; Henrich 33, 34
STOLTZ/STOLZ Anna Barbara 37; Catharina 100; Edmund 100; Georg 38; Henrich 37; Ludwig 11, 38, 65; Margaretha 11, 35; Margretha F. 38; Maria Magdalena 11; Michaem 100; Peter 37
STONER Elis. 29
STONESIFER (See Steinseifer)
STORM Maria Catharina 99; Peter 99; Susanna Maria 99
STORN Elisabetha 91; Wilhelm 91
STORR Barbara 18; Elisabetha 14, 18, 22; Friderich 15; Johannes 15, 22; Maria Marg. 15; Wilhelm 14, 22; William 18

INDEX

STORTZMAN (See Startzman/etc., Sterzman, Stirtzman, Sturtzman) Adam 6; Anna Margaret 6; Daniel 3; David 6; Elisabeth 6; Eva 5; Eva Katharina 7; Fenrich 5; Henry 3; Margaretha 6, 7; Peter 6, 7; Rebecca 3; Susana 5
STORY Catherine 107; John 107
STORZMAN Johannes 11; Marg. 11; Peter 11
STORZMANN Eva 1; Henry 1; Juliana 1
STOUT Nancy 27
STRAHN Elisabeth 21; Michael 21
STRANER Elisabeth 39; Johannes 39; Martin 39
STRANG David 40; Jacob 38; Jeams 38, 40; Magthalena 38, 40
STRAUB Catharina 90; Joseph 90
STRAUS A. Marg. 16; Christ. 13, 19, 24; Christina 13, 16; Eva Marg. 19; Hennerich 13, 16, 19, 24, 25; Joh. Georg 13, 24
STREIN Cath. 23; Fronika 23; Matheus 23
STREIT/STREITT Anna Maria 9; Barbara 9, 11, 12, 93; Cath. 12; David 11; Leonard (Leonhard, Leonhart) 9, 11, 12, 93
STREITHOF Cath. 22; Franz 22
STROHM Elisabetha 95, 97, 102; Johannes 97; Michael 95, 97, 102
STUCKY Elisabeth 65; Martin 65
STUDER Elisabeth 20; Johannes 20; Philip 20
STUHN Catharine 47; Philipp 47
STULL Daniel 64; Holland 64; John 64; Mary 64; Matilda 64
STUM Jacob 58
STUMPF Catharina 60; Ester 60; Georg 26; Jacob 60
STUNG Catharina 58; Elizabeth 58; Jacob 58
STURM Anna Margretha 76; Jacob 76; Maria 44; Maria Margretha 76
STURTZMAN (See Startzman/etc., Sterzman, Stirtzman, Stortzman) Elisabeth 45
STUTER Catharine 48; Elisabeth 48; Elisabetha Schweiser 48; John Philip 48; Philip 47, 48; Philip Jacob 48
SUDER (See Suter) Cath. 22; Joh. Jacob 22; Margretha 33; Martin 33; Peter 22
SUDFORT Anna Maria 51; Challendin 51; Conrad 51
SUIL Elis 48; Martin 48; Sara 48
SUMER/SUMERS A. Barbara 17; A. Cath. 17; Barb. 24; Hennerich (Henrich) 17, 24; Jacob 24
SUTTER (See Suder) Peter 29
SWAILES Sus. 28
SWEARINGEN Catherine 64
SYDEL Hennerich 29
SYGMAN David 58; Jacob 58; Susanna 58
SYSTER Henry 28
SZIER Catharina 62; Nicklaus 62

TAMER (TAMSER?) Susana 73
TAMSER (See Tamer) Johan 68; Johan Adam 68; Susana 68
TANISER Johannes 78; Susana 78
TARD Cath. 27
TAUDENBUSCH Johannes 68; Maria 68; Susana 68
TAUSS Elisabetha 40; Herrich 40; Michael 40
TAYLOR Ignatius 64; Margaret 64
TEIBEL Jacob 65; Margretha 65, 80; Michael 80
TEIMEL Cathrina 73; Philip 71, 73
TEIS/TEISE/TEISS/TISE Barbara 71; Cathrina 69, 71; Daniel 69, 71; Elisabeth 13, 17; Henrich 32; Johannes 13, 17, 32; Maria Salome 69; Mary 29
TEISSINGER Elisabeth 7; Katharina 7; Theobold 7
TEMBERS Robert 30
TEMPEL Conrad 88, 92, 93; Magdalena 93; Margreth 88, 92, 93
THEIL Adam 4, 70, 74; Catharina 68; David 8; Elisabeth 74; Fromia 68, 70, 74; Fronica 2; Georg 2, 68, 70, 74; Jacob 2, 7; John 7; Margaretha 8; Maria 70, 74; Maria Dorothea 4; Samuel 8; Sarah 7
THOMAS David 107, 111; George 107; John 111; Susanna 107, 111
THOR Elizabeth 107; John 107; Margaretha 107
TIDER Anna Maria 36; Eva 36; Jacob 36
TIFENBACH Anna Maria 78; Baltzer 78; Johannes 78
TILE Salomon 27
TIM Cath. 28
TIRR Barbara 33; Catharina 34; Elisabeth 34; Lorentz 36; Michael 34
TIRTH Anna Catha. 82; Peter 82
TISE (See Teis/etc.)
TODWEILER (See Dotweiller, Dutweiler, Tudweiler, Tutweiler) Henrich 81

INDEX

TOLEK Daniel 72
TOMAS Christophel 39; Elis. 26; Jacob 39; Susana 39
TOMER Anna Maria 70, 71, 75; Michael 70, 71, 75
TOMS Catharina 53, 54, 55; Conrad 54; Jacob (Jacobs) 53, 54; John 54; Maria Magdalena 53
TONERAY Esther 29
TRAB (See Trap/Trapp) Catharina 97; Christofel 67; Henrich 67; Jacob 97
TRABINGER Levi 23; Polly 23; Samuel 23
TRAEG Catharine 44; Joseph 44; Margaretha 44
TRAP/TRAPP (See Trab) Barbara 11; Catharina 11, 19, 21, 52; Elisabeth 21; Hennerich 11; Jacob 11, 21, 52; Segina 52; Stophel 11
TRAUB Adam 55; Catharina 55; Maria 55
TRAXEL/TREXEL (See Troxel) Abraham 35; Catharina 34, 35, 69, 71, 77; David 40; Elisabetha 77; Johannes 77
TREXLER Catha. 86; Emanuel 86; Samuel 86
TRISHER Juliana 21
TRISLET Jacob 10; Magd. 10; Wilhelm 10
TRITER Elias 80; Margrethe 80
TROXEL (See Traxel/Trexel) Abraham 32; Elisabetha 67, 77; Georg 67, 77; Johann Daniel 77; Margretha 67
TSCHONS (See Schons, Johns) Anna Maria 34, 35, 38; Barbara 41; David 41; Davis 33; Elisabeth 37, 38, 41; Elisabeth B. 40; Henrich 41; Jacob 38, 40; Johannes 38, 40; Jonathan 37, 38, 40; Magtalena 38, 40; Margretha 33; Maria Magtalena 41; Susana 35, 36; Thomas 38, 40; Wilhelm 34, 35, 38, 39, 40, 41
TSCHORSCH Johannes 39; Joseph 39
TUDWEILER (See Dotweiler, Dutweiler, Todweiler, Tutweiler) Cath. 28
TUERDER Frederic 2; Margareth 2
TUERDES Elisabetha 3; Frederic 3; Margarethe 3
TUTWEILER (See Dotweiler, Dutweiler, Todweiler, Tudweiler) Barbara 13; Elis. 13; Jacob 19; Jonadan 13
TYLE Christina 110; Elisabeth 19; Marg. 20; Nancy 19; Simon 19; Solomon 110; Theodor 20
TYLER Isaac 28
TYRE Bezi 21; Joh. 21; Maria Dorrothea 21
TYS/TYSE Andreas 111; Catherine 111; Joh. 25
TYSNO Benjamin 26

UENSELL Ann Mary 3; John 3; John Jacob 3
ULM Jacob 73; Johan Peter 75; Margretha 75; Peter 75
UMRICHHAUSER Elisabetha 101; Maria 101; Peter 101
UNSEL Anna Maria 70; Elisabeth 70; Johannes 70
UPDEGRAFF Cath. 26
URBAN Catharina 15, 16, 19, 29, 96; Elisabetha 105; Jacob 95, 102; Joh. Jacob 22; Maria 19; Maria Eva 95
UVON Susanna 52
UXOR Anne 89

VACH Becke 27
VALENTINE Frederic 2; Jacob 2; John 2; Margarathe 2; Philippina 2
VANDERMAN Rahel 32
VARNER Mary 30
VAUBOL Anna 59; Jacob 59; Michael 59
VOGELER Christian 104; Elisabetha 104; Susana 104
VOGELGASANG/VOGELGESANG/VOGELSANG (See Fogelgesang) Barbara 22, 45, 46; Catherine 22, 42, 45; Christ. 22; Christian 45, 46, 50; Georg 22, 42; Jacob 50; John 46; Margaret 28; Sovia 30; Susanna 28, 50
VOGLER (See Fogler) Andrew 3; Catharina 61, 93; Christian 93; Ester 3; Heinrich 61; Katharina 3; Susana 93
VOLCK/VOLK Andrea 39; Anna Maria (Anamaria) 10, 95; Cath. 11; Christina 39; Daniel 10, 95; David 10; Eva 10; Eva Elisabeth 11; Henrich 95; Joh. Fridrich 39; Maria 10; Martin 11
VOLD Daniel 7; Susana 7
VOLTZ/VOLZ Anna Maria 48; Daniel 48; George 2; Marg. 15; Mary 2; Peter 2
VROLSS George 8; Hishia 9; Jacob 8; Jesse 9; John 9; Margaretha 9; Maria 8, 9; Melito 9; Michael 9; Otto 9; Peter 8, 9

151

INDEX

WAALER James 50; Jeremiah 50; Maria 50; William 50
WACHER (See Wacker) Elisabeth 69
WACHTEL Catharina 23, 42, 57, 105; Elisabeth 17, 57; Joh. 17; John 57; Jonathan 57
WACHER Elisabetha 73; Jacob 69, 73; Peter 73
WAGELE Elisabeth 15; Joh. Paulus 15; Joh. Paul 24; Marg. 24; Samuel 24
WAGANER/WAGENER/WAGNER A. Maria 25; Adam 62; Anna Maria 78; Catharina 61, 62, 106; Charlota (Charlotho) 70, 75, 77, 78; Christian 106; Conrath 76; Elisabetha 106; Frantz 70, 75, 77, 78; Johannes 70; John 48; Magdalena 66, 95; Margretha 34, 76, 102; Maria Cathrina 75; Peter 25, 34, 66, 76; Susana 95; Valentin 95, 102
WAITMAN Barbara 28
WALCH A. Maria 18, 19; Anna Maria 48; Georg 18, 19, 48; Johannes 18; Matthew 48
WALFAHRT (See Wohlfahrt/etc.)
WALLACE/WALLES James 29, 111; Orth 111; Susana 111
WALTER Abraham 102, 104; Catharina 36; Charity 26; Elisabetha 26, 102, 104; Katharina 2, 3; Maria 101; Maria Magdalena 102; Michael 2, 3, 36; Philipp 101; Samuel 101; Sarah 30
WALTZ Jacob 30
WAREIN Nansi 32
WARLY Cath. 13; Hennerich 10, 13; Sabina Maria 10; Sibile 10
WARNER (See Werner) Eli 105; Elisabetha 105; William 105
WART Anna Maria 14; Sibile 14; Simon 14
WARTH George 49; Simon 49; Sybilla 49
WATRING (See Wothring)
WAVER Frederick 28
WEADDLE (Weddle, Weddel, Wedel, Weidel) Mary 29
WEAVER Nora 44
WEB Elisabeth 87; Peter 87
WEBER Christian 78; Elisabeth 56, 78; Georg 78; Margaret 56; Martin 65; Peter 56; Philipina 26
WEBERLE John 5; Maria 5; Peter 5
WEBERLINGLING Jacob 83; Maria 83; Peter 83
WEGELEIN/WEGELIN/WEGERLEIN Fromia 73; Johann Fridrich 73; Johan Henrich 92; Johan Paulus 92; Margretha 92; Maria 44; Philip 73
WEH Fenrich 8; Maria 8; Sarah 8
WEHR Elisabeth 67, 78, 80; Johannes 80; Julian 78; Martin 67, 78, 80
WEIANT (See Weyan/etc., Wyan) Barbara 98; David 100; Margretha 98, 100; Philip 98, 100
WEICKEL Daniel 13; Hennerich 13, 82; Sly 13; Susana 13, 82
WEIDEL Elisabeth 3; Fenrich 5, 7, 8; George 7; Henry 3, 9; John 3; Katharina 5; Samuel 8; Susanna 3, 5, 9
WEIDER Christofel 40; Elisabeth 40; Jacob 40; Maria 40
WEIDMAN Benjamin 51; Jacob 51; Margaret Eschel 51
WEIGAND/WEIGANT Anna Maria 80; Elisabeth 89; Georg 80; Jacob 89; Joh. Jacob 69; Jose 69; Jost 80, 81; Margretha 69; Maria 81
WEIKEL Henrich 83, 85; Susanna 83, 85
WEIL Ann Sophia 1; Cath. 10, 20; David 14, 20, 26; Elisabeth 19; Georg 72; Jacob 1, 8, 10, 11, 14, 19, 24, 26, 48; Johannes 10, 12; John Frederick 44; Katharina 8; Margretha 72; Philipina 14, 20; Samuel 72; Sophia (Sovia) 11, 44; Susanna 8, 10, 11, 14, 19, 24, 48; William 1, 44
WEIMAR/WEIMER/WEIMARN Anna Maria Salome 11; Christoph 11; Elisabeth 11; Ester 11; Jacob 38, 65, 81, 85; Salome 38, 65, 81, 85; Anna Maria Salome 11
WEIN/WEINN Andreas 92; Annamaria 62; Elisabetha 92; Johannes 92; John 62; Susanna 62
WEINBRENER/WEINBRENNER Anna Maria 87; Christian 87, 91; Christina 87, 91; Elisabeth 89; Jacob 89; Johannes 87; Margretha 89
WEINMAN Christian 66; Elisabetha 66; Johann Ludwig 66
WEINN (See Wein)
WEIRICH Elisabeth 70; Maria 70; Peter 70
WEIS (See Weiss)
WEISEL A. Margaret 111; A. Maria 111; Daniel 110, 111; Eva 104; Margaretha 110; Sara 110
WEISEMANN (See Wisman, Wiessman) Anna Maria 61; Daniel 61; John 61

INDEX

WEISS/WEIS Adam 3; Ann Elisabeth 1; Anna Eve 2; Anna Maria 48, 74, 87; Catharina 85, 97, 100, 103; Christ. 23; Christian 2; Christina 88; Daniel 23; Eva 17, 22; Georg 2, 17, 22, 85; Henrich 72, 97, 100; Jacob 48, 85; Johannes 23, 88, 97; Joh. George 84; John Adam 1; Margaretha 1, 3; Mary Katharina 3; Peter 48; Samuel 100

WEISSHAAR Christian 46; Margareth 46

WEITER Christofel 40; Henrich 40; Jacob 40; Maria 40

WEITMAEN/WEITMAN Abraham 86; Jacob 79, 86; Joh. Jacob 79; Margretha 79; Margretha Elisabeth 86

WEITNER Barbara 89, 90; Cath. 79; Elisabeth 79; Henrich 89; Jacob 79; Michael 89, 90

WEITTURST Cath. 24; Philip 24; Polly 24

WEIZEL Henrich 93; Johanes 104; Maria Magdalena 104; Susana 93

WEL Doretea 79

WELIHER Daniel 42; George 42; Veronica 42

WELLER Elisabetha 93; Georg 89; Johannes 90, 89, 93, 94; Joseph 92; Magdalena 89, 92, 93, 94; Philip 89, 92

WELSH Elizabeth 25; James Maxwell 25; Marg. 25; Maxwell 25

WELTY Cath. 29

WELZ Mary 26

WENTLING Joh. 29

WER Elisabetha 73; Joh. Henrich 73; Martin 73

WERKING Anna Elisabeth 84; Peter 84

WERLE Fenrich 7; Sarah 7

WERLEY Anamaria 94; Henrich 94

WERNER (See Warner) Anna Maria 4, 44; Arnedony 76; Catharine 44; Elisabetha 74, 101; Georg 33, 74; Jacob 3; Johan Jacob 101; Johan Niclos 31; Johannes 33; Magdalena 3, 4, 76; Margretha 33, 74; Maria 31, 44, 70, 85; Maria Christina 101; Mary 29; Nicholas 44, 70; Paul 85; Philip 3, 4, 76; Sara 85

WES Magdalena 104

WESCHENBACH Henrich 67

WESZSTEIN (See Wetzstein/etc.)

WETHMAUER Barbara 109

WETSTEIN (See Wetzstein/etc.)

WETZEL Barbara 107; Catherine 107; John 107

WETZSTEIN/WETZTEIN/WETSTEIN/WESZSTEIN Daniel 44, 46, 47; David 5; Elisabeth 3, 57; Eva (Eve) 2, 3, 5, 38; Frederick 57; George 57; Johannes 38; John 2, 3, 5; John Georg 44; Katharina 2; Maria 44, 47; Maria Bund 46; Maria Cath. 46; Michael 39; Susana 39

WEYAN/WEYAND/WEYANT (See Weiant, Wyan) Ann 28; Christina Gobel 46; Jacob 46; John 47; Jopst 47; Maria Krebs 47

WEYDMAN/WEYMANN Benjamin 47; Elisabeth (Kreel) 46; Elisabeth Kried 47; Eva 46; Matthew 47; Mathias 46

WEYGARD Elisabetha 75; Jost 75; Margretha 75

WEYRICH/WEYRICK Christina 4, 6; Jacob 4, 6

WHITTLE Joh. 27

WHOOER Christian 27

WIBGE Abraham 32; Elisabeth 32; Johannes 32

WICHER Hanna 86; John 86

WICKE Elisabeth 36; Henrich 36; Johannes 36

WICKERT Barbara 11; Maria Barbara 90; Melchor 11, 90

WIESSMAN (See Weisemann, Wiseman) Elisabeth 17; Ludwig 17; Susana 17

WIEST Anna Brbara 61; Elisabeth 61; Leonhart 61

WILBERGER Jacob 32; Johannes 35; Margretha 32, 35; Matheis 32, 35

WILD Catharina 104; Johanes 104; Peter 104

WILIGE Abraham 32; Elisabeth 32; Johannes 32

WILLAR John 64

WILLHELM Mary L. 27

WILLIAMS Elie 64; Joseph 64; Otho 64; Prudence 64

WILLIART Anna Maria 66; Catharina 66; Henrich 66; Peter 66

WILSON Eliz. 25

WILVERBACK Jacob 52; Joseph 52; Josiah 52; Susanna Uvon 52

WINDER/WINDERS Elisabeth 19; George 66; Joh. 19; Samuel 19; Susana 66

WINDROTH Anna Maria 81; Elisabeth 81; Peter 81

WINGERT Anna Catharina 69; Cath. 88; Elisabetha 69; henrich 88; Johannes 88; Peter 69

WINTER Abraham 27

INDEX

WIPEL Engel 84; Magtalena 84; Philip 84
WIRD/WIRT Christina 78, 79; Elisabetha 32, 37; Ester 79; Eva 37; Henrich 79; Hermannes 78, 79; Magtalena 39; Maria 79; Peter 32, 36; Vallentein 32
WIRTEMBERGER Elisa 48; Jacob 48; John Adam 48
WIRTH Elisabeth 1; Peter 1
WISMAN (See Weisemann, Wiessman) Daniel 94; Elisabetha 92, 94; Juliana 92; Ludwig 92, 94
WITHNY A. Maria 17, 22; Arder. 22; Arthur 17; Elisabeth 17; William 22
WITZLER Anna Catha. 77; Elisabetha 77; Wilhelm 77
WITZSTEIN Anna Maria 67; Daniel 67
WOHLFAHRT/WOHLFARTH/WOHLFORT/WALFAHRT /WOLFAHRT/WOLFARTH/WOLFARTT Adam 2, 3, 5, 46, 47, 69, 70; Cath. 19, 69; Catharine Haefel 47; Elisabeth(a) 2, 3, 5, 46, 47, 69, 70; Henrich (Hennerich, Henry) 19, 47, 104; Johanes 99; John Adam 2; John Michael 5; Rosina 3; Samuel 19
WOHLGEMUTH Joh. 89; Maria 89; Susanna 89
WOHLGENERICH Cathrina 32; Joseph 32
WOHLHOREN Anna Cathrina 83; Peter 83
WOHLSCHLAEGER/WOHLSCHLEGER/ WOHLSCHTEGER (See Wollenschlaeger, Wollschlaeger) Anna Elisabetha 81; Anna Maria 81; Cathrina 79, 81, 83; Jacob 78, 79, 81
WOLF Ana 98; Anamaria 102; Andreas 34; Anna Dorothea 4; Anna Margretha 34; Cath. 26, 27; Christina 39; David 57, 87; Dorothea 2; Elisabetha 2, 29, 96; Jacob 39, 87; Joh. Jacob 21; Johanes 96, 99, 102; John 55, 98; Magdalena 21, 34, 55, 57; Magdalena Hagern 99; Maria 96; Michael 18; Michel Hager 102; Nentzi 87; Peter 21, 55, 57; Philppina 18; Samuel 39; Susana 98; Wendel 2, 4
WOLFENSPERGER/WOLFERSPERGER Ana 90; Catharina 91; Elisabetha 90, 91, 106; Johan Peter 106; Johanes 90, 91, 106; Susana 91, 106
WOLFHARTH (See Wohlfahrt)
WOLFINGER Mrs. Jacob 51
WOLFORD/WOLFORT Elis. 30; Mathias 14; Rosina 27
WOLG Catharina 39; Georg 39

WOLLENSCHLAEGER (See Wohlschlaeger/etc., Wollschlaeger) Elisabeth 45; Magdalena 45; Vallentin 45
WOLLER Johannes 85, 87; N. 85, 87; Wilhelm 85
WOLLSCHLAEGER (See Wohlschlaeger/etc., Wollenschlaeger) John 46; Magdalena 46; Vallentin 46
WOLSCHOESER Catharina 69; Jacob 69
WOLST Adam 81; Susana 81
WOLTER Adam 65; Anna Christina 87; Anna Maria 65; Henrich 87; Jacob 65
WOLTZ/WOLZ Anna Maria 13; Bezi 10; Carlota 81; Cath. 28; Charlotta 79, 90; Elis. 26; Georg 22, 79, 81, 90; Maria 79, 90; Metilda 90; Peter 13, 79, 90
WOMERIN Anna Maria 71
WOOD Jams 26
WOODEN Beal 53; Stephen 53; William 53
WOPPBACH Elisabetha 74; Henrich 74
WORT Herman 30
WOTHRING/WOTRING/WOTTRING/WATRING Abraham 42, 54, 83, 88, 91; Catharina 42, 88, 91; Jacob 83; Johanes 97; Margretha (Margaret) 54, 83, 88, 97; Peter 54, 87, 88, 97
WREYACK Amilia 12; Jacob 12
WURTENBERGER Cath Engel 47; Jacob 47
WUSTEBERGER David 30
WYAN (see Weiant, Weyan) Maria Elisabeth 46

YEGLY Elizabeth 57; George 58; Henry 57, 58; Margaret 57, 58
YELIVICHS Rebarbara 30
YERZER Michael 30
YINGLING (Yungling) Anna Margretha 84
YOUNG (See Jung, Yung) Eleonorah 8; Elizabeth 8; George 8; Jacob 8; John George 6; Margaretha 6; Odelia 8; Pastor 8; Susanah 8
YOUNGERS (See Yunker) Mary 30
YTNEIER Doretea 85; Henrich 85; Johannes 85
YUNG (See Jung, Young) Cath. 21; Elizabeth 51; George 51; Henry 51; Ludwich 21; Samuel 21
YUNKER (See Youngers) Christ 26; Maria 28
YUNTER Joh. 30

INDEX

ZACHARIAS Christian 45; Elisabeth 45, 47; Elisabeth Fey 46, 47; Jacob 45, 46, 47; John Georg 46
ZEICHLER (See Ziegler) Barbara 69
ZEILL Henry 110
ZEISTER Elisabeth 7; Fenrich 7; Katharina 7
ZEIT Jacob 81; Johannes 81; Magtalena 81
ZEITENAUES Catherine 107; Richard 107
ZEITNER Margarethe 1; Martin 1; Nicolas 1
ZELL Anna 110; Maria Catherine 110
ZELLER/ZEOLLER/ZOELER/ZOELLER/ZOLLER Anmargreth 94; Anna 110, 111; Anna Maria 107; Catherin(a) 57, 107, 108, 109, 111; Christina 110; David 107, 111; Elisabeth(a) 17, 42, 43, 101; Henry (Henrich) 34, 36, 108, 109; Jacob 32, 35, 36, 42, 43, 57, 94, 111; Johannes 17; John 107; John George 110; Jonas 17, 42, 101; Joseph 108; Magtalena 35; Margretha (Margaret) 34, 36, 38, 43, 57; Margretta 42; Maria 18; Martin 110, 111; Samuel 42, 101; Sara(h) 42, 111
ZENTMYER Barbara 63; John 63; Maria Barbara 63
ZEOLLER (See Zeller/etc.)
ZERCKMAN Esther 29
ZERTLIN Eva 69
ZIEGER Jacob 4; John Phillip 4; Judith 4
ZIEGLER (See Zeichler) Electa 41
ZIMER Mag. 27
ZIMERMAN/ZIMMERMAN/ZIMMERMANN Anna Margretha 85; Anna Maria 34; Barbera 10, 84, 96, 103; Carolina Margretha 96; Carline 84; Catharina Margretha (Cath. Marg.) 88, 94; Catharine 65, 84; Charlotha 84; Elisabeth 21; Eva 20; Georg 88; Gottlieb 20, 23, 28; Henrich 21, 84, 94, 96, 103; Johannes 65, 96; Jost 34, 84, 85, 88, 94, 96; Margretha 21, 34, 85; Maria 23; Mary 28; Sovia 20
ZINN Ann Maria 6; Ann Mary 1, 3; Anna Maria 2, 5, 70, 79; Daniel 8; Elisabeth 2; Georg 1, 2, 3, 6, 70, 79; Jacob 70; Jane 5; John 3; John George 6; Peter 5, 6, 8; William 6
ZIRGER Christofel 65; Margretha 65
ZOELER/ZOELLER (See Zeller/etc.)
ZOELTER Jacob 32; Magdalena 32
ZOLLEERIRD Margaretha 107

ZOLLER (See Zeller/etc.) ZOLLINGER Adam 53, 60; Anna Maria 53, 60; Susan 53
ZOUCK Elis. 23; Jacob 23
ZUCK Elizabeth 109; Jacob 109; John 109
ZUEROHER Christoph 2; Elisabeth 2; Margareth 2

155

Other books by F. Edward Wright:

Abstracts of Bucks County, Pennsylvania Wills, 1685-1785
Abstracts of Cumberland County, Pennsylvania Wills, 1750-1785
Abstracts of Cumberland County, Pennsylvania Wills, 1785-1825
Abstracts of Philadelphia County Wills, 1726-1747
Abstracts of Philadelphia County Wills, 1748-1763
Abstracts of Philadelphia County Wills, 1763-1784
Abstracts of Philadelphia County Wills, 1777-1790
Abstracts of Philadelphia County Wills, 1790-1802
Abstracts of Philadelphia County Wills, 1802-1809
Abstracts of Philadelphia County Wills, 1810-1815
Abstracts of Philadelphia County Wills, 1815-1819
Abstracts of Philadelphia County Wills, 1820-1825
Abstracts of Philadelphia County, Pennsylvania Wills, 1682-1726
Abstracts of South Central Pennsylvania Newspapers, Volume 1, 1785-1790
Abstracts of South Central Pennsylvania Newspapers, Volume 3, 1796-1800
Abstracts of the Newspapers of Georgetown and the Federal City, 1789-99
Abstracts of York County, Pennsylvania Wills, 1749-1819
Bucks County, Pennsylvania Church Records of the 17th and 18th Centuries Volume 2: Quaker Records: Falls and Middletown Monthly Meetings
Anna Miller Watring and F. Edward Wright
Caroline County, Maryland Marriages, Births and Deaths, 1850-1880
Citizens of the Eastern Shore of Maryland, 1659-1750
Cumberland County, Pennsylvania Church Records of the 18th Century
Delaware Newspaper Abstracts, Volume 1: 1786-1795
Early Charles County, Maryland Settlers, 1658-1745
Marlene Strawser Bates and F. Edward Wright
Early Church Records of Alexandria City and Fairfax County, Virginia
F. Edward Wright and Wesley E. Pippenger
Early Church Records of New Castle County, Delaware, Volume 1, 1701-1800
Frederick County Militia in the War of 1812
Sallie A. Mallick and F. Edward Wright
Inhabitants of Baltimore County, 1692-1763
Land Records of Sussex County, Delaware, 1769-1782
Land Records of Sussex County, Delaware, 1782-1789
Elaine Hastings Mason and F. Edward Wright
Marriage Licenses of Washington, District of Columbia, 1811-1830
Marriages and Deaths from the Newspapers of Allegany and Washington Counties, Maryland, 1820-1830
Marriages and Deaths from The York Recorder, 1821-1830
Marriages and Deaths in the Newspapers of Frederick and Montgomery Counties, Maryland, 1820-1830

Marriages and Deaths in the Newspapers of Lancaster County, Pennsylvania, 1821-1830
Marriages and Deaths in the Newspapers of Lancaster County, Pennsylvania, 1831-1840
Marriages and Deaths of Cumberland County, [Pennsylvania], 1821-1830
Maryland Calendar of Wills Volume 9: 1744-1749
Maryland Calendar of Wills Volume 10: 1748-1753
Maryland Calendar of Wills Volume 11: 1753-1760
Maryland Calendar of Wills Volume 12: 1759-1764
Maryland Calendar of Wills Volume 13: 1764-1767
Maryland Calendar of Wills Volume 14: 1767-1772
Maryland Calendar of Wills Volume 15: 1772-1774
Maryland Calendar of Wills Volume 16: 1774-1777
Maryland Eastern Shore Newspaper Abstracts, Volume 1: 1790-1805
Maryland Eastern Shore Newspaper Abstracts, Volume 2: 1806-1812
Maryland Eastern Shore Newspaper Abstracts, Volume 3: 1813-1818
Maryland Eastern Shore Newspaper Abstracts, Volume 4: 1819-1824
Maryland Eastern Shore Newspaper Abstracts, Volume 5: Northern Counties, 1825-1829
F. Edward Wright and Irma Harper
Maryland Eastern Shore Newspaper Abstracts, Volume 6: Southern Counties, 1825-1829
Maryland Eastern Shore Newspaper Abstracts, Volume 7: Northern Counties, 1830-1834
Irma Harper and F. Edward Wright
Maryland Eastern Shore Newspaper Abstracts, Volume 8: Southern Counties, 1830-1834
Maryland Militia in the Revolutionary War
S. Eugene Clements and F. Edward Wright
Newspaper Abstracts of Allegany and Washington Counties, 1811-1815
Newspaper Abstracts of Cecil and Harford Counties, [Maryland], 1822-1830
Newspaper Abstracts of Frederick County, [Maryland], 1816-1819
Newspaper Abstracts of Frederick County, 1811-1815
Sketches of Maryland Eastern Shoremen
Tax List of Chester County, Pennsylvania 1768
Tax List of York County, Pennsylvania 1779
Washington County Church Records of the 18th Century, 1768-1800
Western Maryland Newspaper Abstracts, Volume 1: 1786-1798
Western Maryland Newspaper Abstracts, Volume 2: 1799-1805
Western Maryland Newspaper Abstracts, Volume 3: 1806-1810
Wills of Chester County, Pennsylvania, 1766-1778

www.ingramcontent.com/pod-product-compliance
Lightning Source LLC
Chambersburg PA
CBHW062225080426
42734CB00010B/2029